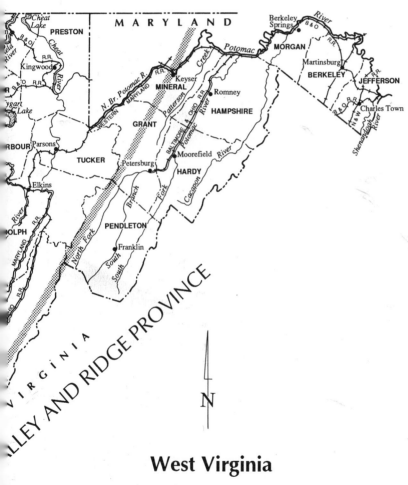

PENNSYLVANIA

MARYLAND

Cheat Lake

PRESTON

Cheat River

Kingwood

R.R.

B & O

N. Br. Potomac R.

WESTERN MARYLAND

Keyser

MINERAL

Creek

Potomac

Berkeley Springs

B & O

MORGAN

Martinsburg

BERKELEY

R.R.

JEFFERSON

Romney

Patterson

HAMPSHIRE

River

Charles Town

N & W

B & O

Shenandoah River

GRANT

BALTIMORE & OHIO R.R.

Potomac

River

RBOUR

Parsons

TUCKER

Petersburg

Moorefield

River

HARDY

Cacapon

Elkins

River

R.R.

North Fork

Branch

Fork

OLPH

MARYLAND

PENDLETON

Franklin

South Branch

South

VIRGINIA

VALLEY AND RIDGE PROVINCE

N

West Virginia

0			50 miles

0			60 kilometers

West Virginia

West Virginia

A HISTORY

Otis K. Rice
Stephen W. Brown

Second Edition

THE UNIVERSITY PRESS OF KENTUCKY

Scholarly publisher for the Commonwealth,
serving Bellarmine College, Berea College, Centre
College of Kentucky, Eastern Kentucky University,
The Filson Club, Georgetown College, Kentucky
Historical Society, Kentucky State University,
Morehead State University, Murray State University,
Northern Kentucky University, Transylvania University,
University of Kentucky, University of Louisville,
and Western Kentucky University.

Editorial and Sales Offices: The University Press of Kentucky
663 South Limestone Street, Lexington, Kentucky 40508-4008

00 99 98 97 96   5 4 3 2

Library of Congress Cataloging-in-Publication Data
Rice, Otis K.
    West Virginia : a history / Otis K. Rice, Stephen W. Brown.
— 2nd ed.
      p.   cm.
    Includes bibliographical references (p.) and index.
    ISBN 0-8131-1854-9 (alk. paper)
    1. West Virginia—History.   I. Brown, Stephen W., 1950-
II. Title.
F241.R515   1993
975.4—dc20   93-17819

For David Neal, Matthew, and Lennie

Contents

Photographs follow pages 54 and 214

Preface

The first edition of *West Virginia: A History,* published in 1985, was designed for informed West Virginians and others interested in the history of the state. The approach was primarily narrative and based upon the belief that most readers desired essential information and a faithful re-creation of the past rather than one predominantly interpretive or analytical.

In this second edition we have retained the same approach, but we have added a chapter on the 1980s and 1990s. We have also updated or amended some material in the text and bibliographical listings. Insofar as possible, we have based this work upon scholarly writings, both past and present, and commented upon their findings and interpretations, while at the same time we have offered our own views when they seemed essential or desirable. Although we subscribe to the belief that history may inform and elucidate the present, we have not attempted to draw out only those threads that seem to exist in the late twentieth century. The past has its own integrity, and recapturing it for its own sake may in the long run be as instructive as winnowings that appear to have special relevance to some later time. We have tried to recognize that integrity without ignoring pertinent threads from the past where they genuinely appear to exist.

In the course of our research, we have relied upon the staffs of numerous libraries, but our greatest dependence has been upon those of the Vining Library of West Virginia Institute of Technology, the West Virginia Division of Archives and History, the Kanawha County Public Library at Charleston, and the West Virginia University Library. They have been unfailingly sympathetic and helpful. The collection and reproduction of photographs have been greatly facilitated by the courtesies of Rodney Pyles, a former director of the West Virginia Division of Archives and History, and his cooperative staff; Rodney Collins, director of the Historical Preservation Unit of the West Virginia Division of Archives and History; Daniel Fowler and Ray Swick of the Blennerhassett Historical Park Commission, Parkersburg; and Professor Raymond Janssen of the Department of Geology of Marshall University. Dr. Kenneth R. Bailey and the West Virginia Institute of Technology Foundation rendered a valuable service by providing funds for preparation of the maps.

We also extend our thanks to Dr. Ken Hechler, West Virginia secretary of state; Dr. Gordon R. Short, vice-president for Academic Affairs, West Virginia Institute of Technology; Kenneth M. Ferguson, Planning and Research Division supervisor, West Virginia Department of Transportation; Sharon Lewis, West Virginia Department of Education; and Sharon Burgess Paxton, research analyst, West Virginia Development Office. Finally, we thank students and other readers for useful comments on the first edition of this work and for encouraging us to undertake a second edition.

1

Prehistoric Times

A Land of Grandeur. In 1784, nearly two hundred years before a popular song referred to West Virginia as "almost Heaven," Thomas Jefferson wrote that the contrast between the "placid and delightful" Shenandoah Valley and the "wild and tremendous" mountains at Harpers Ferry, the Potomac gateway to the state, was worth a journey across the Atlantic Ocean.[1] Jefferson might have found equally awesome beauty in Hawks Nest, a crag towering 585 feet above the turbulent New River, spectacular waterfalls in the Kanawha, Little Kanawha, and Blackwater rivers, the serenity of the Canaan Valley, and numerous other natural formations in West Virginia.

Geological Determinants. The striking physiography of West Virginia has sprung from geological activity. For some four hundred million years, the state lay in a long trough, or geosyncline, that extended from New Brunswick to Alabama, where the Appalachian Highlands are today. The trough was actually an arm of the ocean, which left vast deposits of salt, either as brine or rock salt, in the western parts of West Virginia and limestone, from fossils of marine animals, in the eastern sections.

To the east of the trough rose a continent known as Old Appalachia. From it and other highlands, material washed down into the geosyncline, pressing it downward and forcing the surrounding rock upward. This action weakened the geosyncline and gave rise to a disturbance known as the Appalachian Revolution, in which rock strata were repeatedly folded and uplifted. Prior to the final upheaval much of West Virginia was swampland with luscious vegetation, which decomposed and formed vast beds of coal. About seventy million years ago the state and surrounding areas were part of a peneplain, worn almost flat by erosion. Uplift, nevertheless, continued, and at the beginning of the Ice Age, about one million years ago, streams and erosion had sculptured the landscape of West Virginia essentially as it is today. Continued action, however, has since deepened the valleys and sharpened the contours of the land.

During the Ice Age, which ended only about ten thousand years ago, great polar ice sheets crept southward into the present Ohio Valley. The glaciers did

[1]Thomas Jefferson, *Notes on the State of Virginia,* ed. William Peden (Chapel Hill: University of North Carolina Press, 1955), 19.

not reach West Virginia, but they drastically changed its drainage system. Lake Erie did not exist before the Ice Age, and streams from the Allegheny Plateau flowed in a northwesterly direction into the Erie Basin and then into the ancient Saint Lawrence River. The ice blocked the Monongahela River, which followed roughly its present course toward Pittsburgh before turning into the Erie Basin at Beaver Falls, and impounded its waters in the Monongahela Valley to a depth of about eleven hundred feet. The lake thus formed extended southward to the Little Kanawha Valley and overflowed through a channel approximating modern Fishing Creek. Waters of the lake receded with the formation of the Ohio River, which carved its valley as a marginal glacial stream.

The Teays River, the principal prehistoric stream of southern West Virginia, followed the course of the Kanawha, its successor, westward to Scary, about fifteen miles below Charleston, and turned into the present Teays Valley toward Huntington. This ancient riverbed is only about one hundred feet above the level of the Kanawha. The New River, a tributary of the Kanawha, defied the forces of uplift in the Appalachians and continued its westward course from North Carolina and Virginia even after other streams of the Atlantic slope directed their flow toward the ocean.[2]

Extent and General Location. With an area of 24,282 square miles, West Virginia ranks forty-first among the states. Its greatest distance from east to west is 260 miles and that from north to south is 327 miles. West Virginia has a mean elevation of over 1,500 feet, the highest of any state east of the Mississippi River, but elevations vary from only 247 feet at Harpers Ferry to 4,860 feet at Spruce Knob in Pendleton County.

West Virginia lies within two major physiographic regions of the eastern United States. They are the Valley and Ridge Province and the Allegheny Plateau, both part of the Appalachian Highlands. The two most striking features of the Valley and Ridge section are the Blue Ridge, to the east of the state, and the Appalachian Valley, known locally as the Valley of Virginia, or the Shenandoah Valley. About two hundred miles long, the Valley of Virginia tapers in width from about sixty-five miles on the Maryland border to fifty miles on the North Carolina line. It includes all of Jefferson County and part of Berkeley County, West Virginia, but in some respects most of the upper Potomac River basin is a giant arm of the Valley. Noted for its rich limestone soils and gentle terrain, the Valley is a region of surpassing beauty.

The Allegheny Plateau, separated from the Valley and Ridge section by a bold escarpment known as the Allegheny Front, embraces about five-sixths of West Virginia. The plateau slopes toward the Great Lakes and the Mississippi Valley. One lofty section of Randolph, Pendleton, and Pocahontas counties is the source of numerous streams, including the South Branch of the Potomac,

---

[2]The best short account of the geological history of West Virginia is Raymond E. Janssen, *Earth Science: A Handbook on the Geology of West Virginia* (Clarksburg: Educational Marketers, Inc., 1973), of which pp. 35-43 and 210-226 have been of special value for the above summary.

Cheat, Tygart Valley, Elk, and Greenbrier rivers. The central portion is marked by extremely rugged terrain, where rivers have carved deep, canyonlike channels, and forest-clad hills tower above narrow valleys. Toward the Ohio River, the plateau has a mean elevation of about one thousand feet. There its hills seldom rise above a few hundred feet. Rich alluvial soils dominate lowlands along the Ohio and, through its tributaries, reach like long fingers deep into the heart of the plateau.

Rivers and Lakes. In many mountainous regions of the world, rivers have mitigated difficulites in communication and ameliorated tendencies toward particularism. West Virginia rivers form a large part of its boundaries and give it an irregular shape with two panhandles, but, since they and their tributaries flow in all directions, they have given the state very little unity. The Potomac and its tributaries flow into the Chesapeake Bay; the Monongahela, with its West Fork, Tygart Valley, and Cheat influents, northward to the Ohio at Pittsburgh; and the Little Kanawha, Kanawha, Guyandotte, and Big Sandy in more westerly courses to the Ohio. Each of the Ohio tributaries has its own hinterland. The turbulent New prevents close river ties between the Greenbrier and Bluestone with the Kanawha. Since the Ice Age, West Virginia has had no natural lakes, but in recent decades flood control projects on state streams have created several large artificial reservoirs.

The First Inhabitants. The historic record forms but a small fragment of the story of human occupation of West Virginia. Archaeological findings show that aboriginal man lived or hunted in the state for at least ten thousand years before the arrival of the first Europeans.

Archaeologists long ago discarded theories that the Indians were descendants of the Ten Lost Tribes of Israel or relics from the submerged continent of Atlantis. They now generally agree that the first Americans crossed the Bering Strait from Asiatic Russia to Alaska and gradually fanned out over the American continents. They theorize that the Indians may have crossed the sea in kayaks, walked over an ice cap during the glacial period, or used a land bridge formed by the receding glacier. Those supporting the idea of a land bridge hold that the Pacific Ocean may have been as much as 250 feet lower than it is now. The Indians began their migrations at least fifteen thousand and possibly as much as forty thousand years ago and continued their intercontinental movement for several thousand years.

Diversity in height, body build, and facial structure indicate that the Indians originated in various parts of Asia. Common characteristics, however, such as shovel-shaped incisors, stamp all of them as clearly of "Old Mongoloid" stock. Old Mongoloid man brought with him to America only a few possessions, chief of which were spears, skins for clothing, and scraping and hide-working tools. In time his way of life gave rise to Paleo-Indian culture.

Paleo-Indian Culture. Known also as Early Hunter, Clovis, or Folsum culture, Paleo-Indian life developed on the high plains east of the Rocky

Mountains. It centered on the quest for large game such as mammoths, mastodons, or large hairy elephants, giant sloths, horses, camels, and a large variety of buffalo, all of which became extinct about 6000 B.C. Such hunting was best done by small nomadic groups, and it is likely that the Early Hunters were organized into small family units, perhaps with the oldest male as chief.

The most characteristic artifact left by Paleo-Indian culture was a fluted spearpoint, identified by channels from the base to the tip on each flat side, evidently as an aid in securing the point to the shaft. The discovery of fluted points in the Ohio, Kanawha, and Potomac valleys indicates activity by Early Hunters over much of the state. Fluted points have been found in the greatest numbers along the Ohio River between Saint Marys and Parkersburg, particularly around the latter city.

Archaic Cultures. Forced to adapt to new conditions when the large game became extinct, the Early Hunters either succumbed to lack of food or blended into a new Archaic culture. The Archaic foragers apparently arrived from Asia somewhat later than the Paleo-Indian migrants. They were most numerous from about 7000 to about 1000 B.C., particularly in the centuries following the disappearance of Paleo-Indian culture. Archaic man first lived by gathering nuts, berries, roots, and edible plants and by hunting small game animals. Later, he became somewhat more selective in his food gathering, in some cases concentrating on acorns and small shellfish from the rivers.

Archaeological excavations at Saint Albans in the late 1960s revealed one of the oldest radiocarbon-dated sites in the eastern United States. The stratigraphy, which provided only one type of projectile point at each level, indicated that Indians, perhaps in family groups, had frequented the site since about 7000 B.C. probably to gather shellfish from the Kanawha River. Flooding in unusually wet periods evidently caused interruptions in occupation of the site.

West Virginia had several variants of Archaic culture. The Panhandle Archaic, principally in Ohio, Brooke, and Hancock counties, relied heavily upon freshwater clams from the Ohio River for food. Distinctive spearpoint types, grooved adzes, atlatls, and tools of bone have been found in the large refuse heaps, or middens, at Archaic campsites. Excavations of a 4,000-year-old campsite at Globe Hill, Hancock County, revealed that Archaic people continued to hunt game, especially deer and small animals. The Montane Archaic cultures in the eastern parts of the state made use of quartz, quartzite, hematite, sandstones, and other non-flint rocks to make spearheads and tools normally fashioned from flint. The Buffalo Archaic, at Buffalo, on the Kanawha River, with a comparatively recent radiocarbon dating of 1920 B.C., was probably Transitional Archaic. This stage featured the cultivation of some plants, such as the sunflower and perhaps goosefoot and pigweed, the advent of soapstone and some crude pottery vessels, and the beginnings of burial ceremonialism.

Early Woodland Culture. The fusion of the three elements of cultivation of plants, making of pottery, and burial ceremonialism characterized the cultural stage known as Early Woodland. In essence, Early Woodland was the same as Adena culture, which developed and held sway in the middle Ohio Valley between present Louisville and Pittsburgh in the millenium preceding the birth of Christ.

Early Adena culture lasted from about 1000 B.C. to about A.D. 500. It featured circular houses of poles, wickerwork, and bark. Simple burial mounds contained some stemmed projectile points, plain tubular pipes, whetstones, and pottery that was thick, crude, grit-tempered, and cord-marked, with barrel shapes and flat bottoms.

Late Adena blended Early Adena and Hopewellian cultures, which began to develop in the Illinois Valley about 500 B.C. and in time became the most influential culture in the eastern United States. Late Adena artifacts include whetstones, often carved with abstract bird designs, and carved tubular pipes showing Hopewellian characteristics. Pottery often had incised decoration along round, solid lug handles. Remains of both Early and Late Adena cultures include stone and copper gorgets, shell and copper beads, solid copper bracelets, and cones and hemispheres of stone, usually hematite.

Mounds and Earthworks. The most distinctive Adena legacy in West Virginia and the Ohio Valley consists of hundreds of earthen mounds. The Adena people and their Hopewellian and Mississippian successors built mounds over the remains of chiefs, shamans, priests, and other honored dead or as temples and houses for chiefs. They exposed the bodies of common folk after death, and, once they were denuded of flesh, burned the bones. They then buried the remains in small log tombs on the surface of the ground. The forces of Nature and the cultivation of the soil by European settlers later removed nearly every trace of these burials.

The most striking prehistoric earthwork in West Virginia is the Grave Creek Mound at Moundsville. The largest of its kind in the United States, it originally measured 69 feet high, 295 feet in diameter at its base, and 60 feet in diameter at its flat top. Joseph Tomlinson, the first owner of the site of the mound, refused all proposals to open it. In 1838 a descendant, Jesse Tomlinson, believing that it might hold treasures, consented to its exploration. Excavations revealed that it had been built in two stages on a low natural eminence. A vault, or log tomb, about twelve feet long and eight feet wide, in the center of the original mound contained skeletons of a man and a woman, about 650 circular bone and disc beads, and an atlatl. A timber-covered passageway from the north side of the mound indicated that access to the vault remained for some time after the burials. Thirty-four feet above that tomb, another was found to contain a skeleton, ivory and shell beads, a gorget, copper bracelets, and many pieces of perforated mica. A small, grayish sandstone tablet, about one and one-half by two inches in size and covered with mysterious markings, was allegedly found in the upper vault, but reputable authorities consider the stone a hoax.

Adena mounds were numerous in the South Charleston–Dunbar area of the Kanawha Valley. A mound 35 feet high and 175 feet in diameter at the base, yet standing at South Charleston, was opened in 1883–84 under the direction of the Smithsonian Institution. Excavators found a vault with five skeletons, one in the middle and the other four surrounding it in such positions as to suggest that they may have been live burials. The center skeleton was seven and one-half feet long. With it were bracelets, spearheads of black flint, hematite celts, mica plates, and large quantities of shells and beads. Nearby, another mound held a skeleton surrounded by ten others, extended horizontally with their feet pointed toward the central figure.

Scarcely less interesting are walls and other earthworks of Indian origin. Those at Bens Run, Tyler County, are the most extensive of their kind in the United States. Two parallel circular walls about 120 feet apart enclose some four hundred acres of land, within which are two small mounds, a cross wall running the entire length of the enclosure, and inner walls parallel to but not touching the outer ones. On a nearby hilltop are mounds and other evidences of ancient burial grounds. In another direction two large stone platforms or roadways extend for 192 and 100 feet. Between them is a large earth mound covered with stones in such a manner as to suggest that the area was used for religious ceremonies, possibly some form of sun worship.

Earthworks on top of a mountain overlooking the village of Mount Carbon on the upper Kanawha have baffled archaeologists. Stone walls around the mountain crests partially enclosed rock cairns, flint quarries, and work areas. In the absence of any other acceptable explanation, it must be presumed that they had a religious purpose. Strip mining has virtually destroyed the walls, and a housing development has all but obliterated village remains.

Middle Woodland Mound Builders. The identity of the builders of the earthworks at Mount Carbon and others at Pratt remains uncertain, but they were very likely Armstrong or Buck Garden people, who dominated the Kanawha Valley from about A.D. 1 to 500. The Armstrong culture was a variant of the Hopewellian, or Middle Woodland, culture, which reached its zenith in Ohio about that time. Artifacts from the Murad Mound in Saint Albans and other mounds in the South Charleston area suggest that Hopewellian people moved into the state and mingled peacefully with Adena residents. Many of the latter, however, apparently moved away, possibly to Pennsylvania, Maryland, and New York, or even to Tennessee and Alabama.

The Armstrong people took their name from a creek that flows into the Kanawha River at Mount Carbon, where excavations first identified theirs as a distinct culture. Their villages consisted of scattered circular-shaped houses constructed of poles and woven materials. Cultivation of plants, limited to sunflowers and a few others, had not advanced beyond that of the Adena period. The Armstrong people continued to build small earthen mounds, but they also practiced cremation on a considerable scale. Their pottery, one of the most distinctive features of their culture, was thin, tempered with particles of clay, and fired so that surfaces were oxidized, leaving an orange-yellow color.

The Wilhelm culture, prominent in the Northern Panhandle and adjacent parts of Pennsylvania, coincided with the Armstrong culture on the Kanawha. An excavation in Brooke County first drew attention to the distinctive practice of the Wilhelm people of building small mounds over individual stone-lined graves and then fusing several graves together into a single large mound.

Later Hopewellian variants included the Buck Garden and Watson Farm stone mound builders, who succeeded the Armstrong and Wilhelm cultures, respectively. The change from Armstrong to Buck Garden, first identified at a rock shelter at Buck Garden Creek, Nicholas County, was gradual and under way about A.D. 500. Buck Garden folk probably built many of the stone mounds of central West Virginia, but they also buried their dead under overhanging rock formations. Greater attention to agriculture, into which they introduced the cultivation of corn, beans, and squash, combined with defense needs to foster a more compact village life. Excavations at Mount Carbon have shown that the Buck Garden people were driven from the Kanawha Valley, but they probably continued to live in the hills on both sides of the river for some time. By about A.D. 1200 their culture had all but disappeared.

Watson Farm people dominated the Northern Panhandle and adjacent regions from about A.D. 500 to about 1000. Like their Buck Garden contemporaries, they lived in compact villages and cultivated corn, squash, and beans. They evidently abandoned the use of individual cists and included many burials in one mound. The Watson Farm Mound in Hancock County and the Fairchance Mound near Moundsville have yielded much information regarding their modes of life.

Hopewellian influence among mound builders of mountainous areas of West Virginia is somewhat obscure. Artifacts from mounds at Romney and in the Tygart Valley, in Randolph County, show characteristics indicating that a distinct Hopewellian culture prevailed contemporaneously with the Buck Garden and Watson Farm variants. Nevertheless, the frequent and widespread contacts among earlier Hopewellian peoples began to diminish about A.D. 500. All of the related cultures began to place less emphasis upon moundbuilding and to give greater attention to the living. Warfare became common and gave rise to special concern for defense.

Late Prehistoric Village Farmers. Mississippian culture, which developed around Saint Louis between A.D. 800 and 900, spread eastward and dominated the eastern United States at the time of the arrival of Europeans. In West Virginia, Mississippian influences were strongest in the Ohio and Kanawha valleys. Middle Woodland traits persisted in mountainous areas. The new culture was marked by city-state political organizations, priest-temple cults, compact towns serving as centers for outlying villages, large flat-topped pyramidal mounds for temples or homes, and wattle and daubed houses with thatched roofs. Where it prevailed, permanent villages sprang up, particularly in river valleys, and population increased in density. To sustain the growth, residents turned to a much more intensive cultivation of corn, beans, squash, and other plants.

During the Late Prehistoric period, Fort Ancient people replaced the Buck Garden with a blend of Mississippian and Middle Woodland cultures. They usually lived in oval-shaped stockaded villages of several hundred inhabitants and consisting of a single row of houses built around an open plaza. The houses, about thirty feet long and from eighteen to twenty feet wide, had sidewalls of saplings, probably covered with bark or hides, and roofs of thatch supported by two interior center posts. Some houses had small basin-shaped fire pits inside. Early Fort Ancient burials were inside the village, with the dead usually placed in a flexed position. Sometimes there were grave offerings, such as strings of bone beads with alternating cannel coal pendants.

Villages and houses both became larger in the later Fort Ancient period. As many as three concentric rows of houses appeared inside the stockades, and populations numbered from 1,000 to 1,500. Advances in horticulture and the protection afforded by larger political units in an era of mounting warfare probably account for the greater size of villages. Rectangular houses measured up to fifty or sixty feet long and twenty-five feet wide. Roof supports invariably consisted of three large center posts and six or seven secondary center supports midway between the sidewalls and the main posts.

Later Fort Ancient burials were inside the houses, under the floors. Prolonged use of some houses necessitated the stacking of burials along the inside walls. Grave offerings were rare, except for some pottery vessels, presumably with food for the departed. Other artifacts include shell-tempered pottery, often with strap handles; small crudely worked figurines of human beings and animals; elbow pipes; and a large assortment of flint and bone objects and tools. Toward the end of the period, southern influences led to rather extensive use of lizards and fish in designs.

The Monongahela culture, found in the northern part of the state and in western Pennsylvania, closely resembled the Fort Ancient. Villages, usually smaller than Fort Ancient, seldom covered more than two acres and were enclosed by circular stockades. The dome-shaped houses were of pole and bark construction. Many had pear-shaped pits, probably for storage. Both Monongahela and Fort Ancient people moved their villages often, evidently to find fresh soil for crops and areas where game had not been depleted. The Monongahelans continued to build small stone mounds well into late prehistoric times.[3]

Petroglyphs. All parts of West Virginia have yielded petroglyphs, or rock carvings, made by Indians. One type, often a maze of grooves and commonly called "turkey tracks," is usually found under rock overhangs. Sometimes regarded as a form of picture writing, it now seems more likely that they were made in sharpening stone or bone tools.

[3]Of special value for the preceding summary of prehistoric inhabitants of West Virginia is Edward V. McMichael, *Introduction to West Virginia Archeology,* 2d ed. rev. (Morgantown: West Virginia Geological and Economic Survey, 1968), the best single work relating specifically to the prehistory of the state.

Perhaps more interesting are pictographs with representations of human figures, birds, deer, snakes, puma or dog-like animals, fish, turtles, and abstract designs. Numerous pictographs have been found in the vicinity of Morgantown, in the Northern Panhandle, near Salt Rock in Cabell County, at Beards Fork in Fayette County, and along the Kanawha River. Most of them were probably the work of Fort Ancient or Monogahela people.

The Protohistoric Period. The discovery of glass beads, brass kettles, and iron objects in excavations of some Fort Ancient and Monongahela sites indicates that they were inhabited in historic times, or after the arrival of Europeans in America. Indians of West Virginia who had indirect trading contacts with Europeans are better described as protohistoric rather than pre-historic.

Identification of Fort Ancient and Monongahela cultures with specific historic tribes is at present educated guesswork. The Moneton town on the Kanawha River visited by Gabriel Arthur in 1674 may have been one of the Fort Ancient sites that have yielded European trading goods. The Monetons may have been Shawnee, possibly remnants of the Western Shawnee who appear to have introduced Fort Ancient culture into West Virginia but were living along the Cumberland River in Kentucky and Tennessee when Europeans first found them.

Association of any tribal group with the Monongahela culture is more difficult. One early reference mentions the Honniasonkeronons, or Black Mingua, in the area, but it is possible that the Monongahela culture was that of the Eastern Shawnee whom Europeans first encountered in the Carolinas. The Monongahela people appear to have left the upper Ohio Valley during the protohistoric era for the Potomac Valley, and from there they evidently moved southward.

Artifacts from several sites along the South Branch of the Potomac, including trading goods and pottery, are unmistakably Susquehannock. The Susquehannocks pushed into the area from central Pennsylvania during the Iroquois conquests in the mid-seventeenth century. They remained in the South Branch Valley from 1630 to 1677.

Indians of Historic Times. Although many parts of West Virginia had substantial Indian populations in prehistoric times, the first white explorers and settlers found almost no Indian residents. Popular theories once attributed the exodus of the Indians to devastating epidemics and scarcity of game. A far more plausible explanation is that they were forced out by the Iroquois confederation, which sought domination of the Ohio Valley as part of their effort to control the fur trade with the Dutch, and later the British, at Albany. Armed with superior weapons supplied by the Dutch and the British, the Iroquois reduced numerous tribes in the eastern United States to vassalage.

Small families or tribes of Indians sometimes returned to West Virginia during historic times, but they did so at the sufferance of the Iroquois. They were chiefly Shawnee and Delaware from Ohio. For the Shawnee, the visits may have represented a return to their old homes, but the Delaware had never been native to the state, originating instead in Pennsylvania, New Jersey, and Delaware. Indian villages in West Virginia in historic times included one of Shawnee at Oldtown near the mouth of the Kanawha River and one at Bulltown, on the Little Kanawha, where Delaware, under Chief Bull, made salt in the 1770s.

Indian Trails and Place Names. Networks of trails and scores of place names serve as reminders of Indian occupation of West Virginia. Thousands of years ago wild animals blazed trails in their endless search for grazing lands and salt licks. Indians followed these trails in pursuit of game and in tribal warfare. Later, fur traders, explorers, and settlers used them in their relentless march westward. In time they became packhorse trails, wagon roads, and turnpikes.

The most important north-south trails in the state were the Warrior Path and the Seneca Trail. The Warrior Path, one of the most important in the eastern United States, connected western New York and the Carolina Piedmont by way of the Valley of Virginia. The West Virginia portion roughly paralleled present U.S. Route 11 and Interstate 81. The Seneca Trail, which passed along the South Branch of the Potomac to Elkins, Lewisburg, and Bluefield, is now U.S. Route 219, appropriately called the Seneca Trail.

East–west trails also became routes of modern highways. The Scio-to–Monongahela Trail connected the Lower Shawnee Town in Ohio with the Monongahela Valley, following U.S. 50 for much of its course. The Kanawha, or Buffalo, Trail ran along the north bank of the Kanawha River to Cedar Grove, then through the back-country to Ansted, whence it followed U.S. 60 to Lewisburg and beyond. One branch extended southward along Paint Creek and Flat Top Mountain toward Virginia and North Carolina. Another trail, connecting southern Ohio with the Valley of Virginia, ran along the Big Sandy and its Tug Fork, approximating U.S. Route 52. The McCullough, or Traders, Trail connected the Valley of Virginia and the Monongahela Valley by way of Wardensville, Moorefield, and Mount Storm.

Indian names, many of them of great beauty, have also been preserved in West Virginia. Rivers included the Ohio, "river of whitecaps" or "the white foaming waters"; Shenandoah, "daughter of the stars"; Monongahela, "river of falling banks"; and Kanawha, "place of the white stone" or, in the language of the Shawnee, Keninsheka, "river of evil spirits." The names Potomac, Cacapon, Opequon, Elk, once the Tiskelwah, and perhaps Guyandotte are of Indian origin. Kanawha, Logan, Mingo, Monongalia, Ohio, Pocahontas, and Wyoming counties also are reminders of Indian occupation. Relatively few towns bear Indian names, but Aracoma, Logan, Matoaka, and Monongah are prominent exceptions.

Although much of Indian life in West Virginia remains shrouded in the mists of the past, Indian names, trails, and artifacts serve as reminders that the culture of the state has Native American as well as other origins.

Explorations and Early Settlements

An Unknown West. For about one hundred and twenty-five years after English colonists landed at Jamestown, settlements in Virginia did not extend beyond the Tidewater and Piedmont regions. Virginians kept busy with the burdensome tasks of taming a wilderness and with transplanting and adapting essential political and social institutions. Culturally, they remained tied to England, and English demand for their tobacco and furs formed the economic underpinnings of their colony.

In spite of more immediate concerns, seventeenth-century Virginians had a deep curiosity about the unknown West. Some envisioned the discovery of gold, silver, and other treasures such as the Spaniards had found in Mexico and Peru. Others, with an optimism born of erroneous concepts of North American geography, entertained hopes of following one of the interior waterways a few hundred miles to the South Sea, as they called the Pacific Ocean, and opening a shorter route to China and the Indies. For some, the sheer joy of adventure was enough to lure them into the depths of the great forests.

Indian wars in 1622 and 1644, brought on by the relentless pressure of settlements upon tribal lands, dashed dreams of riches, discovery of the elusive passage to the Pacific, and high adventure. Following appalling massacres of settlers in 1644, Virginia established forts at the falls of the James, Pamunkey, Chickahominy, and Appomattox rivers. Completed in 1646, they guarded the trails by which hostile Indians gained access to exposed settlements. Each fort was erected by a contractor known as an undertaker, who received the fort property, six hundred acres of land adjoining it, and important tax exemptions on the condition that he maintain ten armed men there for three years to defend the frontiers.

Fur Trade and Seventeeth-Century Exploration. The defense posts built by the undertakers became key centers for the expansion of the fur trade in Virginia. In August 1650 Abraham Wood, the builder of Fort Henry at the falls of the Appomattox River, set out for the western country in the company of three gentlemen, their servants, and an Indian guide. Wood's party passed through the land of the Occaneechi Indians, who had acted as middlemen in the fur trade, and beyond the point where the Staunton and Dan rivers unite to form the Roanoke. Although remote tribes evinced some hostility, Wood foresaw possibilities for a profitable trade and placed orders in England for trading goods, including guns, powder, shot, hatchets, and kettles. Edward Bland, a member of the expedition, wrote an account entitled "The Discovery of New Brittaine," later published as a pamphlet in London. It aroused much interest, but unsettled political conditions in England precluded further advancement of the fur trade in the 1650s.

The growth of the Virginia fur trade in the quarter of a century following the Stuart Restoration was part of a great territorial and commercial expansion that absorbed English energies. In three wars between 1652 and 1674, England dealt the Dutch, her old commercial rival, staggering blows, and in a series of navigation acts, particularly those of 1660, 1663, and 1673, she moved the center of European commerce from Amsterdam to London. In 1664 she acquired New Netherland, which controlled the heart of the American fur country. Other evidence of the importance of furs in the British economy stemmed from the organization of the Hudson's Bay Company, the world's largest fur-trading corporation, in 1660.

Spearheading the fur trade and western exploration in Virginia was Sir William Berkeley, who returned to the colony as governor in 1664, and several planter-traders, including Abraham Wood and William Byrd. Their interest in furs resulted in expeditions that later pointed the way toward West Virginia. When King Charles II denied him permission to lead an expedition into the Indian country, Berkeley engaged a young German, John Lederer, then in Virginia, to undertake three journeys into the backcountry. On the third of his expeditions, in 1670, Lederer followed the Rappahannock River to its headwaters, ascended the wooded slopes of the Blue Ridge, and from a point near Front Royal became the first white person of record to gaze upon the Shenandoah Valley. Lederer's accounts suffer from misconceptions and exaggerations, but they quickened interest in the fur trade and exploration.

Of far greater importance to West Virginia history was the expedition dispatched from Fort Henry by Abraham Wood in the summer of 1671. Known for Thomas Batts, its leader, and Robert Fallam, who kept a journal of its progress, it proceeded to the junction of the Staunton and Dan rivers and continued westward until it reached a stream, which, unlike others of the Virginia Piedmont, flowed toward the west rather than into the Atlantic Ocean. The men called the stream Wood's River in honor of Abraham Wood, but it later became the New River. Along their route they saw markings, including the letters M A   N I, on trees, evidence that other white men had already been there. Who their predecessors were remains unknown, but they may have been traders, some of whom they met, sent out by William Byrd from his post at the present Richmond. The Batts and Fallam expedition reached Peters Falls on the New River, near the present Virginia–West Virginia border, before turning homeward. Their journey later had international implications, when England used their discovery of the New River to assert her claim to the entire Ohio Valley.

Wood sent out another expedition from Fort Henry on May 17, 1673, for the purpose of opening a direct fur trade with tribes beyond the Blue Ridge and ending the exactions of Occaneechi middlemen. James Needham, its leader, and his companions visited a village of Tomahittan, now believed to have been Yuchi Indians on the Hiwassee River. They established friendly relations and left Gabriel Arthur, an intelligent youth, with the Indians to learn their customs and language. Arthur later accompanied a Tomahittan war party across southern West Virginia to the Kanawha River, probably by way of the Coal, to a village of Moneton Indians, possibly at either Saint Albans or Buffalo. Arthur thus became the first white person of record to visit the Kanawha Valley. Before he returned home he was captured by Saura, or Shawnee, in Ohio, but he managed a dramatic escape.

In about 1675 disruptive conditions began to impede the fur trade and exploration. In that year war broke out with the Susquehannocks on the frontiers, and an even more serious conflict known as Bacon's Rebellion, brought on by the Indian disturbances and autocratic policies of Governor Berkeley, threatened the Virginia government itself. Severe economic problems also undermined the tranquil atmosphere essential to trade and exploration. In 1680 Abraham Wood died, and during the ensuing decade unsettled conditions in England itself, which culminated in the Glorious Revolution, removed any solid support from the mother country.

Meanwhile, French explorers and traders had penetrated the Ohio Valley. French authorities claimed that the famous explorer La Salle was on branches of the Ohio in 1669, two years before Batts and Fallam reached the New River, and that on the basis of discovery, France had a stronger claim than England to the Ohio Valley. Their claim cannot be substantiated, but there seems little doubt that French traders visited the Ohio Valley during the late seventeenth century and that some of them ventured into the present West Virginia.

Traders from other colonies, who engaged in commerce with the Shawnee and Delaware, also visited West Virginia. In 1692 Arnout Viele, a Dutchman sent out by the governor of New York, followed the Ohio to Shawnee towns along the lower course of the river. By the early eighteenth century several Pennsylvania traders, among them Peter Bezalion, Martin Chartier, and James Le Tort, had become familiar with parts of West Virginia. In 1725 John Van Meter, a New Jersey trader, visited the South Branch of the Potomac with a party of Delaware and was highly impressed with the excellence of its lands.

First Attempts at Settlement. In West Virginia, as elsewhere on the American frontier, the fur trader was usually the precursor of the settler. In 1703 Louis Michel, a resident of Bern, Switzerland, wrote from Germantown, Pennsylvania, that he and "eight experienced Englishmen" proposed to visit western regions described by the Indians as having high mountains, rich minerals, abundant game, and fertile lands. Michel became associated with George Ritter, a Bern druggist, who proposed to plant a Swiss colony in America with some four or five hundred merchants, artisans, manufacturers, traders, and farmers. The plan, however, led to no migrations.[1]

Michel remained interested in West Virginia. In 1706, accompanied by James Le Tort, Peter Bezalion, and Martin Chartier, he visited Harpers Ferry and sketched a map of the area. Upon his return to Switzerland, Michel joined Baron Christopher de Graffenried, another resident of Bern, in a plan to establish a Swiss colony in America. Once again, however, plans for a Swiss colony at the forks of the Potomac failed. The lands desired were claimed by the proprietors of Maryland and Pennsylvania, as well as by Virginia, and the Conestoga Indians warned the government of Pennsylvania against allowing settlers to take up land around Harpers Ferry. When the proprietors of North Carolina offered the Swiss promoters far more attractive terms, they abandoned plans for any settlement in West Virginia.

The Shenandoah Valley continued to beckon Virginians. By the time Alexander Spotswood arrived in the colony as governor in 1710, valuable plantations already covered much of the Piedmont, and buffer settlements west of the Blue Ridge were considered essential to their protection from the French and the Indians. In 1716 Spotswood led an expedition of fifty gentlemen, with servants and Indian guides, across the mountains by way of Swift Run Gap and into the Shenandoah Valley. The discovery of excellent farm and grazing lands by these "Knights of the Golden Horseshoe," as Spotswood later dubbed his companions, clearly foreshadowed an imminent move of the frontier into the Shenandoah Valley.

There are some reasons to believe that settlements may have been made in the Shenandoah Valley section of West Virginia within a year after Spotswood's expedition. In 1717 the Conestoga Indians asked Pennsylvania authorities for information about persons who had taken up lands west of the Blue Ridge. Moreover, records of the Philadelphia Synod of the Presbyterian Church show that on September 19, 1717, residents of "Potomoke, in Virginia" requested a minister. These records further reveal that during the following year the Reverend Daniel McGill visited "Potomoke," where he "remained for some months and put the people in church order." The site of "Potomoke" remains a mystery, but there is reason to believe that it was at or near Shepherdstown.[2]

West Virginians have generally credited Morgan Morgan, a Welshman who

[1]William J. Hinke, trans. and ed., "Letters Regarding the Second Journey of Michel to America, February 14, 1703, to January 16, 1704, and His Stay in America till 1708," *Virginia Magazine of History and Biography* 24(June 1916): 295-97, 301-302.

[2]Charles H. Ambler and Festus P. Summers, *West Virginia, the Mountain State*, 2d ed. (Englewood Cliffs, N.J.: Prentice-Hall, Inc., 1958), 107, which quotes Minutes of the Philadelphia Synod of the Presbyterian Church.

settled on Mill Creek near Bunker Hill, Berkeley County, with the first settle-ment in the state. Assertions that he moved to West Virginia in 1726 are erroneous. Records show that he lived in Delaware in 1729 and did not acquire his West Virginia lands until November 1730. When he migrated to Bunker Hill about 1731, settlers had probably already begun to enter the lower Shenandoah Valley. In fact, Germans may have settled at Shepherdstown, then known as Mecklenburg, as early as 1727. The claim that Morgan Morgan was the first settler in West Virginia, therefore, must be considered tradition rather than established fact.

The Role of the Land Speculator. Concerns with the identity of the first settler or settlers obscure the fact that no substantial number of immigrants could have arrived in West Virginia before about 1730. Unlike migrating families in the Tidewater and Piedmont regions, pioneers west of the Blue Ridge had to cut themselves off from nearly all contacts with former friends and relatives. Only the boldest dared face single-handedly the perils of Indian hostilities, the chilling prospects of isolation in times of sorrow and distress, and the almost insuperable burdens of conquering a wilderness. Most families were willing to move only as part of larger migrations.

With French activity in the Ohio Valley becoming more ominous for her Piedmont settlements, Virginia in 1730 made changes in her land law designed to encourage migrations into the Valley of Virginia. They placed the land speculator between the settler and the wilderness. The law allowed speculators to receive one thousand acres for each family that they seated west of the Blue Ridge, provided they drew the families from outside Virginia and settled them within two years. Most speculators requested grants ranging from 10,000 to 100,000 acres. Some of the grants, including those to John and Isaac Van Meter between the Potomac and the Shenandoah, Alexander Ross and Morgan Bryan northwest of Opequon Creek, and Edward Barradall and John Lewis on the Cacapon River, were wholly or partly in West Virginia.

Most speculators obtained the necessary families from Pennsylvania and New Jersey and from distressed areas of Europe. Large numbers of Germans and Scotch-Irish responded to their offers, but they also attracted English, Welsh, Dutch, and other nationalities. About thirty-five percent of the population of Jefferson and Berkeley counties at the time of the French and Indian War was English, but Germans and Scotch-Irish each accounted for about thirty percent. Martinsburg and Shepherdstown were centers of German population. There were also so many Germans along the South Branch of the Potomac and Patterson Creek that a Moravian missionary, who visited the area in 1748, declared that in order to reach the people a minister should be fluent in both German and English.[3]

[3]William J. Hinke and Charles Kemper, eds., "Moravian Diaries of Travels Through Virginia," *Virginia Magazine of History and Biography* 11(January 1904): 226.

Although some historians have claimed that land speculators impeded the advance of the frontier generally in America, it appears that their influence in the Valley of Virginia and the Eastern Panhandle of West Virginia was, on the whole, favorable, especially before the French and Indian War. By 1750 a population pressure had built up in the Valley of Virginia, and both speculators and settlers were seeking new lands that might drain off surplus numbers. By then about eight thousand persons lived in the Eastern Panhandle.

The success of the Valley and upper Potomac speculators stemmed in part from the excellence of their lands, for both crops and grazing, and from their charges of only three pounds per hundred acres, compared with the five to ten pounds asked for less desirable lands in Maryland and Pennsylvania. The Virginia speculators also extended easy credit terms and took care of legal detail, often at a distant courthouse. These services were important to immigrants who had little or no cash and were often unfamiliar with either the English language or legal technicalities.

The Fairfax Proprietary. The grants in the lower Shenandoah and upper Potomac valleys, including all of those in West Virginia, lay within a tract claimed by an English nobleman, Thomas, Sixth Lord Fairfax. The Fairfax claim originated in a patent made in 1669 by King Charles II to seven supporters of the royal family in its long struggle with Parliament. By 1719, through inheritance and purchase, the entire property had come into the hands of Lord Fairfax, who claimed all the territory between the headsprings of the southern fork of the Rappahannock River and the highest branch of the Potomac. Known as the Northern Neck, it embraced some 5,282,000 acres.

In 1733, shortly after settlers began to move into present West Virginia, Lord Fairfax petitioned the Crown to proclaim his rights and to restrain Virginia from making further grants within the area that he claimed. Three years later, commissioners representing both Fairfax and Virginia were selected to run the boundary, but Virginia held that the Fairfax line extended westward only to the mouth of the Shenandoah and included only 2,033,000 acres. Fairfax, however, proposed a compromise by which the Crown, on April 6, 1745, confirmed his rights. It defined his tract as extending to the headsprings of the Rapidan River and to the westernmost spring of the North Branch of the Potomac, where in 1746 the famous Fairfax Stone was erected. Fairfax recognized all grants already made by Virginia in the area. He retained extensive properties, including all ungranted lands in present Jefferson, Berkeley, Morgan, Hardy, Hampshire, and Mineral counties and substantial parts of Grant and Tucker counties.

Although the frontier, with its abundance of land, was not conducive to the perpetuation of European forms of land tenure, Fairfax did not hesitate to introduce a feudal system into his princely estate. He laid off his land into large manors, such as the South Branch Manor with 55,000 acres and Patterson Creek Manor with 9,000 acres. The majority of his tenants obtained tracts of from about one hundred to three hundred acres under the old plan of lease and release.

They made a down payment, known as composition money, and each year thereafter, on Saint Michaelmas Day, they paid a quitrent varying with the size and value of their holdings. Probably not more than ten percent of those who acquired lands from him held them in fee simple.

The system of tenure introduced by Fairfax apparently did not deter settlers from making contracts with him. By 1747 homesteads extended for sixty miles along the South Branch and along much of Patterson Creek. Families such as the Heaths, Van Meters, Hornbacks, Hites, Harnesses, Armentrouts, Inskeeps, McNeals, Renicks, Shobes, and Cunninghams, which would in time become prominent, either acquired their lands from Fairfax or became his tenants after the resolution of his dispute with Virginia.[4]

Cultural Influences. Pioneers in the lower Shenandoah and upper Potomac valleys escaped much of the crudeness and prolonged reversion to primitive conditions that characterized most of the Appalachian frontier. As elsewhere, religion and education suffered acutely from the erosive effects of the frontier experience. On the other hand, strong family ties and national consciousness, such as that which prevailed among the Germans, helped preserve moral and ethical standards. The requirement that Virginia speculators settle families rather than individuals had a salutary effect and cannot be ignored in any assessment of the significance of the land speculator west of the Blue Ridge.

A quarter of a century in which they remained unmolested by the Indians and favorable geographical conditions also contributed to the preservation of social and economic forms. Like the Bluegrass region of Kentucky and the Nashville Basin of Tennessee, the limestone soils of the Shenandoah and upper Potomac valleys provided unsurpassed grazing lands and promoted a diversified plantation-type agriculture. As early as 1747 Moravian missionaries reported barns along the South Branch large enough to accommodate religious gatherings. In 1762 the Virginia General Assembly incorporated the towns of Mecklenburg and Romney. By the time of the American Revolution, plantations, including Adam Stephen's Bower, Horatio Gates's Traveler's Rest, and Samuel Washington's Harewood, were common in the lower Shenandoah Valley.

Taking advantage of their opportunities, residents of the Shenandoah and upper Potomac valleys transformed a naturally favored land into one of milk and honey. Andrew Burnaby, a British traveler, declared in 1760 that they had "what many princes would give half their dominions for, health, content[ment], and tranquillity of mind."[5]

[4]For the changing relationships between social classes on the Virginia frontier, see Albert H. Tillson, Jr., *Gentry and Common Folk: Political Culture on a Virginia Frontier, 1740-1789* (Lexington: University Press of Kentucky, 1991).

[5]Andrew Burnaby, *Travels Through the Middle Settlements in North-America, in the Years 1759 and 1760, with Observations on the State of the Colonies* (London: Printed for T. Payne, 1775), 33.

3

At the Vortex of
Imperial Conflict

Tension in the Ohio Valley. Unlike the peaceful advance of settlement into the Valley of Virginia, occupation of trans-Allegheny West Virginia proceeded amid considerable peril. French and Indian claimants contested nearly every move by the Virginia settlers into the area. The claims of both England and France to the Ohio Valley, of which trans-Allegheny West Virginia was a part, rested upon principles recognized by international usage. England based her claims upon the discovery of the New River by Batts and Fallam, an extensive fur trade in the region, and settlements along remote tributaries of the Ohio, such as the New and the Greenbrier. France asserted rights emanating from the alleged visit of La Salle in 1669, far-flung trading operations, and settlements in the Illinois country.

In 1742, during King George's War, two Virginians, John Howard and John Peter Salling, perhaps in anticipation of the opening of trans-Allegheny lands, set out for the western country. Howard, who apparently lived on the South Branch of the Potomac, and Salling, then living on the New River, ascended the South Branch and moved westward by way of the New and Coal rivers. At Peytona, on the Coal River, they observed outcroppings of coal. They continued to the Kanawha and followed that stream to the Ohio, where they constructed a bullboat, which carried them on to New Orleans.

Whether Howard and Salling had any official or semiofficial sanction for their journey remains unknown, but skeptical French officials took no chances. They arrested the entire party. Salling managed to escape and make his way back to Virginia. His journal probably provided much of the information on western Virginia used by Joshua Fry and Peter Jefferson in their famous map of 1751. Not so fortunate, Howard and the other men were sent to France and put on trial. The court cleared them of any criminal charges, whereupon they went to London and faded into obscurity.[1]

[1]The background of the Howard and Salling expedition is discussed in Fairfax Harrison, "The Virginians on the Ohio and Mississippi in 1742," *Virginia Magazine of History and Biography* 30(April 1922):203-22.

With her own claims to parts of the Ohio Valley at stake, Virginia took the lead in asserting the rights of England. Her contention that the Iroquois, or Six Nations, had ceded their right to territory west of the Allegheny Mountains in the Treaty of Lancaster of 1744 suggests that even then she was ready to embark upon an aggressive policy in the Ohio Valley. In the wake of the Treaty of Aix-la-Chapelle in 1748, which ended King George's War but proved no more than an armed truce, both Virginia and France stepped up their activities in the Ohio Valley.

The Virginia Land Companies. Convinced that settlements were essential to control of the Ohio Valley, Virginia as early as 1745 turned to the policy that had proved successful in peopling the Valley of Virginia. She offered speculators one thousand acres of land for each family they settled west of the Allegheny Mountains and allowed them four years instead of the customary two to meet their requirements. By the end of 1754, Virginia had granted more than 2,500,000 acres in the trans-Allegheny region, about 650,000 of them in West Virginia. Only three of the recipients, the Greenbrier, Loyal, and Ohio companies, however, achieved any noteworthy success.[2]

The Greenbrier Company came closest to fulfilling its agreement. Its members included John Robinson, Sr., the Speaker of the House of Burgesses, John Lewis, a prominent Valley landowner, and others with political influence and experience in settling frontier areas. In 1745 the company received one hundred thousand acres in the Greenbrier Valley. By 1754 Andrew Lewis, its surveyor, had laid off more than fifty thousand acres.[3]

The Loyal Company, with a grant of eight hundred thousand acres in 1748, consisted of forty prominent Virginians, including Joshua Fry and Peter Jefferson. Its guiding spirit was Dr. Thomas Walker of Albemarle County, who moved to Wolf Hills, the present Abingdon, about 1748. On March 6, 1750, Walker and five companions undertook a search for lands for the company. They passed through Cumberland Gap and into central Kentucky and missed the rich Bluegrass region by only about a day's journey. Walker and his men returned home by way of southern West Virginia and the Bluestone, New, and Greenbrier rivers. By 1754 the Loyal Company had seated about two hundred families on its lands, mostly in southwestern Virginia, but a few apparently settled along the New and Bluestone rivers in West Virginia.

Much closer to the heart of the international conflict in the Ohio Valley was

---

[2]Descriptions of these grants are in H.R. McIlwaine, Wilmer Hall, and Benjamin J. Hillman, eds., *Executive Journals of the Council of Colonial Virginia*, 6 vols. (Richmond: Virginia State Library, 1925-1966): Vol. 5, 172-73, 195, 206, 231, 258, 282-83, 295-97, 377, 409, 426-27, 436-37, 454-55, 470. For a summary, see Otis K. Rice, *The Allegheny Frontier: West Virginia Beginnings, 1730-1830* (Lexington: University Press of Kentucky, 1970), 34-38.

[3]There is no single account of the Greenbrier Company, but useful information can be gleaned from several secondary works, including Patricia Givens Johnson, *General Andrew Lewis of Roanoke and Greenbrier* (Blacksburg, Va.: Southern Printing Company, 1980), 16-19.

the Ohio Company of Virginia. Organized by Thomas Lee and including Thomas Cresap, Augustine Washington, and George Fairfax among its members, it sought a grant of five hundred thousand acres of land in 1747. Governor William Gooch declined to authorize the grant, but yielded after the company carried its case to the English Privy Council. The company received two hundred thousand acres with the stipulation that it settle one hundred families within seven years and build and garrison a fort for their protection. Once it had complied with these terms, it might have an additional three hundred thousand acres on similar conditions. The Ohio Company never specifically located its lands, and its only settlement, of eleven families, was in the vicinity of Redstone, Pennsylvania.

In its quest for land, the Ohio Company dispatched Christopher Gist, a competent North Carolina surveyor and explorer, on two expeditions. On the first, undertaken in 1750-1751, Gist proceeded from the residence of Thomas Cresap, at Oldtown, Maryland, to the Forks of the Ohio, now Pittsburgh. He then followed a circuitous route through Ohio, Kentucky, and southwestern Virginia to a point near his old home on the Yadkin River in North Carolina. On the second expedition, he explored both sides of the Ohio River from the present Pittsburgh to the mouth of the Kanawha. He moved up the Kanawha, where he found excellent lands, and then turned back toward the Ohio and proceeded northward by way of Mason, Jackson, Wood, Pleasants, and Tyler counties.

In the early summer of 1752 Virginia cemented her claims to trans-Allegheny lands by the Treaty of Logstown with Delaware, Shawnee, and Mingo chiefs. Representing her at the conference, held about eighteen miles below the Forks of the Ohio, were Lunsford Lomax, Joshua Fry and Colonel James Patton, a prominent Valley of Virginia landowner. Gist was present to speak for the interests of the Ohio Company. In the Treaty of Logstown the Indians reluctantly accepted the interpretation of the Treaty of Lancaster of 1744 by which Virginia claimed trans-Allegheny lands south of the Ohio River in western Pennsylvania, West Virginia, and Kentucky.

Early Trans-Allegheny Settlements. Following the end of King George's War in 1748, settlers began a cautious advance across the Alleghenies. Their most important moves were into the Greenbrier Valley. Among the first were Jacob Marlin and Stephen Sewell, who resided at Marlinton. According to tradition, they disagreed over religion, and decided that Marlin should remain at their cabin and Sewell should live in a hollow tree as a means of preserving their friendship. Indians later killed Sewell on Sewell Mountain, and Marlin returned to the Valley of Virginia. Sewell was one of eighteen persons who received a grant of land between the Greenbrier and Monongahela rivers in November 1752, and it seems likely that he and Marlin were land prospectors rather than bona fide settlers.

At the beginning of the French and Indian War, about fifty families evidently lived in the Greenbrier Valley. In 1750 Thomas Walker reported several "plantations" and asserted that prospective settlers had already purchased much of the land from the Greenbrier Company. Most of the settlements lay on Muddy, Howard, Anthony, Spring Lick, and Knapp creeks and in the area known as the Sinks rather than along the river itself. Prominent pioneer families included those of John Keeney, James Burnside, Thomas Campbell, Samuel Carroll, Archibald Clendenin, Andrew Lewis, Lemuel Howard, James Ewing, Patrick Davis, William Renick, Felty and Matthias Yocum, and George, Frederick, and John See.

Other pioneers crossed the Alleghenies to the headwaters of the Monongahela. In 1753 Robert Files and David Tygart, for whom Files Creek and the Tygart Valley River are named, settled near Beverly, either on or near the Seneca Trail. The following year Files, his wife, and five of their six children were killed by Indians. A surviving son warned the Tygart family, and together they escaped to settlements on the South Branch of the Potomac. Five years later Delaware and Mingo Indians killed Thomas Decker and other settlers at Morgantown. Meanwhile, in 1756, Gabriel and Israel Eckerlin, ascetic and pacifistic settlers at Dunkard Bottom, on the Cheat River, fell victim to Indian attacks. Settlements beyond the Alleghenies were clearly beyond the perimeter of safety in the 1750s.

French Countermoves. After King George's War, France also began to reinforce her claims to the Ohio Valley. Recognizing the Ohio Valley as a significant political and economic link between Canada and Louisiana, the Comte de la Galissoniere, governor general of Canada, took steps to gain the support of the Indians of the region. In 1748 he dispatched an expedition of about 230 Canadian militiamen and Indians to the Ohio under the leadership of Pierre-Joseph Celoron de Blainville. The expedition descended the Allegheny and Ohio rivers. At prominent points along the route, Blainville buried lead plates with inscriptions asserting the right of France to the Ohio Valley. One plate was later found at the mouth of Wheeling Creek and another at the mouth of the Kanawha. Blainville found numerous English traders but no inclination in the Indians to desert them.

Determined not to lose the Ohio Valley by default, a new governor-general, Marquis Duquesne, in 1753 sent about two thousand Troupes de la Marine and Canadian militiamen to build a road from Lake Erie to the headwaters of the Ohio and to construct forts at strategic places. Captain Pierre-Paul de la Malgué, sieur de Marin, whom Duquesne placed in charge of the work, pressed forward so relentlessly that he and nearly four hundred of his men died. The show of power by the French, however, impressed the Indians. They began to sever their relations with the English, with whom they had already become dissatisfied. By the end of 1753 no Virginia or Pennsylvania traders remained in the Ohio Valley. Moreover, Forts Presqu'Isle at Erie, LeBoeuf at the mouth of French Creek, and Venango at Franklin, Pennsylvania, prevented further English penetrations south of Lake Erie.

Virginia and the Burden of Empire. In Robert Dinwiddie, Virginia had a governor whose boldness and determination matched those of the governors-general of Canada. Believing that the time had come for a showdown in the Ohio Valley, Dinwiddie in October 1753 took imperial affairs into his own hands. He sent George Washington to Fort LeBoeuf with a message to Jacques le Gardeur de Saint-Pierre, the French commandant in the Ohio Valley, charging France with encroachment upon English territory and calling upon her to withdraw. The courtly Saint-Pierre received Washington with becoming dignity, but he denied that France had violated English territory. He declared that France intended to remain in the Ohio Valley.

With uncommon perception for a man only twenty-one years old, Washington concluded that the Forks of the Ohio, at the present Pittsburgh, held the key to control of the Ohio Valley. Convinced that Washington was right, Dinwiddie in January 1754 dispatched Captain William Trent and a work party of thirty-seven men to build a fort at the Forks of the Ohio. In April, Washington, with 150 men drawn largely from Frederick and Augusta counties, set out to provide a garrison for the fort. On the way, Washington met the work party returning home. It reported that a large French force had come down the Allegheny River, taken possession of their partially completed structure, and begun building their own fortification, Fort Duquesne.

For reasons that remain obscure, Washington proceeded on to the Forks of the Ohio. Warned of his approach, Claude-Pierre Pecaudy de Contrecoeur, who was in charge of French forces there, ordered a detachment of thirty-three men under Ensign Joseph Coulon de Villiers de Jumonville to intercept the Virginians and warn them to leave. During the night, however, Washington, with about forty militiamen and Indians, surrounded Jumonville's camp. In an attack at daybreak, Jumonville was killed, and the surprised French surrendered. In anticipation of French retaliation, Washington hurriedly threw up a small defense known as Fort Necessity at Great Meadows, near Uniontown, Pennsylvania. On July 3, 1754, the French assaulted the little fort and forced Washington to surrender. They allowed the Virginians to leave, but they made Washington promise not to attempt further fortifications in the Ohio Valley for at least a year.

The victorious Contrecoeur boasted that with Indian support he would drive the English from the trans-Allegheny country. Reports began to circulate among the Virginia settlements that France intended to establish her defense perimeter along the crests of the Alleghenies rather than the Ohio River. Rumors that four hundred Frenchmen were being assembled to construct forts on the Greenbrier, New, and Holston rivers produced alarm in border settlements.

The Braddock Campaign. Convinced that Virginia alone could no longer deal with the French threat in the Ohio Valley, Dinwiddie appealed to London for help. The British government responded by sending General Edward Braddock and two regiments of British regulars to Virginia. With 1,400 Redcoats and 450 Virginia militiamen, Braddock set out for the Forks of the Ohio by way of

Fort Cumberland and Nemacolin's Trail, a path marked out by the Indian guide who had accompanied Washington to Fort LeBoeuf nearly two years previously.

Braddock faced serious difficulties. He lacked Indian allies, and Virginia supplied a disappointingly small number of militiamen. He had to clear a road for transporting his artillery and moving heavy freight wagons. Moreover, his successes with European military tactics rendered him incapable of adapting to modes of fighting in the American wilderness. Worse still, his underestimation of the strength of French forces at the Forks of the Ohio and his reliance upon the element of surprise proved disastrous. On July 9, 1755, Braddock himself was surprised when he was less than ten miles from Fort Duquesne, and his army was cut to pieces. Braddock was mortally wounded in the attack.

The failure of the Braddock expedition laid border settlements of West Virginia wide open to attack by the French and Indians. In late August 1755, bands of Indians attacked the Greenbrier settlements. They killed twenty-five people, took two captives, burned eleven houses, and slaughtered or drove off about five hundred cattle.[4] Survivors fled across the Alleghenies to the Valley of Virginia. They did not return until 1761, when the Greenbrier region once again seemed safe from attack. Similar conditions prevailed in the upper Potomac Valley. Scores of terrified residents on Patterson Creek, the South Branch, and even the Cacapon River, left for the Shenandoah Valley rather than face annihilation. In October 1755, George Washington, who had been placed in charge of all Virginia militia, visited the region. The scenes of desolation and bitterness of the people over the lack of adequate protection so discouraged him that he contemplated resigning his command.

The Sandy Creek Expedition. No abatement in the perils to the West Virginia frontiers could be expected until the French were driven from the Forks of the Ohio and their control over the Ohio Valley Indians was broken. Although the Virginia General Assembly appropriated forty thousand pounds for defense, Dinwiddie had no illusions that Virginia forces could dislodge the French from their position. After months of steadfast opposition to any expedition against Fort Duquesne or into the Indian country, he finally yielded to a popular clamor and authorized a strike against the Shawnee villages in Ohio. Upon the recommendation of George Washington, he named Major Andrew Lewis to lead the expedition. At Fort Frederick, near Ingles Ferry on the New River, Lewis assembled about 340 men, of whom between 80 and 130 were Cherokee warriors.

From the time that it left Fort Frederick on February 18, 1756, the Sandy Creek Expedition, as the move was known, encountered nothing but difficulty

[4]Preston's Register of Persons Killed, Wounded, or Taken Prisoner . . ., Draper MSS, 1QQ83, State Historical Society of Wisconsin, Madison (Microfilm in West Virginia Division of Archives and History, Charleston). See also Elizabeth Cometti and Festus P. Summers, eds., *The Thirty-Fifth State: A Documentary History of West Virginia* (Morgantown: West Virginia University Library, 1966), 51-56.

and disappointment. Rugged terrain and streams swollen by incessant rains impeded the march by way of the North Fork of the Holston River, Burkes Garden, the upper Clinch, and the Big Sandy River. On February 29, the men crossed the flooded Big Sandy sixty-six times within fifteen miles and had to abandon several packhorses. By March 3, rations had to be reduced to one-half pound of flour per man and whatever game could be killed. With most of the packhorses worn out, morale among the men gone, and desertions increasing, Lewis held a council of war on March 15. Despite his entreaties to continue, the officers voted to abandon the expedition and return home. Organized in haste, inadequately supplied, and dependent upon raw frontier militiamen averse to military discipline, the expedition did nothing to alleviate the distressing conditions on the frontiers.[5]

Grim Days on the Border. About the same time that remnants of the Sandy Creek Expedition began straggling back home, the General Assembly took steps to bolster defenses on the upper Potomac. It authorized a chain of twenty-two forts extending from the Cacapon River to the South Fork of the Mayo. It stipulated that nine of the posts should be built in present West Virginia, on the Cacapon, the South Branch of the Potomac, and Patterson Creek, and that 1,045 of the 2,000 men designated for garrison duty be assigned to them. Meanwhile, on April 18, Indians killed Captain John Mercer and sixteen men at Fort Edwards on the Cacapon River, and crumbling defenses there threatened to expose the Shenandoah Valley to attack. Militiamen ordered to the South Branch sometimes disappeared surreptitiously, and some companies fell apart before the time for departure. Before the summer ended, Indians had made several attacks in the vicinity of Fort George on the South Branch, assaulted Fort Neally on Opequon Creek, and engaged settlers and militia in the bloody battle of The Trough. Most of the attacks, however, involved isolated families, such as that of Samuel Bingaman, who killed eight of his assailants before he lost his own life.

In spite of fears that the upper Potomac frontier might collapse and expose the Shenandoah Valley to attack, settlers on the South Branch held their ground. In recognition of their fortitude, a council of war held at Fort Cumberland in April 1757 recommended that additional troops be posted on the South Branch "in order to preserve that valuable Settlement—to induce the people to plant a sufficiency of Corn; and to prevent by that means, the vale of Winchester from becoming the Frontier."[6] The South Branch residents remained even after Indians in the spring of 1758 killed Captain James Dunlap and twenty-two men at Fort Upper Tract, killed or captured thirty persons at Fort Seybert, and burned Fort Warden.

The Changing Fortunes of War. For the West Virginia frontiers, the storms of war subsided almost as quickly as they had gathered. The relief came partly as

---

[5]Albert H. Tillson, Jr., *Gentry and Common Folk: Political Culture on a Virginia Frontier, 1740-1789* (Lexington: University Press of Kentucky, 1991), 68, 70-71, 72-73.

[6]Quoted in Louis K. Koontz, *The Virginia Frontier, 1754-1763* (Baltimore: Johns Hopkins Press, 1925), 163.

a result of the new and vigorous leadership that Prime Minister William Pitt instilled into the British war effort in 1757. In North America, Pitt laid the groundwork for eventual triumph by advancing such young and capable officers as James Wolfe, Jeffrey Amherst, and John Forbes to high rank and entrusting them with crucial assignments. In 1758 the British launched major campaigns in the Saint Lawrence–Great Lakes area and achieved signal successes in the capture of Louisbourg, which guarded the eastern approach to Quebec, and Fort Frontenac.

The campaign directed against Fort Duquesne in the fall of 1758 had immediate effects on the West Virginia frontier. A British army of six thousand men led by Forbes far outmatched French forces at Fort Duquesne, which had been depleted to provide troops for other fighting fronts. Convinced that he could not withstand an assault by Forbes's army, the French commandant ordered his men to blow up Fort Duquesne and withdraw up the Allegheny River toward Canada. Forbes immediately occupied the strategic position taken from the Virginians four years earlier. Indian tribes of the Ohio Valley began to sever their ties to the French and to seek peace with the British. The fall of Fort Duquesne relieved the pressure on the West Virginia frontiers, and almost at once a few intrepid settlers began to cross the Alleghenies.

Wolfe's capture of Quebec, the great bastion of French military power, in 1759 and the fall of Montreal the following year sealed the French fate in North America. The Treaty of Paris in 1763 settled with finality the question of control of the Ohio Valley, where the nine-year conflict between England and France had begun. Trans-Allegheny West Virginia was to be English. But the Shawnee still claimed the land, and much blood would be shed before settlement could proceed with peace and safety.

4

Advance Across the Alleghenies

The Lure of Transmontane Lands. The English victory over the French in 1763 did not open the Ohio Valley to settlement. On the contrary, in the very year that Forbes occupied the Forks of the Ohio, Sir William Johnson, acting in behalf of Pennsylvania, promised the Iroquois in the Treaty of Easton to close the part of the colony west of the Alleghenies to settlement. Colonel Henry Bouquet, the commandant at Fort Pitt, later extended that commitment to include transmontane Maryland and Virginia.

Angered by the promises of Johnson and Bouquet, Virginia speculators fell back upon a proclamation of Governor Robert Dinwiddie in 1754 setting aside two hundred thousand acres of land west of the mountains for Virginia military officers in the French and Indian War. Several of the officers, including George Washington and George Mercer, declared that they would "leave no stone unturned" in order to acquire the forbidden lands.[1] Governor Francis Fauquier later interceded with the English Board of Trade, but it refused to approve the military grant.

Fauquier achieved more success with respect to the claims of the Greenbrier and Loyal companies. Their lands had been "tolerably seated for some time" but had been vacated during the French and Indian War. The Board of Trade took refuge in ambivalence, declining to render "any explicit Opinion" and enjoining the governor from any action that might arouse the Indians.[2] Both companies and prospective settlers took advantage of official uncertainty to reoccupy their lands. In 1762 Archibald Clendenin settled two miles west of Lewisburg, and Frederick See and Felty Yocum took up tracts on Muddy Creek. By the summer of 1763 more than fifty persons were again living in the Greenbrier region.

Pontiac's Uprising. The British victory in the French and Indian War produced great anxiety among the western Indians. Settlers, often in the guise of hunters, continued to move into the region around Fort Pitt and other parts of the

[1]Stanislaus Murray Hamilton, ed., *Letters to Washington and Accompanying Papers,* 5 vols. (Boston: Houghton, Mifflin and Company, 1898-1902), vol. 2, 159.

[2]Quoted in Jack M. Sosin, *Whitehall and the Wilderness: The Middle West in British Colonial Policy, 1760-1775* (Lincoln: University of Nebraska Press, 1961), 45-46.

Ohio Valley. Moreover, reports reached the Indians that Amherst had advocated infecting the tribes with smallpox and that Bouquet had urged the use of trained dogs to hunt and destroy them. When Amherst announced in 1762 that the customary presents to the tribes would not be distributed during the coming winter, unrest reached a head.

Led by Pontiac, an Ottawa chief, the western Indians laid plans for surprise military attacks that would undermine British power in the Ohio Valley and confine their settlements to areas east of the Allegheny Mountains. On May 7, 1763, Pontiac struck at Detroit, and later that month Shawnee and Delaware laid siege to Fort Pitt. Bands of Indians assaulted other posts, and by the end of July only Detroit, Fort Pitt, and Fort Niagara remained in British hands. An expedition under Captain James Dalyell relieved besieged Detroit, and another, under Bouquet, defeated the Indians at Bushy Run and raised the siege of Fort Pitt. By the summer of 1764 the British had broken the power of the Indian confederacy, but Pontiac did not make peace until the following year.

The Shawnee carried Pontiac's War to the West Virginia frontiers with attacks in the Greenbrier region and on the upper Potomac, particularly along the South Branch and the Cacapon. In the summer of 1763 about sixty Shawnee led by Cornstalk entered the Greenbrier region. Posing as friends, small parties visited the Muddy Creek settlements, including the homes of Frederick See and Felty Yocum, and killed or captured every person there. They moved on to the Big Levels, present Lewisburg, to the house of Archibald Clendenin, where about fifty persons had gathered to feast on three elk that Clendenin had killed. The unsuspecting settlers invited the Indians to join them. After they had eaten, the Shawnee sprang their attack. One man made his escape, but the Indians killed or captured all the other settlers. Governor Fauquier ordered a thousand militiamen under Colonel Adam Stephen and Major Andrew Lewis to man small forts, establish guards at mountain passes, and pursue Indians making forays into the settlements. Peace did not return to the West Virginia frontiers, however, until Bouquet defeated the Indians at Bushy Run and Sir William Johnson concluded peace with the tribes at Niagara.

The Proclamation of 1763. Stunned by Pontiac's uprising and groping for some policy that might mitigate the fury of the Indians, the British government on October 7, 1763, issued a sweeping proclamation forbidding settlement west of the Allegheny Mountains. Its actions angered both prospective settlers and land speculators. The only redeeming feature that they saw in the proclamation was a provision for later review and possible extension of the Indian boundary westward. Their pressures induced Lord Shelburne, the Secretary of State for the Southern Department, on January 5, 1768, to authorize the drawing of a new line of demarcation. On March 12 Lord Hillsborough, the new Secretary of State for the American Department, directed Sir William Johnson and John Stuart, the two Indian superintendents in the colonies, to arrange the necessary conferences with the Indians.

Hillsborough instructed Johnson and Stuart to negotiate a boundary running from the Susquehanna River westward to the Ohio, along the Ohio to the mouth of the Kanawha, and from there in a straight line to Chiswell's Mine, on the New River. The proposed boundary cleared the military grant promised by Dinwiddie in 1754 and most of the lands claimed by the Greenbrier and Loyal companies.

During the autumn of 1768 Johnson and Stuart conducted simultaneous negotiations with the Iroquois and Cherokee, respectively. Stuart, the Indian superintendent for the Southern District, or the colonies south of Pennsylvania, concluded the Treaty of Hard Labor on October 17, by which the Cherokee gave up their claims to lands north of a line drawn from Chiswell's Mine to the mouth of the Kanawha. In the Treaty of Fort Stanwix of November 5, Johnson, the superintendent for the Northern District, or colonies from Pennsylvania northward, went far beyond his instructions. Instead of negotiating the release of Iroquois claims to lands north of the mouth of the Kanawha River, he obtained on November 5 a treaty by which they gave up lands south to the Tenneseee River, confirmed an earlier grant of 200,000 acres to George Croghan, Johnson's deputy, and stipulated that a large tract must be provided a group of Philadelphia merchants calling themselves the Suffering Traders.

Johnson's violations of his instructions produced widespread dissatisfaction. The governments of both Pennsylvania and Virginia refused to recognize the grants to Croghan and the Suffering Traders. Lord Hillsborough informed Johnson that the Crown had no intention of permitting settlement beyond the mouth of the Kanawha. Johnson, however, offered the weak defense that if he had not accepted the provisions for Croghan and the Suffering Traders, as well as the Tenneseee River line, the Iroquois would not have made any agreement. Johnson's action led to pressures to acquire additional territory from the Cherokee.

On October 18, 1770, Stuart concluded the Treaty of Lochaber, by which the Cherokee agreed to a new boundary, which ran from the Virginia–North Carolina border to a point near Long Island in the Holston River and thence in a straight line to the mouth of the Kanawha. The treaties of Hard Labor, Fort Stanwix, and Lochaber completely extinguished the rights of the Iroquois and Cherokee to West Virginia, except a small Cherokee claim in the southwest corner of the state.

A Wave of Trans-Allegheny Settlements. The treaties of Hard Labor and Fort Stanwix opened the floodgates to settlement of the trans-Allegheny region from the northern part of Pennsylvania to the headstreams of the Tennessee River. Beginning in the spring of 1769, thousands of pioneers occupied lands in the Greenbrier, Monongahela, upper Ohio, and Kanawha valleys, as well as choice sites in intervening areas.

The movement into the Greenbrier Valley, the third attempt at settlement, was led by John Stuart, Robert McClanahan, Thomas Renick, and William

Hamilton, who located near Frankford in 1769. Within the next six years, at least three hundred families, drawn largely from the Scotch-Irish population in the southern part of the Valley of Virginia, moved into the Greenbrier area. They included the Boggs, Burnside, Clendenin, Donnally, Handley, Johnson, Keeney, Kelly, Kincaid, Lewis, Mathews, McClung, Nichols, Skaggs, Swope, and Woods families.

Even before 1768, intrepid men had made their way into the Monongahela Valley. In 1761 John and Samuel Pringle, deserters from the garrison at Fort Pitt, took up residence in a large hollow sycamore tree near Buckhannon. Three years later John Simpson arrived in the Clarksburg area. These men, and a few others, lived by hunting and trapping. They were the counterparts of Daniel Boone and other noted Long Hunters who ventured into Kentucky and Tennessee about the same time.

Monongahela Valley settlers originating in New Jersey, Pennsylvania, and parts of Maryland and Virginia followed Forbes's or Braddock's roads to the middle Monongahela and then made their way upstream, while those from the upper Potomac, particularly the South Branch, threaded their way through the mountains to the waters of the Cheat and Tygart Valley. Conspicuous family names along the Monongahela and its West Fork and Cheat tributaries included Cobun, Collins, Davisson, Dorsey, Haymond, Ice, Judy, Martin, Miller, Nutter, Parsons, Pierpont, Scott, Shinn, Stewart, and Wade. Among the early pioneers were Zackwell Morgan, Michael Kerns, and John Evans, who located at Morgantown in 1772.

Like Daniel Boone in Kentucky, the Pringle brothers later turned immigrant guides. They led numerous settlers into the Tygart Valley, which abounded in game animals, wild fruits, and fertile lands. The accretions to the Buckhannon and Hackers Creek settlements were so great in 1773 that the grain crops were insufficient to feed the people, and they suffered a "starving year." Early settlers in the Tygart Valley included the Connelly, Hadden, Jackson, Nelson, Riffle, Stalnaker, Warwick, Westfall, Whiteman, and Wilson families.

Most writers have credited the first settlements in the upper Ohio Valley section of West Virginia to Ebenezer, Silas, and Jonathan Zane, who allegedly arrived at Wheeling in 1769, or even earlier. George Washington, who in his own search for lands passed the site of Wheeling on October 24, 1770, made no mention in his journal of any inhabitants there. Moreover, Ebenezer Zane, David Shepherd, John Wetzel, and Samuel McCulloch, all among the earliest residents of the Wheeling area, stated later that they made their settlements in 1772. Fears that the claims of the Suffering Traders, later known as the Indiana Company, might be upheld retarded occupation of lands between the Ohio and Monongahela rivers.

In 1773 Walter Kelly, and possibly John Jones and William Pryor, settled in the Kanawha Valley. Kelly, a refugee from the Carolina backcountry and a man "of bold and intrepid disposition," located at Cedar Grove, where he was killed by Indians the following year.[3] Shortly afterward, William Morris acquired the tomahawk rights (based on notching of trees along the boundary) of Kelly's widow, who, with the remainder of the family had returned to the Greenbrier settlements prior to the attack. With his large and prolific family, Morris established the first permanent settlements in the Kanawha Valley.

The Proposed Colony of Vandalia. For a time it appeared that the trans-Allegheny settlements of West Virginia would become part of Vandalia, a proposed fourteenth colony. Vandalia had its origins in the grant made to the Suffering Traders, or Indiana Company, in the Treaty of Fort Stanwix. In 1769 the company sent Samuel Wharton to London to press its claim. Through tact and skillful maneuvering, Wharton won the support of several cabinet officials and members of parliament, including Thomas Walpole, an influential London merchant. Some of the English supporters, including Walpole, became members. The organization then took the name of the Grand Ohio Company, but it was more commonly known as the Walpole Company, in honor of its chief English supporter.

The Grand Ohio Company endeavored to purchase 2.4 million acres from the territory ceded by the Iroquois and offered the Crown 10,640 pounds, the exact amount that the government had paid the Indians for the entire cession. Its members were astonished when Lord Hillsborough, whom they expected to place impediments in their path, suggested that they enlarge their request to 20 million acres, or sufficient land to establish a separate colony. Hillsborough probably expected to wreck the scheme by pushing the price up to about 100,000 pounds and by raising further opposition from Virginia. Wharton and Walpole reached an understanding with the Treasury Commissioners on January 11, 1770, however, by which the price remained at 10,640 pounds.

The company proved equally adroit in overcoming opposition in Virginia. Excited by prospects that he might become governor of the new colony, George Mercer negotiated the merger of the Ohio Company of Virginia, of which he was the agent, into the Grand Ohio Company. In addition, the Grand Ohio Company agreed to set aside two hundred thousand acres in one tract for the military grant promised by Dinwiddie in 1754. It eased the fears of men such as Andrew Lewis and Thomas Walker by recognizing the rights of earlier grantees, including the Greenbrier and Loyal companies.

On July 1, 1772, the Committee on Plantation Affairs approved the Grand Ohio Company grant. Lord Hillsborough, who steadfastly opposed the move, was forced out of office, and on the very day that he left, the Privy Council gave its approval. The new colony, named Vandalia in honor of Queen Charlotte, who

---

[3]The only contemporary description of Kelly is in John Stuart, *Memoir of Indian Wars, and Other Occurrences* (Richmond: Virginia Historical and Philosophical Society, 1833; Parsons, W.Va.: McClain Printing Company, 1971), 8-9. The author of this account, a pioneer in the Greenbrier region, is not to be confused with John Stuart, Indian superintendent of the Southern District.

claimed descent from the Vandals, included all of trans-Allegheny West Virginia, the part of Pennsylvania between the Monongahela and Ohio rivers, and all of Kentucky east of the Kentucky River.

Although the setting of the royal seal on the document was the only official action that remained, Vandalia never became a colony. Complaints about vagueness in its boundaries and possible problems in the collection of quitrents arose, but the greatest deterrent was the rapidly developing hostility between England and her American colonies. The Boston Tea Party in 1773 and the Intolerable Acts of the following year wrecked all hopes for Vandalia.

Lord Dunmore and the Land Speculators. Virginia experienced a new surge of land speculation in the wake of the treaties of Hard Labor and Fort Stanwix. Speculators found a warm friend in John Murray, Earl of Dunmore, who arrived as governor on December 12, 1771. When the prospects for Vandalia dimmed, Virginia speculators, encouraged by Dunmore, sprang to action. On the basis of the Dinwiddie commitment of 1754 and the Proclamation of 1763, Dunmore made several important military grants in West Virginia. They included 21,941 acres on the Kanawha between the Coal and Pocatalico rivers to John Fry and others: 51,302 acres at the mouth of the Kanawha to George Muse, Adam Stephen, Andrew Lewis, Peter Hog, and others; 28,400 acres at the mouth of the Little Kanawha to Robert Stobo, Jacob Van Braam, and others; and 26,627 acres along the Ohio and Big Sandy rivers to John Savage and fifty-nine associates.

George Washington, who acquired the rights of numerous French and Indian War veterans, was a prominent beneficiary of Dunmore's policies. In the fall of 1770 Washington personally selected tracts totaling nearly thirty-five thousand acres in the Ohio and Kanawha valleys. On the largest of his tracts, situated on the Kanawha River above Point Pleasant, the proposed capital of Vandalia, he planned to settle immigrants from England, Scotland, Ireland, and the German states. He promised settlers passage money to America, suspension of quitrents for a period of years, and religious freedom. In 1775 he sent James Cleveland and a work party to the Kanawha tract, where it built dwellings, cabins, and a barn and planted a variety of crops and two thousand peach trees. The approach of the American Revolution and the increasing hostility of the Indians forced Washington to abandon his plans.

By the spring of 1773 the land fever in Virginia reached a new intensity. With the blessings of Dunmore, surveying parties led by Thomas Bullitt and James McAfee began to lay off lands in central Kentucky. Bullitt had previously gone to the Shawnee at Chillicothe and gained permission for surveying and settling of lands east of the Kentucky River if the Indians were paid for their claims and retained their hunting rights. Bullitt violated his pledge, however, by surveying tracts as far west as Louisville, some of which Dunmore granted to John Connolly, his agent at Fort Pitt, and to relatives and associates of George Croghan. The provocations in Kentucky did more than anything else to incite the hostilities that broke the peace on the upper Ohio in 1774. Dunmore also upheld the claims of the Greenbrier and Loyal companies by instructing law enforcement officials to evict trespassers on their lands.

The Virginia–Pennsylvania Boundary Dispute. Dunmore, as might have been expected, forcefully asserted Virginia's claim to land around the Forks of the Ohio. The territory had been in dispute between Virginia and Pennsylvania for years, but the influx of settlers after the Treaty of Fort Stanwix gave the problem a new urgency. The charter of Pennsylvania defined her western boundary as five degrees west of the Delaware River, without specifying whether it should follow the meanderings of the Delaware or run due north from a point five degrees west of its mouth. If the former were true, Virginia had a strong claim to the disputed territory; if the latter were the case, Pennsylvania's right was well nigh incontestable.

Pennsylvania made the first moves. In 1769 she opened a land office west of the Alleghenies. Two years later she created Bedford County but designated the town of Bedford, east of the mountains, as its seat. In 1772 she established Westmoreland County, which included all territory west of the Alleghenies. Some six hundred Virginians, led by young Michael Cresap, opposed her assertion of authority and appealed to Virginia to provide them with a government.

In the summer of 1773, Lord Dunmore visited Fort Pitt, ostensibly for a firsthand view of the situation. If he had not already formed that opinion, he now convinced himself that Virginia had jurisdiction over the lands and the right to make grants there. On October 11, after his return to Williamsburg, the council created the District of West Augusta to include all Virginia territory west of the Alleghenies. The Revolutionary War muted the Virginia-Pennsylvania dispute, and in 1784 it was resolved by a westward extension of the Mason-Dixon Line.

At Fort Pitt, Dunmore formed an alliance with George Croghan and John Connolly. Bitter over the refusal of Pennsylvania to recognize his grant from the Iroquois in the Treaty of Fort Stanwix and disappointed in the outcome of the Vandalia project, Croghan accepted the dominion of Virginia over the territory around the Forks of the Ohio in return for which Dunmore honored his title. The governor named Connolly, Croghan's nephew, his agent in charge of both civil and military affairs on the upper Ohio. Dunmore's alliance with Croghan placed at his disposal a man of unsurpassed influence with the Indians, but his liaison with Connolly, who lacked Croghan's tact and judgment, proved disastrous to peace in the Ohio Valley.

Hostilities on the Upper Ohio. The movement of settlers into the trans-Allegheny region and the activities of surveyors in Kentucky led to reprisals by the Shawnee, who had never relinquished their claims. In April 1773 Indians killed George Yeager, who with Adam Strader and sixteen-year-old Simon Kenton, had a hunting camp at the mouth of the Elk River. A band of Shawnee attacked a surveying party under John Floyd at the mouth of the Little Guyandotte and held several of the men for three days. Another party fired upon Kentucky-bound surveyors at the mouth of the Kanawha. The irate men chose Michael Cresap as their leader and urged him to move at once against the Shawnee towns. Cresap prevailed upon them to return to Wheeling until they could find out what steps Virginia authorities proposed to take with regard to the attacks. When Connolly issued an inflammatory circular calling upon residents of the trans-Allegheny region to be prepared to defend themselves, Cresap overcame his reluctance to act. During the ensuing weeks he and his followers participated in several small encounters, commonly known as "Cresap's War."

The most serious and indefensible action on the upper Ohio was the killing of the family of Logan, a Mingo chief, at the mouth of Yellow Creek on April 30. Contemporary accounts vary, but it seems clear that the killing of two Mingoes on the north side of the Ohio River the previous day started the unfortunate chain of events. Four Indians, angry over the killings, crossed the Ohio to a tavern kept by Joshua Baker, where a band of whites led by Daniel Greathouse arrived and plied them with whiskey. While the Indians were in a semidrunken state, Greathouse and his companions killed them. They also killed four other Indians who came to make inquiries. The dead included a brother and a sister of Logan. Their loss turned Logan, an old friend, into an implacable enemy, and he took at least thirteen scalps in retaliation.[4]

Numerous attacks by both Indians and whites occurred during the spring and summer of 1774, and a general war appeared imminent. Responsible officials such as Guy Johnson, John Stuart, and George Croghan became convinced that Dunmore actually desired war with the Indians. Certainly Dunmore's close association with Connally and aggressive Virginia speculators did nothing to ease tensions. Stuart and Johnson used their influence with the Cherokee and Iroquois, respectively, to prevent their participation in a general war. Croghan worked with chiefs such as Kiasutha of the Seneca and Grey Eyes and The Pipe of the Delaware to help restrain most of the tribes northwest of the Ohio River. Isolated, the Shawnee and their friends were almost certain to lose any war with the Virginians.

Dunmore's War. In the summer of 1774 Dunmore took the initiative. In addition to Fort Pitt, now renamed Fort Dunmore, he proposed other defenses. At his direction, Major William Crawford began work on Fort Fincastle at Wheeling. There Colonel Angus McDonald assembled an army of about four hundred men for a strike against the Shawnee. McDonald proceeded without mishap until July 26, when, within six miles of its destination, his army was ambushed by some thirty Indians. Recovering from the surprise, it moved on to the Indian towns, but it found them deserted. McDonald succeeded only in destroying the Indian dwellings and supplies of corn that they had left.

[4]For a summary of events surrounding the killing of Logan's family and responsibility for the murders, see the Introduction to John J. Jacob, *A Biographical Sketch of the Life of the Late Captain Michael Cresap* (Cumberland, Md., 1826; Parsons, W. Va.: McClain Printing Company, 1971), 1-48.

Already, Dunmore had plans for a far larger expedition to "Breake the [Indian] Confederacy."[5] He gathered a force of more than a thousand men, mostly from Frederick, Berkeley, and Hampshire counties, and moved to Fort Dunmore and from there down the Ohio River. On his orders, Andrew Lewis assembled about eleven hundred men from Augusta, Botetourt, and Fincastle counties at Camp Union, at Lewisburg, and moved down the Kanawha Valley to Point Pleasant, with the expectation of continuing up the Ohio to join Dunmore. Their combined forces would then strike the Indian villages.

When Lewis arrived at Point Pleasant on October 6, he found awaiting him a message from Dunmore, who instructed him to join Dunmore's army about twenty-five miles from Chillicothe. Lewis's men opposed leaving the mouth of the Kanawha undefended, since it was a key point on a much-used Indian trail into Augusta, Botetourt, and Fincastle counties.

Meanwhile, Cornstalk, the Shawnee chief, had watched the movements of Dunmore and Lewis carefully. Ascertaining their intentions, he decided to attack Lewis before he could join the governor and then strike at Dunmore as he advanced along the Hocking Valley. Cornstalk concealed between eight and eleven hundred warriors in a densely wooded area along the Ohio, opposite the mouth of the Kanawha. During the night of October 9 he crossed the river to the West Virginia side. About dawn on October 10 some of his warriors fired on Valentine Sevier and James Robinson, who had left Lewis's camp in search of wild turkeys. The two men rushed back to camp and informed Lewis that Indians were lurking about in the woods.

Lewis ordered two parties of about 150 men each, under his brother Charles and William Fleming, to reconnoiter along the Ohio and Kanawha rivers. About sunrise the Indians, consisting of Shawnee, Delaware, Mingo, Ottawa, and others, attacked Charles Lewis's men in full force and mortally wounded Lewis. Realizing the magnitude of the assault, Andrew Lewis dispatched another force under Colonel John Field, who also met his death. By then Fleming's men had also given way, and Fleming had suffered severe but not mortal wounds.

From dawn until evening the battle raged, with Cornstalk calling upon his men to destroy the Virginians. Cornstalk, however, mistook a flanking movement by Isaac Shelby along Crooked Creek for the arrival of more Virginia troops and concluded that he could not win the battle. During the night, therefore, the Indians retired across the Ohio. Lewis lost forty-six men killed and eighty wounded. Indian losses could not be ascertained, since they placed the bodies of their slain in the Ohio River.

Cornstalk now faced one of the most crucial decisions in the history of his tribe. He hastened to his villages on the Pickaway Plains and proposed to his

[5]Reuben Gold Thwaites and Louise Phelps Kellogg, eds., *Documentary History of Dunmore's War, 1774* (Madison: State Historical Society of Wisconsin, 1905; Harrisonburg, Va.: C.J. Carrier, 1974), 97.

people that they either kill all their women and children and fight to the last warrior or that they sue for peace. The warriors favored the latter course. The Cornstalk then sent Matthew Elliott, a white man, to Lord Dunmore to arrange a meeting with the governor.

Unaware of the battle of Point Pleasant and assuming that Lewis was in no danger, Dunmore had meanwhile left a garrison of a hundred men at Fort Gower, a small blockhouse he had thrown up at the mouth of the Hocking River, and moved with the remainder of his army toward the Indian towns. About fifteen miles from his destination, he was met by Cornstalk's emissaries. Dunmore agreed to meet with Cornstalk and the other chiefs and hastily set up quarters known as Camp Charlotte, where he quickly came to terms with the Indians. He sent a messenger to inform Lewis, who, with a hundred men, was en route to find Dunmore. Angry over the governor's action, Lewis's men insisted upon attacking the Indian villages. Dunmore, with about fifty militiamen, and John Gibson, a respected trader, arrived, however, and persuaded the men to return to Point Pleasant.

The Treaty of Camp Charlotte was a temporary agreement. By its terms the Indians gave up all captives; surrendered horses, slaves, and other property that they had taken; and promised to cease hunting south of the Ohio. They also assented to a general conference to be held at Fort Dunmore the following spring for the purpose of concluding a definitive treaty.

The defeat of the Indians and the Treaty of Camp Charlotte did not end the necessity for strong defenses in the trans-Allegheny region. Dunmore placed a garrison of seventy-five men under John Connolly at Fort Dunmore. He directed William Russell to replace the small stockade built by Andrew Lewis at Point Pleasant with Fort Blair, a rectangular structure with blockhouses at two corners. The forts at Pittsburgh and Point Pleasant, along with the one at Wheeling, remained the major bastions of West Virginia frontier defense throughout the Revolutionary War.

Significance of Dunmore's War. The claim made by some writers that Point Pleasant was the first battle of the Revolutionary War has no basis in fact. The defeat of the Indians in the battle and the agreements made at Camp Charlotte and Fort Pitt later had the effect of causing most western tribes to remain neutral in the Revolutionary War until 1777, a circumstance of no small importance.

To deny that Point Pleasant was the first battle of the American Revolution does not necessarily imply that there were no connections between them. As John Shy has pointed out, the long-term causes of Dunmore's War and the Revolutionary War were closely intertwined. Shy emphasizes confusion over western policy within the British government, which allowed Dunmore to pursue his own designs in the trans-Allegheny region. Moreover, the problems of frontier defense and efforts to make the Americans pay part of the costs led to troubles on the seaboard, which in turn accelerated withdrawal of British power from the West, "which predictably blew up in 1774."[6] When viewed in a larger context, the battle of Point Pleasant appears as a major event in the advance of the American frontier. Yet even in these larger dimensions, it has no great significance in Revolutionary War history. At the time it was considered frontier aggressiveness and was condemned rather than applauded by other colonies.

[6]John F. Shy, "Dunmore, the Upper Ohio Valley, and the American Revolution," in Thomas H. Smith, ed., *Ohio in the American Revolution*, Ohio American Revolution Bicentennial Conference Series, no. 1 (Columbus, 1976), 13-16.

The Revolutionary Era

The Response to Revolution. Satisfaction with the intervention of Lord Dunmore in land affairs and the victory at Point Pleasant did not divert the attention of western Virginians from events in Boston and Philadelphia in 1774. On November 5, before they returned home from the campaign, officers and soldiers in Dunmore's War issued the Fort Gower Resolves. They coupled professions of loyalty to King George III and confidence in Lord Dunmore with a declaration that "the love of liberty, and attachment to the real interests and just rights of America outweigh[ed] every other consideration." They pledged exertion of every power within them "for the defense of American liberty."[1] Adam Stephen, who probably convened the men at Fort Gower, declared that "before I would submit my life, liberty, and property to the arbitrary disposal of a corrupt, venal aristocracy, . . . I would set myself down with a few hundred friends upon some rich and healthy spot, six hundred miles to the westward, and there form a settlement, which, in a short time would command attention and respect."[2]

Professions of support for the American cause from westerners, who had their own interests, were no idle boasts. Richard Henry Lee asserted that he could raise six thousand men from the counties of Hampshire, Berkeley, Frederick, Dunmore (now Shenandoah), Augusta, and Botetourt alone. These men had developed "amazing hardihood" from years spent in the woods and such "dexterity" with the Kentucky rifle that they scorned any target within two hundred yards and larger than an orange.[3]

Westerners reacted angrily to reports in April 1775 that Dunmore had removed the powder from the Williamsburg magazine to a British vessel at anchor in the James River. A thousand men from the frontier counties gathered at Fredericksburg to march against the governor, but George Washington dissuaded them from their course.

[1]John E. Robbins, "The Fort Gower Resolves, November 5, 1774," in Thomas H. Smith, ed., *Ohio in the American Revolution,* Ohio American Revolution Bicentennial Conference Series, no. 1 (Columbus, 1976), 21-26.

[2]Quoted in Freeman H. Hart, *The Valley of Virginia in the American Revolution, 1763-1789* (Chapel Hill: University of North Carolina Press, 1942), 85.

[3]Don Higginbotham, *Daniel Morgan, Revolutionary Rifleman* (Chapel Hill: University of North Carolina Press, 1961), 19-20.

When the Continental Congress, on June 14, 1775, called upon Virginia to raise two of the ten companies of riflemen for service in Boston, westerners again demonstrated enthusiasm for the American cause. Upon the advice of Horatio Gates, Washington named two veterans of Dunmore's War, Hugh Stephenson of Berkeley County and Daniel Morgan of Frederick County, to command the companies. The two captains filled their companies within a week, mostly with young men equipped with rifles, tomahawks, scalping knives, and other accoutrements. Morgan left Winchester on July 15, and Stephenson set out from Shepherdstown two days later. Eager to arrive in Cambridge first, and knowing that their simultaneous arrival would give more credit to Stephenson, who outranked him, Morgan ignored an agreement to join Stephenson at Frederick, Maryland, and hastened on to Cambridge, Massachusetts, where he arrived on August 6, five days ahead of Stephenson.

Although there were instances of disloyalty and disaffection during the war, West Virginians generally answered the call of their country with promptness and even enthusiasm. They participated in nearly every major battle, including Quebec, Saratoga, Cowpens, and Kings Mountain. Among the officers who achieved military distinction were Major Generals Horatio Gates and Charles Lee, Brigadier General Adam Stephen, and Captains Hugh Stephenson and William Darke.

Indian Relations. The greatest immediate danger to West Virginia residents lay in the possibility that western Indians might join the British. Peace with western tribes, envisioned in the Treaty of Camp Charlotte, no longer served British interests. In February 1775 Lord Dunmore instructed John Connolly to make the Indians allies. Connolly obtained pledges of friendship from the Delaware and a few of the Mingo chiefs. About a month later Dunmore ordered the disbanding of garrisons at Forts Dunmore, Fincastle, and Blair and the evacuation of the posts.

The defenseless frontiersmen appealed to both the Continental Congress and Virginia authorities for protection. On August 7 the Virginia Convention ordered Captain John Neville and a hundred men from Winchester to Fort Dunmore, now hastily renamed Fort Pitt. Already it had named a commission consisting of Thomas Walker, Andrew Lewis, James Wood, John Walker, and Adam Stephen to confer with tribal chiefs and seek their neutrality. Wood visited the Indian villages at great personal risk and arranged a conference at Fort Pitt in September.

The Treaty of Pittsburgh was essentially a victory for Virginia Indian diplomacy. The Shawnee, Delaware, Mingo, Seneca, Wyandot, Potawatomi, and Ottawa recognized the Ohio River as the new Indian boundary and pledged neutrality in the war between England and the colonies. The tribes generally honored their pledges during the first two years of the war. Their neutrality and the occupation of Fort Pitt by colonial forces encouraged an uninterrupted advance of settlement into the transmontane parts of West Virginia until 1777. Under cover of the strong forts along the Ohio River and dozens of small private forts, trans-Allegheny settlers actually found themselves in a better defensive position in 1777 than they had been at the beginning of the war.

Loyalism on the Upper Ohio. The first major threat to settlers on the upper Ohio was a Loyalist move known as "Connolly's Plot." After he abandoned Fort Dunmore, John Connolly joined the governor aboard a British man-of-war off Yorktown. There he proposed to Dunmore a plan to cut the colonies in two by capturing Fort Pitt with a force of British and Indians, which he would assemble at Detroit. He believed that many settlers, whom he would woo with generous land grants, would join him. Should the plan fail, he proposed to destroy Fort Pitt and Fort Fincastle and rejoin Dunmore at Alexandria. Dunmore referred Connolly to General Thomas Gage, the commander of British forces in America, who also found his plan attractive.

When his route from Boston, where he talked with Gage, to Detroit was cut off by the American capture of Montreal, Connolly disguised himself and set out by way of Virginia and Maryland. John Gibson, a Pittsburgh trader to whom he had confided his intentions, alerted the West Augusta Committee of Safety. Authorities arrested Connolly and a companion as they passed through Hagerstown, Maryland, and their plan, with its danger to the backcountry, ended in failure.

In 1777, when most of the Indians joined the British, Loyalism flared anew on the upper Ohio. Several frontier leaders, among them Alexander McKee, Simon Girty, and Matthew Elliott, espoused the British cause and went to Detroit. Colonel Zackwell Morgan of Monongalia County and five hundred men were needed to quell disturbances in northern West Virginia and southwestern Pennsylvania.

The Indians Join the British. Amid reports that Henry Hamilton, the commandant at Detroit, was exerting pressure upon the Indians to join the British, Virginia took steps as early as 1776 to defend her trans-Allegheny settlements. In the summer of that year Matthew Arbuckle constructed Fort Randolph, a stockade with blockhouses and cabins, to replace Fort Blair, which marauding Indians had burned the previous summer. Arbuckle and his men remained at the post as its garrison. Virginia authorities also placed militiamen at several private forts in the Greenbrier and Monongahela valleys and assigned scouts to keep watch along well-used Indian trails.

Despite all precautions, small bands of Indians terrorized isolated settlements throughout the backcountry beginning in the autumn of 1776. Congress favored a policy of restraint, lest decisive action provoke a general Indian war, but it yielded to the urging of Virginia authorities to the extent of sending Brigadier General Edward Hand to Fort Pitt on June 1, 1777, with orders to coordinate all defense measures on the upper Ohio.

British military strategy for 1777 increased the danger to frontier settlements. The general design called for expeditions from Canada, Oswego, and New York, led by John Burgoyne, Barry St. Leger, and William Howe, respectively, to converge on the Hudson Valley and cut off New England from the remainder of the country. In June Hamilton convened a council of tribal chiefs northwest of the Ohio River for the purpose of enticing them to join the British and engage in diversionary attacks on the trans-Allegheny frontier.

Hamilton won pledges of support from Chippewa and Ottawa chiefs and a few of the Mingo and Wyandot, and other tribes began to waver in their neutrality. Nonhelema, a sister of Cornstalk and a friend of the whites, informed Matthew Arbuckle on July 25 that the Shawnee had called off a visit to Fort Randolph when they heard of the council at Detroit. Four days later David Zeisberger, a Moravian missionary, reported to Hand that all the Indians northwest of the Ohio, except the Delaware, were likely to join the British.

Indian Attacks of 1777. When missionaries and others informed him that the Indians were preparing an attack against some undisclosed target in early August, Hand ordered Colonel David Shepherd, the lieutenant of Ohio County, to take charge of Fort Henry (formerly Fort Fincastle), which had no regular garrison, and to assemble there all militia companies between the Ohio and Monongahela rivers. Eleven companies answered Shepherd's call. The end of August came, without an attack, and Shepherd sent nine of the companies home, leaving only two, under Captains Samuel Mason and Joseph Ogle, with about sixty men, at Fort Henry.

On the night of August 31, about two hundred watchful Wyandot and Mingo, accompanied by a few Delaware and Shawnee, crossed the Ohio River and concealed themselves in a cornfield near Fort Henry. The next morning at about sunrise, six Indians fired upon Andrew Zane, John Boyd, Samuel Tomlinson, and a Negro, who were seeking horses for Dr. James McMechen for his departure to the Monongahela Valley. They killed Boyd, but they allowed Tomlinson and the Negro to escape in order that they might lure others outside the fort. Zane allegedly escaped by leaping over a cliff seventy feet high.

The Indian strategy worked perfectly. Mason left the fort with fourteen men in search of the Indians. Suddenly scores of Indians, instead of the few he had anticipated, fell upon him and his party. Hearing their cries, Ogle rushed to their aid with twelve more men. Of the twenty-six men, who were outnumbered about eight to one, only three, including Mason and Ogle, escaped death. The Indians then besieged the fort for three days and three nights, but its thirty-three defenders stood their ground. After burning about twenty-five houses outside the fort and destroying horses and cattle, the attackers withdrew, leaving most of the people homeless and without food or clothing.

Meanwhile, Hamilton dispatched fifteen bands of Indians from Detroit. Within six months they presented him with 73 prisoners and 129 scalps. They made forays against settlements as much as 150 miles east of the Ohio River, attacking within sight of such defenses as Van Bibber's Fort in the Greenbrier area, Van Meter's Fort on Short Creek, and Coon's Fort on the West Fork of the Monongahela. Scores of families fled eastward, and even the garrison at Fort Henry threatened to leave. One of the most audacious moves of the Indians occurred at McMechen's Narrows, about midway between Moundsville and

Wheeling, on September 26, when they ambushed a scouting party under Captain William Foreman and killed him and twenty of his men.

Hand had hoped to forestall the bloody events of the fall and winter of 1777 by sending an expedition into the Indian country. Only Hampshire County met its quota of men, and Hand, with far less than the two thousand he requested, postponed further action until spring. The only protection he could offer lay in the posting of 150 militiamen in each of the Ohio River counties during the winter.

Mounting Perils. An incident at Fort Randolph added to the tenseness on the frontiers. In November 1777 Cornstalk, with two companions, visited the fort and informed Matthew Arbuckle that the Shawnee had decided to join the British and that he had been unable to dissuade them. Fearing that Cornstalk came for some ulterior purpose, Arbuckle detained him until he could obtain instructions from General Hand. On November 9 Elinipsico, Cornstalk's son, came in search of his father, but he, too, was held. When two hunters from the fort were killed the following day, the enraged militiamen demanded retribution, and in spite of Arbuckle's efforts to restrain them, they killed Cornstalk, Elinipsico, and their companions.

An attack on Fort Randolph on May 16, 1778, was probably not a specific retaliation for the death of Cornstalk. More likely, it was part of a general offensive by British and Indians, which included assaults upon such scattered places as Boonesboro in Kentucky, Fort Stanwix and Oriskany in the Mohawk Valley, and the Wyoming Valley of Pennsylvania. About three hundred Indians, mostly Wyandot and Mingo, demanded the surrender of the fort, but Captain William McKee, who was in charge during Arbuckle's temporary absence, refused to capitulate or to send men outside the stockade. After a frustrating day, in which they killed livestock that ran loose, the Indians announced that they came as friends. McKee directed Nonhelema to read them a proclamation of Governor Patrick Henry, which also expressed a desire for peace. The Indians feigned satisfaction and promised to return to their lands across the Ohio.

When the Indians began to move up the Kanawha, McKee sent John Pryor and Philip Hammond, disguised as Indians, to warn the Greenbrier settlements. Exposed families hastily took refuge at Fort Donnally, which the Indians attacked about dawn the next morning. Dick Pointer, a slave of Andrew Donnally, the owner of the fort, and Hammond, who were on watch, sounded the alarm and prevented the attackers from entering by placing their weight against filled water barrels that had been rolled against the door. The Indians kept up their attack throughout most of the day, but in the midafternoon Matthew Arbuckle and Samuel Lewis arrived from Camp Union with thirty-six men and dispersed the Indians.[4]

[4]Many of those who had sought shelter at the fort supported Dick Pointer in 1795, when he appealed to the Virginia General Assembly that he "in the decline of life shall be at public expense liberated, and enjoy by the bounty of the legislature that freedom he has long sighed for." Greenbrier County Legislative Petition, November 12, 1795, Virginia State Library, Richmond.

Critical shortages of gunpowder, medicines, and other supplies frequently threatened frontier defenses. As early as July 1776 Captain George Gibson and Lieutenant William Linn undertook a mission to New Orleans, where Spanish officials permitted them to purchase twelve thousand pounds of powder, but insisted that the transaction be conducted in a manner to preserve the illusion of Spanish neutrality. Gibson remained in New Orleans in deference to their wishes, and Linn, with fifty-three men, returned to Fort Pitt in May 1777 with the valuable cargo. About nine thousand pounds of powder, landed at Fort Henry, enabled that post to withstand the assault in September 1777.

In the summer of 1778 Governor Henry dispatched David Rogers and about forty men from the Monongahela Valley to New Orleans on additional "Business of Importance" to Virginia and her western settlers. On October 4, 1779, as he was returning up the Ohio River with powder, medicines, and other supplies, Indians led by Simon Girty attacked his party. They killed Rogers and seized the five bateaux carrying his cargo.

George Rogers Clark and the West. During the winter of 1777-1778 George Rogers Clark convinced Virginia authorities that an expedition into the Illinois country could weaken British control over the western Indians, enable Americans to make greater use of the Mississippi River, and enhance Virginia's claims to the Northwest. On June 26, 1778, Clark left Fort Massac, ten miles below the falls of the Ohio, with 175 seasoned riflemen, about 150 of whom were from the Monongahela Valley.

Proceeding overland rather than by the more commonly traveled rivers, Clark surprised the British at Kaskaskia on July 4 and forced their surrender. He repeated his success at Cahokia. Father Gibault, a priest at Kaskaskia, carried the news of Clark's victories to Vincennes and accepted its surrender. The French habitants, pleased by reports of an alliance between the United States and France, gave Clark support, and even a few Indian tribes responded to his bravado and distribution of gifts.

In October Governor Hamilton, with five hundred men, recaptured Vincennes, but heavy rains prevented his moving against the other posts. Rather than risk their loss, the indomitable Clark set out with 172 men for Vincennes. Traveling in rain and icy streams, he reached the post at about dusk on February 23, 1779. Caught completely off guard, Hamilton surrendered, with the thirty-three men who remained with him, after a night of fighting. Clark sent all of them to Williamsburg as prisoners of war.

Meanwhile, in June the Board of War directed Lachlan McIntosh, who had succeeded Hand as commandant at Fort Pitt, to move against Detroit, the key to British power in the West, with 3,000 regulars and not more than 2,500 Virginia militiamen. Many Virginians strongly opposed the plan, partly because they believed that Clark would be able to capture Detroit but also because they feared that reduction of that stronghold by Continental forces might jeopardize Virginia's claim to territory northwest of the Ohio River.

After many delays, McIntosh began his march in October 1778. He paused at the mouth of Beaver Creek to build a large defense, which he named Fort McIntosh. In November, with twelve hundred men, he pressed on to the Tuscarawas River in the land of the Delaware and built Fort Laurens. Expiration of militia terms and inadequate supplies, however, nullified the effectiveness of Fort Laurens, and it was reduced to the necessity of obtaining food from the Delaware. The expedition proved almost entirely fruitless.

Clark's successes, the alliance with France, and bold moves against the Iroquois by General Daniel Brodhead, who replaced McIntosh at Fort Pitt, raised American prestige with the Indians to its greatest height since the beginning of the war. In the fall of 1779 delegations of Wyandot and some Shawnee visited Fort Pitt with a view to negotiating peace. Yet American strength was illusory, as letters captured by the Girtys from David Rogers clearly revealed. The Wyandot soon renewed their friendship with the British, and in February 1781 the Delaware joined them. With the defection of the Delaware, American influence over the western tribes plunged to its nadir.

Fearing an attack by the Delaware, Brodhead, with an army of three hundred men, destroyed the tribal towns of Coshocton and Lichtenau. Although his men killed fifteen warriors and took twenty prisoners and much plunder, they refused to engage in further chastisement of the Indians, and Brodhead had to return to Wheeling.

The shift of the main theater of war to the southern states after 1780 seriously affected trans-Allegheny defenses. Military needs along the seaboard of Virginia, for instance, prevented the establishment of a post at Kellys Creek, about midway between Point Pleasant and the Greenbrier settlements. They may also have been responsible for the abandonment of Fort Randolph in 1779 and its subsequent burning by the Indians.

Preparations by Clark for an expedition against Detroit in the summer of 1781 may have spared the trans-Allegheny region even greater dangers from the British and Indians. Clark proposed to attack Detroit with two thousand men, but militiamen from Berkeley, Frederick, Hampshire, Ohio, and Monongalia counties were generally unwilling to leave their homes and families exposed in order to deliver a blow against Detroit. Clark was able to assemble only four hundred men at Wheeling. Even then he suffered so many desertions that he left without waiting for another hundred Westmoreland men under Archibald Lochry. His plan completely collapsed when he learned that Indians led by Alexander McKee and Joseph Brant had attacked Lochry below the mouth of the Miami River and killed or captured every member of his force.

War Weariness in the Eastern Panhandle. Clark's inability to recruit a force for an assault upon Detroit indicated a war weariness, often mistaken for loyalism, that swept over parts of West Virginia during the closing years of the war. Repeated requisitions for beef, grain, and livestock, payment for their goods in depreciating paper currency, and the sacrifice of their menfolk undermined the enthusiasm with which many frontier residents had entered the war. Virginia authorities experienced increasing difficulty in procuring goods on credit and in many cases even with cash in hand.

Disaffection reached its greatest intensity in 1780 and 1781 east of the Alleghenies and centered in Hampshire County. Angered by the arrival of a tax collector, John Claypool and five or six of his friends announced that they would provide no more beef, clothes, or men, and then obtained whiskey and drank to the health of King George III. Armed with warrants for Claypool and his associates, the sheriff and about fifty men set out to arrest the troublemakers. Claypool, meanwhile, had gathered sixty or seventy men of his own and prepared to resist arrest. In the face of this unexpected defiance, the sheriff accepted Claypool's promise to turn himself over to authorities later.

Armed resistance, largely to taxes and levies, flared up in other parts of Hampshire County. An attack upon militiamen at the mill of John Brake, a member of the insurgents, rumors that Claypool was gathering a thousand men in the Lost River area, and the fears that the lives and fortunes of supporters of the American cause were in jeopardy led to an appeal by Colonel Elias Poston, on May 22, 1781, for three hundred men from Frederick County to quell the disturbances. He pointed out that Claypool had so many friends and relatives that it would be impossible to form an army against him in Hampshire County.

Daniel Morgan, with four companies of infantrymen and other recruits, arrived in Hampshire County and dispersed the rioters. Several rebel leaders fled over the mountains, but Claypool and others sought pardons from the governor. They based their defense upon their isolation and ignorance of events outside their area, the effectiveness of the propaganda of British agents, and their conviction that the taxes and levies upon them were unduly burdensome. Claypool himself elicited considerable sympathy. Peter Hog pointed out that he had five sons who were connected with some of the most ardent supporters of the American cause in the South Branch area and that his prosecution would alienate many patriots. Others attested to his honesty, peaceableness, and good intentions. Morgan pointed out that he was the father of fourteen children, most of them small and dependent upon him. The governor pardoned Claypool and nearly all of his associates, and many of them served faithfully in American armies.

The End of the War. Some of the bloodiest episodes of the war west of the Alleghenies occurred after the battle of Yorktown on October 19, 1781. In retaliation for an attack upon settlements in Washington County, Pennsylvania, in February 1782, Colonel David Williamson led an expedition of about one hundred militiamen against the village of Gnadenhutten, where some of the guilty persons were visiting friendly Moravian Indians. The irate militia, with only eighteen dissenting, agreed to kill every Indian present, friendly or hostile. The following morning they slaughtered about one hundred, including men, women, and children, who had spent the night singing and praying, and destroyed their unharvested crops.

General William Irvine, the successor to Brodhead at Fort Pitt, expected massive reprisals for the atrocity at Gnadenhutten. To forestall additional attacks, which by then extended as far as the Tygart Valley and Greenbrier areas, he dispatched about five hundred mounted men under Colonel William Crawford to the Wyandot town of Sandusky. Crawford found the town deserted, but on June 4 he encountered a large body of Wyandot, and a battle ensued. The arrival of reinforcements for the Indians threw the militia into a panic, and it scattered in wild disorder. About three hundred reached home safely. Most of the others, including Crawford, were captured. Crawford was put to death by slow roasting.

On September 10 about two hundred Wyandot, Delaware, and British, led by Joseph Brant, laid siege to Fort Henry. John Linn, a scout, had discovered their approach and warned residents of the area, who hurriedly took shelter in the fort. Linn's warning did not allow time to remove all the military stores from the house of Ebenezer Zane, which stood about forty yards away. Some of the men were deployed there, with the result that the Indians were subjected to a hazardous crossfire.

During the attack, the Indians suddenly perceived what seemed a singular stroke of fortune. A small boat moving up the Ohio and laden with cannonballs and other supplies for Fort Pitt put ashore at Wheeling. The Indians promptly captured the boat and its cargo. Thereupon they fashioned a cannon by hollowing out a log and filled it with cannonballs. They aimed their new weapon at Fort Henry and fired. Much to their astonishment, the only casualties were Indians.

The defenders of Fort Henry also had problems. Gunpowder was running low, and none of the men could be spared to go to Zane's house, where supplies were ample. At this critical juncture, according to legend, Zane's sister, Elizabeth, or Betty, volunteered to obtain the powder. Braving the enemy fire, she ran to the house and obtained the precious gunpowder. Then, to the amazement of the already disbelieving Indians, she dashed back to the fort. Her feat enabled the fort to withstand the attack. After three days of failure, the frustrated Indians gave up the siege, and about half of their warriors retired across the Ohio.[5]

The remainder of the Indians, numbering about a hundred, moved northward to Rice's Fort at Bethany. Normally the little post gave protection to about a dozen families, but at the time of the assault there were only six defenders. The Indians killed one of them at the outset. The remaining five, in what was one of the most remarkable encounters in the annals of frontier warfare, held out against their attackers for twelve hours and killed several Indians without the loss of any additional men. Despairing of any success, the Indians withdrew.

The sieges of Fort Henry and Rice's Fort, which followed closely the disastrous battle of Blue Licks in Kentucky, marked the last large-scale attacks

[5]There are no contemporary accounts of the alleged action of Betty Zane in the defense of Fort Henry. The first stories appeared years later under circumstances that raise doubts about their reliability, but they cannot be dismissed summarily.

upon the West Virginia frontier during the Revolutionary War. A few weeks later Sir Guy Carleton, the British commander in chief, instructed officers at all of Britain's western posts to desist from further moves against the Americans. After six years of frightful warfare, peace returned. Yet it was a peace on paper only, and more than a decade of strife lay ahead before the Indian menace to West Virginia settlements was entirely removed.

Adapting to a New Nation

A New Immigrant Wave. With the end of the Revolutionary War, Americans, long since grown mobile by habit, resumed their course westward in search of new lands in trans-Allegheny West Virginia, Pennsylvania, Kentucky, Tennessee, and the Old Northwest. Each year thousands of immigrants gathered at Wheeling and Pittsburgh for the journey down the Ohio. Others followed the Valley of Virginia southward to headstreams of the Cumberland and Tennessee. In 1790 about 125,000 Virginians lived west of the Appalachians. More than 70,000 of them were in Kentucky, which experienced a dramatic population upsurge of nearly six hundred percent between 1783 and 1790.

West Virginia had a less spectacular growth. In 1790 her total population was 55,873, but only about 20,000 lived west of the mountains. Yet her subsequent increase was by no means inconsequential. Between 1790 and 1830 it reached 317 percent, compared with a 354 percent growth for the nation as a whole. Much of the expansion occurred in the Monongahela, upper Ohio, and Kanawha valleys. Her population density of 7.3 persons per square mile compared with 7.4 percent for the nation. The population, however, was not evenly distributed, and much of the state remained a mountainous and forested frontier.

County and Local Governments. Expansion of settlement necessitated the organization of additional counties and towns. Only two of West Virginia's fifty-five counties, Hampshire and Berkeley, formed in 1754 and 1772, respectively, existed at the beginning of the Revolutionary War. The remainer of the state was included in Fincastle County, which embraced the territory south of the New and Kanawha rivers; in Botetourt and Augusta counties, which extended across most of the northcentral section to the Ohio River; and the ill-defined District of West Augusta, created in 1773 to assert the authority of Virginia over the Forks of the Ohio region and provide an administrative shelter for its residents and those of the extreme northern parts of West Virginia.

Further county reorganization occurred during the Revolutionary War. In 1776 the General Assembly divided the District of West Augusta into Yohogania, Monongalia, and Ohio counties. It split Fincastle County into Kentucky, Washington, and Montgomery counties, the last of which included the part of West Virginia south of the New and Kanawha rivers. In 1778 the trans-Allegheny portion of Botetourt County became Greenbrier County.

Continued population increases resulted in the formation of additional counties. By 1800 the General Assembly had created Brooke, Hardy, Harrison, Kanawha, Monroe, Pendleton, Randolph, and Wood. The establishment of Cabell, Jefferson, Lewis, Logan, Mason, Morgan, Nicholas, Pocahontas, and Tyler brought the number of counties in West Virginia to twenty-two in 1830. Even then, the creation of new counties failed to keep pace with the expanding population. Moreover, some new counties were so large and their inhabitants were so isolated that their governments could not adequately meet the needs of the people.

The General Assembly also authorized the establishment of numerous towns. It formally established Shepherdstown and Romney in 1762. Berkeley Springs (originally known as Bath), Lewisburg, Martinsburg, and Moorefield were created by the end of the Revolutionary War. Among other new towns established before the end of the century were Beverly, Bolivar, Charleston, Charles Town, Clarksburg, Darkesville, Franklin, Frankfort, Middletown (later renamed Fairmont), Morgantown, Point Pleasant, Salem, Smithfield (Berkeley County), Smithfield (Harrison County), Union, Vienna, Watson, Wellsburg (first known as Charlestown), and West Liberty.

The Continuing Indian Menace. One of the most serious deterrents to the growth of trans-Allegheny West Virginia was the danger from Indians, which did not abate after the Revolutionary War. Between 1785 and 1787 British agents, including Sir John Johnson, Joseph Butler, and Joseph Brant, urged a confederation of tribes in the Northwest. Frontier leaders such as George Clendenin of Kanawha County, Hezekiah Davisson of Harrison County, and John Stuart of Greenbrier County, declared that West Virginia settlers were in greater danger than ever before and that there was likely to be no peace as long as the British retained trading posts in the Northwest, contrary to the Treaty of Paris of 1783.

For scores of families the Indian menace was etched in sad and bitter memories. Two examples suffice to illustrate their suffering and heartbreak. At Wheeling Indians killed young Andrew Zane and captured Isaac, his nine-year-old brother. Isaac grew up among the Indians, married the daughter of a Wyandot chief, and became the father of eight children. He chose never to return to his family. Another captive, Mary Kinnan, settled with her husband near Elkwater, on the Tygart Valley River. In 1791 Indians killed her husband and young daughter and carried the unfortunate woman to their towns in Ohio. Later they took her to the Detroit area, where she became a slave of an old Delaware squaw. After more than two years, she managed to communicate with relatives in New Jersey, and her brother, with the aid of friends, arranged her release.

The Federal Constitution. Indian dangers dominated the thoughts of many of the sixteen West Virginians elected to the Virginia convention, which met in Richmond from June 2 through June 25, 1788, to consider ratification of the federal Constitution. Although they were but a small proportion of the 170 delegates, their importance exceeded their numbers. At the time of their election, eighty-five delegates were Federalists, who gave strong support to the Constitution. Sixty-six were chosen as Antifederalists. Of the remaining nineteen, three had not made up their minds at the time of their election, and the views of the other sixteen were unknown. Four of the latter were from trans-Allegheny West Virginia.

Leaders of both Federalists and Antifederalists exerted pressure upon wavering delegates and those representing frontier counties. Antifederalists, led by Patrick Henry, argued that a strong central government would have the power to bargain away navigation of the Mississippi River, a vital concern to many residents of the trans-Appalachian region. They also contended that a strong government might jeopardize the rights of persons who had acquired lands from the sequestered Fairfax estate. West Virginians, however, found Federalist arguments more compelling. The Federalist leaders, including George Washington, James Madison, George Wythe, Edmund Randolph, and Edmund Pendleton, held that a strong central authority would be more likely to secure navigation of the Mississippi and derided the idea that Virginia might not be able to protect her citizens who had obtained tracts from the Fairfax proprietary.

Although Charles A. Beard and other historians have stressed a close correlation between personal holdings, such as slaves and continental or state securities, and support of the Constitution, it is clear that the dominant consideration of West Virginia delegates was their belief that the new government might deal more effectively with the continuing Indian menace. Of the sixteen West Virginians, eleven had at some time actively engaged in frontier defense, and all had witnessed the horrors of Indian depredations. Fourteen of them voted for ratification. John Evans of Monongalia County, for reasons not known, opposed the Constitution, and Ebenezer Zane of Ohio County did not vote. Given the narrow margin, eighty-nine to seventy-nine, by which Virginia ratified the Constitution, it is clear that the West Virginia vote was of critical importance.

The Seeds of Nationalism. The new government of the United States, which was launched in 1789 with Washington as president, quickly fulfilled the hopes that westerners entertained for it. After disastrous expeditions into the Indian country under Josiah Harmar in 1790 and Arthur St. Clair in 1791, the Washington administration dispatched General Anthony Wayne westward in 1794. Wayne centered his efforts around Fort Miami, on the southwestern shores of Lake Erie, which the British had built for the protection of Detroit. He attacked about two thousand Indians at Fallen Timbers and dealt them a decisive defeat.

Wayne's victory and the Treaty of Greenville, by which the Indians gave up their claims to most of Ohio, ended the threat to West Virginia. Such seasoned frontier leaders as George Clendenin and William Morris, members of the House of Delegates from Kanawha County, informed Governor Henry Lee that the defeat of the Indians had been so complete that one militia company could defend the Kanawha and Greenbrier settlements.

Largely as a result of Wayne's achievement, the federal government won two diplomatic victories that had important effects on West Virginia. Jay's Treaty with the British in November 1794 contained a provision whereby England agreed to vacate the Northwest posts by June 1, 1796, a move that left her no longer in a position to incite Indian attacks upon the frontiers. Less than a year later, in October 1795, Spain agreed, in Pinckney's Treaty, to open the Mississippi River to American navigation and to provide a place of deposit at New Orleans or some other suitable location for goods shipped downstream. The Louisiana Purchase in 1803 gave the United States possession of both sides of the Mississippi River for most of its course and further cemented the ties of West Virginians to the federal government.

The Whiskey Rebellion. The importance that West Virginians attached to efforts of the federal government to pacify the Indians, more than anything else, explains their failure to give general support to the Whiskey Rebellion. The disturbance erupted in the late summer of 1794, when Secretary of the Treasury Alexander Hamilton put into effect an excise tax on whiskey. A revenue measure, the tax was also intended to demonstrate the power of the federal government to act directly upon the individual. Trans-Allegheny farmers, who marketed grains in the form of whiskey, regarded the tax as highly discriminatory and calculated to drain the western country of its already scarce specie.

Discontent centered in the Monongahela Valley sections of western Pennsylvania, particularly Washington County, where irate farmers defied federal authority. In Ohio County, in present West Virginia, opponents of the excise tax attacked Zacheus Biggs, the revenue officer, and forced distillers to ignore the law. About thirty men, with blackened faces, called at the home of the officer in Monongalia County and threatened him with destruction of his property and bodily harm. The collector speedily resigned his commission and fled.

Most West Virginians backed away from open defiance of the federal government. Only in Ohio County did opponents of the tax elect representatives to a meeting at Parkinson's Ferry on August 14, at which Pennsylvania leaders sought to concert action against the measure. The Ohio County delegates— William McKinley, William Sutherland, and Robert Stephenson—however, were among those who later met with federal commissioners and agreed to accept the tax in return for guarantees of general amnesty for paticipants in the uprising. McKinley stated that he had no desire to oppose the tax except "in a Constitutional way." Neither he nor most West Virginians were ready to engage in armed resistance at a time when Wayne's army was advancing into the Indian country.[1]

---

[1]William McKinley to [James] Ross, [Jasper] Yeates, and [William] Bradford, August 23, 1794, John George Jackson Papers, Lilly Library, Indiana University, Bloomington.

The Partisan Spirit in National Politics. The political cleavages engendered by the excise tax deepened in succeeding months. George Jackson of Clarksburg won election to Congress in 1795 partly with the support of anti-excise men in Monongalia, Ohio, and Harrison counties. McKinley and Sutherland achieved positions of trust after their fight against the tax. On the other hand, Daniel Morgan and James Machir, who had supported Hamilton's moves, were elected to Congress from the Eastern Panhandle in 1797.

Political lines hardened following the enactment of the Alien and Sedition acts in 1798. The partisan character of the acts, which aimed at curbing Republican strength and unrestrained criticisms of the Federalist administration, angered Republicans. The Virginia and Kentucky legislatures adopted resolutions charging the administration of Federalist John Adams with violation of its constitutional powers. The resolutions, based on a compact theory of government, asserted the right of the states to take steps leading to repeal of the acts.

West Virginia members of the General Assembly divided in their votes on the Virginia Resolutions. Ten delegates supported the resolutions, and five opposed them. Two opponents, Magnus Tate and John Dixon, both of Berkeley County, contended that the federal government was the "result of a compact, not between the States, but between the People of the United States, and as such not under the control of the State Legislatures, but of the people themselves."[2] One of the staunchest defenders of the resolutions, young John G. Jackson, the son of Congressman George Jackson and a delegate from Harrison County, later referred to them as "the great cause I espoused in 1798 & of which I have never ceased to be the zealous advocate."[3]

Sentiment among the people was equally divided. The Greenbrier County court was so incensed over attacks on the Adams administration that it destroyed copies of the Virginia Resolutions and of Madison's *Report,* which contained replies to arguments against the resolutions. "A True Republican," writing in the Martinsburg *Potomak Guardian,* the only newspaper then published in West Virginia, condemned the Sedition Act as a "dreadful law" that struck at constitutional guarantees of freedom of the press.[4]

Republicans laid careful plans designed to place Thomas Jefferson in the White House in 1800. They established organizations in all counties and set up a central committee in Richmond. In West Virginia, however, much residual Federalist strength remained. Richard Claiborne, a member of the Monongalia County committee, attributed it to "the personal influence of a few old Residents, grown into the character of Federalists by habit or premeditation" and to a

[2]Martinsburg *Potomak Guardian*, January 2, 1799.
[3]Quoted in Stephen W. Brown, *Voice of the New West: John G. Jackson, His Life and Times* (Macon, Ga.: Mercer University Press, 1985), 18.
[4]Martinsburg *Potomak Guardian,* January 24, 1799.

lack of understanding by others.[5] The Republicans, nevertheless, swept Virginia, and Jefferson carried the state with a majority of 13,363 in a total of 20,797 votes.

The Jefferson Era. After the centralization of authority under the Federalist administrations, many West Virginians welcomed the more strict construction of the Constitution during the Jefferson era. Their wholehearted approval of the purchase of Louisiana in 1803, however, demonstrated that they did not object to a powerful central government when it appeared to serve their interests. The acquisition not only promised economic advantages, but it also fanned the flames of patriotism and nationalism by offering seemingly unlimited prospects for future expansion.

West Virginians gave additional evidence of their support for the Jefferson administration during the Aaron Burr conspiracy. When he tied Jefferson for the presidency in the electoral college in 1801, Burr allowed his political ambitions to draw him into a bitter contest in the House of Representatives, which deprived him of much of his influence in the Republican Party. The duel in 1804 in which he killed Alexander Hamilton cost him most of his remaining support in the eastern states and ruined his chances of ever becoming president. His popularity generally remained intact in the West, where Hamilton was held in low esteem. Burr turned to that region to rebuild his shattered career.

The precise nature of Burr's plans remains obscure, but he evidently intended to create a new empire in the Southwest. Presumably it would have included parts of the Spanish possessions west of the Mississippi River and possibly sections of the United States south of the Ohio. In 1805 he made a journey into the southwestern part of the United States, where leaders, most of them unaware of his intentions, received him with warmth and hospitality.

Among those upon whom Burr called was Harman Blennerhassett, who resided on an island in the Ohio River near the mouth of the Little Kanawha. Born into the Irish gentry, Blennerhassett attended Trinity College, Dublin, and studied law at King's Inn, London. He migrated to the United States under some social ostracism arising from his marriage to his niece, Margaret Agnew. On his Ohio River island he built a mansion, provided with elegant furnishings and wings for a library and scientific laboratory and surrounded by handsome gardens. The Blennerhassetts were gracious and welcomed as visitors many of the distinguished travelers on the Ohio River.

Burr's visit ended their idyllic life. Flattered by Burr's attentions, tiring of his isolated life, eager to replenish his dwindling fortune, and dazzled by visions of a high position in some new government, Blennerhassett readily succumbed to Burr's nebulous schemes. Following a second visit by Burr in August 1806, he contracted with a business partner in Marietta for supplies and arranged for

---

[5]W.P. Palmer and others, eds., *Calendar of Virginia State Papers and Other Manuscripts*, 11 vols. (Richmond, 1875-1893; New York: Kraus Reprint Company, 1968), vol. 9, 111-12.

the construction of boats, which he assembled at Blennerhassett Island. As "Querist," he published a series of articles in the Marietta *Ohio Gazette* in September in which he emphasized exploitation of the agricultural West by the commercial East and suggested secession of western areas from the Union.

When reports of the Burr conspiracy began to circulate, cordiality toward Blennerhassett and his wife turned to suspicion and scorn. While they were in Lexington, Kentucky, residents in a mass meeting called by Federalist Alexander Henderson condemned their actions, pledged support to President Jefferson, and laid plans to raise a corps of militiamen in case of an emergency. Almost oblivious to public concern, Blennerhassett returned and continued to oversee preparations for the move down the Ohio and Mississippi rivers. Upon orders of Governor Edward Tiffin of Ohio, Judge Return Jonathan Meigs and General Joseph Buell seized ten boats and confiscated others at boatyards on the Muskingum River. In danger of arrest, Blennerhassett and his associates hurriedly left the island on December 10 aboard four of the boats that they had acquired. The following day Colonel Hugh Phelps and Wood County militia arrived at the island. Despite the entreaties of Mrs. Blennerhassett, they did considerable damage to the property.

Blennerhassett reached the Mississippi Territory, where his wife soon joined him. Later he was arrested in Lexington, Kentucky, and sent to Richmond to stand trial with Burr, who had by then been apprehended. The court, over which Chief Justice John Marshall presided, acquitted Burr, who was not at Blennerhassett Island, where the overt act of treason with which he was charged allegedly occurred. After it acquitted Burr, the court declined to proceed with the indictment against Blennerhassett. Unrealistic to the end, Blennerhassett returned to the island estate, only to behold the destruction and wreckage left by the militia and by looters who had carried away nearly everything of value.

After futile efforts to recoup his fortune as a cotton planter in Mississippi, as an attorney in Montreal, and through literary endeavors by his wife, Blennerhassett returned to the Isle of Jersey, in England, where he died in 1831 of a paralytic stroke. Mrs. Blennerhassett later returned to New York to care for an invalid son and to seek compensation from Congress for the destruction of the island property. She, too, died without relief from the destitute circumstances into which the family had fallen. Many years before, in 1811, the mansion had burned. Sorrowful as was the plight of the family, West Virginians extended them no sympathy.

The War of 1812. The people of West Virginia gave further evidences of their attachment to the federal government in the troubles with England in the Napoleonic era. Federalists, still strong in the Eastern Panhandle and some other parts of the state, criticized policies of the Jefferson and Madison administrations as anti-British, but Republicans, by then the majority in most sections, loyally upheld the government. Congressmen from trans-Allegheny districts generally condemned impressment of American seamen and attacks upon American vessels during the years before the War of 1812 and clamored for defense of the nation's rights and honor. They supported the Embargo, the Non-Intercourse Bill, and Macon's Bill No. 2.

No Congressman was a stouter defender of the Republican administrations than John G. Jackson of Clarksburg. A brother-in-law of James Madison, for whom he often acted as spokesman in the House of Representatives, he excoriated Federalist critics. A clash with highly partisan Federalist Congressman Joseph Pearson of North Carolina, in which Pearson impugned the wisdom and integrity of Jefferson and Madison, resulted in a duel between Jackson and Pearson in 1809. Pearson dealt Jackson a wound that forced him to resign his seat and left him lame for the rest of his life. Had Jackson remained in Congress, he almost certainly would have ranked with Henry Clay, John C. Calhoun, Felix Grundy, and other western and southern War Hawks who entered the House in 1810.

Such was the patriotic spirit in West Virginia that militia captains in the War of 1812 usually filled their companies with ease. Captains Nimrod Saunders and James Laidley from the Parkersburg area expressed the feeling of many members of the fifty-two companies raised wholly or in part in West Virginia, when they wrote Governor James Barbour that they and their men were "members of the Great Union" and would devote their lives to "the security of the whole."[6] More than a thousand men, under General Joel Leftwich, joined William Henry Harrison in northern Ohio after the surrender of Detroit by General William Hull in August 1812. Western forces also hastened to the defense of eastern Virginia when the British invaded the state in 1814.

Land Problems. The federal government had little authority over land questions that lay at the root of many problems in West Virginia during the early nineteenth century and that continued to plague the state. Pioneers who occupied the triangle bounded roughly by the Ohio and Little Kanawha rivers and the Laurel Ridge of the Allegheny Mountains encountered the claims of the Indiana Company. Following the collapse of the Vandalia scheme, the company endeavored to win recognition of its claims by the Virginia legislature. On June 3, 1779, however, the House of Delegates rejected the Indiana claim by a vote of fifty to twenty-eight. Three days later the Senate refused even to hear the plea of the company. No more fruitful was the appeal of the company to Congress, which understandably was unwilling to offend Virginia at a time when her support was of critical importance.

In 1802 the Indiana Company resurrected its claims, threatening the rights of twenty to thirty thousand residents of northern West Virginia. Scores of persons facing the loss of their property signed petitions, which circulated in Monongalia, Harrison, Randolph, Wood, and Ohio counties, asking the legislature to appropriate funds for their defense in suits brought by the company.

[6]Saunders and Laidley to Barbour, May 23, 1812, *Calendar of Virginia State Papers*, vol. 10, 147.

Blackwater Falls is typical of the rugged scenery of West Virginia. West Virginia Division of Archives and History (unless noted otherwise, all succeeding illustrations are from this source)

Harpers Ferry, the lowest point in the state. West Virginia Travel Development Division

Left, Cornstalk, leader of the Shawnees at Point Pleasant. Frost, *Indian Wars of the United States*

Below, Battle of Point Pleasant. Atkinson, *History of Kanawha County*

Bottom, Grave Creek Mound, Moundsville. Historic Preservation Unit, West Virginia Division of Archives and History

Left, Alexander Campbell, educator and founder of the Disciples of Christ. Courtesy of Bethany Press

Below, Jacob Westfall's fort, built in 1774 at the mouth of Files Creek, Beverly

Bottom, Rehoboth Methodist Church, near Union, built in 1786 and said to be the oldest existing church building west of the Alleghenies. Historic Preservation Unit, West Virginia Division of Archives and History

Harman Blennerhassett Mansion, on Blennerhassett Island, near Parkersburg. After Blennerhassett became involved in the western schemes of Aaron Burr, angry neighbors sacked the mansion, which burned in 1811. Blennerhassett Historical Park Commission

"Harewood," home of Samuel Washington, near Charles Town. Here James and Dolley Madison were married.

John Brown defending the fire-engine house at the federal arsenal at Harpers Ferry

Kanawha Salt Works scene about 1845. Howe, *Historical Collections of Virginia*

Above, Philippi, site of what has often been called "the first land battle of the Civil War," in a contemporary sketch by Lafayette Keller

Thomas Jonathan "Stonewall" Jackson, a native of Clarksburg and West Virginia's greatest Civil War general. *Memoirs of Stonewall Jackson*

Francis H. Pierpont, governor in the Reorganized Government of Virginia and "Father of West Virginia"

Below, Independence Hall, site of the Second Wheeling Convention and capitol of the Reorganized Government of Virginia. Preservation Unit, West Virginia Division of Archives and History

Above, John S. Carlile, an insistent advocate of the separation of West Virginia from Virginia

Waitman T. Willey, a leader in the West Virginia statehood movement and a major architect of the postwar Republican party in the new state

George Jackson, a former congressman, declared that the settlers had won their lands from the Indians, occupied them for nearly thirty years, and paid taxes on them. The legislature declined to underwrite the expenses incurred by residents in the dispute, but it reaffirmed its rejection of the Indiana claims.

Even greater troubles for West Virginians grew out of the Virginia Land Law of 1779. The legislation created a land office and provided methods for adjudicating claims to unpatented western lands. It allowed settlers who had taken up lands prior to January 1, 1778, preemption rights to four hundred acres and the option of acquiring an additional one thousand acres at prevailing prices. On the other hand, it disappointed many settlers by recognizing the rights of the Greenbrier and Loyal companies. The politics involved in land questions, however, appeared in the failure of the law to validate the claims of the Ohio Company, on the ground that its surveyors had not been accredited by county surveyors as required by earlier laws.

The most pernicious effects of the Virginia Land Law of 1779 lay in provisions making preemption rights and claims based upon military and treasury warrants transferable. The provisions enabled speculators to acquire millions of acres of land in West Virginia, often for mere pittances. By 1805 some 250 persons or groups, often in interlocking combinations, each acquired ten thousand acres or more. Five of the grantees received princely domains in excess of five hundred thousand acres. They included Henry Banks, a Richmond merchant; Wilson Cary Nicholas, whose land dealings contributed to serious financial troubles for his friend Thomas Jefferson; Robert Morris, the Philadelphia financier; James Welch; and James K. Taylor. Also prominent among speculators were merchants of Philadelphia, Baltimore, Richmond, and other eastern cities, as well as those in West Virginia towns; several members of Congress; at least fifty-two members of the Virginia legislature; and other persons of local importance.[7]

The traffic in lands left much of West Virginia in the hands of absentee owners, who often had more interest in exploitation of their resources than in the region itself. Moreover, since Virginia law did not require surveys of tracts in accordance with the sphericity of the earth, nonresident speculators, as well as others, plastered West Virginia with successive layers of claims, many of them overlapping and ill-defined. The system made land titles highly insecure and kept lawyers busy for decades.

Settlers, faced with the loss of their lands, looked to the legislature for relief. Nicholas County petitioners voiced a typical condemnation of a land system that, "after expelling a man from what he fondly hoped was his freehold and his home, consigns to his tardy but successful rival, and often to the

[7]A general account of Virginia land policies and their effects is in Otis K. Rice, *The Allegheny Frontier: West Virginia Beginnings, 1730-1830* (Lexington: University Press of Kentucky, 1970), 118-49.

merciless speculator, a property acquiring its chief value from the sweat of his brow, and the labour of his hands, without remuneration or recompense to the sufferer for that labour and industry."[8] On the other hand, many speculators found that after they recognized prior settlement rights, they had little useful land left. Nor was all the land of speculators desirable land. Levi Hollingsworth of Philadelphia was told by his local agent that his 13,245 acres in Pendleton County had little value, "inasmuch as no Stage rout approached nearer than 40 miles of this place & the balance of the journey must be made on horseback or in a balloon."[9]

All West Virginia residents, whether or not their own lands were in dispute, suffered from the land system. Speculators often lacked or were unwilling to spend resources to develop their holdings and waited for the state government to provide roads, canals, and other improvements. Much of their land, however, was classified as wild and taxed at abysmally low rates that yielded little money for internal improvements, schools, or other services. The vicious cycle continued when speculators, unable to realize any immediate returns on their investments, failed to pay taxes and allowed their property to revert to the Literary Fund, a condition that afforded the state only tracts of land providing no taxable income at all.

The chaotic land system deprived West Virginia of thousands of desirable immigrants and retarded its economic growth. Although many worthy men and women settled in the state and fought valiantly for its improvement, others preferred the rich farmlands and secure titles of lands farther west to the relatively scarce bottomlands and uncertain prospects south of the Ohio River.

In the long view of history, the land system must be regarded as one of the most unfortunate influences upon the development of West Virginia. Hundreds of tracts acquired by post-Revolutionary War speculators subsequently changed hands, but the patterns of absentee ownership, external control of land and natural resources, and arrested economic development long remained and imposed a colonial economy upon the state. The farseeing statesmanship that Virginians gave the nation in its early days, unfortunately, did not always extend to the state's own internal affairs. As a result the land magnates, the economic royalists of the late eighteenth and early nineteenth centuries, gained an advantage that they have never relinquished.

[8]Kanawha County Legislative Petition, December 17, 1817, Virginia State Library, Richmond. Most petitioners lived in Nicholas County, then part of Kanawha.
[9]Quoted in Rice, *Allegheny Frontier,* 143.

The Quality of Mountain Life

The Mountain Environment. Mountainous regions of the world have always been conservative and slow to change. Isolation from the mainstream of national and world events entrenches within their people beliefs, attitudes, and customs that in more accessible places retreat under the pressure of new ideas and changing interests. West Virginia has been no exception to this pattern. Her confining mountains and lack of broadly unifying river systems discouraged easy communication in early times and fostered a high degree of particularism among her people. Pioneer characteristics long persisted, in some isolated areas even to the twentieth century. The essential features of life in bygone years therefore require some attention in order to understand West Virginians of today.

An Economy of Abundance. Nature lavished her bounties upon West Virginia. The vast forests that originally covered the state provided cover for a great variety of game animals, ranging from bears, deer, and elk to small quarry such as squirrels and wild fowl, including turkeys and pheasants. Reports of hunters who killed a hundred or more bears in a single season were not uncommon. From forest trees came walnuts, butternuts, hickory nuts, chestnuts, and hazelnuts, as well as such wild fruits as the cherry, plum, crab apple, and papaw. Smaller plants added blackberries, raspberries, blueberries, wild grapes, and other delicacies to the pioneer diet. Matching the forests in their abundance were the streams, which teemed with numerous kinds of fish.

Although most families began to clear land for crops immediately, they continued to rely on the forests and streams for part of their sustenance. Joseph Doddridge one of the most discerning observers of pioneer life, recalled a saying that hunting was good in every month that had an *r* in its spelling. François-André Michaux, a French traveler in the Ohio Valley in the early nineteenth century, declared that many residents had developed such a fondness for hunting that they neglected the cultivation of their crops.

The natural abundance and the difficulties in setting the plow to the land appear to have attracted to West Virginia a disproportionate number of the class of settlers that Frederick Jackson Turner, the great frontier historian, called "pioneer farmers." These restless souls seldom remained in one place more than a few years. They lived chiefly by hunting and raising rangy cattle and razorback hogs, which they turned loose to feed upon natural grasses and the mast of the forests. They limited their agricultural production chiefly to corn and a few garden vegetables. They sought only the usufruct of the land and were prodigal of its seemingly unlimited resources.

The Permanent Settler. The casual observer often failed to distinguish between the "pioneer farmer" and the permanent farmer. The former usually left his wilderness home after a few years for greener pastures. The permanent settler had hopes of taming the wilderness and gazing upon his own teeming fields and hardy flocks and herds.

The first abode of the pioneer family, a crude cabin of unhewn logs, was a testimonial to the alliance between family and forest. The pioneer chinked the cracks of his dwelling with grass and mud, laid on a roof of clapboards held in place by heavy poles laid crosswise, and constructed a "cat and clay" chimney of stones held together with clay, sticks, and the down from cattails. Most cabins consisted of only one room and a loft, which was reached by means of a ladder and served as sleeping quarters for the children. Later the ambitious settler replaced the cabin with a house of neatly hewn logs, puncheon floors, a cut stone fireplace and chimney, glass windowpanes, and a neatly shingled roof.

Although many pioneer families long relied upon forests and streams for food, even to considering the breast of the wild turkey and venison as substitutes for bread, most turned increasingly to the produce of their lands. The very first year the pioneer cleared a plot for a cornfield by girdling trees, which he later cut, and removing the undergrowth. Even before he grubbed out the stumps, which might require two or three years, he planted a crop of corn. The very staff of pioneer life, corn was ground into meal for bread, including corn pone and journeycakes, and served as roasting ears, hominy, mush, and dozens of other dishes. It provided food for livestock and was the base of the common "hog and hominy" diet. The planting of wheat had to wait until stumps had been removed and the soil had lost some of the nutrients that caused the grain to mature without forming a head. Oats, rye, and buckwheat, the latter grown chiefly in Preston and Greenbrier counties, were other common grains. Potatoes, beans, squash, pumpkins, and other garden vegetables relieved some of the monotony of mealtime fare.

Pioneer dress was at first simple and unadorned. Men wore hunting shirts, breeches, coonskin caps, and moccasins. The hunting shirt, made of deerskin or linsey-woolsey, a homespun fabric, reached nearly to the knees and bloused over a belt to form a pocket for carrying food and other articles. Moccasins of deerskin were well suited to dry weather but were uncomfortable in rain and snow. Women made their dresses of linsey-woolsey, a material prized for durability rather than beauty. They ordinarily wore sunbonnets throughout the year, and in summer they frequently were barefoot. Children's attire was very much like that of their elders.

An Expanding Economy. Pioneers bore the hardships and privations of frontier life with considerable equanimity, but they aspired to leave behind the most primitive conditions and return to more sophisticated and comfortable ways as soon as possible. With industry and good fortune, their farms could be made to produce a variety of articles that might be sold for cash or traded for needed supplies or even luxuries. Bulky or perishable products could not be transported by packhorse or flatboats and canoes to distant towns, but corn and rye could be made into whiskey, peaches into brandy, and apples into cider. Ready markets existed for all of these, as well as for tallow, furs, hides, saltpeter, ginseng, and many native roots. Moreover, within a few years western residents annually began to drive thousands of livestock, chiefly cattle and hogs, to eastern markets such as Baltimore and Philadelphia.

Cash crops and various native products enabled the pioneer to acquire gunpowder, rifles, salt, and bar iron, the raw material of the blacksmith, but they also provided him and his family with their first luxuries. The records of an unidentified merchant in the Greenbrier Valley in 1784, only fifteen years after settlements were reestablished there after the French and Indian War, are instructive. To his customers the merchant provided fine linen, calico, holland, silk for bonnets, cambric, velvet, broadcloth, check, durant, stock mohair, scarlet cloaks, and apron strings; buttons, needles, and thread; salt, pepper, chocolate, ginger, and coffee; teapots, coffeepots, cruets, soup plates, cups and saucers, knives, tumblers, and pepper boxes; and guns, barlows, jackknives, padlocks, and saddles. The merchant took ginseng for seventy percent of his sales and farm and forest products for most of the remainder. His cash income amounted to only two percent of his sales.[1]

Folkways. Frontier isolation subtly merged into rural life patterns that had an enduring effect upon the outlook and customs of the people. Lonely families welcomed social gatherings and visits from strangers who occasionally passed their way. Normal interest in other people sometimes took the form of excessive curiosity, and the unwary visitor was bombarded with questions about his or her personal circumstances, family, and reasons for travel. Travelers from that day to this, however, have commented upon the friendliness of the people of West Virginia.

Weddings were favorite social occasions. Very often they were held at the house of the bride's parents, who provided a feast as sumptuous as farm and forest could afford, with beef, pork, fowl, bear, venison, and fruits and vegetables that were in season. Some West Virginians indulged in the customs of stealing the bride's shoe or "running for the bottle." A dance often climaxed activities and lasted through the night despite tired, aching feet and a weary fiddler. The infare, held by the bridegroom's parents the following day, continued the festivities.

Most social occasions combined pleasure with work best done through

---

[1]Unidentified Private Account Book, 1783-1785, Monroe County Court Records, Union, W. Va. (Microfilm in West Virginia University Library, Morgantown).

group effort. A prime example was the house-raising. Once the site for a dwelling had been selected, a "fatigue party" cut down trees, hauled the logs to a designated spot, made clapboards for the roof, and hewed puncheons for the floor. A knowledgeable and industrious work force could have the foundations laid before the end of the first day. The next morning four skilled cornermen notched and laid up the logs, while other men laid the floor and built the chimney. By the end of the third day, workers had the structure under roof and ready for occupancy. Churches and schoolhouses were commonly built by the same cooperative endeavor. The women ordinarily prepared meals and refreshments at such times.

Logrollings were common spring events. In preparation, the landowner felled the trees, cut off the branches, notched the trunks at about eight- or ten-foot intervals, and for several days burned dry limbs at each notch until the trunk had been reduced to manageable lengths. On the day of the logrolling, men with handspikes moved the logs to a large heap, where they burned them. Again women provided the meals, which often featured burgoo, a kind of potpie of vegetables and wild meats never reduced to a specific recipe.

Pioneers also relieved the tedium of life with corn shuckings, molasses making, quilting parties, and other common endeavors. Equally exciting were court days, when men gathered to hear both civil and criminal cases, transact necessary business at the county seat, and engage in such tests of dexterity as marksmanship, throwing the tomahawk, and wrestling with no holds barred. Funerals also had their social aspects, with friends and neighbors participating in the "wake" and accompanying the departed to the grave.

Ailments and Their Treatment. A common assumption invests pioneer men and women with robust health and great physical vigor. Actually, they suffered acutely from privation, exposure, disease, and debilitating seasonal ailments. Often without access to doctors and lacking scientific knowledge of anatomy, they relied upon experimentation, the advice of others who had borne similar afflictions, and superstition in the treatment of their ailments. Their folk remedies leaned heavily toward specifics, and they combed the hills and valleys for roots, barks, and herbs, the major ingredients of their medicines. Some proved efficacious, but as Joseph Doddridge, himself a pioneer physician, observed, others did wonders in all cases in which there was nothing to be done.

Fevers and rheumatism caused untold suffering. Treatment of fevers, commonly classified as intermittent, remittent, and ague, consisted of an assortment of drinks, particularly those made from cherry, dogwood, or poplar bark. In 1803 Dr. Gideon Forsythe introduced calomel and Peruvian bark into the Wheeling area. Victims of rheumatism bathed the affected parts with oil, including that of rattlesnakes, geese, wolves, bears, raccoons, groundhogs, and skunks. Some rheumatics favored crude petroleum, often called Seneca oil. Others preferred to bathe in water dipped from an open stream before sunrise on Ash Wednesday or to turn their shoes upside down before going to bed.

Cough remedies were numerous. Many made use of spikenard and elecampane. Virginia snakeroot was considered effective for coughs of all kinds. Another remedy consisted of a mixture of Indian turnip and honey, but many users believed that the Indian turnip must be scraped from the top down to be of any benefit. Also useful were teas, particularly those made from horehound or bear's-foot, the latter a superlatively bitter concoction that required a "good nerve" on the part of the consumer. Favorite treatments for inflammation of the chest included demulcent liquids and rubefacients. Comfrey, spikenard, sassafras pith, and slippery elm bark provided soothing drinks, and horseradish and mustard the poultices used to relieve difficulty in breathing.

Many pioneers considered childhood diseases inevitable and exposed their children to milder ones, such as chickenpox, as early as possible in the belief that the younger the victim the less severe the disease. Smallpox, however, held terror for old and young alike. Vaccination was used in some areas by the 1820s, but most sections lacked that protection, and many residents would have rejected it had it been available.

Annoying skin problems elicited remedies reflecting both common sense and superstition. The itch, a common affliction, usually responded to a mixture of sulfur and lard. Chapped lips might be cured, so it was said, by kissing the middle rail of a five-rail fence.

Pioneers often recognized that good health was related to proper diet, pure water, and clean air. They noted that flooding in the Ohio and its tributaries brought fever, probably typhoid. Never suspecting the mosquito, residents along the West Fork of the Monongahela opposed the erection of locks and dams in the stream in the early nineteenth century on the ground that they would create ponds of stagnant water that would exude vapors harmful to health. Henry Ruffner, president of Washington College, returned to a mountaintop farm in his native Kanawha Valley where pure air and physical activity might repair "a constitution broken by 30 years of constant labor in a literary institution."[2]

Early doctors ranged from woefully ignorant and unprincipled quacks to men whose knowledge and skill matched those of the most advanced areas of the country. Wheeling, Charleston, Clarksburg, Morgantown, and populous towns of the Eastern Panhandle drew some of the most capable practitioners. Even the best physicians engaged in bleeding, a practice recommended by no less an authority than Dr. Benjamin Rush, the eminent Philadelphia physician and teacher. Joseph Doddridge declared that in many ailments the danger was not that the lancet might be used too freely, but too sparingly. Most communities lacked doctors but had men or women possessing some skill in the medical arts.

Persons whose means permitted patronized the numerous mineral springs of the state, including White Sulphur and Old Sweet Springs. Drinking or

---

[2]Quoted from Henry Ruffner, "The Kanawha Country," in the Henry Ruffner Papers. Historical Foundation of the Presbyterian and Reformed Churches, Montreat, N.C.

bathing in their waters may or may not have been efficacious, but the social seasons must have proved powerful psychological restoratives. Most residents, however, continued to rely upon familiar home remedies and patent medicines purchased at the country stores. They retained an honored place on many home medicine shelves long after other sources of medical attention had become available.

Superstition. Most pioneers brought into the mountains with them an accumulation of superstitions, many of them of European origin. Such beliefs long continued to influence the thinking and fire the imaginations of people in isolated sections, and some still survive. Given to the stories of love and tragedy, early settlers were almost inevitably attracted to tales of witchcraft and the supernatural. They often blamed strange happenings and incurable diseases, especially those of children, upon witchcraft. Accused persons never paid the supreme penalty, such as New England leaders meted out a century earlier, but some suffered sorely for their alleged activities.

Many superstitions concerned everyday occurrences. A black cat crossing one's path meant that bad luck would follow, but it could be averted by walking backward across the cat's path. Breaking a mirror entailed seven years of bad luck, unless the pieces were placed under running water, in which case the bad luck would last only seven days. A bird flying into the house was an omen of death. Such superstitions, as well as a belief in the special importance of dreams, served as constant reminders of the influence of supernatural forces. Far more exciting were reports of ghosts, and scarcely a family escaped some alleged experience with the occult.

The Role of Churches. Often closely related to belief in supernatural intrusions was the influence of religion in the daily lives of pioneers. Most accepted the basic tenets of Christianity and acknowledged the value of Christian principles, even though they might violate them in their own conduct.

Throughout the colonial period and until 1786, when the legislature accepted the principle of separation of church and state, the Anglican or the Protestant Episcopal Church, was the official religious establishment of Virginia. Yet for more than half a century, religious toleration had been extended to the trans-Allegheny country in order to promote settlement of the backcountry. There a variegated religious complexion prevailed. Along with Anglicans were large numbers of Presbyterians, Lutherans, German Reformists, Quakers, and Dunkers and scatterings of other denominations.

Isolation and the exigencies of prolonged frontier life eroded old denominational ties. Before the Revolutionary War few settlements had resident ministers, and most pioneers depended upon infrequent and uncertain visits by itinerant preachers for marriage, baptism, and funeral services. Recognizing their neglect, Moravian missionaries began as early as 1747 to visit settlers along the South Branch of the Potomac and Patterson Creek. There they emphasized the bounties of God's love and preached a doctrine of free grace that "tasted well" to their listeners. They usually refused, however, to perform marriages and baptisms for persons whom they did not know and thereby denied them two of the services they most desired of the church.

The weakening of existing church ties in West Virginia coincided with the Great Awakening, a religious revival that began in New England in the 1720s and swept southward during the following decades. The revival, which affected most denominations, stressed the importance of emotions and personal conversion over ritual and ceremony, the need for evangelical work in religiously neglected regions, and more itinerancy among ministers. Disruptive though it was, the movement proved highly invigorating by infusing new zeal into older denominations and providing the impetus to others that until then had attracted but few adherents. Already prepared by a profound piety and a blurring of doctrinal differences, West Virginians formed "the plastic material for the revivalist who found them receptive to a gospel which taught a direct personal relationship between Christ and the believer."[3]

The Revolutionary War era gave religious dissent a respectability that it had not previously enjoyed in Virginia. Beginning in the 1770s, Methodists and Baptists especially, in successive waves of revivalism, reached out to the frontiers and gathered a harvest of souls. Within the next half century they gained a preeminence in West Virginia that they have never lost. In 1850 Methodists had 281 and the Baptists 115 of the 548 congregations in West Virginia. The Presbyterians trailed far behind with 61 congregations and the Protestant Episcopal, formerly the Anglican, Church had only 22. Older denominations such as the Quakers, Lutherans, German Reformists, and Dunkers were reduced to very small fractions of church members in the state.

The Baptists. Of the major denominations in present West Virginia, the Baptists were the first to gain a solid foothold. In 1743 they established the Mill Creek church at Gerrardstown, which was broken up during the French and Indian War but later revived and took the lead in forming the Ketocton Regular Baptist Association in 1765. Two New England ministers, Shubal Stearns and Daniel Marshall, who visited the Eastern Panhandle in 1754 with the intention of establishing a base for spreading the ideas of Separate Baptists throughout the South, encountered a chilly reception. Most listeners objected to their "animated" preaching, and they moved on to Sandy Creek, North Carolina, which in time became a center of Baptist influence in the South.

During the Revolutionary War Baptist ministers crossed the Alleghenies to exposed and isolated settlements. In 1774 John Sutton founded the Simpson Creek Church at Bridgeport, and the following year John Corbly established the Forks of Cheat Baptist Church. John Alderson took up residence in the Greenbrier Valley in 1777 and organized the Greenbrier Baptist Church at Alderson in 1781. The courage of such ministers, who braved great personal danger and

[3]Wesley M. Gewehr, *The Great Awakening in Virginia, 1740-1790* (Durham, N.C.: Duke University Press, 1930), 26-27.

hardships in the midst of a raging war to plant their faith, did much to win converts.

Another strength of the Baptists lay in their democratic organization. Their heroic struggle for separation of church and state, stoutly resisted by authorities during the colonial era, was vindicated by postwar legislation. The Baptists extended concepts of democracy to the congregation, which selected its own minister and established its rules of decorum. Baptist churches could not be accused of elitism, since their often uneducated farmer-preachers came from the same elements as the congregations, which in early years were likely to represent the poorer economic classes of society.

The Baptists suffered two disadvantages, particularly with respect to the Methodists. Partly because of the lack of a strong central authority capable of resolving doctrinal issues, Baptist congregations often split on relatively minor matters. Divisive issues in the early nineteenth century included missions, education, temperance, and Freemasonry. Another handicap was the Calvinistic doctrine of predestination, and as time passed, the Baptists began to emphasize a doctrine of general atonement.

The Methodists. In contrast with other denominations, the Methodists had an organization ideally suited to conditions in West Virginia and to the needs of an expanding frontier. Like the Baptists, they had a strong grass roots base. Small congregations were served by a lay reader, or lay leader, who lived in the community and conducted services. Periodically, however, they received visits from a circuit rider, a regularly appointed minister whose charge included several churches. In the organizational pyramid, circuits were grouped into quarterly conferences, which in turn formed annual conferences. The entire structure was capped by the authority and prestige of the bishop. As settlements expanded, new congregations were added to existing circuits, which could be rearranged to accommodate shifting populations. With the best features of both centralization and decentralization, the Methodists remained close to the people but escaped many of the disruptions that plagued the Baptists.

In some respects the circuit riders were the key figures in the Methodist organization. These dedicated men traveled hundreds of miles each year over arduous mountain trails, braved the perils and hardships of storms and freezing weather, faced dangers from ferocious animals, and suffered great physical discomfort. The rewards for their labors were most often spiritual rather than monetary. They belonged, "like the early founders of Christianity, to the toiling classes of the community. They were taken from the plow, the loom, the bench, the anvil." They proved singularly effective in setting forth "those soul-saving truths which brought the sinner to dust, and raised the fallen to the blessings of pardon and salvation."[4]

Complementing the work of the circuit riders was that of the indefatigable

[4]John B. Finley, *Sketches of Western Methodism: Biographical, Historical, and Miscellaneous, Illustrative of Pioneer Life*, ed. W.P. Strickland (Cincinnati: Methodist Book Concern, 1855), 250.

Bishop Francis Asbury, who frequently left the beaten paths "to seek the outcasts of the people."[5] Between 1776 and 1815 Asbury made at least thirty-four journeys to the frontiers, setting out from Baltimore and swinging westward to the outer fringes of settlement. His close association with the people themselves does much to explain the vitality of early West Virginia Methodism.

Although Methodism continued to appeal to the masses, it also drew support from the natural aristocracy of the areas into which it advanced. It began as a movement within the Church of England in 1739 under the spirited leadership of John Wesley. The first three Methodist missionaries arrived in the colonies in 1766, but during the Revolutionary War all except Francis Asbury returned to England. Asbury remained and took the lead in establishing the ecclesiastical independence of American Methodists from their English counterparts. Yet American Methodism retained a measure of the prestige that had attached to the Anglican Church. Locally prominent families, such as the Zanes, McMechens, McCulloughs, Doddridges, and Wellses in the Northern Panhandle and Edward Keenan in the Greenbrier region, could readily become Methodists without feeling alienated from all previous spiritual values.

Other advantages of the Methodists derived from their own hymnody, the social qualities of their class meetings, and their effective use of the camp meeting. The origins of the camp meeting are usually traced to the famous Cane Ridge revival in Bourbon County, Kentucky, in 1801, and to techniques used by James McGready, a Presbyterian minister. The quarterly meetings of West Virginia Methodists, however, had long been marked by assemblages of circuit riders, local preachers, class leaders, and communicants, often numbering in the hundreds, and by an emotional uplift produced by spirited preaching, love feasts, and the singing of Methodist hymns. It was but a short step from the quarterly gathering to the camp meeting, which in Methodist hands assumed the flavor of a great religious crusade.

The Methodist Protestant Church. Although West Virginia Methodists did not experience the fragmentation of the Baptists, they did not entirely escape disruption within their ranks. As early as 1792 discontent was voiced over the power and life tenure of the bishops, the lack of lay representation in the General Conference, and the arbitrary assignment of ministers and other church officials. Years later, several reformist ministers circulated a petition called *Mutual Rights* and were expelled from the church. At the Baltimore Conference in 1827 discontented elements drew up a new petition for presentation to the Pittsburgh Conference the following year and called for reinstatement of the expelled ministers.

Despite eloquent pleas by such leaders as Henry Bascom, who had begun his ministry on the rugged Guyandotte Circuit of West Virginia, and Asa Shinn,

---

[5]Francis Asbury, *The Journal and Letters of Francis Asbury,* ed. Elmer T. Manning, J. Manning Potts, and Jacob S. Payton, 3 vols. (Nashville: Abingdon Press, 1958), provides details on Asbury's journeys to West Virginia.

a prominent Methodist leader in the northern part of the state, differences between church authorities and reformers remained unresolved. Several congregations dominated by reformers severed their connection with the Methodist Episcopal Church and in November 1830 officially established the Methodist Protestant Church. In West Virginia support for the reformers centered largely in the Monongahela Valley. The chief congregations were at Fairmont, under Thomas Barns, a brother-in-law of Shinn, and at Hacker Valley, under John Mitchell and David Smith. In 1855 West Virginia members numbered 3,036 of whom more than half were in the Morgantown, Pruntytown, Evansville, Jackson, and Braxton circuits. The Greenbrier Circuit, the largest in southern West Virginia, had seventy members.

The Presbyterians. Considering the fact that about half of the five hundred Presbyterian churches in the colonies in 1776 were in areas from which West Virginia settlers were drawn, the state might well have become predominantly Presbyterian. In fact, during the early 1780s Presbyterianism seemed to take on new life in the Eastern Panhandle. Moreover, Presbyterians were in the vanguard of intrepid ministers who crossed the Allegheny Mountains to carry the gospel to the frontiers. In 1775 John McMillan visited the Greenbrier and Tygart Valley settlements. In 1783 John McCue organized three congregations in the Greenbrier region. Other missionaries began to appear in the Kanawha, Monongahela, and upper Ohio valleys.

Unfortunately, the structure and philosophy of the Presbyterian Church was ill adapted to the requirements of frontier areas. Lacking both the flexible organization of the Methodists and the local orientation of the Baptists, it suffered a distinct disadvantage. In 1800 nearly all of its twenty-two congregations were in the Eastern Panhandle, the Northern Panhandle, and the Greenbrier Valley. As late as 1830, ten large counties of northcentral West Virginia, with a population of sixty thousand, had no settled Presbyterian minister with the exception of Asa Brooks, the pastor of the church at French Creek.

Without doubt, the greatest handicap to the Presbyterians in increasing their numbers lay in their insistence upon an educated ministry. Men such as John McElhenney at Lewisburg, Henry Foote at Romney, and Henry Ruffner at Charleston also had to spend as much time in teaching and administering academies in their respective towns as in strictly religious endeavors. Encumbered with educational baggage as well as insistence upon trained ministers, the Presbyterian Church found itself unable to keep pace with advancing settlements in the manner of the Methodists and Baptists.

The Episcopal Church. Even less a proselytizing denomination than the Presbyterians was the Episcopal Church. In 1840 West Virginia had only eleven Episcopal churches west of the Allegheny Mountains. Most of them were in larger towns such as Charleston, Wellsburg, Wheeling, Moundsville, Follansbee, Morgantown, and Clarksburg. The nuclei of the congregations often consisted of well-to-do members whose families had historic ties with the

Episcopal Church and its Anglican antecedents. An example was Judge George W. Summers, who provided a little church, Saint John's in the Valley, at his farm at Scary on the Kanawha River. Others owed their existence to some devoted minister, such as Joseph Doddridge, who founded three of the churches in the Northern Panhandle.

The Disciples of Christ. Although the Disciples of Christ had relatively few members in West Virginia before the Civil War, Alexander Campbell, one of its founders, spent most of his adult life in the state. Born in County Antrim, Ireland, Campbell studied at the University of Glasgow. In 1809 he migrated to America, where his father had assumed charge of a church in Pennsylvania. Young Campbell deplored the spirit of intolerance that he found among American churches and tried to promote a more ecumenical approach to religion through the Christian Association of Washington (in Pennsylvania). Believing that the manners and morals of the people needed reform, the Campbells and their followers organized a full-fledged church at Brush Run, Pennsylvania. Campbell's acceptance of congregational government of each church and infant baptism enabled his church to become a member of the Redstone Baptist Association, but the Baptists did not consider Campbell rigid enough in his Calvinism to qualify as a minister.

Campbell continued his battle against sectarianism after his removal to Buffalo Creek, present Bethany. He held that the simple language of the Bible could explain all the basic aspects of Christianity and unite all who accepted its teachings. In a successful publication, the *Christian Baptist,* founded in 1823, he attacked missions, Sunday schools, and sectarian societies. When in 1826 Baptist associations began to cut off the Campbellites, they, ironically, formed a new denomination, the Disciples of Christ.

In time Campbell made Bethany a center of religious influence in America. In 1816 he founded Buffalo Academy, and in 1840 he established Bethany College, which he nourished with devotion and financial support. He founded a press, from which he issued the *Christian Baptist* and its successor, the *Millenial Harbinger,* as well as dozens of religious books and tracts. Campbell himself wrote many of the works he published and translated a new edition of the English Bible. Widely traveled and skilled as a debater of theological issues, Campbell was in many respects the greatest religious leader residing in West Virginia in the early nineteenth century.

Enduring Patterns of Life. The modes of life established in the late eighteenth and early nineteenth centuries set patterns that endured in many parts of West Virginia for well over a century. Religious affiliations in 1990, for instance, show striking similarities to those of 1850 or earlier. Many beliefs, folkways, and speech forms common in the early nineteenth century survived well into the twentieth and may even yet be encountered in parts of the state. The essential rurality of life until comparatively recent times explains the persistence of older patterns. For many areas the pioneer heritage has even yet an unusual vitality.

8

Educational and Cultural Foundations

A Sea of Illiteracy. When West Virginia separated from Virginia in 1863, the Old Dominion had no statewide system of free schools. Illiteracy prevailed throughout the state and was appalling in mountainous sections. Robert Hager, a Boone County representative in the West Virginia constitutional convention of 1861, asserted that he knew men and women in his county who had never even seen a schoolhouse. An agent of the American Tract Society, who visited the hill country around Fairmont in 1845, declared that his experience was "like a translation from sunlight into darkness—from a high civilization into one of ignorance and superstition, with here and there a family of wealth and refinement."[1]

The educational climate in West Virginia probably reached its nadir in the two or three generations preceding the Civil War. Available evidence, which is extremely sketchy, suggests that the first generation of pioneers had greater concern for education than did their children and grandchildren. Before the end of the French and Indian War settlers established schools at Shepherdstown, in sparsely inhabited parts of the Greenbrier and South Branch valleys, and even in isolated sections of Pendleton County. Within a few years after settlers crossed the Alleghenies, schools existed in such widely scattered places as the Forks of Cheat, Buzzard's Glory near Pruntytown, West Liberty in the Northern Panhandle, and Cedar Grove on the Kanawha River.

The rising illiteracy stemmed partly from the exigencies of surviving in a wilderness. Because of the arduous and almost unending labor required, pioneers came to place greater value upon knowledge and skills gained in the home, on the farm, and in the forest than upon formal instruction. Book learning appeared to have less immediate usefulness, and in time a popular apathy toward schooling developed. In some parts of West Virginia these attitudes continued until well into the twentieth century.

Subscription Schools. For nearly three quarters of a century after settlement

---

[1][John Cross], *Five Years in the Alleghanies* (New York: American Tract Society, 1863), 57-58.

began in West Virginia, the only schools available were of the subscription type. These schools were established by a contract between a schoolmaster and subscribers, or parents who had the desire to provide education for their children and the means to pay tuition. School terms usually lasted about two months, and tuition ranged from two to three dollars per pupil per term. Some teachers were very competent, but others were barely literate and capable of only the lowest order of instruction. Statistics on enrollments of early subscription schools are meager, since few of them kept records. Probably not more than half the children of West Virginia attended these schools.

Convinced, like many other leaders, that education was the cornerstone of the new American republic, Governor Thomas Jefferson in 1779 called upon the legislature to authorize the division of each county into districts known as hundreds and the estabishment of a free school in each hundred. After the Revolutionary War, unfortunately, much of the enthusiasm for free schools abated.

The Literary Fund. The triumph of Jeffersonian democracy in the United States in 1800 excited renewed interest in public schools. During the first decade of the nineteenth century several states provided for instruction of children of indigent families. In 1810 Virginia joined their ranks by creating the Literary Fund. Western leaders resisted efforts of influential persons in the Tidewater and Piedmont to draw off part of the money for a proposed state university, and about $45,000 annually was set aside for the education of poor children.

Administration of the Literary Fund rested with the second auditor, who served as superintendent. The law also required that each county appoint from five to fifteen commissioners, who were charged with responsibility for determining the number of poor children eligible for benefits and given authority to construct buildings and employ teachers. The commissioners ordinarily used their limited funds to pay tuition for poor children at existing subscription schools. In some localities, where the number of paying children was insufficient for a school, the addition of those supported by the Literary Fund made schools possible for the first time.

School attendance remained low in spite of opportunities provided by the Literary Fund. Many parents considered the fund a form of charity and refused its benefits. Some desired to send their children to school but could not afford the clothing needed during winter months. Still others, untouched by formal education themselves, held schools in contempt and kept their children at home. Even where positive attitudes prevailed, the population, particularly in mountainous sections, was often too sparse to support schools.

Qualified teachers long remained scarce, and many counties employed almost any person professing an ability to teach if he gave evidence of good moral character, a criterion regarded as important as academic preparation. Perhaps a high percentage of the teachers, like those of Harrison County, could be described as "generally men of good moral character but not . . . men of high literary acquirements."[2] By 1840 several counties had begun to employ women as teachers of small children.

Schools of West Virginia did not differ substantially from those in other parts of the United States. Most of them emphasized reading, writing, spelling, and arithmetic. Worn copies of the Bible and the New Testament served for textbooks in many classrooms. Both teachers and parents believed in rigid discipline, and the ability to keep order and maintain respect was considered the mark of a good teacher.

District Free Schools. Prospects for free schools brightened in 1829, when the General Assembly provided for the division of counties into school districts and the establishment of a free school in each district. Unfortunately, the legislation was permissive rather than mandatory, and few counties cared to tax themselves for free schools. The first West Virginia county to attempt the plan was Monroe, which established a free school at Sinks Grove in 1829, but it abandoned the system in 1836. Influential men still believed that free schools simply saddled "the liberal and just" with the burden of educating the children of the "parsimonious and niggardly."[3]

An address by Governor David Campbell to the legislature in 1839 detailing widespread illiteracy and revelations of the census of 1840 that the problem was actually increasing galvanized advocates of free public schools into action. They held a series of educational conventions, the most important of which were at Clarksburg, Lexington, and Richmond.

The Clarksburg Convention, held September 7 and 8, 1841, attracted 114 persons, most of them from northern West Virginia. George Hay Lee, an eminent barrister of Clarksburg, served as chairman. The gathering drew wide support from political, religious, social, and journalistic leaders. Fourteen members were at the time or would soon become state legislators. Prominent newspapermen in attendance included Benjamin Bassel of the Clarksburg *Scion of Democracy* and Enos W. Newton, who founded the Charleston *Kanawha Republican* less than three months later.

Alexander Campbell and Henry Ruffner delivered two of the major addresses to the convention. Blending Jeffersonian liberalism and Christian idealism, Campbell called for an educational system based upon a "common Christianity" and stressing piety and morality. He branded the principles underlying the Literary Fund humiliating and proclaimed that "we do not want poor schools for poor scholars, or gratuitous instruction for paupers; but we want schools for all at the expense of all."[4] Ruffner, a prominent Presbyterian

---

[2]Virginia, *Second Auditor's Report on the State of Literary Fund, for the Year 1837, and Proceedings of the School Commissioners in the Different Counties, for the Year Ending September 30, 1836* (Richmond, 1837), 22.

[3]Quoted in Charles H. Ambler, *A History of Education in West Virginia from Early Colonial Times to 1949* (Huntington, W.Va.: Standard Printing & Publishing Co., 1951), 44.

[4]Charles H. Ambler, ed. "The Clarksburg Educational Convention of September 8-9, 1841," *West Virginia History* 5(October 1943):7.

minister and educator, proposed public education financed through a general property tax and administered by a state superintendent. The convention urged rich as well as poor to support the free school movement as essential to the preservation of American democracy and appealed to the legislature to establish district free schools "good enough for the rich" in order that "they may be fit for the poor."[5]

The Clarksburg Convention stirred interest in free schools as never before. West Virginians watched closely the conventions held in Lexington and Richmond later that year. The Richmond Convention, dominated by Thomas Ritchie, editor of the Richmond *Enquirer*, rejected Ruffner's plea for a general property tax and the creation of state normal schools for the training of teachers, but it endorsed free public schools for all white children of school age and support for academies and colleges. Western leaders feared that inclusion of academies and colleges might divert attention from the pressing need for elementary schools, but they conceded that the agitation would at least keep the free school issue alive.

Responding to mounting public clamor, the legislature in 1846 provided methods whereby the counties might institute the district free school plan either through action of the county courts or petition of their citizens. The lawmakers did not mandate the plan, however, and left financing at the county level. Kanawha County adopted the district free school plan in 1847, Jefferson and Ohio soon followed suit, and at least six others were contemplating it when the Civil War came.

Most West Virginians, unfortunately, remained apathetic toward education. The thousands of petitions addressed to the legislature emphasized material interests, such as roads, bridges, ferry franchises, tax relief, and other mundane matters, and relatively few mentioned education. Moreover, some Virginians took advantage of statistics on crime, illiteracy, and economic fluctuations in the northern states, including New York and Massachusetts, to reflect favorably upon conditions in their own state and to foster a deadening complacency that counteracted efforts at reform.

Academies. Education for most West Virginians ended with the common school. Only the middle and upper classes could afford attendance at academies, with their tuition and costs, for many students, of boarding and lodging away from home. Motivated by patriotic and religious ideals, founders of academies believed that middle class virtues and moral principles constituted the underpinning of the American republic. They did not subscribe to a social leveling theory of education, and they believed that the republic itself would be in jeopardy if the middle classes sank to the status of the poor. Education should assure political, social, and economic opportunity; uphold property rights and class distinctions; provide enlightened leadership; and produce knowledgeable and responsible citizens.

[5]Ibid., 52-53.

Although academies served youths with diverse interests, many empha-sized the training of ministers. Protestant churches, particularly Presbyterian and Episcopalian, were active in their establishment. Outstanding clerical leaders included Alexander Campbell, the founder and benefactor of Buffalo Academy at Bethany; Henry Ruffner, the chief promoter and first instructor at Mercer Academy at Charleston; John McElhenney of Lewisburg Academy; Gordon Battelle of Northwestern Academy at Parkersburg; Alexander Martin of Preston Academy at Kingwood and later first president of West Virginia University; and Dr. Henry Foote of Romney Academy.

Between the founding of Shepherdstown Academy about 1784 and the Civil War, some sixty-five academies were established in West Virginia. The first ones were mostly in the eastern and northern parts of the state at such places as Shepherdstown, Martinsburg, Charles Town, Romney, Morgantown, Clarks-burg, Wheeling, West Liberty, and Wellsburg. Stable academies in the more thinly populated southern sections included Mercer, Lewisburg, Marshall at Huntington, and Union at Alderson.

Except for granting charters, authorizing lotteries for fund-raising, and extending occasional aid from the Literary Fund, the legislature of Virginia gave little support to academies. Randolph Academy, founded at Clarksburg in 1787, was an important exception. The legislature anticipated that in time it would become the state-supported college for the Allegheny section of the state, just as the College of William and Mary served the Tidewater and Piedmont and Transylvania Seminary served the Kentucky area. Despite its distinguished board of trustees and diversion of part of the surveyors' fees from several counties to its use, Randolph Academy never fulfilled its promise, and by 1830 its days were numbered.

Most academies offered English grammar, ancient languages, history, natural philosophy, moral philosophy, and mathematics, and several added practical subjects such as geography, surveying, navigation, and astronomy. The Wheeling Lancastrian Academy, founded in 1814 and later renamed Linsly Institute, made use of a monitorial system on the premise that more effective teaching could be combined with economies in operation. Financed by a bequest from Noah Linsly, it may have been the first private institution chartered in a slave state for the education of the poor.

Higher Education. With their stress upon the availability of education for all children, many West Virginians were downright hostile toward expenditure of state money for higher education, which they considered elitist. Few West Virginia youths attended either the University of Virginia or Virginia Military Institute, the nearest state institutions to them. Those from northern counties generally preferred Dickinson College at Carlisle or Allegheny College at Meadville, both in Pennsylvania. Those in southern counties usually attended colleges in Ohio or Kentucky, with Ohio University at Athens a favorite.

Several academies in West Virginia aspired to collegiate status. As early as

1823 Mercer Academy advertised that its courses were taught "by lecture precisely in the mode adopted in the College of William and Mary."[6] In 1824 it added chemistry, political economy, and natural, national, and municipal law to its curricula and in 1826 other "Collegiate branches." By mid-century, Monongalia Academy at Morgantown contemplated elevation to collegiate rank. Already, in 1846 Romney Academy had become Romney Classical Institute and Brooke, at Wellsburg, in 1852 had merged with Meade Collegiate Institute. Emerging from the trend were Weston College at Weston, Union College at Union, Levelton Male and Female College at Hillsboro, Allegheny College at Blue Sulphur Springs, and Marshall College at Huntington, all chartered from 1858 to 1860.

In spite of the tendency to upgrade academies, collegiate education in West Virginia was limited before the Civil War. Bethany, founded in 1840 by Alexander Campbell, was the strongest college in the state. Its preeminence stemmed from its ability to attract students from areas outside West Virginia, its affiliation with the rapidly growing Disciples of Christ Church, and, perhaps most of all, the devoted leadership of Campbell, who gave it much of his time and personal fortune. Rector College, a Baptist institution founded at Pruntytown in 1839, also flourished for a time. The Reverend Charles Wheeler, its principal, lavished attention upon it, but his death in 1851 accelerated a decline that had already set in.

Even before the Civil War West Virginians evinced an interest in practical education. John Cook Bennett, an educator of questionable principles, tried in vain during the 1830s to persuade the legislature to establish Wheeling University, with a medical college as its main component. Efforts to establish an agricultural college in western Virginia had the support of Professor Robert Richardson of Bethany College, who advocated a broad curriculum that included chemistry, geology, botany, natural science, zoology, and bookkeeping. Richardson pioneered activities that led to the Morrill Act of 1862, which provided for land grant colleges to teach agricultural and mechanical arts. In southern West Virginia, several residents, including the author Thomas Dunn English, incorporated Aracoma Polytechnic College, at Aracoma, now Logan, for instruction in agriculture, mining, and other useful arts, as well as languages, literature, arts, and sciences.

Except for Bethany, West Virginia's oldest surviving institution of higher learning, and Marshall, now grown into a university, antebellum colleges of West Virginia were generally weak and unstable. Poor transportation, arrested economic development, and inadequate financing combined with popular indifference to higher education to keep enrollments low and operations tenuous. Flourishing colleges were almost impossible in a milieu so inimical to higher education.

[6]Charleston *Western Courier,* April 8, 1823.

Literary Societies and Libraries. Often working in close association with academies and colleges were literary societies. At Harpers Ferry, Romney, Lewisburg, Charleston, Wheeling, and Wellsburg they served as sponsors or patrons of academies. The Buffalo Creek Farmers Library Company, in operation by 1812, and the Morgantown Circulating Library, chartered in 1814, may have been instrumental in the founding of Monongalia Academy at Morgantown in 1814.

Perhaps no literary society did more to affect the cultural climate of a community than that at Romney. Organized in 1819 and incorporated in 1822, it accumulated more than three thousand books and scientific apparatus by 1860. It provided public lectures on agriculture, manufacturing, mechanical arts, ethics, and political philosophy and until 1846 operated Romney Academy.

More impressive than the small subscription libraries found in many towns were the college collections. One of the finest libraries was that of Alexander Campbell, which became the nucleus of the Bethany College holdings. Rector College had about two thousand volumes when it closed, part of which were evidently from the large collection of Charles Wheeler.

Men of learning and refinement were to be found in nearly every part of West Virginia. John G. Jackson of Clarksburg, a member of Congress and federal judge, left a collection of 725 books at his death in 1825. A man of catholic interests, Jackson owned works on law, politics, eloquence, and medicine, as well as novels, textbooks, and miscellaneous titles. John Hite of Berkeley County owned a modest ninety-three books, but they included works of Pope, Milton, Congreve, Addison, and Steele and titles in ancient, medieval, and modern history.

Families not of the professional classes seldom possessed more than a few books. Most depended upon the stocks of merchants in the towns and country crossroads, whose selections seldom extended far beyond Bibles, Testaments, almanacs, and school textbooks. For most literate families the two most common possessions were the Bible, very likely well worn, and an almanac, almost certainly tattered from use.

Newspapers and Periodicals. Interest in political issues and events led to a rapid expansion of newspapers in the United States during the late colonial and early national periods. The press made its entry into West Virginia in 1790, when Nathaniel Willis, a Boston newspaperman who had participated in the famous Tea Party, moved to Shepherdstown and founded the *Potowmac Guardian and Berkeley Advertiser,* later known as the *Potomak Guardian.* Aware of agreements between Thomas Jefferson and Alexander Hamilton regarding the ultimate location of the United States capital, Willis probably expected Shepherdstown to become the seat of government of the new nation. When the District of Columbia was chosen, Willis moved his press to Martinsburg, where he remained until 1810.

The staunch Jeffersonian position of the *Potomak Guardian* made a rival organ in the lower Shenadoah Valley, where Federalists were strong, almost a certainty. In 1799 John Alburtis founded the *Berkeley Intelligencer* at Martinsburg. The paper continued, under at least ten different titles, until the Civil War. Seven other newspapers, most of them short-lived, were established at Shepherdstown by 1830. Other noteworthy publications of the Eastern Panhandle and the dates of their establishment were the Martinsburg *Republican Atlas,* 1800; Charles Town *Patriot,* 1803; *Harpers Ferry Free Press,* later the *Virginia Free Press,* 1821; and the Romney *Hampshire and Hardy Intelligencer,* later the *South Branch Intelligencer,* 1830.

In trans-Allegheny West Virginia thirty-five years elapsed between the beginnings of settlement and the founding of the first newspaper. In 1804 Joseph Campbell and Forbes Britton began publication of the *Monongalia Gazette and Morgantown Advertiser* at Morgantown. Britton and his brother gave Clarksburg its first newspaper, the *Bye-Stander,* in 1810. By 1830 four other newspapers had been founded at Morgantown and six others at Clarksburg. Gideon Butler introduced the press at Weston, with the *Western Star,* in 1820 or 1821.

Wheeling initially proved less hospitable to newspapers. The *Wheeling Repository,* started in 1807, lasted less than two years, and for about a decade the town had no newspaper. In 1818, the year the National Road was completed to Wheeling, Thomas Tonner founded the *Va. North-Western Gazette,* later the *Wheeling Gazette,* which dominated the Wheeling press for the next quarter of a century. It had no rival until the establishment of the *Virginia Statesman* and the *Compiler* in 1828 and 1829, respectively. Wellsburg supported the *Charlestown Gazette,* later the *Wellsburg Gazette,* begun in 1814, and its successors.

The press took root slowly elsewhere in West Virginia. In 1820 Herbert P. Gaines, who later became principal of Mercer Academy, founded the *Kenhawa Spectator* at Charleston. Its four successors and the Lewisburg *Palladium of Virginia, and the Pacific Monitor*, begun in 1823, were the only newspapers in the southern part of the state before 1830. Because of widespread illiteracy, circulation problems arising from poor transportation, and scarcity of money, most of the forty-five newspapers attempted in West Virginia prior to 1830 were short-lived. The social ferment between 1830 and 1860, however, provided fertile soil for the press. By 1860 at least thirty-nine towns, ten of them in the southern counties, had established at least one newspaper.

Religious journals enjoyed considerable popularity. The *Lay-Man's Magazine,* founded at Martinsburg in 1816, was an organ of the Protestant Episcopal Church. The *Christian Baptist,* published by Alexander Campbell at Bethany from 1823 to 1830, and its successor, the *Millenial Harbinger,* which continued to 1870, expounded Disciples of Christ views and were among the most widely read religious periodicals in the country. Between 1850 and 1861, seven other religious journals, most of them by Methodists and Baptists, were published at Morgantown, Charleston, Parkersburg, Fairmont, and Harrisville. The *Mountain Cove Journal and Spiritual Harbinger,* begun in Fayette County in 1852, was the voice of a millenialist group that had migrated from New England and the Burned-Over District of western New York a few years earlier.

Agricultural periodicals naturally appealed to rural West Virginians. The Charles Town *Farmers' Repository,* established in 1808, was the first agricultural newspaper west of the Virginia Blue Ridge. It was followed by the Martinsburg *Farmers' Museum and Berkeley and Jefferson Advertiser* in 1827; the Morgantown *Monongalia Farmer* in 1833; the Brandonville *Silk Culturist and Farmers' Manual* in 1839; and the Union *Farmers' Friend, and Fireside Companion* in 1853. Later publications coincided with a growing interest in scientific agriculture.

Exactly how many early newspapers were partisan political journals is difficult to determine, but probably very few remained neutral on the burning questions of their times. Between 1840 and 1850 Wheeling, Charleston, Clarksburg, Brandonville, and Moorefield each had one or more prominent Whig journals. The *Wheeling Intelligencer* remained for years the leading organ of the Republican Party in the state. Staunch Democratic newspapers included the Buffalo *Star of the Kanawha Valley,* founded in 1855 and known after its move to Charleston in 1857 as the *Kanawha Valley Star,* and the *Morgantown Shield,* begun about 1843. The Morgantown *American Union,* established in 1855, expressed the views of the American Party.

Athough the press of antebellum West Virginia was generally Unionist and antislavery, most sections also had pro-Southern newspapers. The *Kanawha Valley Star* upheld Southern views, as did the Point Pleasant *Independent Republican,* the Philippi *Barbour Jeffersonian,* and the Pruntytown *Family Visitor,* all established between 1854 and 1858. The most vehement antislavery newspaper in southern West Virginia was the Ceredo *Crescent,* founded in 1857 in connection with Eli Thayer's attempt to make Ceredo a pilot antislavery community in a slave state.

The western terminus of the National Road, a thriving river port, and an industrial town, Wheeling had the most cosmopolitan population and the most diversified press in antebellum West Virginia. It was the only town to support a daily newspaper before the Civil War. Its first daily, the *Gazette,* appeared in 1835, but seven others, some short-lived, were launched by 1860. In 1829 William Cooper Howells, the father of William Dean Howells, founded the *Eclectic Observer and Working People's Advocate,* a journal devoted to the rights of labor and free schools, and *The Gleaner, or Monthly Miscellany,* with Ann Cooper Howells as its editor. Ann Cooper Howells took up her editorial labors two years before Anne Newport Royall, regarded by many as the first woman newspaper editor in the country, established *Paul Pry* in Washington, D.C. The *Arbeiter Freund,* a German-language newspaper, appeared at Wheeling in 1848 to meet the needs of German residents and transients, some of whom may have been refugees from the German revolutions of that year. In 1860, as the *Virginische Staats-Zeitung,* it became the first German-language daily in West Virginia.

Books and Pamphlets. In addition to newspapers and journals, 168 other items, mostly books and pamphlets, issued from West Virginia presses prior to 1830. Nearly one thousand more appeared between 1831 and 1863. Many of these early imprints were of a religious nature. The first book printed in the state, *Christian Panoply; Containing an Apology for the Bible in a Series of Letters Addressed to Thomas Paine,* published at Shepherdstown in 1797, attacked Deism and defended the Bible. Between 1823 and 1861 Alexander Campbell published more than sixty-five titles at Bethany, most of them religious tracts and sermons.

In the early nineteenth century, Wheeling became a center of some importance for the publication of school textbooks. The firm of Davis and McCarty produced the *Murray English Readers,* widely used in West Virginia schools. Albert and Edwin Picket published readers, spellers, and grammars, of which their father, a prominent educator, was the principal author.

West Virginia Writers. Works of more than ordinary literary, historical, and scientific value emanated from the pens of early West Virginia writers. *A Short Treatise on the Application of Steam* by James Rumsey was published somewhere in Virginia in 1787 and reprinted in Philadelphia the following year. Both it and *A Plan Wherein the Power of Steam is Fully Shown,* published by Rumsey in 1788, were attacked by John Fitch, who was also interested in steam navigation, and led to "a war of pamphlets" between Fitch and Rumsey.

Nineteenth century West Virginians took immense pride in their ancestors who had conquered a wilderness and sustained a new nation. The *Journal of the Lewis and Clark Expedition* by Patrick Gass, a resident of Wellsburg and the last survivor of the expedition, naturally excited interest. The journal was first published at Pittsburgh in 1807 and later in Philadelphia and London. Aware of interest in Gass himself, John G. Jacob, editor of the *Wellsburg Herald,* published *Life and Times of Patrick Gass* at Wellsburg in 1859.

No early West Virginia writer has received more acclaim than Joseph Doddridge. Nearly every historian of the American frontier has acknowledged a debt to his *Notes, on the Settlement and Indian Wars, of the Western Parts of Virginia & Pennsylvania,* published at Wellsburg in 1824. Theodore Roosevelt, known for his *Winning of the West,* pronounced Doddridge's *Notes* "the most valuable book we have on old-time frontier ways and customs."[7] Born at Friend's Cove, Bedford County, Pennsylvania, in 1769, Doddridge grew up in southwestern Pennsylvania and later moved to Wellsburg. His own frontier experiences, vivid memory, and integrity enabled him to depict faithfully the life and folkways of the trans-Allegheny region. An Episcopal minister and physician, Doddridge also wrote a noted *Treatise on the Culture of Bees* (Wellsburg, 1813) and *Logan, the Last of the Race of Shikellemus* (Buffaloe Creek [Bethany], 1823), the latter a drama in which he sought to immortalize a much-wronged Mingo Indian chief.

[7]J. Merton England, "Some Early Historians of Western Virginia," *West Virginia History* 14(January 1953):95.

Another work of importance to trans-Allegheny frontier history has been *Chronicles of Border Warfare* by Alexander Scott Withers. Based upon tradition and upon writings and notes of generally reliable antiquarians, including Hugh Paul Taylor, Judge Edwin S. Duncan, Noah Zane, and John Hacker, the *Chronicles,* published at Clarksburg in 1831, inspired Lyman C. Draper to undertake the immense task of gathering source materials for trans-Appalachian history at the State Historical Society of Wisconsin. Withers lived in Clarksburg from 1827 to 1861 and died at the home of a daughter in Parkersburg in 1865.

Colonel John Stuart of Lewisburg was the most important chronicler of pioneer history in southern West Virginia. One of the first permanent settlers of the Greenbrier region, Stuart was an organizer of Greenbrier County and a major figure in its political, social, and religious life. In 1799 he wrote *Memoir of Indian Wars, and Other Occurrences,* with details of Greenbrier history and the battle of Point Pleasant. His *Memoir* was first published in 1833.

Anne Newport Royall left perceptive but sometimes biting descriptions of life in the Greenbrier and Kanawha valleys in *Sketches of History, Life and Manners in the United States* (New Haven, Connecticut, 1826). A survivor of the famous Hannastown, Pennsylvania, massacre, Anne married Major William Royall and lived for several years at Sweet Springs, Monroe County, and later in Charleston. Left in straitened circumstances after her husband's death, she turned to writing and published several works, including *Paul Pry,* a gossipy Washington newspaper.

Two other prose works merit note. Philip Pendleton Kennedy provided a vivid picture of life in the West Virginia mountains in the *Blackwater Chronicle* (New York, 1853). His cousin David Hunter Strother, like Kennedy a resident of Martinsburg, illustrated his work. Strother, with the nom de plume of "Porte Crayon," was also well known as an essayist and illustrator for *Harper's* magazine. Of unknown authorship, *Young Kate* (New York, 1845) has been attributed to John Lewis. Reissued ten years later as *New Hope, or the Rescue: A Tale of the Great Kanawha*, its sketches of pioneer characters, leading families, dealings in land, and modes of life reveal intimate knowledge of the early Kanawha Valley.

A few West Virginians wrote poetry of merit. Joseph Doddridge was the author of "A Dirge," inspired by the death of George Washington, and "An Elegy on the Family Vault" (Wellsburg, 1824), a successful imitation of Thomas Gray's more famous elegy. Margaret Blennerhassett, the wife of Harman, published *The Widow of the Rock and Other Poems* (New York, 1824) in the hope of providing income for her needy family. "The Deserted Isle" portrayed her life at Blennerhassett Island. Thomas S. Lees of Wheeling stressed the beauty of the Ohio River in *Musings of Carol* (Wheeling, 1831). Perhaps the best of antebellum West Virginia poetry was *Froissart Ballads and Other Poems* (New York, 1847) by Philip Pendleton Cooke, whose "Florence Vane" was one of the most popular love songs in the English language.

The literary endeavors, the increasing diffusion of the press, the establishment of academies and colleges, and the acceleration of the free school movement during the early nineteenth century were evidences that the light of knowledge had begun to penetrate the mountain darknesses. They inspired hope that illiteracy and ignorance might be dispelled from those regions where they yet prevailed.

Antebellum Economic Life

Economic Diversity. Throughout most of the nineteenth century, economic life in West Virginia centered on agriculture. The amount and distribution of rainfall, length of the growing season, retention of moisture and soil fertility by vast forestlands, and exceedingly rich lands along the streams and in mountain valleys favored the cultivation of a wide variety of crops and the promotion of animal husbandry. Except for a few sections, notably the Eastern Panhandle, where large landowners with diversified plantations made use of slave labor, most of West Virginia remained a land of yeoman farmers. These farmers often had prosperous holdings, but in the recesses of the mountains farms were often of marginal quality and provided little more than mere subsistence.

Although tied to agriculture, West Virginians perceived something of the possibilities of coal, timber, iron, salt, clay, and other resources. Inadequate investment capital, critical problems in transportation by both land and water, the absence of developed markets, and in some areas shortages of labor seriously retarded the development of natural resources. When West Virginia became a state, industry was yet in its infancy, but salt, timber, coal, and iron production even then offered a glimmer of a future in which the industrial sector of the economy would take precedence over the agricultural.

Agricultural Advances. The simple agrarian-woods economy of pioneer times continued to satisfy many West Virginia families, but most aspired to a more sophisticated, or at least a more comfortable, existence. Their aspirations required greater attention to horticulture and stock raising and to the production of marketable products. German farmers set a worthy example for improvement of agricultural practices. Unlike others, who depleted the soil through wasteful methods, they strove to preserve its fertility and made successive plantings on tracts for fifteen years or longer. They sheltered and fed their livestock in winter and gave special attention to the construction of their barns.

Perhaps the first improvements in stock breeding in West Virginia were carried out by Matthew Patton, who lived on the South Branch of the Potomac in Pendleton County. At the end of the Revolutionary War, Patton purchased improved English cattle through a Maryland importing firm. He crossed the English cattle with native stock to produce "Patton cattle," highly regarded for their size and milking qualities. Patton cattle later became favorites in the

Bluegrass region of Kentucky, to which Patton and members of his family migrated in 1790.[1]

Cattle raising quickly assumed a place of importance in animal husbandry. Cattlemen, particularly along the South Branch, drove herds each spring to mountain pastures, where they grazed upon nutritious natural grasses throughout the summer. Many residents contracted with Kentucky and Ohio cattlemen to graze animals en route to Baltimore, Washington, and Philadelphia markets in order that they might reach their destinations in better condition. The completion of the Baltimore and Ohio Railroad to Wheeling in 1852 stimulated cattle raising west of the Alleghenies. The village of Lost Creek in Harrison County, for instance, in time became one of the largest cow towns on the rail line.

Farmers also gave attention to other livestock. By 1825 thousands of Merino sheep roamed the hillsides of the Northern Panhandle. John G. Jackson of Clarksburg, an agricultural reformer better known for his political and industrial activities, had by then made improvements in his ovine stock. Horses were first used only as pack or draft animals, but as personal wealth accumulated, the demand for carriage and riding horses increased. Anne Royall noted that by 1823 the Greenbrier region had large numbers of horses conspicuous for their size and beauty, whereas only a few years before such animals were rare.

Striking as improvements were, in most mountainous areas farming changed but little before the Civil War. Peter H. Steenbergen, John Lewis, and Lewis Summers, prominent promoters of scientific agriculture in the lower Kanawha Valley, declared in 1840 that "with some exceptions the tillage of cleared lands has not advanced beyond the first rudiments of husbandry."[2]

Farm-Related Industries. Among farm-related industries that developed beyond the domestic stage during the nineteenth century were milling, textile manufacturing, and distilling. As early as 1795 the tub mill, which replaced hand mills and horse mills, began to give way to the water gristmill, and by 1825 improved merchant mills were common throughout much of the state. Flour milling was centered in the Monongahela Valley and in the Eastern and Northern panhandles. Wellsburg, for example, exported some thirty to forty thousand barrels of flour annually to New Orleans. Wheeling had three steam flour mills, and West Liberty had six mills within a three-mile radius.

Most families made their own linsey-woolsey, with flax providing the "chain" and wool the "filling," until the first decade of the nineteenth century, when fulling and carding machines began to appear. These machines produced more durable and attractive yarn, cloth, blankets, linsey-woolsey, and stockings. Carding machines at Wellsburg and in Monroe County were prototypes of

[1]Otis K. Rice, "Importations of Cattle into Kentucky, 1790-1860," *Register of the Kentucky Historical Society* 49(January 1951):35-47.

[2]Mason County Legislative Petition, December 23, 1840, Virginia State Library, Richmond.

others installed in more than a dozen towns soon afterward. Wellsburg boasted not only a carding machine but also woolen, cotton, and rug factories.

Distilling generally remained in a semidomestic stage. Many farmers continued to manufacture their corn and rye into whiskey and their peaches and apples into brandy and cider. The Monongahela Valley produced "the best and greatest quantity of rye whiskey," marketed as "Old Monongahela."[3] As a result of the temperance movement, which gained momentum after 1830, many distillers were forced to divert some of their energies into other channels.

The War of 1812 Era and Manufacturing. Interruptions in international trade during the Napoleonic Wars aroused Americans to a keen awareness of their dependence upon Europe, particularly England, for manufactured goods and of their economic vulnerability. During the War of 1812 establishment of domestic manufactures assumed the character of patriotic duty, and economic independence was equated with continued political freedom.

In a climate relatively free of foreign competition, hundreds of small industries sprang up west of the Alleghenies from 1807 to 1815. After the war, nationalistic tariff legislation extended them further protection. From 1816 to 1824 protective tariffs were considered necessary to national security, but after that time they rested upon the principle that the federal government had an obligation to promote an economy conducive to national self-sufficiency. Tariff policies fostered the nationalistic feeling that West Virginians had evinced since the administration of George Washington.

The Salt Industry. Until the War of 1812 the salt industry remained in early infancy. The basic techniques of boiling brine had been used by Indians, who for centuries had frequented salt springs at the mouth of Campbells Creek, near Malden, on the Kanawha River, and at Bulltown, on the Little Kanawha. In 1797 Elisha Brooks leased the Malden area salt marshes from Joseph Ruffner and erected the first commercial saltworks in the Kanawha Valley. Upon the death of Ruffner in 1802, his sons, David and Joseph, inherited the salt property. By sinking deeper wells and improving drilling methods, they increased production from the 150 pounds a day made by Brooks to 1,250 pounds in 1808. When British West Indian salt supplies were cut off during the war, the Kanawha "red salt" had already become a favorite in the Ohio and Mississippi valleys for curing meats and butter.

The success of the Ruffners and the increasing demand for salt in the West led to a frenzy of activity in the Kanawha Valley. Suspecting that a vast saline reservoir lay beneath rock strata of the valley, Tobias Ruffner bored a well 410 feet deep and reached brine so rich that forty-five gallons produced a bushel of salt. By 1815 fifty-two salt furnaces lined the banks of the Kanawha for a distance of ten miles east of Charleston. They yielded between 2,500 and 3,000

---

[3]Zadok Cramer, *The Navigator; Containing Directions for Navigating the Monongahela, Allegheny, Ohio, and Mississippi Rivers* (Pittsburgh: Cramer, Spear and Eichbaum, 1814), 15.

bushels of salt a day, making the Kanawha Valley one of the major salt-producing centers of the United States.

At the end of the war the British dumped vast quantities of West Indian salt on Mississippi and Ohio valley markets, and new operations developed around Pomeroy, Ohio. Hoping to avoid disastrous competition among themselves, Kanawha saltmakers in 1817 formed the Kanawha Salt Company, a combine often called the first trust in the United States. They gave the new organization authority to assign production quotas to members, regulate the quality of salt sold, prescribe proper packaging, set prices, and establish a joint sales agency. Their action failed, however, to revive the near monopoly of western markets that they had enjoyed during the preceding decade.

Kanawha salt production continued, nevertheless, to increase and in 1846 reached its peak year, when 3,224,786 bushels were manufactured. Moreover, rising demands stimulated production elsewhere in West Virginia. From 1790 until 1823 John Haymond and Benjamin Wilson, as well as others, manufactured salt at Bulltown. In 1814 John G. Jackson opened a well three miles from Clarksburg on the West Fork of the Monongahela. None of the brines matched those of the Kanawha Valley, and local demands absorbed the entire production.

The salt business had a significant impact upon other industries in the Kanawha Valley. It diversified the economic life of the valley, which until then had been essentially a region of yeoman farmers. In addition to workers at the furnaces, some two hundred men found employment in 1830 in making barrels and hoop poles for shipping salt. Hundreds of others provided timber or coal for fueling the furnaces. Scores of others built flatboats or served as boatmen in transporting salt downstream.

Equally important, the salt industry transformed the social structure of the upper Kanawha Valley. The demand for labor drew to the saltworks hundreds of landless and transient workers, whose manners and morals drew considerable criticism from observers such as Henry Ruffner and Anne Royall. It also led to industrial slavery in the valley. On the other hand, it created a new aristocracy in which members of the Ruffner, Lewis, Shrewsbury, Dickinson, Donnally, Noyes, Brooks, Tompkins, and other families constituted a new elite.

Iron Manufacturing. Numerous small furnaces throughout West Virginia produced bar iron, the raw material of the blacksmith, and metal for farm implements and household utensils. Thomas Mayberry probably manufactured the first iron in the state at Bloomery, on the Shenandoah River, in 1742. Peter Tarr erected a furnace on King's Creek, near Weirton, in 1794, which was apparently the first in trans-Allegheny West Virginia.

One of the most important pre–Civil War iron operations was the Jackson Iron Works at Ice's Ferry, on the Cheat River, reputedly the best in Virginia and probably in the western country in 1830. The Ellicott family of Maryland, who acquired the Cheat operations nine years later, constructed a rolling mill, puddling and boiling furnaces, nail factory, foundry, and shops, as well as houses for their employees, who numbered several hundred. This nearby source of iron made Morgantown a center of some importance for the manufacture of plows, nails, stoves, grates, cane mills, and other iron products.

Wheeling early achieved first place in iron manufacture in the Northern Panhandle. In 1835 it had four foundries and four steam engine establishments, which employed 140 men. The Wheeling Iron Works made nails and bar, boiler, sheet, and hoop iron. Smaller productions in the Eastern Panhandle included an iron and brass foundry at Martinsburg and forges at Glencoe and Moorefield.

Coal Mining. Unlike iron ore, coal resources of West Virginia remained almost untouched for many years. The first significant industrial use of coal occurred at the Kanawha saltworks, where the Ruffner brothers, at the urging of John P. Turner, introduced it as a fuel for their salt furnaces. Their success led all major saltmakers to abandon wood for coal. By 1846 nearly six million bushels were required at the Kanawha Salines. To supply the demand, landowners opened small mines for a distance of twenty miles above the saltworks and sent their coal down the Kanawha by flatboat. The saltworks consumed most of the coal mined in the Kanawha Valley before the Civil War. Kanawha coal was seldom sent to markets in Cincinnati, Louisville, and Mississippi River towns because the Kanawha River was usually so low in summer and fall months that boats had to be held until winter and spring.

Local industries also consumed most of the coal elsewhere in West Virginia. Mines from the Northern Panhandle fed the industrial machines of Wheeling, where by the 1830s ironworks, foundries, paper mills, glass factories, distilleries, cotton and woolen factories and other enterprises required about one million bushels of coal annually. Most of the limited amount of coal mined east of the Alleghenies was shipped down the Potomac to the Harpers Ferry arsenal and to Georgetown and Baltimore.

The discovery of cannel coal at Cannelton in the winter of 1847–1848 produced a mild boom in the coal industry of the Kanawha Valley. Cannel, a rare variety of coal, was prized as a parlor fuel because of its cleanness. It was valued even more as a source of superior illuminating oil and lubricants. The northeastern states, the major consumers of cannel coal, imported most of their supplies from Scotland, the source of most cannel coal, but only the wealthy could afford it. The discovery at Cannelton touched off extensive prospecting on the Kanawha. Within a few years mines were in operation at several places, including Cannelton, Paint Creek, Mill Creek on the Elk River, and Peytona.

Operators along the Kanawha and Elk rivers converted cannel coal into crude oil, which had several times the value and less bulk than the coal itself. The Union Coal and Oil Company factory at Cannelton made about half the oil produced in the Kanawha Valley, shipping most of its products to Boston. Other companies sought western markets. Under the leadership of William Madison Peyton, the Coal River companies organized the Coal River Navigation Company, which, with the aid of the state, built nine locks and dams that gave the river four feet of water at all seasons. On the eve of the Civil War, the cannel coal companies of the Kanawha and Elk valleys were making about five thousand gallons of oil a day. Coal River companies, benefiting from the improvements in that stream, were shipping out about 1,500,000 bushels of coal annually.

Other Early Industries. One of the oldest West Virginia industries was the construction of flatboats. Settlers bound for Ohio, Indiana, Kentucky, and other western regions acquired flatboats on the Monongahela, upper Ohio, and Kanawha at such places as Morgantown, Wheeling, and Cedar Grove. Flatboats transported large amounts of farm produce to market, and in 1829 the Kanawha saltworks alone required three hundred. Construction of keelboats, used for upstream as well as downstream travel, required greater skill and was less extensive.

Pottery and glassmaking establishments appeared in West Virginia quite early. Morgantown had a pottery works in 1785, which served household and distilling needs. Wheeling and Wellsburg manufactured both pottery and glass. Isaac Duval opened a glass factory at Wellsburg in 1813. A Wheeling factory built in 1820 produced window glass, bottles, and dishes. Both the pottery and glass industries used primitive methods that did not differ substantially from those of Biblical times.

The oil and gas industries were little more than dreams before the Civil War. Only Kanawha Valley saltmakers made any practical use of natural gas. Oil, first used for medicinal purposes by Indians and early residents, was sold commercially in Marietta as Seneca oil for treatment of rheumatic afflictions. The commercial oil industry was born on the eve of the Civil War, shortly after the success of the Drake well in Pennsylvania, but its history properly belongs to the postwar era.

Banking and Capital. The economic development of West Virginia required sound banking establishments and availability of adequate capital, neither of which existed in the antebellum era. A general shortage of money, so acute in some sections that residents regularly paid their taxes by bounties on wolves' heads, further impeded economic advancement.

At the close of the War of 1812 not a single incorporated bank existed in present West Virginia. Businessmen resorted to establishment of unincorporated banks. Private facilities, all industrially oriented, were established at Wheeling, Morgantown, Charleston, and Clarksburg in 1814. Typical was the Virginia Saline Bank at Clarksburg, which was expected to improve the Monongahela River; encourage the manufacture of salt, iron, and woolen and cotton goods; and promote agriculture. The Bank of the South Branch of the Potomac, founded at Romney in 1815, had as its prime purpose the extension of credit to farmers engaged in grazing and stall-feeding of beef cattle for eastern markets.

The lack of adequate banking facilities exacerbated relations between eastern and western Virginia. Responding to mounting clamor from westerners, who obtained most of their negotiable paper from Ohio and Pennsylvania banks, the legislature in 1817 authorized the establishment of two banks west of the Blue Ridge. They were the Northwestern Bank of Virginia at Wheeling, with authority to establish branches at Wellsburg, Morgantown, and Clarksburg, and the Bank of the Valley of Virginia, with power to create a branch in Jefferson, Berkeley, Hardy, or Hampshire county. In 1832 the legislature established a branch of the Bank of Virginia at Charleston.

The establishment of banks under the law of 1817 only temporarily allayed sectional tensions arising from monetary problems. When President Andrew Jackson refused to recharter the United States Bank in 1836, the Whig-dominated General Assembly assumed responsibility for promoting stable currency and policing banking institutions in the state. It refused to set up additional banks in the West. Later, Democratic legislatures waged bitter war against the state banks, with the result that when the Whigs regained control they authorized new state banks for the West, permitted them to issue notes in denominations of less than five dollars, and made the notes legal tender for payment of taxes and state debts. These moves, along with the introduction of the federal Independent Treasury plan, calmed western fears of an eastern financial monopoly and essentially removed banking from the sectional conflict in Virginia.

The problem of obtaining capital for large-scale industry, nevertheless, remained acute, particularly in the coal industry, which needed support from New York, Philadelphia, and other cities, as well as from England. The experiences of William H. Edwards, a young New Yorker who bought a controlling interest in the 86,000-acre Wilson Survey in the upper Kanawha Valley for a trifling sum, were typical. Lacking capital to develop his lands, which included some of the richest coal tracts in southern West Virginia, Edwards subdivided his property and went to England, where he formed several companies, with his English partners providing the capital and Edwards the coal tracts. By 1861 at least five coal companies had begun work on parts of the Wilson Survey. One of them, the Paint Creek Coal and Iron Mining and Manufacturing Company, engaged Ralph Swinburn, an associate of George Stephenson, to build a narrow-gauge railroad from its mines to the Kanawha River. Through the efforts of Edwards and others, capital slowly began to flow into the state.

East–West Transportation. On October 10, 1784, George Washington wrote to Governor Benjamin Harrison urging that Virginia take steps to draw the area between the Ohio River and the Great Lakes into her own economic orbit and prevent its leaning toward either Spain or Great Britain. Harrison laid the proposal before the General Assembly, which in 1785 chartered two corporations, known in time as the James River and Kanawha Company and the Chesapeake and Ohio Canal Company. Ten years later petitioners in the Monongahela and Cheat valleys used the arguments set forth to urge the legislature to build roads that would connect them with the Potomac River and the Virginia seaboard and lessen their dependence upon the uncertain Mississippi River trade.

The federal government, rather than Virginia, achieved the first notable success in linking trans-Allegheny Virginia and the seaboard with the completion of the National, or Cumberland, Road from Cumberland, Maryland, to Wheeling in 1818. Wheeling, a village of only 120 houses and eleven stores in 1810, became by 1830 the largest town in northwestern Virginia. In 1822 a total of 4,681 wagonloads of goods, averaging 3,500 pounds each, unloaded their cargoes at Wheeling, but that number probably constituted no more than one-tenth of the traffic passing through the town. The results confirmed the prediction of Congressman John G. Jackson in 1816 that the road would promote national unity. It became also a "visible symbol of the power and fostering care of the national government."[4]

When federal interest in internal improvements waned during the Andrew Jackson administration, Virginia kept the hopes of westerners alive. Already in 1816, the legislature had created an internal improvements fund, to be kept separate from other state monies, and established a Board of Public Works with the authority to subscribe state funds to the stock of approved companies. In 1820 it authorized the James River and Kanawha Company to construct a road from Dunlap Creek to the falls of the Kanawha at a cost of one hundred thousand dollars and to improve the Kanawha River from its falls to the Ohio to accommodate boats drawing three feet of water. The road, known as the James River and Kanawha Turnpike, followed an older thoroughfare, the "Old State Road," which had been built to the falls in 1790. The new road was opened to the falls in 1826 and extended to the mouth of the Big Sandy four years later. For the next twenty years it was one of the busiest commercial arteries in Virginia, but traffic began to decline in 1852.

Unfortunately, road building in Virginia suffered from rampant partisan politics in the 1830s. During the early part of the decade the Whigs, who were in power, staunchly supported the James River and Kanawha Company, whose operations lay in Whig territory. Once the Democrats gained power in 1835, the Kanawha area received less attention.

The most improved road built into West Virginia in the 1830s was the Northwestern Turnpike, which connected Winchester and Parkersburg. Chartered partly for the purpose of offsetting the depressing effects of the National Road upon remote areas, it was completed in 1838 by Charles B. Shaw, under the general direction of Colonel Claudius Crozet. The Northwestern Turnpike stimulated the growth of such towns as Capon Bridge, Romney, Rowlesburg, Grafton, Pruntytown, Bridgeport, Clarksburg, Salem, West Union, Pennsboro, and Murphytown.

The last of the four major east–west turnpikes across West Virginia, the Staunton and Parkersburg, did not reach completion until 1847, largely because counties through which it passed were slow to raise their shares of the money for

[4]Dan Elbert Clark, *The West in American History* (New York: Thomas Y. Crowell Company, 1937), 291.

its construction. Nevertheless, it promoted the growth of the numerous towns, among them Monterey, Beverly, Buckhannon, and Weston.

Water Transportation. Welcome as the turnpikes were, rivers remained an essential means of transportation for much of West Virginia. When the National Road reached Wheeling, steamboats had already become common on the Ohio River, and they would soon be familiar sights on its major tributaries. Indeed, a West Virginian, James Rumsey of Bath, or Berkeley Springs, had devised as early as 1783 a "mechanical boat," which deeply impressed George Washington. In 1787 he exhibited another kind of boat on the Potomac at Shepherdstown and astonished curious crowds by moving it upstream under its own power. Rumsey went to England to enlist financial support and there formed a company to promote his invention. Unfortunately, he fell dead at a meeting of the stockholders, and plans for building boats on his model ended.

The launching of the *New Orleans* at Pittsburgh in 1811 by the Robert Fulton interests, following the success of the *Clermont* on the Hudson four years earlier, introduced steam navigation to the inland rivers. Built by Nicholas J. Roosevelt, the *New Orleans* went into service after a maiden voyage in which it successfully navigated the treacherous falls of the Ohio and survived the New Madrid earthquake. It remained for the 403-ton *Washington* to demonstrate beyond the shadow of a doubt that the day of steam navigation had arrived on the western rivers. Built at Wheeling in 1816 of timbers from dismantled Fort Henry, the *Washington* made the journey upstream from New Orleans to Louisville in twenty-five days.

The advent of steamboats led to new demands from trans-Allegheny West Virginia for river improvements. Saltmakers on the Kanawha addressed urgent appeals for navigational aids when the *Robert Thompson* was unable to ascend the river above Red House shoals in the summer of 1819. By 1823 work on the river enabled the *Eliza,* built especially for the salt trade, to go into service. Ten years later at least half a dozen other steamboats regularly engaged in the salt traffic.

Improvements in the Monongahela River were first made by the Monongalia Navigation Company, chartered in 1816 through the efforts of John G. Jackson and a few other businessmen of the Clarksburg area. The legislature granted the company authority to build locks and dams in the Monongahela and West Fork to provide eighteen inches of water at all seasons, to condemn sites for dams, and to collect tolls on river traffic. Bitter opposition to the company developed, with critics charging that the rise in water level would destroy valuable fording places, require a greater volume of water to enable flatboats and rafts to pass over the dams, and produce health hazards by creating ponds of stagnant water in the lowlands. Opponents also branded the plan monopolistic and aristocratic. The controversy was rooted in part in a clash between agrarian and industrial interests and in deep personal and political animosities between factions headed by Jackson and Benjamin Wilson.

Virginia lagged behind other states in the building of canals and railroads. The success of the Erie Canal in New York and the Pennsylvania Main Line Canal, connecting Philadelphia and Pittsburgh, raised hopes among western Virginians that they, too, might reap benefits from that mode of transportation. In 1812, a twenty-two–member commission headed by John Marshall examined a proposed route for linking the James and Kanawha rivers by a canal along the New River. Two years later Ballard Smith, a congressman from Kanawha County, sought authorization for the federal government to subscribe two-fifths of the stock in any company Virginia might charter for connecting the two rivers, but his proposal fell on deaf ears.

In the summer of 1823 Potomac Valley residents held mass meetings at which they urged federal support for internal improvements, and in 1828 western sections of the state strongly endorsed John Quincy Adams for president largely because he favored internal improvements at federal expense. The General Assembly of Virginia, however, opposed federal involvement and in the late 1820s cut off further appropriations to the Chesapeake and Ohio Canal Company for that reason. Obstructed by Jacksonian politics, the canal was never built into the trans-Allegheny part of West Virginia.

Although construction of internal improvements accelerated in the decades before the Civil War, the industrial climate of the transmontane region generally remained unfavorable. Transportation remained a critical problem for many areas, as did the lack of capital and other requisites for industrial growth. At mid-century, economic retardation remained a serious source of tension between eastern and western Virginia.

Conflict with Eastern Virginia

The Seeds of Diversity. The dramatic separation of West Virginia from Virginia during the Civil War sprang from no sudden impulse but from an accumulation of differences and grievances. Physiographically, economically, and culturally, the Eastern Panhandle was an integral part of the upper Potomac Valley and, like adjacent parts of Virginia and Maryland, a hinterland of coastal areas with an Atlantic orientation. On the other hand, the Allegheny Plateau, which encompassed nearly eighty percent of West Virginia, was dominated by rugged, mountainous terrain that precluded the plantation economy common in parts of the Eastern Panhandle as well as in Tidewater and Piedmont Virginia. Hill country farms, which combined a diversity of crops with animal husbandry, prevailed in the plateau area. There, too, abundant timber, coal, salt, oil, natural gas, iron, and silica resources pointed toward an industrial rather than an agricultural way of life.

Virginia land policies accentuated differences created by natural conditions. The requirement that Valley of Virginia speculators recruit settlers from outside Virginia drew large numbers of Germans and Scotch-Irish and sprinklings of Welsh, Dutch, and other nationalities to the Valley and upper Potomac regions. From the great post-Revolutionary migrations, trans-Allegheny West Virginia drew thousands of settlers from Pennsylania, New Jersey, New York, and New England, as well as from the British Isles. Most of the new immigrants had no prior ties to Virginia and no ingrained loyalties to the Old Dominion.

Too much can be made of differences between eastern and western Virginia. Diversity of background and resources may indeed add strength to a state, and wiser leaders with more enlightened policies might have welded the East and West together. Unfortunately, many Virginia leaders did not bring to bear on state problems the same statesmanship that they mustered in dealing with national issues. Nor did impatient westerners always appreciate the mounting economic difficulties of eastern Virginia as the nineteenth century advanced. Internal improvements, land policies, taxes, education, and political rights and aspirations became increasingly divisive issues, and few government officials had the vision or political support to deal with them effectively. Conflicts and tensions repeatedly threatened the unity of the state and finally broke the Old Dominion asunder during the Civil War.

Political Awakening of the West. Throughout the first half of the nineteenth century western discontent focused on political issues such as voting rights, representation in the General Assembly, and methods of choosing state and local officials. Like most Americans, West Virginians believed that political power held the key to the solution of most problems and to the advancement of society. Their own political weakness vis-à-vis that of the planter aristocracy was a continuing source of frustration.

The constitution of Virginia, adopted in 1776 under the stress of wartime necessity, was a bulwark of eastern power. It incorporated a property qualification for voting, allotted each county, irrespective of population, two seats in the House of Delegates, and provided an undemocratic system of county government. It created twenty-four state senatorial districts but allowed the trans-Blue Ridge country only four of them. Actually, western counties suffered no discrimination in representation, in respect to their population, but by 1829 an estimated 31,000 out of 76,000 men of voting age in Virginia were disfranchised, with the western proportion increasing.

The first West Virginian to speak out in the legislature for reform of the state constitution was John G. Jackson, who in 1798 won election to the House of Delegates from Harrison County. In one of his first actions, the twenty-one-year-old Jackson presented a petition from his county calling for amendments to the constitution, particularly sections relating to suffrage and representation in the General Assembly, but the legislature rejected the memorial.

Writing in the *Richmond Examiner* under the pseudonym of "A Mountaineer" in 1803, Jackson set forth arguments on which westerners thereafter rested the case for reform. He contended that the property qualification for voting violated the Virginia Bill of Rights, which declared that "all men having sufficient evidence of permanent interest with, and attachment to the community have the right of suffrage, and cannot be taxed or deprived of their property for public uses, without their own consent, or that of their Representatives so elected, nor bound by any law to which they have not *in like manner, assented* for the public good." Those who paid taxes on property other than real estate and were denied the right to vote, he maintained, were taxed without their consent and denied a right guaranteed them. Jackson branded the provision allowing each county two seats in the House of Delegates the most serious flaw in the constitution. Warwick County, he pointed out, had the same number of delegates as Frederick, which had sixteen times as many people. Such inequities made other defects in the constitution "dwindle into insignificance." He blamed constitutional flaws for retardation of trans-Allegheny sections of Virginia.[1]

The Staunton Conventions of 1816 and 1825. Sentiment for a constitu-

---

[1]"A Mountaineer" in *Richmond Examiner*, January 15, 1803. See also Stephen W. Brown, *Voice of the New West: John G. Jackson, His Life and Times* (Macon, Ga.: Mercer University Press, 1985), 207-209.

tional convention gained ground following the War of 1812. In 1815 the House
of Delegates passed a bill for that purpose by the narrow margin of ninety-three
to eighty-nine, but it failed in the Senate. In June 1816 twenty-two prominent
residents of the Valley and trans-Allegheny counties met at Winchester and
published an address calling for a convention to end inequities in representation.
They pointed out that forty-nine eastern and southern counties, whose 274,766
white inhabitants were 73,138 less than half the total for the state, had a majority
in the House of Delegates. They reminded the people that "their right to
assemble in convention is not derived from the *Legislature,* but from a higher
source" and called upon each county to elect two delegates to a convention to
meet at Staunton on August 19.[2]

Some easterners also took up the cause of reform. In a famous letter to
Samuel Kercheval in July 1816, Thomas Jefferson called for representation
based on white population, free white male suffrage, and popular election of
most state and county officials. Richmond newspapers such as the *Enquirer* and
Virginia Argus also urged reform, particularly in representation in the legislature.

Sixty-three delegates representing thirty-six counties gathered at Staunton
on August 19. Almost immediately they divided into those who, like James
Breckenridge of Botetourt County and James McDowell of Rockbridge County,
favored a limited convention empowered to deal only with specific questions,
such as representation, and those who, like John G. Jackson, wanted to consider
"every point on which [the existing constitution] shall be found to be defective."[3] The convention compromised by addressing a memorial to the legislature in which they passed over "many lesser evils" and confined their
attention to representation, "not doubting that the same remedy which will be
applied to it, will at the same time be extended to every principle in the
constitution inimical to the rights and happiness of an independent people."[4]

On December 12, 1816, Philip Doddridge of Brooke County reported for a
select committee to which the House of Delegates referred the memorial. The
committee recommended a constitutional convention authorized to deal only
with representation and taxation. The House of Delegates adopted the report by
a vote of seventy-nine to seventy-three, but the Senate defeated it.

Advocates for constitutional revision continued to press for a convention.
Jackson emphasized the arrested development of western Virginia and the
unlikelihood of its obtaining adequate roads, banking facilities, river improvements, and educational institutions as long as political power remained in the
hands of an eastern minority. Writing as "Anti-Monarchist" in the Clarksburg
Republican Compiler, he declared that, according to principles set forth in the
Declaration of Independence and the Virginia Bill of Rights, two-thirds of the

[2]Charles Town *Farmer's Repository,* March 21, 1816.
[3]Journal of the Staunton Convention, in *Farmer's Repository,* September 11, 1816.
[4]Ibid.

white male population of Virginia was not bound to respect and obey the laws of the state. The Wheeling *Va. North-Western Gazette* commended him for his effort to change a political system that continued to "shackle and cramp" the energies of the state.[5]

Although it refused to authorize a constitutional convention, the legislature attempted to appease western feelings. In the wake of western disappointments in 1816, it reapportioned the Senate on the basis of white population, provided for more equitable assessments of land, created a Board of Public Works with authority to plan roads and canals, appropriated additional money for internal improvements, and established banks at Wheeling and Winchester. Men such as Jackson, however, viewed such favors as attempts to subvert the constitution and lull westerners into an unwarranted sense of security.

In 1824 and 1825 mass meetings were held in various sections of Virginia to reharness the forces of reform. They culminated in the Staunton Convention of July 1825. Its delegates, numbering more than one hundred, again demanded representation on the basis of white population and suffrage for all white males over twenty-one years old. Unfortunately, the reformers again split over the power of any convention to deal with all matters at issue or only those specified in the enabling legislation. Conservatives in the legislature took advantage of their division and for the next two years beat down all moves for a convention.

The Constitutional Convention of 1829–1830. Yielding to continued clamor from the West, the legislature in 1828 agreed to a popular referendum on a constitutional convention. The vote, 21,896 to 16,646, was a clear-cut victory for supporters of a convention. Nearly all the Valley voters and about three-fourths of those of the trans-Allegheny region favored a convention, but seven-eighths of the Tidewater and one-half of the Piedmont voters opposed any change. After weeks of debate, in which western members strove for representation in the convention on the basis of a new census, the legislature directed each of the state's twenty-four senatorial districts to select four delegates. These districts, drawn in accordance with the census of 1810, left western sections at a serious numerical disadvantage in the convention.

In men of talent and distinction, no state gathering has ever matched that which assembled at Richmond on October 5, 1829. Members included two former presidents of the United States, James Madison and James Monroe; two United States senators, John Tyler, later to become president, and Littleton W. Tazewell; distinguished jurists such as Chief Justice John Marshall and Abel P. Upshur, later to serve as secretary of war and secretary of state; eleven congressmen, among whom were John Randolph of Roanoke, Charles F. Mercer, Philip P. Barbour, and Philip Doddridge; and prominent lawyers such as Benjamin W. Leigh, Chapman Johnson, and Lewis Summers. Great things were expected of such men, and observers from throughout the country converged on

[5]Wheeling *Va. North-Western Gazette,* August 29, 1818.

Richmond to witness what promised to be a landmark in the history of the Old Dominion and even the nation.

After unanimously electing James Monroe president, the convention set up four committees, each consisting of one member from each senatorial district. The committees and their chairmen were Bill of Rights, Samuel Taylor; Legislative, James Madison; Executive, William B. Giles; and Judiciary, John Marshall. Conservatives dominated all except the Legislative Committee. The committees deliberated behind closed doors and kept no official minutes.

The issues of most immediate importance to western delegates, representation in the legislature and extension of suffrage, lay within the province of the Legislative Committee. Reformers, led by Doddridge, insisted upon representation in both houses in accordance with white population, but Benjamin W. Leigh, the chief spokesman for the conservatives, held out for a mixed basis, using both white population and direct taxes. Madison voted with the reformers to recommend basing the House of Delegates on white population, but he opposed it for the Senate. The committee also favored an extension of suffrage.

When the report of the Legislative Committee reached the floor of the convention, Judge John W. Green moved to amend the section relating to representation to provide the mixed basis for both houses of the legislature. Reformers drew upon the Declaration of Independence, with its concepts that men are born free, that they have inalienable rights, that governments exist for their common good and derive their powers from their consent, and that the people have the right to abolish governments that fail to serve their interests. Older conservatives such as Madison, Monroe, Randolph, Tazewell, and Giles subscribed to these theories, but they were apprehensive about the rising power of the western parts of the state.

More extreme conservatives, including Leigh and Upshur, contended that the acquisition and possession of property was one of the inalienable rights of man. Upshur argued that there properly existed a "majority *in interest,* as well as a majority in number" and that "those who have the greatest stake in the Government, shall have the greatest share of power in the administration of it."[6] The French Revolution, he declared, had demonstrated that universal male suffrage could spell ruin for a nation. Moreover, adoption of the white population basis would make it virtually impossible for Virginia to defend the three-fifths ratio for representation in the United States House of Representatives. Chapman Johnson of Augusta County and Alexander Campbell of Brooke County took the lead in refuting conservative arguments. Campbell held that if property rights must be represented, there should also be provision for intellect, physical strength, literary art, scientific accomplishments, and other acquirements which were as important to some men as material possessions.

[6]Virginia, *Proceedings and Debates of the Virginia State Convention of 1829-1830,* 2 vols. (Richmond, 1830: New York: Da Capo Press, 1971), vol. 1, 66.

During the three weeks of debate, power gradually slipped into the hands of the extreme conservatives. On November 14, with the Piedmont delegates voting with the conservatives, the convention rejected representation on the basis of white population by a margin of one vote. Seeking a way out of the impasse, however, it turned to a plan advanced by William F. Gordon of Albemarle County, which rested on no particular principle. With some modification, it set the number of senators at thirty-two, with nineteen from the Tidewater and Piedmont and thirteen from the Valley and trans-Allegheny regions. Of the 134 seats in the House of Delegates, thirty-six were alloted to the Tidewater, forty-two to the Piedmont, twenty-five to the Valley, and thirty-one to the trans-Allegheny counties. The plan provided for reapportionment in 1841 if two-thirds of each house of the legislature approved, but it limited the number of senators to thirty-six and delegates to 150. The vote on the Gordon plan was fifty-five to forty-one, with most western members in opposition.

An equally acrimonious debate centered around suffrage, which reformers contended was a natural right. Conservatives held that it was a conventional right and should be restricted to those capable of exercising it judiciously. They refused to yield to arguments that twenty-two of the twenty-four states had already abandoned property qualifications for voting or that military service, long residence, and payment of taxes indicated an interest in government as great as that originating from ownership of land. As a result, the right to vote was extended only to small numbers of leaseholders and householders.

The reformers suffered defeat on other points. A proposal by Doddridge that the governor be elected by popular vote received the endorsement of Upshur and other conservatives but failed to pass by a single vote. The convention also rejected popular election of judges. Marshall insisted that their election by joint ballot of the General Assembly or appointment by the governor was traditional and essential to prevent their becoming political figures. The final document, which was not entirely satisfactory to any faction, was approved by a vote of fifty-five to forty, with thirty-nine of the negative notes cast by delegates representing districts west of the Blue Ridge.

Western Reactions. Predictably, westerners viewed the work of the convention with outrage. Alexander Campbell contemplated assembling western delegates in a separate convention and considered the possibility of secession of the western counties from Virginia. Residents of Wheeling, in a mass meeting, declared that western delegates should have withdrawn as soon as it became clear that the convention had "definitely determined . . . to disregard the basis of white population in organizing the popular branch of the Legislature."[7]

Similar reactions greeted publication of the amended constitution. The Wheeling *Compiler* presented the constitution to its readers with "unfeigned sorrow" and without any "hopes of a rejection of this MONSTER." Participants

[7]*Wheeling Compiler*, December 23, 1829.

in a mass meeting in Ohio County declared the document "unfit for the government of a free people." A writer in the *Wheeling Gazette* called for a division of the state 'peaceably if we can, forcibly if we must.'"[8]

Despite western opposition, the constitution was ratified by a vote of 26,055 to 15,556. Every county east of the Blue Ridge, except Warwick and Lancaster, voted overwhelmingly for it, but parts of the Piedmont and the Shenandoah Valley gave it its strongest support. All counties of trans-Allegheny West Virginia voted heavily against it. In Ohio County it received only three affirmative votes out of 646, and in Brooke, the home of Campbell and Doddridge, it did not win a single favorable vote. Only eight of the 1,128 voters in Harrison County favored it.

Ratification of the constitution gave rise to renewed talk of dismemberment of Virginia. A mass meeting at Wheeling on October 1, 1830, proposed that the part of West Virginia north of a line drawn from the southwestern corner of Maryland to Parkersburg be added to Pennsylvania. A series of articles by "Senex" in several newspapers set forth the view that separation from Virginia offered the only hope of maintaining the integrity of the trans-Allegheny section. Many eastern Virginians and even some Valley residents favored allowing the western counties to depart in peace.

The revelation by the census of 1840 that ten senators and fifty-six delegates represented 271,000 white persons living west of the Blue Ridge and that nineteen senators and seventy-eight delegates represented 269,000 east of mountains led to new western demands for reapportionment. In May 1842 proponents of reform from ten counties held a meeting at Clarksburg and called upon the legislature to take the sense of the people on the question of a convention. A similar meeting at Charleston set up committees of correspondence, enjoined westerners to field their own ticket in the election of 1842, headed by James McDowell as their candidate for governor, and to send delegates to a convention in Lewisburg. The Lewisburg Convention assembled on August 1, 1842, with twenty counties represented by eighty delegates, but it declined to draw up a state ticket and merely appealed to the legislature for a popular referendum on a constitutional convention. As usual, the legislature remained unmoved.

Amelioration of tensions came, at least temporarily, not through statesmanlike deliberation and compromise but through the workings of party politics. In the election of 1845 Tidewater and Piedmont Democrats, styled the "Richmond Junto," entered into an alliance with the Valley organization known as the "Tenth Legion." Trans-Allegheny Democrats generally supported the new alliance. They achieved a tangible victory when the legislature chose James McDowell governor and Isaac Pennybacker, also a Valley resident, a United States senator.

---

[8]Ibid., January 27, 1830; *Wheeling Gazette*, April 6, 1830.

Westerners also scored another victory. Prior to 1845 the legislature ada-
mantly refused to allow the Baltimore and Ohio Railroad to extend its lines
southward through the Valley of Virginia and westward by way of the Kanawha
Valley, lest Baltimore reap economic advantages at the expense of Richmond
and Norfolk. After threats by representatives from thirteen western counties,
who met at Clarksburg in 1845, that they would vote against all appropriations
for railroads and canals in Virginia, the General Assembly relented. It agreed
that the Balitmore and Ohio might build its lines from Cumberland, Maryland,
to the Ohio River, provided that they did not touch the Ohio "at any point further
south than the mouth of Fish Creek" in Wetzel County.

The Reform Convention of 1850–1851. Political and economic concessions never entirely diverted attention from the need for constitutional
revision. In 1850 the legislature yielded to demands for a convention, but only
after cleavage between Whigs and Democrats in the West indicated that the East
could control it through election of delegates on a mixed basis. Under that
arrangement, eastern counties chose seventy-six delegates and the western
counties fifty-nine. Had the white population basis been used, eastern counties
would have had sixty-one delegates and western counties seventy-four.

The Reform Convention, as it was generally called, met in Richmond on
October 14. It did not include a single participant in the convention of
1829–1830 and gave dramatic evidence of the decline in quality of political
leadership in Virginia. Several members, including M.R.H. Garnett, John
Minor Botts, John Janney, John Letcher, John S. Carlile, Benjamin R. Floyd,
Waitman T. Willey, and Charles James Faulkner, attained prominence during the
Civil War era, but at the time of the convention most had achieved no more than
local reputations.

The positions of most delegates on critical issues were marked by a rigidity
that held little promise of acceptable solutions. Following the selection of a
president and the formation of committees, westerners succeeded, by a four-
vote margin, in forcing an adjournment until January 6, 1851, when data from
the 1850 census were expected to be available. When it reassembled, the
convention was wracked by acrimonious debate, and on May 10 it actually
adjourned for a day, not knowing whether the delegates would ever agree on
essential constitutional changes. It also seemed likely to break up on other
occasions.

The first signs of progress appeared when a compromise based purely on
political expediency broke the impasse over representation. Members agreed to
reapportion the House of Delegates according to white population as shown in
the census of 1850. The decision allowed counties west of the Blue Ridge 83 of
the 152 seats. In return the East was awarded 30 of the 50 Senate seats. The
compromise empowered the legislature to reapportion seats in both houses in
1865 on the basis of white population. If it did not do so, the governor was
required to submit the question of a white population or mixed basis of

representation to the people. Expecting that by 1865 they could also control the Senate, western delegates accepted the plan.

The West won other important political concessions. All white males over twenty-one years old received the right to vote. Multiple voting, which enabled men who owned property in more than one city or county additional votes, was abolished, but viva voce procedures were retained. Numerous political offices, both state and local, then appointive or filled by legislative action, were made elective. They included the governor, lieutenant governor, judges, and all major county officials. Other provisions extended the term of the governor to four years, reformed the jury system, and limited the power of the General Assembly with respect to much personal legislation.

Although westerners hailed the constitutional changes as a victory for democracy in Virginia, they bought their gains at a heavy price scarcely realized at the time. The constitution required taxation of all property at its true and actual value, except slaves, which were assessed at three hundred dollars if they were over twelve years old and were not taxed at all if they were under that age. As slave prices advanced, the impact of the provision, which shifted a disproportionate share of state taxes to the West, became increasingly clear. Moreover, the legislature was forbidden to pledge the credit of the state to defray obligations of any company or corporation and dealt a serious blow to internal improvements still vitally needed in the trans-Allegheny region. It prohibited lotteries, which some educational institutions and churches had used for raising money. Restrictions were also placed upon the creation of new counties which required that they be at least six hundred square miles in area and that those from which they might be carved be left with at least that area.

Many residents of the Tidewater and Piedmont believed that the East had yielded too much, but Virginians generally approved the reforms. They ratified the changes by the overwhelming majority of 75,784 to 11,063. Only five counties, all in the East, gave majorities against ratification. During the 1850s sectional tensions eased perceptibly, but eastern and western Virginians remained distrustful of one another and differences occasionally rose to the surface. During the national secession crisis of 1861, they erupted into the most serious events in the history of the Old Dominion.

Politics and Slavery

Conciliatory Politics. The decade of the 1850s began on a note of harmony in Virginia. The constitutional reforms of 1850–1851 removed some of the political issues that had divided eastern and western sections of the state for half a century. Whigs and Democrats had drawn closer together as a result of threats to Southern "rights" and the "peculiar institution" perceived in the Wilmot Proviso. As sectional tensions in the nation deepened, most Virginians, including present West Virginians, opposed extremism and supported compromise proposals before Congress.

Although John C. Calhoun urged Virginia to support the Nashville Convention, called to protest congressional action regarding slavery in California and New Mexico, the legislature leaned toward Daniel Webster, who in his famous Seventh of March Address in 1850, called for support of the Union. The legislature declined either to select delegates to the Nashville gathering or to pay expenses of those chosen by other methods. It left the selection of any delegates to congressional district conventions, held in May. Only seven of the fifteen districts elected delegates, and of the fourteen persons chosen only six went to Nashville. Jefferson was the only county in present West Virginia even to send representatives to a district conference.

In the gubernatorial election of 1851 both Whigs and Democrats endorsed the Compromise of 1850, but with varying degrees of enthusiasm. George W. Summers of Kanawha County, the Whig nominee, echoed Unionist sentiments of John Minor Botts, who not only denied the right of secession but also urged the president to use force against South Carolina if she attempted to withdraw from the Union. The Democratic candidate, incumbent governor Joseph Johnson of Harrison County, assumed a more moderate attitude and carried even the extreme northwestern part of the state by a majority of over six thousand votes.

Johnson, the first popularly elected chief executive of Virginia and also the first from the trans-Allegheny section, had been in politics since 1815, when he won election to the House of Delegates. A protégé of John G. Jackson, he defeated the influential Philip Doddridge for congressman from the First District in 1823. He served, with several interruptions, six terms as congressman. In 1847 and 1848 he returned to the House of Delegates. As governor-elect by legistative choice, he participated in the Constitutional Convention of 1850–1851.

Transportation Improvements. Johnson's governorship produced tangible as well as psychological gains for the West. During his tenure the General Assembly incorporated ten independent banks west of the Blue Ridge. From 1850 to 1854 it incorporated more turnpike and railroad companies for internal improvements in the West than in all previous history. In addition, the state itself made liberal appropriations for western turnpikes, although it contributed even more to railroads east of the Blue Ridge. Johnson told the lawmakers in 1855 that northwestern Virginia was "most happily situated" and that her network of macadamized turnpikes and feeder roads provided "all the facilities for travel and transportation the most fastidious could desire."[1]

Of special importance to transportation were the Baltimore and Ohio and Northwestern Virginia railroads, which placed residents of Wheeling and Parkersburg within sixteen hours of Baltimore and even closer to Alexandria. Grafton and Fairmont, on the Baltimore and Ohio, developed into industrial centers, and nearly every village and farm along the rail line felt the exhilaration of contact with the world beyond its environs. Towns along the Northwestern Virginia, such as Clarksburg, Salem, West Union, Pennsboro, and Cairo, also experienced industrial and business growth. The arrival of the railroads in Wheeling and Parkersburg further stimulated their development as Ohio River towns.

Southern West Virginia, particularly the Kanawha Valley, evinced new interest in railroad construction. An internal improvement convention at White Sulphur Springs in 1854 endorsed the Covington and Ohio Railroad, which proposed to connect the James River with the Ohio by way of the Kanawha Valley. Supporters of the railroad emphasized its importance to the economic development of the Kanawha Valley, but many easterners feared that it would divert western trade to Baltimore by way of the Shenandoah Valley unless it joined the Virginia· and Tennessee Railroad, of which Richmond was the eastern terminus. Moreover, residents of northern West Virginia, who enjoyed the advantages of the privately built Baltimore and Ohio and Northwestern Virginia lines, had no desire to tax themselves for a railroad through the southern part of the state.

Spurred in part by threats of secession of the Southern states in the 1850s, the legislature of Virginia recognized a need to bind western parts of the state more firmly to the Old Dominion. At its 1857–1858 session it appropriated $800,000 toward the construction of the Covington and Ohio Railroad. The following year it added $2,500,000, part of it to prepare a roadbed between Charleston and the "Mouth of Sandy," or present Kenova. In a burst of unwarranted optimism, the Charleston *Kanawha Valley Star* declared, "It is in

[1]Quoted in Charles Henry Ambler, *Sectionalism in Virginia from 1776 to 1861* (Chicago: University of Chicago Press, 1910), 301.

the power of this Legislature in five years to build up cities and fleets, and an immense commerce both home and foreign."[2]

Stockholders of the James River and Kanawha Company stoutly opposed the Covington and Ohio line. Those who favored a canal contended that only a water connection between the James and the Kanawha rivers could provide a feasible means of transporting heavy freight, such as lumber, building stones, and coal, eastward to the ocean. Their arguments eventually swayed the General Assembly, which at its 1859-1860 session authorized the James River and Kanawha Company to borrow $2,500,000 and vested entire control of its affairs in its stockholders. The legislature also took steps to transfer the property to Messrs. Bellot des Mínìeres, a French corporation that, under an agreement with Virginia, organized the Virginia Canal Company and pledged itself to complete a waterway from the James River to the Ohio and to maintain a regular steamship line between Virginia and France.

Discussion of the proposed canal naturally drew attention to the unsatisfactory condition of the Kanawha River. The existing sluice and wing dam navigation provided sufficient water only in winter and spring months for moving coal from the upper Kanawha to Ohio Valley markets. Coal shippers maintained that at least four feet of water was needed at all seasons. The construction of nine locks and dams on the Coal River, to provide four feet of water at all times, had demonstrated the truth of their assertion. The hope that the legislature would subscribe three-fifths of the stock for improvement of the Kanawha, as it had done with respect to the Coal River Navigation Company, however, was never realized.

Social and Economic Conditions. As the 1850s drew to a close, westerners began to realize that political power could not always be turned to economic advantage. The salt industry of the Kanawha Valley reached its zenith in 1846, and the Ohio Salt Company, which obtained supplies from Mason County, (West) Virginia, and Meigs County, Ohio, was already on its way to domination of western markets. Droves of cattle and hogs, which had once clogged West Virginia turnpikes on their way from the Ohio Valley to eastern centers, almost disappeared. The number of ironworks, sawmills, and spinning and weaving operations also decreased. Travelers interested in mountain scenery preferred to obtain their views from railroads rather than endure arduous stagecoach journeys, which most West Virginia travel entailed. The Panic of 1857 further strained old economic patterns and undermined confidence in the immediate future.

In spite of the gloomy outlook, underlying conditions provided ground for encouragement. Between 1850 and 1860 the population of present West Virginia increased by nearly 75,000, with counties served by the Baltimore and Ohio Railroad and navigable rivers scoring the largest gains. The slave population

[2]Quoted in Charles H. Ambler and Festus P. Summers, *West Virginia, the Mountain State*, 2d ed. (Englewood Cliffs, N.J.: Prentice-Hall, Inc., 1958), 174.

declined by more than twelve percent, dropping from 20,500 in 1850 to less than 18,000 in 1860, but free Negroes increased from slightly more than 2,000 to about 3,000.

Population increases were reflected in the formation of new counties and towns. New counties included Pleasants and Upshur, formed in 1851; Calhoun, Roane, and Tucker, 1856; McDowell and Clay, 1858; and Webster, 1859. Among the score or more towns incorporated were Saint Marys, 1851; Harpers Ferry, Ravenswood, and Shinnston, 1852; Benwood, Bethany, Bruceton Mills, and Fetterman, 1853; Glenville, Grafton, Mannington, Mason, and Piedmont, 1856; Ceredo, 1857; Rowlesburg and Spencer, 1858; and Terra Alta, 1860.

Political Trends. National tensions over slavery disrupted the political and sectional harmony that prevailed in Virginia during the early years of Johnson's governorship. The Whig Party, unable to take a strong stand on the Compromise of 1850, entered a period of decline. By means of a gerrymander, Democrats carried the state for Franklin Pierce over his Whig opponent, General Winfield Scott, in 1852. The following year the state sent a solidly Democratic delegation to Congress.

The Democratic party gained considerable strength in western Virginia. Large numbers of Irish immigrants, who had worked as construction crews on the Baltimore and Ohio Railroad and then settled along its route, added to party ranks. Although West Virginia was overwhelmingly Protestant, few Democrats defected to the American, or Know-Nothing, Party, despite its strong nativistic and anti-Catholic position. Moreover, pro-Northern Democrats of the West and pro-Southern Democrats of the East had learned that cooperation enabled them to carry state elections and reap mutual benefits.

The gubernatorial election of 1855 reflected the rising influence of the West in state politics. Its support of Henry A. Wise, the Democratic candidate, provided most of the 10,180-vote majority by which he won over Know-Nothing Thomas S. Flournoy of Halifax County. Wise, a resident of Accomac County, had impressed western voters with his stand on internal improvements, representation in the legislature, and education in the Reform Convention of 1850–1851. The West also regarded him as a staunch Unionist, although many party leaders and the Democratic press sought to align the party with the South. Most western counties endorsed Wise for the presidency in 1856, but they loyally supported James Buchanan, who received the largest majority that Virginia had yet given to a Democratic nominee for that office. With westerners emphasizing its anti-abolitionist proclivities, the party also won every congressional seat in Virginia.

The Slavery Issue. Although they escaped the disintegration that overtook the Whig party, the Democrats in Virginia also proved unable to palliate the deep divisions produced by slavery. Most westerners clung to the spirit of the Declaration of Independence and the ideas of Thomas Jefferson and James Madison, but they rejected the abolitionist doctrines set forth by William Lloyd Garrison and others of similar persuasion.

After a period of dormancy, the slavery issue had erupted in Virginia in 1831, when Nat Turner, a slave preacher claiming divine inspiration, led an insurrection in Southampton County. The uprising resulted in the death of sixty-one white persons, most of them women and children, spread terror throughout much of Virginia and the South, and gave rise to numerous petitions to the legislature to consider the problem of slavery in the state. Thomas Jefferson Randolph advanced an amended proposal of his grandfather Thomas Jefferson to emancipate slaves born after July 4, 1840, at the age of twenty-one if male and eighteen if female. The abolitionist movement in the North was just beginning, and Virginia emancipationists generally based their arguments on economic detriments to the state and its people, and not upon moral principles.

Actually, the questions surrounding slavery were exceedingly complex. Many who favored freedom for the slaves focused almost exclusively on the evils of the institution itself. Others, who believed that free Negroes would be as repellant as slaves to opponents of manumission, viewed the matter as a Negro rather than slave problem. Proposals for abolition of slavery, therefore, were often accompanied by calls for deportation of freedmen from the state. There also remained the questions of property rights and compensation to owners of emancipated slaves.

Eastern defenders of slavery bitterly attacked western emancipationists. W.O. Goode, a member of the House of Delegates from Mecklenburg County, called George W. Summers of Kanawha County, who advocated the use of money from the sale of public lands to pay the costs of manumission, the "Byron of the West, walking on the mountain tops and gazing on the desolation which burns in the plains below."[3] Goode urged dismemberment of Virginia if abolitionist sentiment became widespread in the mountainous sections, lest the contamination spread to other areas.

After the spirited debates of 1831–1832, the General Assembly never again evinced the same concern over criticisms of the "peculiar institution." In 1832 Thomas R. Dew, a professor at the College of William and Mary, drew together the proslavery arguments in a small volume, *Review of the Debates . . . in the Legislature of Virginia in . . . 1831 and 1832*. Dew contended that all great civilizations had rested upon a mudsill of labor and cited such diverse sanctions for slavery as Aristotle and the Bible. He held that deportation of Negroes, whether slave or free, was not feasible and that slavery offered the best solution to problems relating to the economy of the South and control of the blacks, whom he believed unlikely to attempt insurrection as long as they were outnumbered by whites.

The Ruffner Pamphlet. Dew's intemperate writings actually helped crystallize antislavery impulses in the South. Men such as Jesse Burton Harrison, James G. Birney, Daniel R. Goodloe, and Cassius Marcellus Clay drew attention with their publications attacking the evils of slavery. In Virginia John Hampden

[3]Quoted in Ambler, *Sectionalism in Virginia*, 198.

Pleasants, the editor of the *Richmond Whig,* eloquently stated the case for emancipation, and Samuel Janney, a Quaker, attacked slavery in essays in the Leesburg *Washingtonian* in 1849. Both men suffered for their views. Janney was tried for violation of Virginia law in claiming that "owners had no right of property in their slaves," but he was acquitted. Pleasants was killed in a duel with the son of Thomas Ritchie, a rival editor, who accused him of being an abolitionist.

Among the most significant antislavery writings of the 1830s and 1840s was *An Address to the People of West Virginia* by Henry Ruffner, president of Washington College at Lexington, Virginia. The Ruffner Pamphlet, as it was commonly called, grew out of an address to the Franklin Society of Lexington in 1847. Several of those who heard Ruffner, including John Letcher, Samuel McDowell Moore, James A. Hamilton, and John Echols, were so pleased that they urged him to publish the address. According to Letcher, however, Ruffner altered the text and changed it from "a calm argument on the social and political influence of slavery upon agriculture and mechanical development of western Virginia" to one that "contained many things so exceptional that those . . . who called upon him to publish the speech refused to contribute to the cost of publication of the pamphlet."[4]

Ruffner, himself a slaveholder and a descendant of a prominent Kanawha Valley saltmaker, attacked slavery on the grounds that it kept immigrants out of Virginia; retarded industry, agriculture, and commerce; and hampered education. He called for gradual emancipation of slaves west of the Blue Ridge, but only if property rights were protected and steps were taken to make the freedmen "industrious, intelligent, and religious beings." The pamphlet received but slight support in the Valley, where many considered it "ill-timed while northern abolition was raging," but it found considerable favor in most trans-Allegheny sections of the state.[5]

Slavery and Churches. Until about 1840 the slavery controversy had relatively little impact upon the churches of West Virginia. After abolitionists transformed their movement into a moral crusade, however, the churches almost inevitably became involved. Tensions were especially great among Methodists, Baptists, and Presbyterians, the three largest denominations in West Virginia.

Dissension was especially acute in the Methodist Church, which in 1850 included about sixty percent of the congregations in West Virginia. Most of the territory now in the state lay within the Baltimore, Philadelphia, Pittsburgh, and Ohio conferences, which forbade ministers to hold slaves. The laws of Virginia,

[4]Letter of Letcher, June 25, 1858, in *Richmond South,* June 28, 1858; See also Henry T. Shanks, *The Secession Movement in Virginia, 1847-1861* (Richmond: Garrett and Massie, 1934), 57-58.

[5]Quoted from Charleston *Kanawha Republican,* July 15, 1858, in William G. Bean, "The Ruffner Pamphlet of 1847: An Anti-Slavery Aspect of Virginia Sectionalism," *Virginia Magazine of History and Biography* 61(July 1953):275.

however, not only permitted ministers to have slaves but forbade manumissions. The General Conference of the church in 1840 attempted to resolve the dilemma by permitting ministers to retain slaves in states that did not allow emancipation or refused liberated slaves the right to enjoy freedom. When the Baltimore Conference flouted the decision and suspended John A. Harding, one of its ministers, for failure to comply with its ban on slave ownership, tensions in the church increased. They led in 1844 to a split in the Methodist Church and the formation of the proslavery elements into the Methodist Episcopal Church, South.

Acrimonious contests over church properties and preaching places ensued between the two branches of the church. Suits over property were filed in many towns, including Parkersburg, Charleston, and Malden. Local courts usually upheld the parent Methodist Episcopal Church, but the Virginia Supreme Court reversed their decisions and held that church properties belonged to local societies. The competition between rival ministers was described by Sam Black, a prominent circuit rider of Fayette and Greenbrier counties. In 1847 Black found himself "in the hot of battle" with a Northern competitor on his circuit. Black soon proved the victor, winning all but two congregations and expecting to have them eventually. In one locality he won 110 Methodists to his side, leaving "only one northern man and that a woman" to the Northern Methodist minister.[6]

Southern Methodists refused to accept the "Plan of Separation" of 1844, which awarded the northern branch the territory north of a line running from a point near Lynchburg almost due west to the headwaters of the Big Sandy and along that stream to the Ohio. Determined to push their domain northward to the Mason and Dixon Line, they dispatched the indefatigable Sam Black to a northern West Virginia circuit in 1852. Within a few months, Black reported, his enemies were "as silent . . . as frogs in the month of January."[7] One local paper urged that the work continue "until the whole Valley and the Western portion of Virginia are cleansed of this foul leprosy of anti-slavery Methodism."[8] In 1861 both Northern and Southern Methodists had churches deep within rival territory.

Many Methodists deplored the politicization of their church. When the Northern conferences denounced slaveholding as a sin, Gordon Battelle, a prominent minister and educational leader, declared that Negro slavery was a national and civic institution beyond the authority of the church. Mass meetings were held in numerous West Virginia towns to protest the increasingly virulent abolitionism of the Methodist press. A Boothsville, Marion County, gathering called upon the church to "send among us only such ministers as have wisdom and grace enough to enable them to preach the gospel without meddling with

[6]S[am] Black to George W. Smith, June 7, 1847, George W. Smith Papers, West Virginia University Library, Morgantown.

[7]Sam Black to George W. Smith, April 9, May 27, 1852, George W. Smith Papers.

[8]Quoted in Shanks, *Secession Movement in Virginia,* 80.

our civil institutions."[9] A Parkersburg grand jury presented the *Western Christian Advocate* of Cincinnati on a charge of inciting slaves to insurrection and forbade its circulation.

The Ceredo Experiment. Antislavery sentiment in West Virginia was sufficiently widespread to attract the attention of Eli Thayer, a Massachusetts abolitionist. Thayer's experiences as a congressman and prime mover in the New England Emigrant Aid Society and its activities in Kansas during the 1850s had convinced him that the battle against slavery would never be won in legislative halls. Turning to an economic approach, he proposed to establish industrial enterprises and colonies of northern emigrants in slave territory, preferably in Virginia, and to demonstrate the superiority of free labor over slave labor. Since small numbers of emigrants widely diffused among the Southern population, he believed, tended to adopt Southern viewpoints on slavery, he anticipated a contingent large enough to withstand proslavery pressures and to provide the impetus to the gradual disappearance of slavery.

After considering invitations for his industrial enterprises from several localities in western Virginia and eastern Kentucky, Thayer chose Ceredo, Wayne County, for his first endeavor. With a charter from the Massachusetts legislature, funds provided by New York investors, and the support of James Gordon Bennett's New York *World,* he launched his "friendly invasion" of Virginia in 1857. During the next three years he constructed dwelling houses, a church, a schoolhouse, and various industrial establishments, including a grist and flour mill, carriage factory, match factory, saltworks, blacksmith shop, and glass factory, and founded a newspaper, the *Crescent.* The emigrants, mostly from New England and New York, may have numbered as many as five hundred.

Thayer's activites drew mixed responses from local residents and from the Virginia and Southern press. The Charleston *Kanawha Valley Star* declared that the goals of Thayer were "diametrically opposed to the cherished institutions" of Virginia, while the Petersburg (Virginia) *Southside Democrat* urged him to use his "pseudo-pious zeal and pharisaical philanthropy" for the benefit of Northern society. The *Wellsburg Herald,* however, expected free labor and an increase in population and land values to enable western Virginia to assume its proper place in the councils of the state and the nation and perhaps "drag the balance of the Commonwealth into prosperity." The Ashland, Kentucky, *American Union* held forth "a brother's hand and a brother's welcome" to Northern emigrants.[10]

The Ceredo experiment, like others before it, ended in failure. Some of the investors failed to meet their financial commitments, the Panic of 1857 presented further difficulties, and many of the emigrants themselves became

[9]Charleston *Kanawha Valley Star,* September 15, 1857.

[10]Ibid., June 30, 1857; Petersburg, Va., *Southside Democrat,* March 9, 1857; Wellsburg Herald, quoted in Boston *Daily Evening Traveller,* August 17, 1857; Ashland, Ky., *American Union,* May 28, 1857.

disillusioned. The Civil War contributed to its collapse, and in 1865 not more than 125 of the original "neighbors," as Thayer called the settlers, remained. In 1894 only ten of the original number were left.

Slavery and Politics. During the last years of Wise's governorship political differences between eastern and western Virginia sharpened, as did those between radical and conservative Democrats. In the gubernatorial contest of 1859 the Wise faction, including eastern radicals, supported Judge John W. Brockenbrough, identified with eastern slave interests, for the Democratic nomination. Conservative Democrats, led by Robert M.T. Hunter, favored John Letcher. Eastern newspapers generally endorsed Brockenbrough. The *Richmond Enquirer,* edited by O. Jennings Wise, son of the governor, denounced Letcher as an abolitionist. It condemned his support of the Ruffner Pamphlet at a time when slavery was under attack by the Wilmot Proviso and questioned the sincerity of "sound" views that he expressed later.

After the Virginia congressional delegation agreed to support Letcher, Sherrard Clemens, a congressman from Wheeling, called upon Brockenbrough and obtained from him a declaration that he was not a candidate. Clemens then wrote the *Richmond Enquirer* that Brockenbrough had authorized him to withdraw his name. Brockenbrough angrily denied that he had authorized Clemens to speak for him and stated that, although he was not an active candidate, he would accept the nomination if it were offered. The episode resulted in heated correspondence between Clemens and O. Jennings Wise and a duel in which Clemens received a near-fatal wound. In the ensuing congressional elections, proslavery forces sought to unseat Clemens, but anti-Wise feeling in his district was so intense that the popular congressman won easily.

Letcher won the gubernatorial nomination without serious difficulty. Of the fifty counties comprising present West Virginia, he carried only twenty, but he drew substantial support from northwestern counties and from "Southern rights" groups, who had given Hunter, his leading supporter, a preponderant power in party affairs.

With improved party organization, divisions among the Democrats, and defections to the American party behind them, the Whigs saw an opportunity to return to power. They nominated William L. Goggin of Bedford County, who was "sound" on slavery and a states' rights advocate, for governor and Waitman T. Willey of Monongalia County for lieutenant governor. Their attacks upon Letcher as "unsound" on slavery and their circulation of the Ruffner Pamphlet incensed western Whigs, and Francis H. Pierpont of Marion County threatened to cease campaigning for Goggin. Out of deference to their feelings, the Whigs did not distribute the pamphlet in western counties, and Goggin confined his addresses to eastern parts of the state. Speechmaking in western counties was left to Willey, who ignored the slavery issue and concentrated on alleged Democratic indifference to internal improvements in the West.

Letcher defeated Goggin by only 5,569 votes. Western counties gave him a majority of 4,500, but Goggin carried most of southcentral and southeastern West Virginia and part of the Northern Panhandle. The *Richmond Whig* ungraciously attributed Letcher's victory to "Yankeeism and Black Republicanism of the Pan Handle."[11]

Both Hunter and Wise had presidential ambitions, but neither was able to control the choice of Virginia delegates to the Democratic National Convention when it met in Charleston, South Carolina, in 1860, leaving each of the congressional districts free to choose between them. Hunter stood squarely behind the James Buchanan administration, the admission of Kansas under the Lecompton Constitution, and the principles of states' rights enunciated in 1798. Wise repudiated all of these principles in favor of Southern rights and the unequivocal right of slaveholders to take their property wherever they chose. Hunter won nearly all of the delegates from districts west of the Blue Ridge and substantial numbers from the eastern part of the state. Recognizing his clear victory, Virginia delegates at Charleston, under the unit rule, voted for him to the last.

The Whigs, convinced that the slavery issue was dead and that they should unite with conservative Republicans to overcome Democratic strength, took new heart. Prominent trans-Allegheny members, including Willey, John S. Carlile, and George W. Summers, worked with Goggin and Thomas S. Flournoy of the Piedmont and Alexander H.H. Stuart and William B. Preston of the Valley to further the optimistic spirit that imbued the party.

John Brown and Harpers Ferry. Considering the relative moderation with which residents west of the Blue Ridge reacted to the burning national issues, it is ironic that one of the most incendiary events of the antebellum decade occurred on the soil of present West Virginia. The central figure was John Brown, a rabid abolitionist who had gained national attention during the Kansas troubles. Believing that "slavery was so dark a sin . . . that it should be wiped out by the blood of the masters," Brown began to lay plans for a Negro republic in the mountains of Virginia.[12] In 1858 he drew up a constitution for his proposed state, which was adopted by a convention of Negroes and whites at Chatham in the Canadian province of Ontario. He envisaged the state as a center of guerrilla activities against slaveholders that might incite a vast slave insurrection throughout the South. Without revealing the exact nature of his plans, Brown succeeded in enlisting financial support from Gerrit Smith and other abolitionists, known as the Secret Six.

Brown rented a farm on the Maryland side of the Potomac River and laid plans for an attack upon the federal arsenal at Harpers Ferry, on the opposite shore. Posing as a peaceful farmer, he gathered an army of sixteen white men, three of them his sons, and five blacks. From the arsenal he expected to obtain

[11]*Richmond Whig*, June 7, 1859.

[12]Clement Eaton, *A History of the Old South: The Emergence of a Reluctant Nation*, 3d ed. (New York: Macmillan Publishing Co., Inc., 1975), 483.

arms and ammunition for the slaves, anticipating that they would rise in rebellion. He also believed that his move would draw the moral armor of the world to his cause. As an added assurance, he engaged a local blacksmith to make one thousand iron pikes for the use of revolting slaves.

On the night of Sunday, October 16, 1859, Brown seized the arsenal with no difficulty. Shortly afterward he arrested Colonel Lewis Washington, a great-grandnephew of George Washington, and freed his slaves. In this historic act, he took from Washington a sword which Frederick the Great of Prussia had presented to George Washington with the compliments of "the oldest general in the world to the greatest."

Contrary to Brown's expectations, only a few slaves joined him, and they did so with reluctance. Although he had cut telegraph wires and detained an eastbound Baltimore and Ohio express, a general alarm was sounded, and residents of Harpers Ferry and the surrounding countryside armed for resistance. When a local militia company cut off avenues of escape, Brown and his men took refuge in the fire engine house on the arsenal grounds. During the disturbances seven deaths occurred. They included a free Negro baggagemaster at the railroad station, the mayor of Harpers Ferry, the railroad station agent, three of Brown's followers, and, ironically, a Negro slave.

About dawn on October 18 a company of marines arrived, under the command of Colonel Robert E. Lee and Captain J.E.B. Stuart. When Brown refused their order to surrender, the marines attacked. A small party led by Lieutenant Israel Green battered down the door of the fort and Green wounded Brown with the hilt of his sword. Brown surrendered and was taken to the Charles Town jail. Although he could have been tried in federal courts, the temper of the times was such that, since he had also invaded the soil of Virginia, he was turned over to state authorities to stand trial for treason against the commonwealth.

The immediate reaction to John Brown's raid was one of incredulity. In an attempt to regain some of his lost popularity in western Virginia, former governor Wise visited Brown in his jail cell and concluded that, in spite of attempts by his family to prove insanity, he should stand trial. When the role of the Secret Six became known and prominent Northerners such as Ralph Waldo Emerson, Henry David Thoreau, and Wendell Phillips rose to Brown's defense, Southern alarm increased. On December 6 the *Richmond Whig* declared that "never before, in the history of this commonwealth, were the people so aroused, and so bent on maintaining their rights and honor, *at any cost!*" The Charleston *Kanawha Valley Star*, one of the most pro-Southern organs in the western part of the state, advised citizens to lock their houses, stables, and barns "to see that none of these incendiary wretches are secreted for mischief."[13]

Amidst growing apprehension, westerners remained remarkably cautious

[13]Charleston *Kanawha Valley Star*, November 28, 1859.

and moderate in their attitudes. Several counties passed resolutions condemning the legislature for urging a boycott of Northern goods. Moreover, whether because of the relatively small slave population or antislavery attitudes, militia companies of the trans-Allegheny and Valley districts, raised in response to legislative action, tended to be smaller than those of the Tidewater and Piedmont.

Western counties vigorously opposed proposals for a convention of Southern states, advocated by fire-eater Edmund Ruffin and others. In one of the most forceful speeches in the General Assembly, George M. Porter of Hancock County stressed the advantages of remaining in the Union and cooperating with moderate elements of the North. With the exception of the *Kanawha Valley Star,* almost every newspaper of present West Virginia counseled moderation. Western votes contributed to sizable majorities by which both houses of the legislature rejected participation by Virginia in any secessionist convention.

The trial and execution of John Brown on the gallows at Charles Town on December 2, 1859, did not end tensions between the North and South. Historians James G. Randall and David Donald have declared that "the results of the John Brown raid are to be measured in terms of social psychology" rather than as a genuine menace to the South. Clement Eaton, a leading authority on the Old South, held that the raid "was an important factor in destroying the fraternal feelings and bonds of sentiment that held the Union together." Finally, as Francis B. Simkins and Charles P. Roland have pointed out, "in death he [Brown] became greater than in life" and *John Brown's Body* "became a standard under which a million men marched to destroy slavery" in the nation's most tragic war.[14]

[14]J.G. Randall and David Donald, *The Civil War and Reconstruction,* 2d ed. rev. (Lexington, Mass.: D.C. Heath and Company, 1969), 125; Eaton, *History of the Old South,* 485; Francis Butler Simkins and Charles Pierce Roland, *A History of the South,* 4th ed. (New York: Alfred A. Knopf, 1972), 202.

Secession and Reorganized Government

Political Parties in Crisis. At the end of the 1850s national events far overshadowed the internal affairs of Virginia. Disruptive events such as the Kansas–Nebraska Act, the civil strife in Kansas, the Dred Scott decision, and John Brown's raid at Harpers Ferry became "wedges of separation" between North and South. Until 1850 the two great national political parties had been able to accomodate divergent sectional views, but the disintegration of the Whig party after the Compromise of 1850 left only the Democratic party with a national character.

The Republican party rose out of the ashes of the Whig party. Founded at Ripon, Wisconsin, in 1854, it grew with unprecedented rapidity. Its unyielding opposition to further extension of slavery in the territories and commitment to a high protective tariff for American industry made it anathema to the South. In Virginia the only significant number of Republicans was in the Northern Panhandle and trans-Allegheny areas with sizable numbers of northern immigrants. Hoping to use this nucleus to advance their party into other parts of Virginia, nationally known Republicans, including William H. Seward, provided financial support for the *Wheeling Intelligencer,* which in 1856 came under the guidance of Archibald Campbell, one of the builders of the party in West Virginia.

The Election of 1860 in Virginia. The presidential election of 1860, one of the most critical in the nation's history, was marked by great uncertainty in Virginia. Robert M.T. Hunter and his supporters at the Democratic national convention at Charleston, South Carolina, were forced to endorse William L. Yancey's "Alabama Platform," which demanded full federal protection for slavery, the issue that broke up the convention. They reaffirmed their position in the Constitutional Democratic Convention, a gathering of Southern extremists in Richmond, although C.W. Russell of Wheeling, the chairman of the Virginia delegation to the national convention, and Governor John Letcher opposed their stand.

When the reassembled national convention at Baltimore refused to seat the old Alabama and Louisiana delegations, Russell led supporters of both Hunter and Henry A. Wise out of the hall. Twenty-three of the state's thirty delegates joined 232 from seventeen other states in the "Seceders Convention" and nominated John C. Breckinridge of Kentucky and Joseph C. Lane of Oregon for president and vice president, respectively. The national convention then nominated Stephen A. Douglas and Herschel V. Smith, a Georgia moderate, for the respective offices.

In Virginia the real beneficiary of the split in the Democratic party was the new Constitutional Union party, pledged to support the "Constitution of the Country, the Union of the States and the enforcement of the laws," a broad platform susceptible to various interpretations. Its candidates, John Bell of Tennessee and Edward Everett of Massachusetts, won the electoral vote of Virginia, but with a plurality of the popular vote and only 1,144 more than Breckinridge.

Breckinridge led in popular votes in present West Virginia, receiving 21,961 compared with 21,175 for Bell and 5,112 for Douglas. The Kanawha Valley and southeastern counties, normally Whig, supported Bell, but the usually Democratic northcentral sections gave majorities for Breckinridge. Abraham Lincoln, the Republican victor, received only 1,929 votes in Virginia, about 1,200 of them in the Northern Panhandle. Douglas won a plurality of votes only in Wayne County, where the northern immigration to Ceredo was substantial. Most West Virginians who voted for Breckinridge evidently did so in the belief that he stood for both the Union and Southern rights.

The Secession Crisis. The election of Lincoln led to the secession of South Carolina on December 20, 1860, and six other Cotton States by February 1. On November 7, only a few days after the election, ninety-four members of the Virginia legislature petitioned Governor Letcher to call a special session to consider the crisis produced by Lincoln's election. Letcher had already agreed, several weeks previously, to a session to consider the sale of the rights and properties of the James River and Kanawha Company to a French corporation. On November 15 he issued the call for a special session, but he scheduled it for January 7, 1861, nearly a month later than the petitioners desired.

Letcher recognized the strength of forces for moderation, which often coupled support for the Union with calls for defense of Southern rights. The *Richmond Whig* advised "a masterly inactivity,"[1] and the *Richmond Examiner* urged the state to take the lead in securing concessions from the North before other states seceded, a view shared by many Virginians, even those east of the Blue Ridge.

In present West Virginia sentiment was generally Unionist. At Wheeling on December 14, Congressman Sherrard Clemens branded South Carolina as having been "an unruly member" of the Union since 1832 and pictured the disasters ahead for Virginia and her people in the event of the establishment of a Southern confederacy.[2] On January 5, 1861, a meeting of workingmen at

[1]*Richmond Whig*, November 13, 1860.
[2]*Wheeling Intelligencer*, December 16, 1860.

Wheeling endorsed the compromise proposals advanced by John J. Crittenden in the United States Senate and pledged opposition to any man "known to entertain disunion sentiments."[3] The "largest and most enthusiastic" assembly ever held in Wood County up to that time gathered at Parkersburg on January 1, 1861. After addresses by John J. Jackson, Arthur I. Boreman, and others, its participants resolved that "our national prosperity, our hopes of happiness and future security, depend upon preserving the Union as it is, and we see nothing in the election of Abraham Lincoln to the Presidency of the United States—as much as we may have desired the election of another—as affording any just or reasonable cause for the abandonment of what we regard as the best Government ever yet devised by the wisdom and patriotism of men."[4]

Prominent leaders also warned against hasty action. In a letter to the Clarksburg *West Virginia Guard,* dated December 26, 1860, Waitman T. Willey of Monongalia County predicted that secession by Virginia would expose her western sections to devastation and ruin. He also opined that internal dissension in the Republican Party would render it relatively harmless and that Lincoln's own Whig background would cause him to be "a conservative Chief Magistrate . . . faithful to the Constitution."[5] John J. Davis of Harrison County, nevertheless, foresaw a convention, called by the legislature, in which secessionists, by "dexterous and never tiring" trickery and "wire-pulling" would win over "the worst and most depraved portion" of the population. Virginia would then "be dragged out of the Union" against the wishes of her representative citizens, most of whom favored a conservative course.[6] A Union meeting in Tyler County declared that "we are in favor of striking West Virginia from eastern Virginia and forming a state independent of the South, and firm to the Union."[7]

Secessionists also held mass meetings in at least twenty-one counties in present West Virginia. A Ritchie County gathering on January 12, 1861, condemned federal coercion, endorsed a secession convention, and branded "the division of the State by any line North and South, East or West . . . as worse than a dissolution of the National Union."[8] A meeting of "Southern Rights Men" in Harrison County on April 26, led by former governor Joseph Johnson, declared that Lincoln's call for men had initiated "a most fearful, terrible and devastating war."[9] Disunionist activities indicated a substantial minority of Secessionists in Harrison, Jackson, Kanawha, Marion, Ritchie, Taylor, Upshur,

[3]Ibid., January 7, 1861.

[4]Ibid., January 4, 1861.

[5]For Willey's background and this letter, see Charles H. Ambler, *Waitman T. Willey: Orator, Churchman, Humanitarian* (Huntington, W.Va.: Standard Printing & Publishing Co., 1954), 1-35.

[6]Quoted in Granville Davisson Hall, *The Rending of Virginia: A History* (Chicago: Mayer & Miller, 1902), 144.

[7]*Wheeling Intelligencer,* February 4, 1861.

[8]*Parkersburg News,* January 24, 1861.

[9]Quoted in Richard Orr Curry, *A House Divided: A Study of Statehood Politics and the Copperhead Movement in West Virginia* (Pittsburgh: University of Pittsburgh Press, 1964), 48.

Wayne, and Wood counties. Eleven other counties—Barbour, Braxton, Calhoun, Clay, Gilmer, Nicholas, Pocahontas, Randolph, Roane, Tucker, and Webster—approved the secession ordinance and vigorously opposed any dissolution of the state.

Letcher and the Legislature. In his address to the legislature on January 7, Letcher adopted a moderate tone. He condemned both abolitionist New England and secessionist South Carolina and warned that he would not permit federal troops to cross Virginia in order to coerce the seceded states. He failed to please the Secessionists but drew strong approval in much of West Virginia. On his recommendation, the legislature on January 19 invited all the states to send representatives to a Peace Convention in Washington on February 4. The Virginia delegation consisted of John Tyler, William Cabell Rives, John W. Brockenbrough, George W. Summers, and John A. Seddon. Only Summers was from present West Virginia. Letcher hoped that the conference would use "every reasonable means" of averting a dissolution of the Union and allow time for friendly reaction to develop in both North and South.

The Peace Convention seemed doomed from the beginning. The six Cotton States, as well as seven midwestern and western states, refused to send delegates, leaving only twenty-one states represented. After considerable disagreement, the convention adopted resolutions based upon the Crittenden Compromise but differing from it in some respects. On February 28, John Tyler, the president, submitted its recommendations to Congress, but a Senate committee rejected them by a vote of twenty-eight to seven, and the Speaker of the House refused to suspend the rules to consider them.

Meanwhile, on January 14, the Virginia legislature had authorized a convention to meet in Richmond on February 13. It unanimously adopted resolutions denying the right of the federal government to use force against a state, and by majority vote in both houses asserted that Virginia should join the Cotton States if moves toward reconciliation failed. As concessions to the West, the legislature provided that delegates to the convention should be chosen on the white population rather than the mixed basis and that the convention should also consider reforms in state government. The concessions had little effect.

The Virginia Secession Convention. The Virginia convention consisted of 152 members, chosen from districts corresponding with those for the House of Delegates. Secessionists predominated among those from the Tidewater and Piedmont, but most delegates from the Valley and from central, eastern, and southern sections of West Virginia took no firm stand on the issues prior to their election. Candidates from northwestern Virginia had to promise unflinching support for the Union. The successful aspirants at Wheeling pledged themselves to vote against secession and to support a division of the state if the convention adopted such an ordinance.

Moderates dominated the convention at first, with some seventy members. Unionists numbered about fifty and Secessionists about thirty. The convention had its share of prominent men, but it lacked stellar quality. Leading Secessionists included John Tyler, Henry A. Wise, Lewis E. Harvie, Robert L. Montague, and George Randolph. Among the strong Unionists were George W. Summers, John S. Carlile, Waitman T. Willey, and Sherrard Clemens from trans-Allegheny counties and Jubal A. Early, Alexander H.H. Stuart, John Janney, John B. Baldwin, William Ballard Preston, and Samuel McDowell Moore of the Valley. Janney, who was nominated by Summers, defeated his Secessionist opponent, W. V. Southall, for chairman by a vote of seventy to fifty-four.

The crucial decisions of the convention fell to a Committee on Federal Relations appointed by Janney. Clemens, Willey, Samuel Price of Greenbrier County, and William McComas of Cabell County were the only members from present West Virginia. In the debates on secession and coercion of a state, Willey declared that secession would not stop Northern attacks upon slavery and that it would encourage fugitive slaves by providing friendly and permanent places of safety in Northern states. He maintained that the Supreme Court had already guaranteed Southern rights in the territories and that Congress could have tied the hands of Lincoln had the Cotton States not left the Union. He rejected the notion of an "irrepressible conflict" between North and South and warned of special dangers to Virginia if the Union were dissolved.

Westerners injected the issue of constitutional reform into the convention. Franklin P. Turner, who represented Jackson and Roane counties, called for a special committee to study the taxation of slaves on the same basis as other property. Later, Willey presented resolutions for tax reforms and using the white population basis for representation in both houses of the legislature. Carlile of Harrison County, James Burley of Marshall County, and even Secessionists Alpheus F. Haymond and Samuel Woods of Marion and Barbour counties, respectively, joined their pleas. The *Richmond Enquirer* accused western delegates of blackmail in seeking redress of grievances before voting on a secession ordinance.

On the question of Virginia's relation to the Union, which always took precedence over reform, the tide ran in favor of the Secessionists. Appeals of commissioners from Georgia, Alabama, and Mississippi to the convention made a profound impression. Moreover, it became clear that the Peace Convention sponsored by Virginia would fail and that Lincoln's inaugural address presaged the use of force against a state, a threat condemned by virtually all members of the convention.

Rumors that Lincoln intended to relieve Fort Sumter sent a surge of secessionist feeling through Virginia and the convention. On April 3 Lincoln sent for George W. Summers, who was unable to leave Richmond and asked John B. Baldwin to go in his place. The conference proved disappointing, and Lincoln reportedly told the Virginian, "You have come too late."[10] As Virginia moved closer to secession, Burley reminded the convention that "the right of

[10]Quoted in James C. McGregor, *The Disruption of Virginia* (New York: The Macmillan Company, 1922), 164.

secession . . . can be exercised as well by a portion of the citizens of a State against their State government as . . . by the whole people of a State against their Federal government."[11] Willey warned that disunion would result in division of Virginia.

Despite western admonitions, the convention on April 17 adopted a secession ordinance by a vote of eighty-five to fifty-five. Based on states' rights philosophy, it repealed the acts by which Virginia had ratified the federal Constitution in 1788 and subsequent amendments and reclaimed sovereignty for the state. It required ratification by the people in the spring elections on May 23.

Without waiting for the referendum, Letcher named Robert E. Lee to command the military and naval forces of Virginia and on April 19 informed President Jefferson Davis that Virginia desired to enter into "an alliance, offensive and defensive" with the Confederate States. On April 24 ex-President John Tyler concluded a treaty with the Confederacy, and on April 29 Virginians elected five persons to represent them in the Confederate congress. Virginia formally entered the Confederacy on May 7, and in June the new Southern government moved its capital from Montgomery, Alabama, to Richmond.

West Virginia and the Secession Ordinance. Forty-seven members of the Virginia Convention of 1861 were from West Virginia counties. Thirty-two opposed the withdrawal of Virginia from the Union, eleven voted for it, and four did not vote. Two of those who did not vote later signed the ordinance. After Lincoln called for volunteers, two opponents of secession, concerned about federal coercion, also signed the ordinance.

Feeling among West Virginia delegates ran deep. Observing that he was an old man who had served the state for many years and lost between $15,000 and $20,000 in slaves enticed away by abolitionists "along the Ohio borders," John J. Jackson declared that "I feel to-day as if I was at . . . the funeral of my country." Waitman T. Willey predicted that "if this secession ordinance goes out naked and alone, it will either be voted down by the people, or it will dissolve this State." William G. Brown expressed fears that his own Preston County, which adjoined Fayette County, Pennsylvania, with three times the population and "nothing but a wood fence" between them, would be overrun "once the dogs of war are let loose." Residents of other border counties shared his fears. Henry L. Gillespie of Fayette and Raleigh counties asserted that the reading of the secession document "fell upon my ear like an avalanche." Allen T. Caperton of Monroe County, however, was certain that Virginians would vote for secession and any conference of border states would afford advantages to the North.[12]

Convinced that Virginia had taken an irrevocable step, Unionist delegates

[11]George H. Reese, ed., *Proceedings of the Virginia State Convention of 1861, February 13-May 1*, 4 vols. (Richmond: Virginia State Library, 1965), vol. 1, 724.

[12]Statements of Jackson, Willey, Brown,and Gillespie are, in order, in *Proceedings of the Virginia State Convention*, vol. 4, 30, 52, 80-81, 96.

from West Virginia had no alternative but to return home. Carlile, the most conspicuous, left Richmond for Clarksburg on April 19. He had already received threats of violence, and one evening a mob surrounded his house and pointedly threw a noose over the limb of a tree. His departure, however, stemmed not from fear but from a desire to arouse without delay the forces of resistance to Virginia's course. He proceeded by way of Washington, D.C., and may have been the first to inform Lincoln and his cabinet of the passage of the act of secession.

The day after Carlile left, more than a dozen northwestern Unionists under the leadership of Jackson met at the Powhatan Hotel in the room of Sherrard Clemens. Convinced that it was both dangerous and useless for them to remain in Richmond, they agreed to return home and rally the forces of opposition to the action of the convention. They secured safe conduct passes from Governor Letcher and left Richmond early on Sunday morning, April 21. At Alexandria they experienced demonstrations of disapproval. One or two reached Washington, but most proceeded homeward by way of Manassas Junction and Staunton or Winchester.

Grass Roots Reaction to Secession. Once the ordinance of secession was adopted, the government of Virginia put the state on a military footing. Richmond took on the character of a city at war, with enthusiasm at a high pitch. Virginia forces seized the arsenal at Harpers Ferry. Officials acted as though secession was a fait accompli and the popular referendum a mere formality.

The response in most of western Virginia was different. Numerous officials resigned their posts, and civil government began to disintegrate in many counties. Bands of armed men, taking advantage of the confusion, roamed the countryside and intimidated peaceful citizens. Sensing a great moment in history, farmers left their plows, blacksmiths their anvils, and merchants their shops to gather and discuss the uncertainties of the future and courses of action.

By the time that delegates to the Virginia Convention returned home, public opinion had already begun to crystallize, and Union meetings again became the order of the day. The most significant of these mass meetings was organized by John S. Carlile at Clarksburg on April 22. There some twelve hundred persons assembled with only forty-eight hours' notice. The Clarksburg Convention adopted a "Preamble and Resolutions" calling upon the people of each of the northwestern Virginia counties to select no less than five of their "wisest, best and discreetest" men to meet at Wheeling on May 13 to determine a course of action in the "fearful emergency." The Clarksburg *Western Virginia Guard* printed the "Preamble and Resolutions," along with an "Address" to the people in an extra edition. Expressmen on horseback rushed copies to towns in nearby counties, and the Baltimore and Ohio Railroad carried others westward to Parkersburg and Wheeling and eastward to Martinsburg and the lower Shenandoah Valley.

Divisionist sentiment was clearly in the air from Barbour County to Wood and from Marshall to Mason and beyond. Chester D. Hubbard of Ohio County wrote Willey that he "should like to show those traitors at Richmond . . . that we are not to be transferred like the cattle on the hills or the slaves on their plantations, without our knowledge and consent." John W. Mitchell informed the governor that Secessionists at Wheeling "might grace a lamp post" at any time.[13]

On April 27 the *Wheeling Intelligencer* carried a formal call for the Wheeling Convention to assemble on May 13. Two days later it declared the state "in revolution now" and called upon the people to let history record that "there was one green spot—one Swiss canton—one Scottish highland—one province of Vendée, where unyielding patriotism rallied . . . and won a noble triumph." Many westerners, however, remained opposed to Lincoln's call for troops. Dissidents, even though against secession, interrupted several Union meetings to condemn his action. Some Virginia authorities believed that this hatred of federal coercion would combine with political and economic gains of westerners during the 1850s to prevent a disruption of the state. Others considered dismemberment inevitable and favored allowing the westerners to depart.

The First Wheeling Convention (May 13–15, 1861). The First Wheeling Convention, sometimes called the May Convention, assembled in Washington Hall on May 13. Of the 436 "delegates" present, 162 were from the Northern Panhandle. Members represented twenty-seven counties, all of which except Frederick became part of West Virginia. Only Wayne was south of the Kanawha River and only Berkeley, Frederick, and Hampshire were east of the main ridges of the Alleghenies. The delegates included nearly every leading Unionist of northwestern Virginia, among them Carlile, Jackson, Willey, Hubbard, John S. Burdett, Campbell Tarr, Marshall M. Dent, and George M. Porter, who had served in the Richmond Convention, as well as Archibald Campbell, editor of the *Wheeling Intelligencer,* Francis H. Pierpont, Daniel Polsley, and Daniel Lamb. Eight large metropolitan newspapers from New York, Chicago, Cincinnati, Cleveland, and Pittsburgh sent correspondents to cover the convention.

Shortly after the convention chose William B. Zinn, "a rugged old mountaineer" from Preston County, temporary chairman, a note of discord appeared. Aware that most of the members had been elected irregularly or had no popular mandate whatever, Jackson moved to receive all as delegates, but he urged that the convention be sure that it had "our whole people with us" before taking any momentous action.[14] It should, he declared, set forth the mistakes and usurpations of Virginia and consider means of defeating the secession ordinance in the May 23 elections. Only after peaceful methods of resolving the crisis with Virginia were exhausted would he favor a division of the state.

[13]Statements of Hubbard and Mitchell are quoted in Curry, *A House Divided,* 35.

[14]Virgil A. Lewis, *How West Virginia Was Made: Proceedings of the First Convention of the People of Northwestern Virginia at Wheeling, May 13, 14, and 15, 1861, and the Journal of the Second Convention of the People of Northwestern Virginia at Wheeling* (Charleston: News-Mail Company, 1909), 37.

Carlile, the most influential member, challenged Jackson's position. He declared that he and his colleagues from Harrison County had been elected to represent the people and had not been handpicked by any courthouse clique. He insisted that the convention had full power to act and that if it had "merely met . . . to consult and adjourn and go home," he had no further interest in it.[15] The sharp exchanges between Carlile and Jackson stemmed less from differences regarding ultimate goals than from questions of procedure and timing. They did not prevent the convention from effecting the establishment of a permanent organization, with Dr. John Moss of Wood County as president. Moss thereupon appointed a Committee on Credentials and another on State and Federal Relations.

Once the "duly certified" members were seated, Carlile proposed that the Committee on State and Federal Relations be instructed to report an ordinance dissolving the connection between the thirty-two counties of the Tenth and Eleventh congressional districts and Wayne and the remainder of Virginia and to draw up a constitution for a state to be known as "New Virginia." He argued that the procedure would enable the convention to comply with provisions of the United States Constitution for carving a new state from territory of an existing state. He held that once the secession ordinance was ratified Virginia could not grant permission without the consent of the Confederate government and that the creation of a new state would be jeopardized.

The Committee on State and Federal Relations rejected Carlile's plea and recommended that a second convention meet at Wheeling on June 11 if the people ratified the secession ordinance on May 23. The counties should hold elections on June 4 and choose twice the number of their representatives in the General Assembly. The June Convention should have power to "devise such measures and take such action as the safety and welfare of Virginia may demand." Encouraged by strong support from the galleries, Carlile opposed further delay. Willey objected, and Pierpont moved adjournment of the convention until the next morning.

On May 15 tensions deepened. Carlile pressed for his proposal and its submission to the voters on May 23. Willey branded the plan "triple treason." Pierpont accused Carlile of trying to drive all who disagreed with him "from the field" and charged that the cheers of the spectators when Carlile spoke were intended to intimidate the convention. James S. Wheat of Ohio County, an opponent of Carlile, challenged Pierpont's statement, which he termed a "gross injustice" and a misjudgment of "the temper of . . . citizens of Wheeling."[16]

When the afternoon session began, Carlile, in a move to prevent further factionalism, agreed to postpone action on the new state question until after the referendum on May 23. With the temporary restoration of harmony, the convention adopted with only two dissenting voices the report of the Committee on State and Federal Relations. It set up a Central Committee of five members with

[15]Ibid., 39.
[16]Ibid., 53, 55, 58-60.

Carlile as chairman to prepare an address to the people urging them to defeat the secession ordinance. In case of emergency, the Central Committee might summon the convention, which adjourned shortly afterward, back into session. Ending the gathering on a dramatic note, Carlile again voiced his conviction that even though the future might bring "scenes of blood," a new state was the only hope for the people of northwestern Virginia. "Come life or death," he declared, "it shall be accomplished."[17]

The Referendum on Secession. When the First Wheeling Convention adjourned on May 15, only a week remained until the referendum on secession. Carlile prepared an address to the people which circulated through newspapers and in pamphlet form. He fervently appealed to them to reject secession, but he said nothing about the creation of a new state.

Precise statistics on the vote on secession in present West Virginia cannot be determined. Charles H. Ambler placed the vote at about 48,000, with some 44,000 in opposition to secession. Richard O. Curry rejects Ambler's figures as having "absolutely no basis in fact" and holds that the total vote was some 53,978, with 34,677 for and 19,121 against secession. Although Curry's conclusions rest upon extrapolations derived from incomplete data, they seem more realistic, but they, too, must be used with some reservation.

Nine counties of southern West Virginia—Greenbrier, Monroe, Fayette, Raleigh, Mercer, Boone, Wyoming, McDowell, and Logan—voted rather solidly for secession, and sentiment in that direction was evidently stronger in the Eastern Panhandle than statistics indicate. Henry Mason Mathews, later a governor of West Virginia, wrote Governor Letcher that "There is but one sentiment here" and that "every man, young & old, was ready to defend the Commonwealth." The Fayette County court appropriated $5,000 for arming and equipping volunteers and pledged that after "money and property are exhausted . . . we will eat roots . . . and still fight for our liberty unto death."[18] Jefferson, Hampshire, Hardy, and Pendleton counties ratified the ordinance, but Berkeley and Morgan rejected it.

Twenty-four of the thirty-five counties of northwestern Virginia gave substantial majorities for the Union, but eight of the thirty-three counties that Carlile would have included in New Virginia—Barbour, Tucker, Randolph, Webster, Braxton, Gilmer, Calhoun, and Roane—and three others—Nicholas, Pocahontas, and Clay—favored secession. In secessionist counties, however, large numbers of Unionists were intimidated and refrained from voting. Thomas M. Harris of Braxton County declared that there "a Union man dare not open his mouth," and Spencer Dayton of Philippi stated that in that town it was "personally hazardous" to favor the Union.[19] Except for Barbour, most secces-

[17]Ibid., 66.

[18]Statements of Mathews and the Fayette County Court are quoted in Curry, *A House Divided*, 50-51.

[19]Harris and Dayton are quoted in Curry, *A House Divided*, 48, 50; see also pp. 141-47.

sionist counties in northwestern Virginia were thinly populated, and the region as a whole was predominantly Unionist, perhaps by as much as three to one.

The Second Wheeling Convention (June 11–25, 1861). The Second Wheeling Convention, sometimes called the June Convention, assembled on June 11 with 105 delegates, many of them chosen by irregular methods, including military intervention. The delegates represented thirty-eight counties, five of which were east of the Allegheny Mountains. Two of them—Fairfax and Alexandria—never became part of West Virginia. Fifteen of the trans-Allegheny counties, or more than one-third of the area of West Virginia, sent no delegates.

The convention chose Arthur I. Boreman, a Parkersburg attorney, as president. In the first formal action, Carlile offered a resolution thanking federal authorities for "the prompt manner in which they have responded to our call for protection." The convention also expressed appreciation to General George B. McClellan for saving northwestern Virginia from "destruction and spoliation." More importantly, as a gesture of courtesy and expediency, Carlile was named chairman of the Committee on Business to consider all questions of state and federal relations. From that vantage point he established himself as the real leader of the convention and the new state movement.

Although Dennis B. Dorsey of Monongalia County offered a resolution for making necessary preparations for separate statehood on the ground that it would not impose upon the West "the calamity of an overburdening State debt," sentiment had shifted away from immediate statehood.[20] On June 13 Carlile, on behalf of the Committee on Business, presented "A Declaration of the People of Virginia," which proclaimed the offices of all state officials who had favored secession vacant and called for a reorganization of the government of Virginia on a loyal basis. The next day the committee presented a proposal under which the convention elected a governor, lieutenant governor, and council and constituted Unionists who had been elected to the General Assembly on May 23 as the legislature of the Reorganized, or Restored, Government to be located at Wheeling.

Carlile hastened to reassure Dorsey and others that he was still as much committed to separation as he had been at the May convention. Now that the Richmond government had been repudiated, he urged the assembling of a loyal legislature that might proceed, with recognition by the federal government, as "the true, legal, constitutional representatives of the people of Virginia." He admitted that "In relation to this thing of dividing, I find that even I, who first started the little stone down the mountain, have now to apply the rubbers to other gentlemen who have outrun me in the race, to check their impetuosity."[21]

The convention adopted the ordinance for reorganization of the state government on June 19 by a vote of seventy-six to three. That night a caucus

[20]Lewis, *How West Virginia Was Made,* 83.
[21]Ibid., 109, 125.

chose Francis H. Pierpont "Governor of Virginia," and members of the convention formally elected him to that office by unanimous vote the following day. Daniel Polsley was elected lieutenant governor and Daniel Lamb, James W. Paxton, Peter G. Van Winkle, William Lazier, and William A. Harrison members of the governor's council. The convention adjourned on June 25 with the provision that it would reconvene at Wheeling on August 6.

Launching the Reorganized Government. On the day of his election, Pierpont called the legislature of the Reorganized Government into session on July 1. The following day he requested additional military aid from President Lincoln, who informed Congress that "These loyal citizens, this government is bound to recognize, and protect, as being Virginia."[22] Lincoln's recommendation was in effect an official recognition of the Reorganized Government.

The new legislature immediately proceeded to elect state officials not included on Virginia's short ballot, enact laws to deal with chaotic conditions prevailing in much of northwestern Virginia, and select two United States senators. On July 9 it elected Carlile, without opposition, for the long Senate term ending March 3, 1865. It chose Waitman T. Willey over Van Winkle and Lamb for the short term ending March 3, 1863. On July 11 the United States Senate formally declared the seats of Robert M.T. Hunter and James Mason vacated, and two days later Andrew Johnson of Tennessee presented the credentials of Carlile and Willey. Over objections of Senator James A. Bayard of Delaware, the Senate voted thirty-five to five to seat them. Nine days earlier Carlile, William G. Brown, and Kellian V. Whaley had taken seats in the House of Representatives. Convinced that a constituent assembly should take the first moves toward the creation of a new state and conscious of the deep divisions over the status of slavery in the proposed state, the General Assembly declined to take immediate action toward statehood for West Virginia.

The Second Wheeling Convention, Adjourned Session, (August 6–21, 1861). Military conditions gave momentum to separatist sentiment at Wheeling. The battles of Rich Mountain (July 11) and Corricks Ford (July 13), following earlier successes of Union forces, pushed Confederate troops out of the Monongahela Valley, and General Jacob D. Cox drove the Confederates out of the Kanawha Valley. On the other hand, the Confederate victory at Bull Run, or Manassas, raised the danger that unless proponents of the new state acted quickly, western Virginia might find itself, against its will, included in the Confederacy.

On the very day, August 6, that it reassembled in adjourned session, the Second Wheeling Convention created a Committee on a Division of the State, consisting of one member from each of the thirty-three counties represented. Daniel D.T. Farnsworth of Upshur observed that the legislature had refused its assent to a new state, as required by the Constitution, and proposed that the

---

[22]Quoted in Curry, *A House Divided*, 73.

convention adjourn. Carlile submitted resolutions instructing the Committee on Business to report an ordinance for a separate state with thirty-eight counties, five of them in the Valley of Virginia, and any contiguous counties in which a majority of the people desired to be included. He also asked that the committee be empowered to draw up a constitution for the new state. He argued that division of Virginia was essential as a defense measure, that northwestern Virginia might again be subjected to domination by eastern Virginia if the rebellion were suddenly crushed, and that opponents of immediate action really hoped to defeat the statehood movement. The convention tabled his resolutions.

Prospects for the new state brightened on August 13, when the Committee on a Division of the State reported a dismemberment ordinance. Its inclusion of nearly every county west of the Blue Ridge as well as Potomac River counties in the vicinity of Washington, D.C., however, lessened its chances of adoption. William J. Boreman offered a substitute motion to postpone the question until January 1862, when voters in the counties affected could express their views. Had it been adopted, Boreman's substitute, which was defeated by the narrow margin of forty-two to forty, could have wrecked the new state plans.

After five days of wrangling over boundaries, the convention referred the question to a committee consisting of three new state advocates—Carlile, Farnsworth, and James Paxton—and three opponents—Van Winkle, Lamb, and Charles Ruffner. On August 20 the committee proposed a compromise whereby a new state, to be known as "Kanawha," would include thirty-nine counties, with the provision that Greenbrier, Pocahontas, Hampshire, Hardy, Berkeley, Morgan, and Jefferson would be added if the majority of their voters approved. Other counties contiguous to them might also apply for admission. The question would be put to the voters on the fourth Thursday in October, at which time they would choose delegates to a constitutional convention to convene at Wheeling if they approved the dismemberment ordinance. The convention adopted the committee recommendations by a vote of fifty to twenty-eight.

Before announcing adjournment, President Boreman told members of the convention, "You have taken the initiative in the creation and organization of a new state." He expressed his hope that the action would not engender strife among the people and that "its most ardent advocates" would "realize their fondest hopes of its complete success." On that note he adjourned the convention.[23]

[23]Hall, *Rending of Virginia*, 383.

The Agony of War

The Crystallizing of Allegiances. The adoption of a secession ordinance by Virginia, the firing upon Fort Sumter, the call of President Lincoln for volunteers, and events at Wheeling in early summer 1861 produced deep divisions among West Virginians. The crises "arrayed brother against brother, father against son, and neighbor against neighbor," heightening the tragedy of civil war.[1]

Unionists and Seccessionists in trans-Allegheny West Virginia vied for men and materiel. Secessionists hastened to comply with state directives to activate militia companies, but Unionists refused to serve in those destined for Confederate service and formed their own. Both attempted to gain control of state firearms stored in western jails and armories in the wake of John Brown's raid at Harpers Ferry. At Parkersburg, for instance, Unionists engaged in a pitched battle with Secessionists for muskets with which to arm a home guard company. Seccessionists seized the muskets at Sisterville, but Unionists captured two cannon placed there for border defense. Union arms in northwestern counties were augmented by two thousand Minié rifles sent by Secretary of War Simon Cameron and another two thousand secured by a loan negotiated by John S. Carlile and the Central Committee of the First Wheeling Convention with the governor of Massachusetts.

At the outset of the war the Secessionists appeared to have a slight advantage in West Virginia. By early May, however, Union companies were drilling in Wheeling, Clarksburg, Grafton, and other towns, and by the middle of the month the First Virginia Volunteer Infantry, commanded by Colonel Benjamin F. Kelley, became the first Virginia unit to answer Lincoln's call for volunteers. State forces at Grafton, Charleston, and Guyandotte threatened Unionists with seizure of property and imprisonment, but the Unionists gained strength and in the Wheeling area warned that they would retaliate against such actions.

The number of West Virginians who fought in the Civil War cannot be determined precisely. Estimates of Union strength, based upon records of the

[1]Charles H. Ambler and Festus P. Summers, *West Virginia, the Mountain State*, 2d ed. (Englewood Cliffs, N.J.: Prentice-Hall, Inc., 1958), 207.

adjutants general of the Reorganized Government of Virginia and the state of West Virginia and the report of the quartermaster general of West Virginia, range from twenty-eight to thirty-six thousand, with recent studies pointing toward the higher figure. Of the total, 212 were "Colored Troops." The number of Confederate troops from West Virginia, once placed at seven to nine thousand, was later revised upward to between ten and twelve thousand. More recent studies suggest far less disparity between the numbers of Union and Confederate soldiers from West Virginia than was once accepted by students of the Civil War. In addition, there were hundreds of independents and scouts, as well as "bushwackers" who used the war for personal advantage.[2]

Northwestern Virginia, 1861. On May 9, four days before the First Wheeling Convention assembled, the secretary of war added the part of West Virginia north of the Kanawha River to the Department of Ohio, under the command of General George B. McClellan. While McClellan laid plans for an advance into northwestern Virginia, Colonel George A. Porterfield, the Confederate commander in the Monongahela Valley, occupied Grafton and ordered the destruction of Baltimore and Ohio Railroad bridges between there and Wheeling.

McClellan responded with a directive for a two-pronged attack on Grafton, with Colonel Benjamin Kelley and the First Virginia Infantry, supported by companies of the Second Virginia Volunteers and the Sixteenth Ohio, moving eastward from Wheeling by way of the Baltimore and Ohio and the Fourteenth and Sixteenth Ohio regiments proceeding from Parkersburg by the southern branch of the railroad. Knowing that he could not withstand an assault, Porterfield withdrew to Philippi, where Southern sentiment appeared stronger. Kelley occupied Fairmont and on May 30 took Grafton, an important rail junction, without firing a shot.

Shortly after dawn on June 3 Kelley and Colonel Ebenezer Dumont sprang a surprise attack on Philippi. When their six-pounders heralded their approach at one end of the town, the Confederates fled by the other. Neither side lost a single life, but Kelley was severely wounded in what has been called "the first important inland engagement of the Civil War." Discredited by the "Phillipi Races," as the action was humorously dubbed, Porterfield retreated to Beverly. On June 8 he was replaced by Brigadier General Robert S. Garnett.

Hoping to remain within striking distance of the Baltimore and Ohio Railroad, Garnett established strong defensive positions on the west side of Laurel Hill near Belington and ten miles to the south at Rich Mountain Pass not far from Beverly. His advantages were offset by the arrival of McClellan in Grafton on June 22 to take personal command of Union operations. McClellan convinced many mountain folk, who gathered on railway platforms to see him, that he came as their friend and protector. By the end of June his forces,

[2]Ibid., 208-209; Boyd B. Stutler, *West Virginia and the Civil War* (Charleston: Education Foundation, 1963), pp. vi, 2.

augmented by four regiments under Brigadier General William S. Rosecrans, added Buckhannon, Weston, and Rowlesburg to Monongahela Valley towns in Union hands.

Reassured by his far superior numbers, the usually cautious McClellan struck at Laurel Hill and Rich Mountain Pass at once. His strategy called for Union demonstrations in front of Laurel Hill, the stronger of the two positions, that would force Garnett with some five thousand men to remain in camp and allow McClellan to assault Rich Mountain Pass, defended by Colonel John Pegram and about fourteen hundred men. McClellan believed that by reducing the Rich Mountain fortifications, he could occupy Beverly, prevent Garnett from retreating by way of the Staunton and Parkersburg Turnpike, and thrust the main Confederate force between two larger Union armies.

McClellan's plan worked perfectly. With David Hart, a local youth, as a guide, Rosecrans led a flanking detachment of two thousand men along a nearly forgotten road through heavy timber to the crest of Rich Mountain on July 11. The Confederates fought gallantly, but their position was hopeless, and they were swept from the mountain. When Pegram surrendered at Beverly on July 13, the Union netted 623 prisoners, including 33 officers. Informed of the rout of Pegram, Garnett ordered an immediate retreat of Confederate forces. Learning that Union occupation of Beverly had cut off escape by the Staunton and Parkersburg Turnpike, he frantically pressed his men back to Leadsville, where a mountainous road led to the Northwestern Turnpike at Red House, Maryland. Although he was slowed by a cold rain, mud, and heavy wagon transports, he arrived at Shavers Fork of the Cheat River on July 12. He broke camp next morning, with Union troops in hot pursuit. Before the day ended the Confederates suffered another defeat at Corricks Ford, where Garnett himself lost his life.

Had not inexperienced Union officers made numerous mistakes, they might have captured Garnett's entire command, which was near exhaustion from forced marches and lack of sleep. Their ineptness, however, allowed most of Garnett's troops to escape to Monterey by way of Greenland Gap, although they captured nearly a hundred wagons, eight pieces of artillery, several hundred tents, more than two hundred horses and mules, and ammunition and camp equipment.

Union victories in the Monongahela Valley were of more than ordinary significance. The Confederates were never again able to conduct more than sporadic raids into northwestern Virginia. Their inability to mount a successful campaign made possible events at Wheeling that led to the formation of the Reorganized Government of Virginia and the creation of the state of West Virginia. They also drew McClellan to the attention of the nation and made him a logical choice for commander of the Army of the Potomac after the Union defeat at Bull Run.

The Kanawha Valley. Before McClellan assumed his new post, he telegraphed Governor Francis H. Pierpont that he intended to move troops into the

Kanawha Valley "to complete our work and establish your authority."[3] Unlike the Monongahela region, the Kanawha Valley had a well-organized Confederate element, with Secessionists conspicuous among its political leaders and officeholders. Many residents, however, attempted to maintain a neutral position in the conflict. George W. Summers, their most prominent spokesman, warned that most of the people of the Kanawha Valley would regard the entry of Union forces as an invasion and unite in repelling it. McClellan was impressed by the views of Summers and delayed the dispatch of troops to the Kanawha.

On July 6 Brigadier General Henry A. Wise arrived in Charleston to take charge of Confederate forces of Virginia in the Kanawha Valley. The "Wise Legion," consisting largely of recruits gathered along the way, was joined by the Kanawha Riflemen under Colonel Christopher Q. Tompkins and several hundred militiamen to make a total command of some twenty-seven hundred men. Wise planned to drive the enemy from the Kanawha Valley and move up the Ohio River and break up the Reorganized Government at Wheeling. His flamboyant personality and domineering attitude, however, antagonized even Confederate sympathizers in the Kanawha Valley and undermined much of his original support.

On orders of McClellan, General Jacob D. Cox invaded the Kanawha Valley on July 9 with three Ohio and two Kentucky regiments. The Ohio regiments occupied Point Pleasant on July 10. The Kentucky regiments, protecting the flanks of the main force, crossed the Ohio at Guyandotte and Ravenswood and joined the Ohioans, who moved up the river by steamboat, below Charleston. On July 17, Union and Confederate scouting parties surprised each other at Scary Creek, fifteen miles below Charleston. After initial confusion, the Confederates occupied the position, and Union forces returned to their camp near the mouth of the Pocatalico River. Then, in the belief that Union reinforcements were on the way, the Confederates themselves withdrew. McClellan described the engagement, minor in nature, as "something between a victory and a defeat" for the Union, while Wise claimed "a glorious repulse of the enemy, if not a decided victory."[4]

Without hope of additional recruits, Wise abandoned strong defensive positions on Tyler Mountain and at Charleston, whose mayor formally surrendered the town to Cox on July 25. Wise beat a retreat up the Kanawha, burned the sturdy covered bridge that spanned the Gauley River, and, after establishing cavalry patrols at Gauley Bridge, Fayetteville, and Summersville, continued by way of the James River and Kanawha Turnpike to White Sulphur Springs. By then at least five hundred of his men from the Kanawha Valley, who refused to leave their homes, had slipped away into the surrounding hills. Cox occupied Gauley Bridge and erected earthworks, blockhouses, and gun emplacements at strategic points.

[3]Quoted in Ambler and Summers, *West Virginia, the Mountain State*, 216.
[4]Ibid.

Closing the Ring. Sound military strategy required that Union forces open communications between the Monongahela and Kanawha valleys, particularly between headquarters at Clarksburg and Gauley Bridge. On July 25 Colonel Erastus B. Tyler left Bulltown with fifteen hundred men and, after posting a substantial garrison at Sutton, arrived at Summersville on August 7. His new position placed him within easy communication of Cox at Gauley Bridge.

Confederate efforts to prevent territory along the James River and Kanawha Turnpike east of Gauley Bridge from falling into Union hands spawned a tragicomedy that almost ensured another serious defeat. Authorities in Richmond directed General John B. Floyd, who had been secretary of war in the cabinet of James Buchanan, to reoccupy the Kanawha region and ordered Wise to attach his troops to those of Floyd, who outranked him. Wise rankled under subordination to Floyd, interpreted his most innocuous orders as insulting, and maintained that his command was an independent unit operating under the authority of General Lee. Floyd severely criticized Wise in letters to President Jefferson Davis. He insisted that Wise's blundering had caused the Confederates to lose the Kanawha Valley and that Wise would never cooperate in efforts to regain it.

Plans devised by Floyd threatened Cox's forces at Gauley Bridge with encirclement, particularly if he moved from the James River and Kanawha Turnpike to the upper Gauley River by way of the Wilderness Road, which led to Hughes's Ferry, and on to Summersville, or by the Sunday Road, which extended to Meadow River and on to Carnifex Ferry on the Gauley. Rosecrans, in charge of Union occupation forces in the Monongahela Valley, endeavored to prevent the Confederates from outflanking Cox and cutting off his retreat down the Kanawha by placing Ohio regiments at Summersville to cover the Wilderness Road and at Keslers Cross Lanes to check any movement along the Sunday Road.

On August 21 Floyd conferred with Wise at the foot of Gauley Mountain. They agreed that Wise would march at once via the Sunday Road to Carnifex Ferry, while Floyd guarded the trains and supplies at Dogwood Gap. For some reason, Floyd changed his plans. On the morning of August 22 he arrived at Carnifex Ferry and ordered Wise to return to Dogwood Gap. Upon hearing of Floyd's arrival, Tyler, then guarding a road along Twenty Mile Creek, hastened back to Keslers Cross Lanes and bivouacked within two miles of the Confederate camp. On August 26, Confederate forces surrounded Tyler's men while they were eating breakfast and killed twenty and captured about one hundred of them. Tyler, with about two hundred, fled to Gauley Bridge, and another four hundred, led by Major John S. Casement, crossed the mountains to the Elk River, which they followed to Charleston.

Following the engagement at Keslers Cross Lanes, Floyd sent one regiment to occupy Summersville and with the remainder took up a position on high ground north of Carnifex Ferry. Fearing an assault by way of Gauley Bridge, he ordered Wise to send an infantry regiment and part of his artillery to Carnifex Ferry and to drive the Union troops from Gauley Bridge with the remainder. Wise insisted that he retain all of his men and occupy Cotton Hill, south of the New River. Infuriated, Floyd on September 1 directed Wise to proceed immediately to Carnifex Ferry with his entire command. When Wise neared his destination, however, a messenger met him with information that he was no longer needed and instructions to return to Dogwood Gap at once. Angered by Floyd's indecision and repeated change of orders, Wise on September 2 drove the Union forces from the Hawks Nest area.

Following the battle of Keslers Cross Lanes, Rosecrans left his headquarters at Clarksburg and moved south by way of Weston, Bulltown, and Sutton for an assault upon the Confederates at Carnifex Ferry. On September 9 his army camped only eight miles from Summersville. After futile efforts to secure reinforcements from General Lee or eight hundred men from General A.A. Chapman, who commanded a militia south of the New River, Floyd directed Wise to furnish one thousand infantrymen and a battery of artillery. Still smarting under Floyd's conflicting commands and filled with doubts about his plan, Wise did not comply immediately with Floyd's new directive.

On the afternoon of September 10 the Union forces reached Keslers Cross Lanes. They advanced toward Floyd's camp under a screen of heavy foliage, but after preliminary encounters Rosecrans decided to postpone the main attack until the next morning. Although he had lost no men and had only twenty men, including himself, wounded in action up to that point, Floyd became convinced that he would ultimately have to capitulate to superior numbers. He withdrew across the Gauley River in good order and continued along the Sunday Road to Dogwood Gap. There, dazed and bewildered, he conferred with Wise, and on September 13 both moved to Big Sewell Mountain. Floyd then took up the most defensible position between Meadow Bluff and Lewisburg, but Wise refused to leave. Their occupation of Carnifex Ferry gave Union forces firm control of the Kanawha Valley and closed the gap between the Kanawha and Monongahela valleys.

Other Mountain Campaigns of 1861. A critical need for troops on the Potomac front forced McClellan to reduce sharply the Union forces in western Virginia. To protect Union gains in northwestern Virginia, Brigadier General Joseph J. Reynolds set up his main camp at Elkwater on the Huttonsville–Huntersville Road and established a strong post near the crest of Cheat Mountain on the Staunton and Parkersburg Turnpike. After Garnett's defeat at Corricks Ford, the Confederates, under Brigadier General William W. Loring, relied upon fortifications at Middle Mountain on the Huttonsville–Huntersville Road and at Allegheny Mountain on the Staunton and Parkersburg Turnpike. Loring also placed Brigadier General Henry R. Jackson in command of an advance post where the turnpike crossed the Greenbrier River.

Recognizing the importance of the mountain front to the Confederate cause,

Lee undertook "a tour of inspection and consultation" on a plan of campaign to drive Union forces from Elkwater and Cheat Mountain. Its success would again place the Confederates within striking distance of the Baltimore and Ohio Railroad, which Lee considered the equivalent of another army. Lee proceeded with remarkable patience and serenity in the face of insurmountable problems that included interminable rains, muddy roads that mired down wagons and supplies, an epidemic of measles, and an intransigent Loring, who chafed at serving under Lee, his former subaltern.

Although Confederate commanders made use of obscure mountain roads to move troops to the rear of Union positions at Cheat Mountain, their men were "too wet and too hungry" to fight. They were repulsed at Cheat Mountain and unable to mount an offensive against Elkwater, but they beat back a Union attack upon their own camp at Allegheny Mountain on December 13.

Lee found the same demoralizing conditions in the New River area, which he visited after the Cheat Mountain campaign. Fortunately for Confederate troops on Sewell Mountain, Union forces facing them also suffered from sickness, and Rosecrans, with even fewer numbers, withdrew to Gauley Bridge. Lee urged Wise and Floyd to settle their differences, by then a public scandal. Already, on September 20, President Davis, convinced that their vendetta would undermine the success of any Confederate moves in the Kanawha Valley, ordered Wise to turn over his command to Floyd and return to Richmond.

While on his tour, Lee devised a plan whereby Floyd would cross to the left bank of the New River, descend the Coal to Saint Albans, and cut Cox's communications with Ohio. Loring, who had succeeded Wise, could then attack Rosecrans and defeat him or force him to retreat toward Clarksburg. When Floyd reached the top of Cotton Hill on October 28, he found the men who had been under Wise too demoralized to provide assistance. Moreover, Loring's army was needed elsewhere along the mountain front. These circumstances forced Lee to abandon his plans for the Kanawha Valley.

The initiative passed to Rosecrans, who made several flank attacks on Floyd at Cotton Hill, which, though unsuccessful, caused Floyd to fear entrapment and to move to Dublin Station on the Virginia and Tennessee Railroad. When several of his regiments were ordered to other fronts, Rosecrans himself began to leave the New River area about the end of November. He left Cox in charge of the Kanawha Valley, with a brigade at Fayetteville, another at Charleston, and smaller detachments at other places and set up new headquarters at Wheeling.

By the winter of 1861–1862 guerrilla activity and bushwhacking, with extensive vandalism and murder, had become common in central West Virginia, particularly in Roane, Calhoun, Gilmer, Braxton, Webster, and Pocahontas counties, and in the southwestern parts of the state. In December a band of guerrillas occupied and burned the town of Sutton, but Union troops chased them out and killed about half a dozen. Another Union force struck at a guerrilla base in the Glades of Webster County, killing twenty persons and burning twenty-six houses. In January 1862 Colonel Edward Siber of the Twenty-seventh Ohio Infantry made an unsuccessful search for a band known as the Black Striped Company that had terrorized the Guyandotte Valley. Siber destroyed numerous farmhouses and burned the courthouse and other public structures at Logan on the ground that they had once sheltered Confederate cavalry.

The Upper Potomac and Valley Front. The military situation in much of the Eastern Panhandle in 1861 was unstable. Harpers Ferry, with its armory and arsenal, drew special attention. Colonel Thomas J., later "Stonewall," Jackson, who commanded Confederate forces there, urged that it be defended with all the vigor possible, but his successor, Brigadier General Joseph E. Johnston, regarded it as indefensible against a strong attack and favored more mobile units that could intercept any Union forces attempting a crossing of the Potomac River. Union leaders were equally divided with respect to Harpers Ferry. General Robert Patterson held views similar to those of Jackson, but General Winfield Scott in mid-June ordered him to provide all of his regular troops and his artillery for the defense of Washington. When Patterson failed to halt Johnston's army in the Valley of Virginia during the threat to Washington and announced his intention to march toward the capital city, Scott then insisted that he hold Harpers Ferry and replaced him.

Much of the military activity in the Eastern Panhandle centered around the Baltimore and Ohio Railroad. When Johnston abandoned Harpers Ferry and moved his troops to Winchester, he directed Stonewall Jackson to make the railroad useless to the enemy. On June 13 Colonel Lew Wallace with Indiana troops operating out of Cumberland, Maryland, seized Romney, a key point on the railroad, but he held the town for only an hour. After the defeat at Bull Run, Union generals gained a new appreciation of the railroad, and in the autumn an independent military district was created to cover the part of the line from Harpers Ferry to Cumberland. On October 26 Brigadier General Benjamin F. Kelley reoccupied Romney. By early November, however, Jackson's scouts were harassing Union troops, and his work parties were removing the railroad tracks between Harpers Ferry and Martinsburg, burning crossties and saving the rails for use on lines in the South.

Significance of Military Events of 1861. By the end of 1861 Union and Confederate lines in West Virginia had been established along fronts that remained relatively stable for the next two years. The main front ran roughly along the Alleghenies from Flat Top Mountain in the south to Sewell Mountain and northward to Cheat Mountain. The Union held the territory west of the line, except southwestern West Virginia, and usually controlled the Baltimore and Ohio Railroad despite Confederate efforts to disrupt its service. The Confederates occupied territory east of the mountain front, including the Greenbrier Valley and the New and Bluestone regions to the south. Their less secure hold on the upper Potomac Valley was reflected in the case of Romney, which changed hands no less than fifty times during the war. Neither side made more than ephemeral incursions into the territory of the other.

The lines established in 1861 enabled the supporters of the Reorganized Government of Virginia and the new state makers at Wheeling to proceed with confidence that most of the territory to be included in West Virginia was already in Union hands. Moreover, Union control of most of the trans-Allegheny region dealt a severe blow to Confederate Virginia, which was unable to maintain the political integrity of the Old Dominion.

Stonewall Jackson and West Virginia, 1862. As commander of the Valley District, Stonewall Jackson repeatedly demonstrated his military genius and value to the Confederacy. Born at Clarksburg into West Virginia's most distinguished political family, Jackson was a graduate of the United States Military Academy at West Point, served with distinction in the Mexican War, and in 1851 became professor of artillery tactics at Virginia Military Institute. Deeply religious, fearless, and dedicated to Virginia, he won the respect and devotion of his men. When Jackson died at the age of thirty-eight as a result of wounds accidentally received at Chancellorsville, Lee allegedly remarked that he lost his "right arm."

At the beginning of 1862 Jackson proposed to drive Union forces from his district and complete the destruction of the Baltimore and Ohio Railroad. He would then sweep across the Alleghenies, drive the enemy from mountain passes, and recover northwestern Virginia. He achieved his first success with the occupation of Romney, which Kelley was forced to abandon after Union failures to dislodge the Confederates from their outpost at Blues Gap, or Hanging Rocks. By then weather forced a cessation of military action. Jackson placed Loring in charge at Romney and went into winter quarters at Winchester.

Jackson's greatest problem of the winter originated at Romney. Unhappy with his assignment, which he considered far from commensurate with his importance, Loring allowed the bleak days and boredom to undermine the morale of his men. On January 25 eleven of his officers signed a round robin intimating that Jackson had made a serious mistake in occupying Romney and asking that they be moved to a more acceptable location. Loring sent their appeal directly to Secretary of War Judah P. Benjamin, who handed it to President Davis. Although Joseph E. Johnston, Jackson's superior, made a cursory investigation that vindicated his decision and criticized Loring, Benjamin had already, on January 30, instructed Jackson to evacuate Romney and move Loring's command to Winchester. Jackson complied with the order, but he considered it so destructive of his plans that he asked Governor John Letcher for permission to return to his professorship or to resign from Confederate service. Letcher and Johnston protested to Davis against the exercise of military authority by Benjamin and appealed to Jackson to withdraw his resignation. Jackson agreed, but he charged Loring with neglect of duty and conduct subversive of good discipline. Shortly afterward Loring and his men were transferred from the

Valley District. Union forces, however, had already reoccupied Romney, and by March 30 they had reopened the Baltimore and Ohio from the Ohio River to the Chesapeake Bay.

Meanwhile, on March 28, Major General John C. Fremont arrived in Wheeling as commander of the new Mountain Department, embracing most of West Virginia and parts of Kentucky, Tennessee, and Virginia. The department was designed to protect the Baltimore and Ohio Railroad and facilitate the destruction of the Virginia and Tennessee, which connected Richmond and Knoxville. Fremont intended to shift his base to Gauley Bridge, strike at the Virginia and Tennessee, and occupy Knoxville. Lincoln, however, ordered him to the Valley of Virginia to assist in efforts to trap Stonewall Jackson, who for several weeks had engaged in troublesome hit and run actions against Nathaniel P. Banks of the Department of the Shenandoah.

Fremont proved no match for Jackson. Although his subordinates occupied several towns, including Franklin, and Fort Allegheny, which the Confederates abandoned, Jackson continued to elude and baffle Banks. In mid-May Jackson attacked Union forces near Franklin but stopped short of a decisive victory. He returned to the Valley, struck at the Union garrison at Front Royal, and forced Banks out of Virginia and into Maryland. After the failure of a Union plan to trap him, Jackson and General Robert S. Ewell won a significant victory at Cross Keys. Lincoln then consolidated the commands of Fremont and Banks under Major General John Pope. Declaring that his honor would not permit him to serve under Pope, the flamboyant Fremont resigned his commission and on June 27 was relieved of his command.

Plans for the destruction of the Virginia and Tennessee Railroad, equally unsuccessful for the Union, produced considerable activity in southern West Virginia. Anticipating an attack, Brigadier General Henry Heth, the Confederate commander in the New River area, placed about one thousand men along a line running from Packs Ferry to Flat Top Mountain and another four hundred on Muddy Creek, about seven miles west of Lewisburg, on the James River and Kanawha Turnpike. General Cox, with about twelve thousand men at his disposal, directed Colonels Eliakim P. Scammon and Augustus Moore to advance on Princeton and Colonel George Crook to move against Lewisburg. Lieutenant Rutherford B. Hayes led a regiment of Scammon's brigade in a brief occupation of Pearisburg, and Union forces under Cox engaged in indecisive fighting at Princeton, after which the Confederates retreated toward Lewisburg and Cox dropped back toward Beckley.

Meanwhile, on May 12 Crook entered Lewisburg. Believing that Heth was in retreat, he moved to strike the Virginia Central Railroad at Jackson's River. When he learned that Heth was returning to Lewisburg, Crook hastened back to cut off his advance. On May 23 Heth attacked the Union camp west of Lewisburg, and the main street of the town soon became the scene of fierce fighting. Panic seized the Confederates when they suddenly confronted Crook's main army, and, in the colorful language of the time, they "broke for Dixie."[5]

In spite of the Union victory at Lewisburg, the bright promise of the Mountain Department had faded in southern West Virginia. Cox declined to move against the Virginia and Tennessee Railroad without additional protection to his rear. By then "the long shadow of Stonewall Jackson reached even to the banks of the New and Greenbrier rivers," and Crook himself fell back to Meadow Bluff lest Jackson cut off his retreat.[6]

Later Confederate Offensives, 1862. Following the Second Battle of Bull Run, or Manassas, on August 29 and 30, Lee concentrated his attention upon an invasion of Maryland. Stonewall Jackson's success in driving Union troops from Harpers Ferry on September 15 encouraged him to hold his positions. On September 17 his army of less than fifty thousand men withstood an assault by eighty-seven thousand Union troops under McClellan at Antietam, but it suffered heavy casualties. Believing that the enemy would soon receive reinforcements, Lee withdrew on September 18 to the southern shores of the Potomac by way of the fords near Shepherdstown.

Fearing for the safety of Washington, General-in-Chief Henry W. Halleck ordered Cox to send all of his men except five thousand from the Kanawha Valley. On August 14 Cox dispatched about five thousand from Camp Piatt, near Belle, to Parkersburg by river steamer. There they entrained for Washington. Union troops in the Kanawha Valley were left under the command of Colonel Joseph A.J. Lightburn, a boyhood friend of Stonewall Jackson, with whom he shared many personal qualities.

In preparation for an invasion of the vulnerable Kanawha Valley, a Confederate cavalry troop numbering nearly six hundred under Brigadier General Albert Gallatin Jenkins swept through the area north of the river in a daring raid that rivaled the exploits of Jeb Stuart. Jenkins, a Cabell County farmer, attorney, and former congressman, left Salt Sulphur Springs on August 24, crossed Valley Mountain to the headwaters of the Tygart Valley River, and threaded his way across Rich Mountain to Buckhannon. There he dispersed the Union garrison of about two hundred men and captured or destroyed a large quantity of supplies. He continued his successes at Weston, Glenville, Spencer, and Ripley, where he captured the federal paymaster and confiscated $5,525. He continued to Ravenswood, where part of his men crossed to the west bank of the Ohio, and reunited the two bodies at Point Pleasant. From there he moved to Buffalo and then scouted friendly areas around Barboursville, Logan, Wyoming Court House, and the Coal River. In his raid Jenkins captured or destroyed considerable amounts of arms and ammunition, paroled several hundred Confederate prisoners, and recruited about three hundred men for Confederate service.

By September 10 Lightburn's position at Gauley Bridge was precarious.

---

[5]Quoted in George E. Moore, *A Banner in the Hills: West Virginia's Statehood* (New York: Appleton-Century-Crofts, 1963), 159.
[6]Ibid.

The Jenkins raid forced him to increase the strength of his detachment at Summersville, which guarded his left flank, and to pull back others from Beckley to Fayetteville and from Camp Ewing to Gauley Bridge. Even then, he feared that the raiders would cut his connections with Ohio. When General Loring attacked his advance post at Fayetteville and forced Colonel Edward Siber to withdraw to Montgomery's Ferry on the Kanawha, Lightburn ordered a general retreat and established his headquarters at Charleston. Loring attacked on September 13 and Lightburn withdrew to Ravenswood and Point Pleasant. Cox described the retreat, the most serious Union reversal in West Virginia, as panicky and unworthy of military criticism.

Loring's occupation of Charleston and the upper Kanawha Valley produced few benefits for the Confederacy. He succeeded in sending supplies of much-needed salt from the Kanawha Salines to eastern Virginia, but he failed to recruit any substantial number of men. On September 25 Lee directed Loring to advance into the Monongahela Valley by way of Clarksburg, Fairmont, and Morgantown and to destroy bridges and tunnels on the Baltimore and Ohio Railroad. Loring digressed from Lee's orders to such an extent that Lee removed him from his command and replaced him with General John Echols.

Appeals for protection from Governors Pierpont of Virginia and David Tod of Ohio led to the creation of the District of Western Virginia, with Cox in charge. Determined to drive the Confederates from western Virginia, Cox ordered Lightburn and General George Morgan to advance up the Kanawha; General George Crook to move southward from Clarksburg by way of Summersville to Gauley Bridge; Brigadier General Robert H. Milroy to follow the Staunton and Parkersburg Turnpike to Beverly; and Colonel Jonathan Cranor to seek out Floyd's state troops in Logan County.

Cox's plans met with general success. On October 29, after a brief skirmish, Jenkins's cavalry, left by Loring to guard the Kanawha Valley, abandoned its outpost on Tyler Mountain and retreated up the Kanawha. Union troops moved into Charleston, and the Confederates withdrew by way of Cotton Hill and Fayetteville to Princeton, which they occupied. In early November Cox announced that the region between Clarksburg, Sutton, and Cheat Mountain was also free of Confederates. Numerous guerrilla bands remained in the region between the Kanawha and Guyandotte rivers and along the headwaters of the Little Kanawha. When the armies went into winter quarters, the military situation in West Virginia did not differ substantially from that of a year before.

A Time of Military Reassessment. By the spring of 1863 both Unionists and Confederates had suffered property losses and personal indignities, and vandalism and retaliation had produced bitter animosities that remained long after the war ended. Enthusiasm for the Reorganized Government had begun to wane in some areas, and, with the encouragement of Lee, some Confederates in Union territory organized resistance movements against local officials, particularly sheriffs and municipal authorities identified with the Pierpont government. In this context, whole counties lapsed into anarchy, bushwhacking flourished, and courts were broken up. Moreover, the Emancipation Proclamation appeared to many westerners to transform the war from a defense of the Constitution into a crusade for the abolition of slavery, which Waitman T. Willey had warned as early as July 1861 would be highly detrimental to the Union cause in western Virginia.

By the spring of 1863 both Union and Confederate commanders had concluded that western Virginia was of less value to their strategy than they had previously believed. Union leaders placed less emphasis upon bases for attacks on Virginia and Tennessee and more on protection for the Reorganized Government and support for the proposed state of West Virginia. Their interest in the Potomac region, which they once saw as a gateway to the heart of the Confederacy, shifted to greater protection for the Baltimore and Ohio Railroad. Confederate authorities gave up concerns for occupation of territory beyond the Greenbrier and New rivers on a permanent basis. They redefined their principal military objectives in western Virginia as destruction of the Baltimore and Ohio Railroad, interference with the operations of the Reorganized Government, and activities relating to recruiting, forage, and supply. In light of their altered objectives, both sides made changes in their military leaders in western Virginia, and Confederate commanders shifted their strategy from reliance upon armed might to bold and destructive raids upon Union territory.

The Jones-Imboden Raid. By far the most important Confederate operations in northwestern Virginia in 1863 were the raids carried out in April and May by Brigadier Generals William E. Jones and John D. Imboden. In keeping with the new strategy, Imboden devised a plan for destruction of all Baltimore and Ohio Railroad bridges and trestles between Oakland and Grafton, defeat of Union detachments at Beverly, Buckhannon, and Philippi, enlistment of men for Confederate service, harassment of the Reorganized Government, and exertion of influence upon the May elections.

On April 20 Imboden left Shenandoah Mountain with about 3,400 men, of whom 700 were cavalry, and moved down both sides of the Tygart Valley River toward Beverly. He drove back defenders of Beverly under Colonel George R. Latham and occupied both Beverly and Buckhannon, where he purchased cattle and grain with Confederate money. Faced with reinforced Union troops at Grafton and Clarksburg and nearly impassable roads, Imboden remained relatively inactive and awaited the arrival of Jones, his superior officer.

Jones, who struck into western Virginia from Rockingham County with about twenty-five hundred cavalry, forced his way through stoutly defended Greenland Gap and onto the Northwestern Turnpike. He inflicted serious but not irreparable damage on the Baltimore and Ohio Railroad, including the burning of the bridge at Oakland, but he failed to destroy the Cheat River bridge, his major objective. His raiders descended upon Morgantown on April 27 and 28, forced its surrender, and narrowly missed capturing Waitman T. Willey, who escaped by way of Brownstown and Pittsburgh to Washington, D.C. On April 29 Jones defeated Union troops at Fairmont, demolished an important railroad bridge, and burned the library of Francis H. Pierpont. The following day he dashed to Philippi by way of Shinnston, Clarksburg, and Bridgeport. Sending Colonel A.W. Harman to Beverly with large numbers of cattle and horses that he had taken, he then led his main force to Buckhannon, where he joined Imboden on May 2.

The Jones–Imboden raids produced widespread panic in western Virginia and even Pennsylvania. Governors Pierpont and Andrew Curtin frantically called for aid in ejecting the invaders, but Lincoln was convinced that the Confederates were acting on "the screwhorn principle, on purpose to divert us in another quarter." Actually, federal authorities had undertaken defensive moves almost as soon as the raids began. General Kelley rushed reinforcements to Grafton, Pierpont mustered the militia of the Reorganized Government, Governor Tod of Ohio provided several hundred state troops, and Lightburn moved into Fairmont on May 2.

Meanwhile, in anticipation of an attack on Clarksburg, Jones and Imboden moved their base to Weston. There they found strong Southern feeling, and after ascertaining unexpected Union strength at Clarksburg, decided against an attack upon the town. Imboden then moved south to Summersville by way of the Weston and Gauley Bridge Turnpike, destroying Union barracks and block-houses at Bulltown, Sutton, and Big Birch Mountain en route. On the night of May 12 his advance units drove Union forces under Scammon out of Summersville, which Imboden occupied the following day.

After leaving Weston, Jones and his raiders proceeded along the Staunton and Parkersburg Turnpike to Cairo, destroying railroad bridges and tunnels as they went. From Cairo they moved to "Oiltown" in the newly opened Burning Springs field. There they destroyed all available oilfield equipment and burned an estimated 150,000 barrels of crude oil. In a vivid description of the spectacular scene, Jones wrote that "By dark the oil from the tanks on the burning creek had reached the [Little Kanawha] River, and the whole stream became a sheet of fire. A burning river, carrying destruction to our merciless enemy, was a scene of magnificence that might well carry joy to every patriotic heart."[7] Satisfied with his accomplishments, Jones then sped by way of Glenville and Sutton to Summersville, where he arrived only a few hours after Imboden.

The daring destruction of Jones and Imboden once again sent waves of alarm through western Virginia. An attack on West Union by Harman's detachment unleashed rumors of an impending assault upon the Northern Panhandle. Kelley himself rushed to Grafton, and other changes were made in the Union command in the Monongahela Valley, but by then the Confederate raiders had spent their strength, and both Jones and Imboden knew that their exhausted men

[7]Quoted in Moore, *A Banner in the Hills,* 189.

could endure no more. They recrossed the Alleghenies by diverse routes to the Valley of Virginia.

On balance, the Jones–Imboden raid must be considered an important success. The raiders killed at least twenty-five men, wounded three times that many, and captured more than seven hundred, while losing only ten killed, forty-two wounded, and fifteen captured. They claimed destruction of twenty-one railroad bridges and a tunnel, three turnpike bridges, oil, oilfield equipment, military barracks and blockhouses, and vast amounts of military stores. Through confiscation and purchase they acquired about five thousand cattle and two thousand horses. In addition, they recruited some four hundred men for Confederate service. Finally, their threats to the Baltimore and Ohio Railroad tied up Union troops that might have been used elsewhere.

Union Recovery, 1863. Following the departure of Jones and Imboden, Colonel John McCausland, a prominent landowner of the lower Kanawha Valley and a former professor at Virginia Military Institute, attacked Union positions at Fayetteville. From there he planned to move into the Kanawha Valley to obtain much-needed salt. The arrival of Union reinforcements on the night of May 18, however, forced him to withdraw. The battle at Fayetteville marked the first use of indirect fire, in which Sergeant Milton W. Humphreys discharged a cannon over an intervening forest to rout Union troops.

Intent upon holding and fortifying mountain passes overlooking the Appalachian Valley, General William W. Averell undertook to drive the Confederates from the Greenbrier Valley, their last major stronghold in West Virginia. He advanced by way of Cheat Mountain to Bartow and the Little Levels at Hillsboro to Droop Mountain, where General John Echols and two thousand troops were entrenched. Averell's approach to the Confederate position lay across an expanse of cultivated fields, but low hills and "bewildering ravines" near the base of the mountain provided cover for his men. Amid an artillery demonstration on the Confederate right, Union forces made their way up the mountain along an obscure path and burst upon the surprised enemy, early in the afternoon of November 6. The outflanked Confederate lines crumbled, and by five o'clock they were in retreat down the south side of the mountain toward Lewisburg. Averell's victory broke the back of Confederate power in the Greenbrier Valley and produced a considerable degree of congruency between territory within the boundaries of the new state of West Virginia and that actually under the control of its authorities.

Later Military Events. The arrival of Confederate cavalry under Imboden at Covington and a severe snowstorm prevented Averell from striking immediately at the Virginia and Tennessee Railroad. On December 8 he left Keyser with about twenty-five hundred cavalry to cut the supply lines of General James Longstreet, who had a Union army under General Ambrose E. Burnside under siege at Knoxville, Tennessee. On December 16 he destroyed supply depots and wrecked sections of the rail line at Salem, Virginia. Confederate commanders failed to intercept or trap him, and on Christmas Eve he was safely back across the Alleghenies at his base at Beverly. His "Big Salem Raid" not only saved Burnside's army but gave the Confederates a serious psychological setback.

The Confederates retaliated for the raid on Salem in numerous forays of their own. In January 1864 Fitzhugh Lee invaded the South Branch of the Potomac, and Thomas Rosser attacked Union troops at Greenland Gap, where he took twenty prisoners, including Major Nathan Goff, Jr. On May 10 Imboden defeated the "Ringgold Cavalry" at Lost River. The most spectacular achievement, on July 30, was the invasion of Pennsylvania and the burning of Chambersburg by Generals John McCausland and Bradley T. Johnson.

Standing out among the numerous strikes and counterstrikes of 1864 was the "Dublin Raid." With the Virginia and Tennessee Railroad as his objective, General George Crook on May 9 attacked Confederates under McCausland and Jenkins near Dublin, Virginia. In the resulting battle of Cloyd's Mountain Jenkins received a wound that led to his death twelve days later.

One of the most daring of all Confederate raids involved the McNeill Rangers, organized in 1862 by Captain John Hanson McNeill of Hardy County. He and his son, Jesse, had been captured by the enemy but had escaped. The Rangers attracted a bold set of young men, mostly from Hardy, Hampshire, and Rockingham counties and from Allegany and Baltimore counties in Maryland, who made Moorefield their base of operations. On the morning of February 21, 1865, a detachment led by Jesse seized Generals Crook and Kelley in their hotel rooms in Cumberland, Maryland, in the very shadow of four thousand Union troops, and sent them as prisoners of war to Richmond. The colorless Kelley viewed his misfortune with great solemnity, but Crook, appreciative of the humor in the situation, described it as "the most brilliant exploit of the war." Even Colonel John S. Mosby declared that "This surpasses anything I have ever done."[8]

Of far greater importance than the dramatic raids in the Valley of Virginia were military decisions on distant battlefields. Confederate strength reached its high tide at Gettysburg, and thereafter the Confederacy suffered one defeat after another. With the war in the West already won, with Sherman leaving a swathe of devastation through Georgia and the Carolinas, and with Grant and a reinvigorated Army of the Potomac closing in on Lee and the Army of Northern Virginia, events in West Virginia could hardly have had any great impact on the course of military affairs. When on April 9, 1865, Lee surrendered to Grant at Appomattox, West Virginians, like most Northerners and Southerners, were weary of war and rejoiced at the return of peace.

[8]Statements of Crook and Mosby are quoted in Ambler and Summers, *the Mountain State,* 228.

The Thirty-Fifth State

The Voters Approve Dismemberment of Virginia. On October 24, 1861, after most of northwestern Virginia was safely behind Union lines, residents of the thirty-nine counties named in the ordinance adopted by the Second Wheeling Convention, along with those of Hampshire and Hardy, voted on the dismemberment of Virginia. Less than thirty-seven percent of the approximately fifty thousand eligible voters in the forty-one counties cast ballots. Of those who did, 18,408 favored a new state and only 781 opposed division of the Old Dominion.

Although the *Wheeling Intelligencer* professed to see an "astonishing unanimity" of sentiment in the vote, in reality the returns reflected the deep division of feeling in western Virginia and intimidation on the part of supporters of the new state.[1] Seventeen counties giving majorities for dismemberment had ratified the Virginia secession ordinance earlier in the year. Only five of the forty-one counties reported more than fifty votes against a new state, and three of them—Brooke, Hancock, and Ohio—were in the Northern Panhandle, where overwhelming public support obviated the need for tightly controlled balloting and allowed freer expression. Eleven counties, including Boone, Braxton, Clay, Gilmer, Hardy, Putnam, Raleigh, Roane, Tucker, Upshur, and Wetzel, did not record a single vote in opposition. Eighteen others, among them Barbour, Cabell, Doddridge, Hampshire, Harrison, Jackson, Kanawha, Lewis, Monongalia, Pleasants, Preston, Randolph, Ritchie, Taylor, Tyler, Wayne, and Wirt, reported less than twenty negative ballots. Six predominantly secessionist counties provided no returns.

The Constitutional Convention: Personnel and Organization. At the same time that they voted on dismemberment, residents of counties named in the ordinance elected delegates to the First Constitutional Convention of West Virginia. Altogether, sixty-one persons were chosen, with fifty-three serving in the regular session (November 26, 1861–February 18, 1862) and fifty-six in the recalled session (February 12–20, 1863). Webster and Monroe counties sent no delegates to either session. Disturbed conditions interfered with voting in Calhoun, Clay, Fayette, Logan, McDowell, Mercer, Nicholas, and Wyoming

---

[1]*Wheeling Intelligencer*, October 26, 1861.

counties, which were represented by petitioning groups under the influence of either the military or the Methodist Church. Delegates from Greenbrier, Morgan, Pendleton, and Pocahontas counties, who attended only the recalled session, were chosen by irregular methods. For instance, Dr. D.W. Gibson of Pocahontas County was elected by refugees at Buckhannon in Upshur County.

Among the delegates were twenty-three farmers, seventeen lawyers, and fourteen ministers or licensed exhorters. Whatever their callings, most were churchgoers and influenced by the evangelical tone of western religion. Charles H. Ambler and Festus P. Summers held that had not the lawyers, notably Peter G. Van Winkle of Wood County, imposed "purposeful and practical objectives" upon the convention, the new state "could and probably would have been sponsored by religious zealots."[2] They denied the oft-asserted claim that the Methodists made West Virginia, but they acknowledged that Methodist ministers exercised both direct and subtle influences.

Leaders of the convention included John Hall of Mason County, who was chosen president over conservative James H. Brown of Kanawha County, and Ellery R. Hall of Taylor County, who was elected secretary. Keenly aware of the historical importance of the debates and proceedings of the convention, Van Winkle suggested at the outset that they be reported and published, but the convention failed to take the necessary action. Fortunately, Granville Davisson Hall, a reporter for the *Wheeling Intelligencer,* kept complete stenographic notes of both sessions, and the delegates, at the urging of Van Winkle, authorized their transcription, but they failed to provide funds for immediate publication. Hall preserved his precious notes and copies of every document printed for the convention until 1906, when, through the efforts of Virgil A. Lewis, the first historian and archivist of West Virginia, they were purchased by the state. In 1942 they were finally published, with Charles H. Ambler, chairman of the history department of West Virginia University, as the principal editor.

Name and Boundaries. On December 2 the constitutional convention took up the question of a name for the new state. Motivated in part by sectionalism, some members contended that the name Kanawha, which appeared in the dismemberment ordinance adopted by the Second Wheeling Convention, was hard to spell, already borne by a county and two rivers, and had less claim than one that would preserve the name Virginia. After considerable wrangling, the convention chose West Virginia, which received thirty of the forty-four votes cast. Kanawha received nine votes, Western Virginia and Alleghany two each, and Augusta one.

Determination of a proper boundary for West Virginia produced far more acrimonious debate. Since Chapman J. Stuart of Doddridge County, chairman of the Committee on Boundary, had actually tried to obstruct division of Virginia

[2]Charles H. Ambler and Festus P. Summers, *West Virginia, the Mountain State,* 2d ed. (Englewood Cliffs, N.J.: Prentice-Hall, Inc., 1958), 230-31.

in the Second Wheeling Convention and most committee members had been moderates in the statehood movement, delegates were amazed when the committee report, made on December 5, called for inclusion of thirty-two counties beyond the thirty-nine named in the dismemberment ordinance.

The committee divided the additional counties into four groups, or districts. Advocates of the first district, which included Pocahontas, Greenbrier, Monroe, Mercer, McDowell, Buchanan, and Wise counties maintained that it was essential to a well-rounded boundary. Opponents pointed to strong secessionist sentiment in most of them and to the creation of a southern panhandle for West Virginia if Buchanan and Wise were included. Over strenuous opposition of Chapman and Brown of Kanawha, the delegates approved the first district counties except Buchanan and Wise, but agreed to consider the two with counties in the second district.

The committee recommended that annexation of the other three districts be determined by a plebiscite on the third Thursday in April 1862. The second district comprised the southwestern counties of Craig, Giles, Bland, Tazewell, Russell, Scott, and Lee, and the third district the lower Shenandoah and upper Potomac counties of Jefferson, Berkeley, Frederick, Morgan, Hampshire, Hardy, Pendleton, Highland, Bath, and Alleghany. Together the two districts formed an unbroken tier of counties from the Maryland border to the Tennessee line. The fourth district, consisting of Clarke, Warren, Shenandoah, Page, Rockingham, Augusta, Rockbridge, and Botetourt, lay in the Valley of Virginia, immediately west of the Blue Ridge, which some delegates insisted was the true dividing linc bctwccn castern and western Virginia.

Strong opposition developed immediately to inclusion of counties in the second district. William E. Stevenson of Wood County noted that they were socially, economically, and traditionally tied to eastern Virginia. Brown of Kanawha County attempted to prevent rejection of the counties by offering an amendment to consider the second and third districts simultaneously, but his proposal was decisively defeated by a vote of thirty-five to ten.

Many delegates had deep apprehensions regarding demographic changes that the inclusion of the thirty-two counties would make in the proposed state. The original thirty-nine counties had 272,759 white and 7,932 black residents, including 6,894 slaves. The thirty-two additional counties included 48,634 black persons, 42,303 of them slaves, and 255,182 white inhabitants. John H. Powell of Harrison County voiced the fear that the inclusion of fifty thousand slaves in the proposed state "would destroy us in Congress."[3]

Many members also expressed concern over seccessionist sentiment in several of the thirty-two counties. Stevenson had no objection to including counties known to be loyal, but he feared that the extensions proposed would

[3]Charles H. Ambler, Frances Haney Atwood, and William B. Mathews, eds., *Debates and Proceedings of the First Constitutional Convention of West Virginia (1861-1863)*, 3 vols. (Huntington: Gentry Brothers, 1942), vol. 1, 388-89.

"imperil, and probably in the end defeat, this whole new State movement."[4] Robert Hager of Boone County contended that every secessionist county added lessened the likelihood of approval of the constitution, since Secessionists in the original thirty-nine counties would unite with those in the proposed counties in opposition to the new state.

Although concerns for geographical unity, objections to a substantial slave population, fears of adding strength to secessionist elements, and some genuine reluctance to resort to blatantly undemocratic procedures influenced many members, economic considerations usually proved decisive. Granville Parker of Cabell County pointed out, for instance, that inclusion of Alleghany County would require West Virginia to repay more than four million dollars that Virginia had spent on the Covington and Ohio Railroad in that county and additional sums used for the James River and Kanawha Canal. His sobering admonition contributed to rejection not only of Alleghany County but to the entire second district, which was adjacent to it.

Lower Shenandoah and upper Potomac Valley counties, on the other hand, promised great economic advantage to the new state. Specious arguments that West Virginia should extend eastward to include the tomb of George Washington or to the gates of the national capital carried little weight, but most members of the convention recognized the importance of the Baltimore and Ohio Railroad, a private corporation, to its economic viability. Van Winkle, the president of the Northwestern Virginia Railroad, a subsidiary of the Baltimore and Ohio, declared that the material prosperity and progress of the state depended upon "a suitable avenue of communication with coastal areas." He also predicted, along with other members, that Virginia authorities would impose "all sorts of crippling legislation, all sorts of restrictions" upon the railroad in order to serve the interests of Richmond and Norfolk.[5]

On December 13, after ten days of debate, the convention by a vote of thirty-two to eleven included in West Virginia the thirty-nine original counties and Pocahontas, Greenbrier, Monroe, Mercer, and McDowell. It provided for the addition of Jefferson, Berkeley, Frederick, Morgan, Hampshire, Hardy, and Pendleton if their voters approved. Of the latter seven, all but Frederick ratified the constitution, but out of more than eleven thousand voters, only 1,610 cast ballots, and only thirteen voted against the constitution. In spite of claims that the extended debate over boundaries reflected a "fundamental cleavage" in Union ranks regarding statehood itself, it seems more likely that there were sincere differences of opinion among members of the convention concerning the desirable territorial limits of the new state.

The Fundamental Law. The members of the constitutional convention had no intention of initiating radical changes in the structure of government. They

[4]Ibid., 412.
[5]Ibid., 451.

rejected, however, by a decisive vote of forty-one to two a proposal by Thomas W. Harrison of Harrison County merely to modify the constitution of Virginia and leave the drafting of a new frame of government to the future.

The convention attempted to ensure democratic procedures and account-ability of public officials to the people by making state and county offices elective. The term of the governor was set at two years, but he was eligible to serve as many terms as the people might desire. The existing judicial system, with its supreme court of appeals, circuit courts, and inferior tribunals, had functioned well and was retained.

The legislature, which in Virginia met in biennial sessions of ninety days, was required to meet annually for forty-five days. Representation in both houses was based on white population, and suffrage was guaranteed to all white males over twenty-one years old. Religious influences accounted in part for the absence of restrictions, as existed in Virginia, upon the right of ministers and priests to serve in the legislature and for legislative authority to regulate or prohibit the sale of intoxicating liquors.

Reflecting the long struggle for free public education, the constitution required the legislature to "provide, as soon as practicable, for the establishment of a thorough and efficient system of free schools" and to designate certain funds for their support. It vested administration of the schools in part in townships, a controversial new unit of government. Counties were divided into not less than three nor more than ten townships, each with a minimum of four hundred inhabitants.

Members of the convention generally agreed that West Virginia should assume part of the public debt owed by Virginia in 1863. They differed widely, however, in their calculations of benefits received by West Virginia and in assessments of the proper share that West Virginia should assume. They finally agreed to accept "an equitable proportion" of the public debt of Virginia and to require the legislature to provide "as soon as practicable" for its liquidation by establishing a sinking fund sufficient to pay the principal and interest in thirty-four years.

The specter of sectionalism that had wrenched the Old Dominion began almost at once to hover over the new state. Delegates from the Kanawha Valley, where railroad and river improvements were needed, pressed for constitutional authorization for a bonded state debt. Delegates from the northern part of the state, where such facilities were generally satisfactory, had no desire to incur state debts for improvements in southern sections. Van Winkle, moreover, held that private capital was available for building a railroad from Charleston to Grafton. The convention rejected by a vote of twenty-five to twenty-three any constitutional sanction for bonded indebtedness for internal improvements. At the last moment a compromise, accepted without debate, provided that the state might subscribe to the capital stock of associations or corporations, a practice long accepted in Virginia, but it required payment at the time of the subscription or from taxes levied for the ensuing year in an amount sufficient to cover the full subscription. The compromise allowed the convention to end on a note of harmony.

The Shadow of Slavery. A few days after the convention assembled, Hager, a minister, declared slavery "incompatible with the Word of God" and called for its abolition.[6] On December 14 Gordon Battelle, a Methodist minister, introduced resolutions forbidding the entry of additional slaves into West Virginia once the constitution was adopted and providing gradual emancipation for those already in the state. According to Granville Parker, a native of Massachusetts with antislavery views, "when Mr. Battelle submitted his resolutions, a kind of tremor—a holy terror, was visible throughout the house!"[7] Most members saw in the resolutions, which were tabled, no immediate threat to the statehood movement. On December 16 Henry Dering of Monongalia County informed Waitman T. Willey that Van Winkle believed there would be no trouble "in keeping the vexed question out of the Convention."[8]

Moved by humanitarian impulses and a conviction that the statehood bill could not get through Congress unless steps were taken to end slavery, Battelle persisted. On January 27, 1862, he introduced new resolutions calling for freedom for all children born of slave parents after July 4, 1865, provision for apprenticeship during their minority, and later colonization, as well as for exclusion of additional slaves and free Negroes. Failing that, he sought a referendum on a gradual emancipation clause when the people voted on the constitution, with the clause to become part of that document if it were approved. His proposal was tabled, but by the close vote of twenty-four to twenty-three. By then Dering expressed to Willey fears that Battelle and "his little party" would continue to bring up the subject, even though it did not carry, and produce disturbance in the convention, in the state, and even in Congress.[9]

The strength of free state sentiment made compromise necessary. As finally drafted, the constitution provided that "no slave shall be brought, or free person of color permitted to come into the State for permanent residence." Like others who hoped to prevent the adoption of Battelle's resolutions, Brown of Kanawha County voted for Negro exclusion only with the understanding that it was a "full settlement" of the matter.[10] The compromise had little effect other than allowing the convention to proceed with its work.

Opinion regarding slavery steadily hardened. On December 9 Archibald

[6]Ibid., 56.

[7]Granville Parker, *The Formation of the State of West Virginia, and Other Incidents in the Late War* (Wellsburg, W.Va.: Glass & Son, 1875), 78.

[8]Quoted in Richard Orr Curry, *A House Divided: A Study of Statehood Politics and the Copperhead Movement in West Virginia* (Pittsburgh: University of Pittsburgh Press, 1964), 90-91.

[9]Quoted in Curry, *A House Divided*, 91.

[10]Ambler, Atwood, and Mathews, eds., *Debates and Proceedings of the First Constitutional Convention of West Virginia*, vol. 3, 431.

Campbell, editor of the *Wheeling Intelligencer,* declared that Congress would never consent to a division of Virginia merely to create another slave state. On February 21, 1862, he predicted that the issue would lead to defeat for West Virginia in Congress. In a similar vein, Granville Parker charged that the vehement proslavery element in the convention aimed at nothing less than blocking the formation of the state. Moderate leaders such as Dering and Willey, on the other hand, construed the compromise exclusion clause as a "providential arrangement" that would be acceptable to Congress and the people.

The compromise failed to settle the slavery issue. When the constitution was voted upon by the people on April 4, "Radicals" in favor of gradual emancipation took an informal poll in several counties. The results showed 6,052 in favor of emancipation and only 616 against it. Richard Curry, a careful student of the statehood politics, considers the poll, which represented rejection of the decision of the convention and thrust the issue into the hands of Congress, "a turning point in the history of statehood politics."[11]

Virginia Grants Approval. On February 18, 1862, the convention approved the constitution by unanimous vote. Instead of adjourning *sine die,* however, it set up an interim committee empowered to reconvene the delegates if necessary. Disturbed conditions prevented people in many townships in the proposed state from voting and contributed to the usual one-sided results, with 18,862 ballots cast in favor of the constitution and only 514 against it.

In obtaining the consent of Virginia, as the United States Constitution required, the new state makers turned to the Reorganized Government at Wheeling rather than to authorities in Richmond. Pierpont convened the General Assembly on May 6. He set the tone for the session by pointing to the mountain barriers between eastern and western Virginia, the dissimilarity of the two sections "in their social relations and their institutions," and the long history of conflict between them.[12] On May 13 the General Assembly gave its consent to the formation of West Virginia. The act named forty-eight counties and provided for inclusion of Jefferson, Berkeley, and Frederick when they ratified the constitution.

Congressional Approval. On May 29 Waitman T. Willey presented a formal petition to the United States Senate for the admission of West Virginia to the Union without conditions. The petition was referred to the Committee on Territories, of which Benjamin F. Wade of Ohio was chairman. The House of Representatives took parallel action five days later.

The drafting of the statehood bill was entrusted, as expected, to John S. Carlile, a new state enthusiast from the beginning and a member of the Committee on Territories. Carlile took nearly a month to complete the bill, which was reported on June 23. The bill astounded West Virginians. Carlile,

[11]Curry, *A House Divided,* 97.
[12]Pierpont's message is in *Wheeling Intelligencer,* May 7, 1862.

who had previously insisted upon a small state embracing only trans-Allegheny counties, added fifteen more to the forty-eight included in the constitution. Jefferson, Berkeley, and Frederick, for which the constitution made provision, were among the additions, but the constitutional convention had already rejected the other twelve. The bill required a new constitutional convention representing all sixty-three counties and the gradual abolition of slavery. Once the voters ratified the new constitution and the Reorganized Government gave its consent, the statehood bill would go directly to the president, who was authorized to proclaim the admission of West Virginia to the Union without further delay.

When Wade called up the statehood bill on June 26, Charles Sumner offered an amendment requiring emancipation of all slaves in West Virginia on July 4, 1863. His amendment was decisively defeated. On July 1, Willey offered a substitute that omitted all mention of additional counties, a new convention, and referenda and called for admission of West Virginia as soon as the original constitutional convention reconvened and accepted the emancipation clause in the committee bill that all children born of slave mothers after July 4, 1863, should be free. Wade moved an amendment by which slaves under twenty-one years old on July 4, 1863, should be free when they reached that age, which was adopted despite opposition from both Willey and Carlile.

Carlile raised strenuous objections to Willey's proposal. He insisted that gradual emancipation be approved by a majority of the registered voters in the territory embraced in the new state in 1860. Willey maintained that approval should be by majority of votes cast, to which Carlile reluctantly agreed providing that the referendum were held in all West Virginia counties. Carlile declared that none of the Wheeling conventions had been representative of the people of the new state and that a majority of the voters had never expressed their opinion on the question by electing delegates to the conventions or in referenda on convention decisions. Wade, chagrined at what he termed Carlile's "extraordinary action," pointed out that during the month of committee deliberations he had raised none of the concerns he now voiced. Wade asked other senators not to disappoint the loyal people of Virginia or "yield weakly to the perversity of any of its representatives."[13]

Discussions by several leading senators led to a compromise, worked out by Wade and Willey. Known as the Willey Amendment, it provided that all slaves under twenty-one years old on July 4, 1863, should be free on arriving at that age. Carlile then moved to admit West Virginia without conditions, but his proposal lost by a vote of twenty-five to eleven. The Willey Amendment passed without a recorded vote, and on July 14, 1862, the statehood bill was enacted by a vote of twenty-three to seventeen, with Carlile voting against it.

Willey assumed, and deserves, much credit for the success of the statehood

[13]*Congressional Globe,* 37th Cong., 2d sess., 3316.

bill in the Senate. His biographer, Charles H. Ambler, regards his role as second only to that of Wade. In speaking for his amendment, Willey declared, "Today, when the loyal people come with a united voice, I stand here, where my colleague does not stand, representing the voice of the people of Virginia," while Carlile "gets up here on the very eve . . . of the passage . . . of the [statehood] bill . . . and interposes an objection, to postpone and defer our long cherished hopes and desires." He stated that the fifty-year controversy between eastern and western Virginia grew out of social, geographical, commercial, and industrial distinctions and antagonisms "that never can be reconciled by the power of man," for "The Almighty, with His eternal hand" had "marked the boundary between us."[14]

Assessments of Carlile. The course pursued by Willey won him the plaudits of friends of the new state and later generations of West Virginians; that of Carlile mystified his contemporaries and continues to baffle historians. Wade termed Carlile's "conversion greater than that of St. Paul."[15] Granville Davisson Hall believed that his deviation from "the straight path" was due to the influence of his closest friend in the Senate, Waldo P. Johnson of Missouri, a nephew of a former governor of Virginia, Joseph Johnson of Bridgeport. James C. McGregor wrote half a century later that Carlile's "most clever apologist could scarcely make out a good case for him, although he cannot be condemned solely on the ground that he changed his opinion."[16]

In 1937 Charles H. Ambler speculated that Carlile's desertion of the new state movement may have resulted from "pro-slavery leanings, or his vacillating and generally unstable character, or the current anti-union trend."[17] Seventeen years later he still saw in Carlile's call for approval of the constitution by both a convention and a majority of the voters in each county in the state no consistent adherence to "fundamental principles of democratic government," since Carlile had earlier urged a declaration of statehood by a convention to which most delegates had not even been elected by popular vote.

George Moore, a student of Ambler, placed some credence in Carlile's insistence that "a re-enactment of the various steps preliminary to application for statehood" was necessary to "invoke the principle of majority rule." Carlile's arguments that the initiative for making a state constitution should come from the people and not from Congress and that the Willey Amendment gave them no opportunity to approve or reject the changes in their basic law, Moore believed, was "an early manifestation of resistance to Radical usurpation."[18]

[14]Ibid., 3317.

[15]Ibid., 3318.

[16]Granville Davisson Hall, *The Rending of Virginia: A History* (Chicago: Mayer & Miller, 1902), 298.

[17]Charles H. Ambler, *Francis H. Pierpont, Union War Governor of Virginia and Father of West Virginia* (Chapel Hill: University of North Carolina Press, 1937), 178.

[18]George Ellis Moore, *A Banner in the Hills: West Virginia's Statehood* (New York: Appleton-Century-Crofts, 1963), 197.

Richard Curry, the most recent student of the period, attempts to reconcile seeming inconsistencies in Carlile's behavior by setting it in the context of the Copperhead movement. Curry sees Carlile as but one of several prominent conservative Unionists of West Virginia, among whom were John J. Davis, Andrew Wilson, John C. Vance, Sherrard Clemens, William W. Brumfield, and John S. Burdett. They, like other Copperheads, became alarmed when the war for the preservation of the Union took on the character of a crusade to end slavery. Curry notes that Daniel Lamb became an opponent of statehood in 1862 when the slavery issue was injected and that Van Winkle also criticized congressional dictation but confessed to Willey that he could support emancipation once West Virginia became a state and could treat the matter as "home policy." Curry concludes that Carlile's behavior was not an aberration but consistent with that of others who, unlike the majority, were unwilling to accept statehood if it meant acceding to "abolitionist fanaticism" and "Congressional dictation."[19] Curry's use of the broader context of Copperheadism does not answer all questions, but it offers a rational basis for Carlile's actions. In fact, since no substantial body of Carlile's papers has survived, his real motivations may never be known.

Lincoln Decides for Statehood. On December 15 Senator Orville H. Browning of Illinois carried the statehood bill to President Lincoln for his signature. Lincoln was "distressed by its passage" and on December 23 asked members of his cabinet for written opinions regarding the constitutionality and expediency of the admission of West Virginia to the Union. Caleb B. Smith, secretary of the interior, had recently resigned, and the other six members divided evenly.

In opposing statehood, Attorney General Edward Bates contended that the Reorganized Government was provisional in nature and without power to authorize erection of a new state. He objected to the irregular boundaries of West Virginia, alleged technical flaws in the statehood bill, and the precedent that it might set for creation of additional states in the South. Secretary of the Navy Gideon Welles and Postmaster General Montgomery Blair also held that the Reorganized Government was provisional and had none of the legal attributes of statehood.

Of those favoring the measure, Secretary of State William H. Seward held that the Reorganized Government was in law and in fact the government of Virginia with full plenary powers. He declared that "if it be a state competent to be represented in Congress and bound to pay taxes, it is a state competent to give the required consent."[20] Secretary of the Treasury Salmon P. Chase advanced arguments of expediency, with emphasis upon the necessity of encouraging men loyal to the Union and discouraging secessionism. Secretary of War Edwin M.

---

[19]Curry, *A House Divided*, 106-119. See also Richard Orr Curry, "A Reappraisal of Statehood Politics in West Virginia," *Journal of Southern History* 28(November 1962):419-21.

[20]Quoted in Hall, *Rending of Virginia*, 490.

Stanton seemed most impressed with the constriction of slavery implicit in the bill.

Lincoln agonized over the statehood bill, but, pressed by Senator Willey and Congressmen William G. Brown and Jacob B. Blair, he signed it on December 31, 1862. He convinced himself that it was constitutional and that the Reorganized Government, like others, derived its power from those who exercised the franchise, although they were a minority. He attached greater importance to recognizing the claims of loyal people of West Virginia than concerns about future difficulties in restoring secessionist Virginia to the Union. Moreover, approval of the bill might aid in reconciling many western leaders to the Emancipation Proclamation.

Lincoln announced his decision and showed the signed document to Jacob B. Blair, who, in response to his request of the previous day, called at the White House on the morning of New Year's Day, 1863. Elated, Blair returned to his hotel and informed Willey. From there the two went to a telegraph office and wired Governor Pierpont that success had at last crowned their efforts.

Approval of the Willey Amendment. As a condition for admission to the Union, West Virginia had to reassemble the constitutional convention to add the emancipation clause and provide for a referendum on the amended document. Vacant seats were filled, including those of President Hall, who had resigned after killing Lewis Wetzel, editor of the *Point Pleasant Register,* and Battelle, who had recently died. The people of Greenbrier, Monroe, Morgan, Pendleton, and Pocahontas counties, who had not been represented in the regular session, were urged to select delegates to the convention. Conservative Unionists and free state advocates waged spirited campaigns in counties in which elections were held.

On February 12 the constitutional convention reassembled, with eight new members. After electing Abraham D. Soper, the oldest delegate, president, it heard an address by Willey, who attended to present the case for his amendment. Willey refuted charges of federal dictation by noting that Congress, even before the Civil War, had imposed conditions for the admission of other states. He argued that statehood must be placed above politics and that a free state constitution would best serve the interests of the people of West Virginia.

A temporary difficulty arose with respect to compensation to masters deprived of slave property. At the request of delegates from the Kanawha Valley, the committee appointed to consider the amendment was instructed to study the possibility of compensation. Van Winkle, its chairman, recommended unqualified acceptance of the Willey Amendment and adoption of a resolution advising the legislature to compensate loyal slaveholders, with payments to begin four years after ratification of the constitution and extending over seventeen years. The resolution was tabled by a vote of twenty-eight to twenty-six. Chapman J. Stuart probably summed up the sentiments of many members when he declared, "If we lose the new State, we lose that which is of vast importance to us. It certainly surpasses any little interest I may have in a few little negroes."[21] On February 17 the convention approved the Willey Amendment by a vote of fifty-four to nothing, with three delegates abstaining. The next day it accepted the constitution as amended by a vote of fifty-two to nothing. On February 20, 1863, it adjourned *sine die*.

In spite of the unanimity of the vote, the conservatives, led by Carlile, Davis, Jackson, and Clemens, attempted to prevent ratification on March 26. Free state advocates tried to break up meetings at which they spoke. At Parkersburg and Middlebourne they threatened Clemens with violence, and they denied Jackson the use of the courthouse in his native Parkersburg. At the same time Willey, Van Winkle, and Pierpont stumped the hills and valleys drumming up support for the amended constitution.

The voters ratified the constitution by an overwhelming 28,321 to 572. Significantly, Union soldiers cast 7,828 of the favorable ballots but only 132 of the negative votes. Calhoun, Greenbrier, Logan, McDowell, Mercer, Pocahontas, Raleigh, Webster, and Wyoming counties sent no returns. The results were certified at once to President Lincoln, who on April 20, 1863, issued a proclamation that sixty days after that date West Virginia would become a state.

The Question of Constitutionality. Although Lincoln convinced himself of the constitutionality of procedures in the formation of West Virginia, the question continued to disturb historians. As early as 1922 James C. McGregor wrote of its "farcical nature."[22] James Garfield Randall, a leading authority on constitutional problems under Lincoln, maintained that the First Wheeling Convention was nothing more than a mass meeting and that the Second Wheeling Convention was "revolutionary." He considered neither the Second Wheeling Convention nor the legislatures of the Reorganized Government, which had many members in common, as representative of the state of Virginia, for which they "presumed to act." Randall concluded that "The irregular method by which the new State was formed, and the adoption of a mere fiction [in the Reorganized Government] as a basis for claiming fulfillment of a constitutional provision . . . presented an example of a measure which even its supporters did not wish to be emulated elsewhere or used as a precedent."[23]

Critics of the new state makers, including Randall, have generally agreed that continued debate over the constitutionality of their methods is largely academic. Charles H. Ambler and Festus P. Summers pointed out that the Supreme Court of the United States, although never rendering a specific opinion on the matter, has in several cases, such as those relating to Jefferson and Berkeley counties and the Virginia debt question, accepted the formation and admission of the state as a fact.

Some historians have credited irregularities in the achievement of statehood

[21]Quoted in Ambler and Summers, *West Virginia, the Mountain State*, 245.

[22]James C. McGregor, *The Disruption of Virginia*, (New York: The Macmillan Company, 1922), 206-223, passim.

[23]J.G. Randall, *Constitutional Problems Under Lincoln*, rev. ed. (Urbana: University of Illinois Press, 1951), 437-44, 473.

with enduring effects upon West Virginia. Ambler and Summers maintained that instead of promoting a state consciousness they were "unwholesome on the body politic which was thus denied traditions such as those which tend to immortalize the founders of Jamestown and the Pilgrim Fathers."[24] John A. Williams attributes two "unfortunate traditions" to the manner in which West Virginia became a state. One was "an official cynicism, a propensity to ignore the spirit of democratic institutions as long as the form was observed. The other was an apologetic posture, a defensiveness that made West Virginia overly eager for friendly national attention and for outsiders' approval but overly sensitive to bad publicity and criticism, whether it came from within or without."[25] If such characteristics exist—and the question is moot—it seems more likely that their roots lie in the inferior status of West Virginia during the decades that it was part of the Old Dominion and perhaps in the industrial autocracy which developed in the new state after the Civil War.

Launching the State. On May 6–7 a nominating convention of 235 delegates of the Constitutional Union Party met at Parkersburg and chose a slate of candidates for the eight elective state offices provided by the constitution. When Willey declined the honor, the convention nominated Arthur I. Boreman of Parkersburg for governor. Its other four nominees for excutive offices were Jacob E. Boyers of Tyler County, secretary of state; Campbell Tarr of Brooke County, treasurer; Aquilla B. Caldwell of Ohio County, attorney general; and Samuel Crane of Randolph County, auditor. James H. Brown of Kanawha County, William A. Harrison of Harrison County, and Ralph L. Berkshire of Monongalia County were selected for the supreme court of appeals.

With a fair balance of sectional and factional differences, the Constitutional Union ticket won without opposition in the elections on May 28. Boreman, with between twenty-four and twenty-six thousand votes, led all other candidates. Cabell, Calhoun, Clay, Fayette, Greenbrier, Logan, McDowell, Mercer, Monroe, Nicholas, Pocahontas, Raleigh, Tucker, Webster, and Wyoming counties, representing about one-third of the territory of the state, however, made no returns.

On June 20, 1863, West Virginia became the thirty-fifth state of the Union. The ceremonies held at Wheeling, the capital, featured a farewell address by Pierpont, who proclaimed West Virginia one of the states of the Union. He expressed regrets that the rebellion against the United States had not yet been crushed and urged loyal West Virginians to fight "as long as a mountain presents a site for a battery or a grotto remains to serve as a rifle pit." Pierpont then introduced Governor Boreman, whom he declared to be "as true as steel."[26] In his inaugural address Boreman reverted briefly to some of the issues of the day and asserted his intention to make West Virginia an honored and respected state.

[24]Ambler and Summers, *West Virginia, the Mountain State*, 248.
[25]John Alexander Williams, *West Virginia: A Bicentennial History* (New York and Nashville: W.W. Norton & Company, Inc., and American Association for State and Local History, 1976), 86.
[26]Ambler and Summers, *West Virginia, the Mountain State*, 251.

Responding to calls from the audience, Senator Willey also made brief remarks.

Decisions on the Boundary. West Virginia entered the Union with forty-eight counties. Following authorization by the Reorganized Government to hold referenda on their inclusion, the people of Jefferson and Berkeley counties on May 28, 1863, voted 238 to 2 and 665 to 7, respectively, to become part of West Virginia. Pierpont certified the results of the election to Boreman, and the legislature of West Virginia formally annexed them. Lingering doubts as to their status were dispelled on March 6, 1866, when Congress, by joint resolution, gave specific assent to their inclusion in West Virginia.

Large numbers of residents of the two counties, chiefly ex-Confederates, opposed attachment to West Virginia and charged voting frauds and insufficient polling places. Encouraged by the popular clamor, the first legislature of Virginia elected after Pierpont went to Richmond repealed by unanimous vote the acts of the Reorganized Government under which the counties were transferred.

Soon afterward Virginia brought suit in the United States Supreme Court to recover the two counties. The court held, in a clear victory for West Virginia, that the legislature of the Reorganized Government had acted legally in consenting to the formation of West Virginia and that the act of Congress admitting the state to the Union was informal approval for addition of other counties.

The First Legislature. The first legislature of West Virginia did much to establish precedent and set the tone for the future. For the United States Senate, it chose Waitman T. Willey, a senator from Virginia until the preceding March 4, and Peter G. Van Winkle, who won out over Archibald W. Campbell, editor of the *Wheeling Intelligencer* and an outspoken Radical. In addition to routine duties, it provided machinery for dividing counties into townships; created a Board of Public Works on the Virginia model; established a plan for a system of free schools; arranged to take advantage of the Morrill Act which donated lands for promotion of education in agricultural and mechanical arts; enacted a new plan of property assessments and taxation; engaged Daniel Lamb to codify the laws of Virginia applicable to West Virginia; and authorized Joseph H. Diss Debar to design a state seal.

West Virginia embarked upon statehood with high hopes. Her achievement represented a dream of more than half a century. Victory, however, could not erase deep sectional rivalries and animosities or wartime hatreds and suspicions; nor could it in itself solve economic, political, and social problems that were generations in the making. The magnitude of the challenges, however, was matched by a confidence, whether justified or not, that the destiny of the state was now in the hands of its own people.

Tensions of Reconstruction

The Legacy of War. Although West Virginia was a Union state during the last two years of the Civil War, her political and social history during Reconstruction was scarcely less traumatic than those of the states of the former Confederacy. Most of the tensions and hatreds were rooted in the war and produced permanent schisms even among Unionists. Unconditional Unionists, such as Arthur I. Boreman, Archibald W. Campbell, Waitman T. Willey, and Chester D. Hubbard, were ready to accept emancipation of slaves, imposed by Congress, and wartime proscriptions, including suspension of habeas corpus, of the Lincoln administration in return for statehood. Conservative Unionists, including John S. Carlile, Sherrard Clemens, John J. Jackson, and John J. Davis, would jeopardize statehood rather than bow to a government that they perceived as dictatorial and abolitionist. This fundamental cleavage in Unionist ranks produced in the Radical-oriented government of West Virginia a profound sense of insecurity.

West Virginia authorities anticipated further troubles with the return of Confederate veterans, mostly Democratic, at the end of the war. In 1863 the legislature provided for confiscation of the property of enemies of the state. The act was never seriously enforced, but it encouraged home guards and irregular marauding bands to wreak vengeance upon Confederate sympathizers and to use unsettled conditions for personal advantage. An oath of allegiance to the governments of the United States and West Virginia, required of state and local officials and later of attorneys, schoolteachers, and school trustees, served as a weapon for discrimination and persecution. In addition, numerous persons with Confederate leanings were arrested and detained, and some were sent to Camp Chase at Columbus, Ohio, as prisoners of war.

The Election of 1864. Even when allowances are made for campaign oratory and excesses, there can be no doubt that West Virginia authorities had considerable apprehension that Democrats and conservative Unionists might destroy the new state. On March 15, 1864, Ralph L. Berkshire wrote Willey that he expected the Copperheads to make "great exertions" in both national and state elections. He had no doubt that they would fail nationally, but he feared that their machinations might result in a Democratic victory that would leave no hope for the state. Willey later declared that a conspiracy "has been organized to wipe out West Virginia" and that he and others stood ready to combat the effort.[1] Archibald Campbell condemned the Democratic party in the columns of the *Wheeling Intelligencer* as a "Rebel Aid Society," which did not recognize the new state.[2]

The *Wheeling Register,* the leading conservative newspaper of West Virginia, refuted the "prevarication and deception" of its rival. Lewis Baker, its editor, pointed out that only the Supreme Court could change the status of West Virginia. He reminded his readers that "our Abolition friends labored to defeat the manner proposed by conservatives for its formation and succeeded in doing so; they formed it in their own way, and now they seem wonderfully alarmed about its perpetuity."[3]

In the presidential election of 1864 Lincoln carried West Virginia over Democrat George B. McClellan by a vote of 23,152 to 10,438. His vote, however, fell more than five thousand short of the 28,321 cast for the Willey Amendment the previous year. It indicated that many Unionists who reluctantly supported a necessary condition for statehood wanted no part of Lincoln's war measures and that Carlile, Clemens, Davis, and others were laying the ground for a conservative organization that might collaborate with the Democrats to become a powerful force in West Virginia politics.

The assassination of Lincoln raised new fears for the future of West Virginia. Governor Boreman hastened to Washington, and he and Senator Willey called upon President Johnson, who assured them that the position of the state would remain secure. Johnson also stated that he would recognize the Pierpont government at Alexandria as the *de jure* government of Virginia after the war. These guarantees facilitated the move of Unconditional Unionists into the Republican Party.

Unsettled conditions, marked by violence by Confederates or pseudo-Confederates, also caused authorities continued concern. In his annual message to the legislature on January 17, 1865, Boreman drew attention to robberies "committed on a large scale in many parts of the State" and the murder of some of the "best citizens" of Harrison and Marion counties. He charged that disloyal persons who had remained at home fed and harbored "these marauders and murderers, knowing their purpose." Boreman urged loyal West Virginians to organize for their own protection, authorized them to kill "these outlaws wherever found," and promised free arms and ammunition for that purpose.[4] He asked the legislature to enact more stringent laws with severe punishments for the guilty but with safeguards to protect the innocent.

[1]Berkshire's letter is quoted in Richard Orr Curry, *A House Divided: A Study of Statehood Politics and the Copperhead Movement in West Virginia* (Pittsburgh: University of Pittsburgh Press, 1964), 131. For Willey's remark, see *Wheeling Intelligencer,* October 7, 1864.

[2]*Wheeling Intelligencer,* September 8, 1864.

[3]*Wheeling Register,* October 10, 1864.

[4]West Virginia, Senate, *Journal, 1865,* 6-7.

Political Proscriptions. The legislature responded quickly to dangers described by Boreman and to the anticipated return of Confederate veterans at the end of the war. One of its most galling acts, passed on February 25, 1865, provided for "voters' test oaths." Under the law, a voter might be challenged at the polls and prevented from voting until he had affirmed, under oath, that he had never voluntarily borne arms against or held an office hostile to the United States, the Reorganized Government of Virginia, or the state of West Virginia; that he would support the constitutions of the United States and West Virginia; and that he took the oaths freely "without any mental reservation or purpose of evasion." Opponents of the oaths held that they violated the West Virginia constitution, which granted suffrage to all white male citizens, but defenders justified them as an essential war measure.

The same legislature enacted other laws that struck at the civil liberties of Confederate sympathizers. They provided that court cases arising in pro-Southern counties might be moved to neighboring counties loyal to the Union; allowed tax collectors extra commissions and made other provisions for the collection of taxes in secessionist counties; and prescribed yet another test oath for suitors who had participated in the rebellion.

Most Confederates, encouraged by the tone of Lincoln's Second Inaugural Address and the generosity of Grant at Appomattox, hoped that the Boreman administration would relax its war measures with the return of peace. In many localities Confederate veterans, eager to bind up the nation's wounds, took part in the organization of governments, and their Unionist neighbors, believing the proscriptions against them unwise, unnecessary, and unjust, welcomed their participation. Radical elements, however, resented moves by the Virginia legislature for reunification of the state or at least the recovery of Jefferson and Berkeley counties. They held mass meetings in several counties in the summer of 1865 and called for even sterner actions to prevent their former foes from returning to West Virginia. Hostility toward ex-Confederates was, in fact, so great in some areas that federal troops had to be called in to protect them from their unforgiving neighbors.

Radical leaders were alarmed by victories of former Confederates in the elections of 1865, a clear indication that the test oaths had not had the desired effect in many counties. Henry Mason Mathews of Greenbrier County, a major in the Confederate Army, was elected to the state Senate, but that body denied him his seat. Boreman refused a commission to Samuel Price of the same county and the wartime lieutenant governor of Virginia in Richmond, who was elected judge of the Ninth Judicial Circuit, which included Greenbrier, Pocahontas, Monroe, and other border counties. The legislature removed Judge John M. Kennedy of the Tenth Judicial Circuit, made up of Jefferson, Berkeley, and Morgan counties, on charges that he appointed rebels to office and derided the Reorganized Government and the government of West Virginia. On the other hand Circuit Judge Nathaniel Harrison of the district embracing the Greenbrier and New River areas, prosecuted former Confederates with such lack of discrimination that only his resignation prevented his removal.

Boreman was convinced that "the spirit of rebellion still reigns in the breast" of former Confederates. On January 16, 1866, he told the legislature that they were eager "to repossess themselves of place and power" and "too impatient under the safe-guards that it has been deemed necessary to adopt for the protection and preservation of the Government."[5] At his urging, the legislature enacted a voters' registration law and a law requiring a test oath for lawyers and agreed to a disfranchisement amendment to the constitution. The amendment, approved by the voters on May 24, 1866, by a majority of 7,236, disqualified between fifteen and twenty-five thousand voters and legalized the removal of ex-Confederates from state and local offices.

None of the proscriptive acts produced more bitterness than the voters' registration law, under which the governor appointed a three-member registration board for each county, which in turn named a registrar for each township. The county boards could refuse to register any person suspected of disloyalty even though he was willing to take the loyalty oath. Under changes in the law in 1867, willingness to take the oath no longer assured the right to register.

Registrars, as might have been expected, often acted with unrestrained arrogance and remarkably poor judgment in removing voters from the rolls. In Lewisburg, for instance, the registrar, Dr. J.F. Caldwell, erased so many names from the lists that he earned the nickname "Old Scratch" and is said at one time to have reduced the voters to seven persons, including himself, his son, two Irishmen, and three Negroes.

With as many as eighty-five percent of the voters disqualified in some counties, organized resistance to the registration law steadily mounted from 1867 to 1870. Threats and attacks upon registrars and registration boards were common. Some Radical leaders attributed the violence to the Ku Klux Klan. Undoubtedly such charges were sometimes made in order to obtain state and federal troops, which were used on numerous occasions, particularly in Monroe, Randolph, Tucker, Barbour, Marion, Cabell, Wayne, and Logan counties.

Beginnings of a "Let Up" Policy. Signs of relaxation in restrictions against ex-Confederates began to appear in 1868, when the legislature relaxed the application of test oaths for lawyers and teachers. In the gubernatorial race Republican William E. Stevenson of Wood County won over Democrat Johnson N. Camden of the same county by a vote of 26,931 to 22,052, but with the smallest margin in the short history of the state. Recognizing the futility of "waving the bloody shirt," Stevenson, in a forward-looking inaugural address, dwelt upon the need for railroads and river improvements, expansion of industry, and immigration. He noted that "Deeply rooted prejudices, which here-

[5]Quoted in Charles H. Ambler and Festus P. Summers, *West Virginia, the Mountain State*, 2d ed. (Englewood Cliffs, N.J.: Prentice-Hall, Inc., 1958), 267.

tofore repelled immigration, are rapidly disappearing" and urged discontinuance of voters' test oaths as a means of improving the economic climate as well as easing tensions that lingered in the state.[6]

The ratification by the legislature on March 3, 1869, of the Fifteenth Amendment to the United States Constitution almost inevitably tied enfranchisement of former Confederates to the granting of the vote to Negroes. As late as the summer of 1868 Waitman T. Willey had declared from the steps of the courthouse in Weston that "Negro suffrage should never be forced upon the citizens of West Virginia,"[7] but events had moved rapidly in the succeeding months. The anomaly of granting the vote to eighteen thousand blacks, many illiterate and unprepared for the duties of citizenship, while denying it to some twenty thousand ex-Confederates, including hundreds with education and demonstrated leadership, gave rise to a spirited debate on the whole suffrage question in 1869.

As early as May 12, 1869, the *Wheeling Intelligencer* expressed the view that "the enfranchisement of the blacks . . . is already assured" and predicted that the "question of enfranchising ex-Rebels will grow in prominence until some way a solution is reached." The *Intelligencer* declared, prophetically, "It is our Banquo's ghost; it will not down at our bidding." In a letter to the same newspaper, Horace Greeley warned, "Every year one thousand of your rebels die, and one thousand more of their sons become of age,—you can't disfranchise them. You have now five thousand majority. Six years from now convert this into a rebel majority of one thousand. The rebels will be enfranchised in spite of you."[8]

Liberal Republicans, who favored easing restrictions against former Confederates, recognized the dilemma faced by the party in West Virginia. If the measures were ended immediately, the party was certain to lose power; if they were not, it faced a bleak future for years to come. Granville Davisson Hall, who succeeded Campbell as editor of the *Wheeling Intelligencer,* wrote to Charles Sumner that "our wisest and best Republicans" believed that "our only hope of perpetuating Republican ascendancy in the State is by a magnanimous policy which shall bring a portion of the ex-Rebels into co-operation with us when they become voters. A very large number of them were old line Whigs before the war. They do not like the Democracy and they would come to us if we gave them the ballot. But if we wait for the Democrats to enfranchise them, they will of course fall into that party."[9]

[6]Quoted in Milton Gerofsky, "Reconstruction in West Virginia," Part I, *West Virginia History* 6(July 1945):325.

[7]Quoted in Gerofsky, "Reconstruction in West Virginia," Part I, 327-28.

[8]*Wheeling Intelligencer,* May 12, 1869.

[9]Quoted in Richard O. Curry, "Crisis Politics in West Virginia, 1861-1870," in Richard O. Curry, ed., *Radicalism, Racism, and Party Realignment: The Border States During Reconstruction* (Baltimore: Johns Hopkins Press, 1969), 98-99.

The elections of October 1869 demonstrated that "Radical control had exasperated West Virgnia."[10] In the legislative races, Radicals faced opposition from Liberal Republicans, who were joined by many Conservatives in the party, and Democrats. They lost control of the Senate, winning only four seats, while the Liberals captured thirteen and the Democrats five. Democrats won twenty-three of the fifty-six seats in the House of Delegates. Victories of Liberal Republicans Daniel Lamb and William H.H. Flick and Democrats John J. Davis and James M. Jackson clearly presaged a mood for change.

An End to Political Proscriptions. Governor Stevenson, in a statesmanlike address to the legislature on January 18, 1870, urged removal of political disabilities against ex-Confederates. He expressed confidence that if the legislature approached restoration of voting rights with "a sincere desire to advance the true interests of the State rather than organize the success of a party," many of the difficulties would disappear.[11] In keeping with his recommendation, the legislature on February 7 struck down test oaths for teachers and attorneys. More important, it approved an amendment to the constitution, offered by Flick, conferring the right to vote on all males over twenty-one years old by removing "white" as a requirement for voting. The House of Delegates defeated proposals by George C. Sturgiss to retain disfranchising clauses for ex-Confederates and by John J. Davis to restrict suffrage to white males, and the Senate defeated a white suffrage substitute by Henry Gassaway Davis.

The Flick Amendment was a major issue in the Democratic convention, which met at Charleston in June 1870. The majority report of its Committee on Resolutions held that the Fifteenth Amendment to the federal Constitution had settled the matter of Negro suffrage and recommended adoption of the Flick Amendment. The convention, however, followed the lead of Henry S. Walker, editor of the *Charleston Courier,* who in a ringing address declared that "it was the duty of the Democrats to maintain the honor and dignity of the Caucasian race, and, as this is a white man's country so it should be a white man's government."[12] By a vote of 324 to 242, it adopted the minority report and gave the Conservatives a signal victory.

The Democratic platform excoriated the national Republican party for removing suffrage from the control of the states and "calling to power an alien and inferior race" and rejected all suggestions for social equality of the races. It invited "intelligent white men to join with us in asserting the principle that the white race is the ruling race of the Republic." The platform also called for the abolition of all test oaths, protection against "outrages" committed by registrars, preservation of the public schools on a racially segregated basis, and a reduction in the number of officials. As a result of the bitter fight, it contained no

[10]Jacqueline Balk and Ari Hoogenboom, "The Origins of Border State Liberal Republicanism," in Curry, ed., *Radicalism, Racism, and Party Realignment,* 242.

[11]Quoted in Gerofsky, "Reconstruction in West Virginia," Part I, 331.

[12]*Wheeling Register,* June 11, 1870.

mention of the Flick Amendment, but it denounced "the injustices and disgrace incident to the disfranchisement of twenty-five thousand of our own race while Negroes exercise the right of suffrage without hindrance or condition."[13]

As their candidate for governor, the Democrats chose John J. Jacob of Hampshire County, a congressman not identified with either faction of the party. Described by the *Wheeling Intelligencer* as "a man of good common sense," whose chief recommendation was "that nothing can be said against him," Jacob was expected to follow a moderate course and perhaps to heal party wounds.[14]

The Republican convention assembled at Parkersburg on June 22, with between twelve and twenty Negroes among its delegates. It gave mild endorsement to the Flick Amendment, but it pledged the party to enforce laws against former Confederates as long as they were on the statute books. As its gubernatorial candidate the party chose the incumbent, William E. Stevenson.

During the campaign the Democrats turned the Enforcement Act, passed by Congress on March 30, 1870, to put the Fifteenth Amendment into effect, to their advantage. In test cases, United States District Judge John J. Jackson, a Democrat, ruled that the act fully protected the voting rights of all citizens, white as well as black. United States Circuit Judge Hugh Lennox Bond, a Republican, held views diametrically opposite those of Jackson, but a special act of Congress had invested the district court for West Virginia with circuit court powers, with appeals directly to the Supreme Court. Although Stevenson urged registrars to uphold the laws of the state, Jackson's ruling led to numerous arrests and prevented registrars from exercising the wide discretionary authority they had formerly used.

The Democrats made a clean sweep of the 1870 elections. Jacob won over Stevenson by a majority of 2,010 votes. They won a majority of two in the Senate and twenty-four in the House of Delegates. Democrats also replaced Republicans in the state's congressional seats. Republicans attributed their defeat to intimidation of registrars, lack of law enforcement at polling places, failure of many party members to vote, and dissension within their own ranks. Actually, since 1868 the Democratic Party had increased its strength by about 6,500 votes, with significant gains in Unionist–Republican counties of the northwest, where they added 3,300 votes.

The new legislature, which convened on January 17, 1871, turned at once to removal of political disabilities of ex-Confederates. The Senate concurred unanimously in the action of the previous legislature in passing the Flick Amendment. Conservatives in the House of Delegates, led by Charles Lewis and E. Willis Wilson, sought to restrict suffrage to whites, but liberals, under the leadership of James M. Jackson and Henry Brannon, joined with Republicans to pass the amendment once again by a vote of thirty-eight to seventeen. On

[13]Ibid.
[14]*Wheeling Intelligencer,* June 10, 1870.

April 17 the voters by an overwhelming 23,546 to 6,323 approved the Flick Amendment. The legislature ended proscriptions against former Confederates with laws stripping the registration act and voters' test oaths of most of their potency.

The Constitution of 1872. In 1871 the Democrats were clearly in the ascendancy in West Virginia. They maintained their majorities in the legislature at fourteen in the Senate and twenty-three in the House of Delegates. When the term of United States Senator Willey expired, Democratic legislators replaced him with one of their own number, conservative Henry Gassaway Davis.

On August 24, 1871, West Virginians voted 30,220 to 27,658 in favor of a constitutional convention, regarded by conservative Democrats as essential for removing the last vestiges of Radical Republican rule. A new frame of government would avoid repeated amendments to the existing constitution, which some feared would become "a tissue of patches and inconsistencies."[15]

The constitutional convention assembled at Charleston on January 16, 1872. Only twelve of its seventy-eight members were Republicans. Only Republican Waitman T. Willey had served in the First Constitutional Convention, and he exerted but minor influence in the 1872 convention. The strength of the Redeemers was shown when the convention chose as its president Samuel Price, the Confederate lieutenant governor of Virginia, who three years before had been disqualified for a judgeship to which he had been elected. Democrats rejected a resolution by Archibald W. Campbell to move the convention to Wheeling on the ground that no genuine reforms could be accomplished in that "iron-hearted" city.

Early in the convention unreconstructed Rebels engaged in several moves, amusing in retrospect, that exasperated liberal Democrats and Republicans, including an unsuccessful attempt to change the names of Lincoln and Grant counties to Davis and Lee. Moderate ex-Confederates, such as Price and Charles James Faulkner, exerted restraining influences, but the constitution bore the marks of bitter war and statehood experiences in branding test oaths repugnant to principles of free government and in prohibiting the establishment of voter registration boards.

A proposal to make the constitution conform to the federal Constitution by omitting the word "white" in setting qualifications for voters drew spirited responses before it was adopted. Benjamin F. Martin of Taylor County expressed the hope that the hand that attempted to strike out the word would be palsied, for without it the legal voters would be "carpet baggers, negroes, mulattoes, Chinese, Dutch, Irish, coolies, Norwegians, scalawags with a few of the native population of the country."[16] John J. Thompson of Putnam County maintained that Negroes were less capable of self-government than the buffalo of the plains. The method of voting itself aroused lively debate, and the convention finally

[15]*Wheeling Register,* July 24, 1871.

[16]Quoted in James Morton Callahan, *History of West Virginia, Old and New,* 3 vols. (Chicago: American Historical Society, Inc., 1923), vol. 1, 416.

adopted a compromise that gave the voter the choice of an open, sealed, or secret ballot.

The constitution vested executive power in the governor, elected by the people for a term of four years, without the right of succeeding himself. Executive power was shared with the secretary of state, superintendent of schools, auditor, treasurer, and attorney general, all serving four-year terms, and, with the exception of the secretary of state, elected by the people. The constitution made no provision for a lieutenant governor.

Substantial changes were made in the legislative and judicial branches of government. In line with current practice, annual sessions of forty-five days replaced biennial meetings of the legislature. Terms of members were set at two years for delegates and four years for senators, with one-half of the latter elected every two years. Among persons debarred from membership were salaried officers of any railroad company, a restriction growing out of resentment of the power and influence of the Baltimore and Ohio Railroad. Daniel D.T. Farnsworth, who served six days as governor in 1869, expressed fears that the entire state might come under control of the railroad, which could divert much needed immigration from West Virginia to the Ohio Valley. The judicial system consisted of a state supreme court of appeals with four judges elected for twelve-year terms, circuit courts, county and corporation courts, and justices of the peace. The relative autonomy of the justices of the peace, who were freed from supervision by the circuit courts, was an essentially reactionary feature.

Inevitably, the much criticized township system was abandoned. It was replaced by a modified county court with three commissioners entrusted with fiscal, administrative, and judicial powers. Alpheus F. Haymond of Marion County held that the new system provided opportunities for young members of the legal profession to display "their youthful geniuses . . . before the as-sembled people,"[17] but John Marshall Hagans of Monongalia County believed that the state would do better for would-be attorneys to establish a law school.

Some of the most significant provisions of the constitution dealt with land and, in the words of James Morton Callahan, "may be regarded as a monument to a mistake of the dead but living past."[18] The constitution recognized titles obtained under the laws of Virginia and those of West Virginia before it went into effect. Although clauses relating to lands later gave rise to numerous expensive lawsuits and contributed to the transfer of titles to mining and lumber companies, there appears to have been no basis for the charge that they were "a contrivance gotten up to make litigation the principal business of West Virginia—to the great impoverishment of suitors and the enrichment of swarms of one-horse political lawyers that now feed upon the body politic."[19]

[17]Quoted in Callahan, *History of West Virginia,* vol. 1, 418-19.
[18]Ibid., p. 419.
[19]Quoted from *New York Times* in John Alexander Williams, *West Virginia: A Bicentennial History* (New York and Nashville: W.W. Norton & Company, Inc., and American Association for State and Local History, 1976), 92.

On August 22, 1872, the people of West Virginia ratified the constitution by a vote of 42,344 to 37,777. The *Wheeling Register* proclaimed that it was "in all respects an admirable one" and that it marked "the beginning of a new era in the progress and prosperity" for the state. Of all the victories won by the Democrats in the new state, the newspaper considered this "the crowning work, . . . the greatest and the most enduring."[20] It is the constitution under which West Virginia is still governed.

The State Capital. Political changes and sectional conflicts affected decisions on a permanent capital for West Virginia. Wheeling, preeminent in size and economic advantages, was located in the Northern Panhandle and identified with Republicanism and hated features of Radical Reconstruction. For six years Governor Boreman pleaded in vain with the legislature to select a permanent site as a means of allaying intensifying sectional rivalries and as an evidence of permanence of the new state.

In 1869 the first legislature relatively free of Radical domination designated Charleston as the state capital. On April 1, 1870, the date set for the transfer, state officials left Wheeling aboard the steamer *Mountain Boy* for the new seat of government. Charleston, a town of slightly more than three thousand without a railroad or substantial river improvements, was hardly adequate to the demands that the state government would make upon it. A group of prominent citizens had formed a corporation and erected a temporary capitol, but it was not ready for occupancy for several months. Dr. John P. Hale, one of the leading industrialists and businessmen, built Hale House, a modern and commodious hotel, for the express purpose of accommodating legislators, government officials, and others with business in the town. The completion of the Chesapeake and Ohio Railroad westward to Huntington in 1873 and other advances left little doubt, moreover, that substantial growth and development lay ahead.

Complaints about the inaccessibility and inadequacies of Charleston continued, and in 1875, in a somewhat hasty surprise move, the legislature accepted overtures from Wheeling that included a building to serve as an interim capitol and voted to return the capital to that city. Governor John J. Jacob did not sign the bill, but it became law without his signature. On May 23 and 24 state officials moved to Wheeling aboard the *Emma Graham* and *Chesapeake*.

Disappointed Charlestonians, headed by John Slack, Sr., obtained a restraining order to prevent removal of public archives and other state property to Wheeling. The supreme court of appeals, however, dissolved the injunction on August 13, 1875. State properties were dispatched to Wheeling aboard barges towed by the *Iron City*. Until public buildings could be completed, Linsly Institute served as the capitol, with the legislature meeting in Washington Hall.

In February 1877 the legislature agreed to submit the question of a permanent capital to the people, who were to choose among Charleston, Clarksburg, and Martinsburg. In the referendum held in August 1877, Charleston received

---

[20]*Wheeling Register,* August 29, 1872.

41,243 votes; Clarksburg, 29,442; and Martinsburg, 8,046. Governor Henry M. Mathews thereupon proclaimed that the transfer would take place in 1885.

On May 2, 1885, state officials again boarded the *Chesapeake,* and state records and movable property were placed on a barge towed by the *Belle Prince,* all bound for Charleston. There the old Statehouse Company had turned over its properties to the West Virginia Board of Public Works, which had erected a handsome brick structure with eighty-five rooms in downtown Charleston. At last the new state had a permanent seat of government, just as it stood on the threshold of a new era in its political, economic, and social development.

The Bourbon Ascendancy

The Democratic Party. When it took over the reigns of government in West Virginia in 1871, the Democratic Party was essentially a coalition of diverse interests. Ex-Confederates mingled with former Unionists, and lifelong Democrats welcomed to their ranks former Whigs who found the Republican Party unacceptable. The party included a strong infusion of Bourbons, devoted to Southern agrarian ideals but eager to reap advantages from the emerging industrial age.

Traditional approaches to politics persisted among Democrats. Despite the change wrought by war and Reconstruction, postwar leaders recognized continuities in the social and economic life of the new state, particularly in its eastern and southern counties. Many were strongly attuned to local or sectional interests and easily won backwoods support with a folksy attention to the everyday life and concerns of the people and with speeches at court days and other assemblages. Both politicians and the people felt comfortable with this brand of politics, which nurtured and reinforced conservatism. Thousands of West Virginians, according to the opinionated *New York Times*, were Democrats "because they don't know any better."[1]

At least four major elements could be discerned within the Democratic Party, but the lines dividing them were somewhat blurred. John A. Williams has identified them as Regulars, Redeemers, Agrarians, and the "Kanawha Ring." The Regulars were strongest in the northern and western sections of the state. They were represented by industrialists Johnson Newlon Camden and Henry Gassaway Davis, who drew upon their business experiences to modernize the organization and methods of the party and began to undermine the old informal style of politics that had generally prevailed.

The Redeemers and Agrarians appealed to rural voters. The Redeemers, who upheld older political practices as well as social and economic patterns of the past, counted upon former Confederate politicians and sympathizers. Strongest in eastern, southern, and interior counties, they regained much of their former influence following the Democratic victory of 1870. The Agrarians, found mostly along the Baltimore and Ohio Railroad and in the Kanawha Valley,

[1]*New York Times*, October 8, 1876.

generally disdained Redeemer emphasis upon the evils of Reconstruction and sought a more forward-looking approach to politics.

Party Organization. Democrats such as Lewis Baker, editor of the *Wheeling Register,* recognized the need for a disciplined party organization as early as the 1860s. For leadership they looked first to older Democrats such as Benjamin H. Smith of Kanawha County, the Jacksons of Wood County, and William G. Brown of Preston County, but they gradually turned to Camden and Davis, both relative newcomers to the party. Camden and Davis were vigorous men in their forties, and neither had a controversial political record. Their industrial empires provided them ample funds to give needed financial vitality to their party.

Although leadership in the Democratic Party was diffused, Camden was its titular head form 1868 to 1875. Born in Wood County, he attended the United States Military Academy at West Point and later practiced law. Steering clear of statehood and Reconstruction politics, he concentrated on business interests. Camden became one of the first oil producers in the Burning Springs field in Wirt County, erected his own refinery at Parkersburg, and in 1875 sold his interests to the Standard Oil Company. The epitome of the business monopolist in West Virginia politics, he lobbied diligently with both the legislature and congress to advance the interests of the Standard Oil Company and to assure it almost complete control over the oil industry of West Virginia.

For several years high political office eluded Camden. He was the Democratic nominee for governor in 1868 and 1872, but he was defeated both times. He was disappointed in his desire for a United States Senate seat in 1875, when the legislature chose Allen T. Caperton of Monroe County as a means of placating the Kanawha Valley for its decision to move the state capital back to Wheeling, and again in 1877, when after Caperton's death Republicans threw their support to Davis.

In 1881, when he was in complete command of the Democratic Party organization, Camden at last won the coveted Senate seat. Despite his indulgence in and support of monopolistic business practices, he rendered important services, including sponsorship of the provision of the Interstate Commerce Act of 1887 which forbade railroads to charge more for short hauls than long hauls, thereby removing discriminations against West Virginia shippers. Convinced that a tariff for revenue, with incidental protection to industry, was adequate to the needs of West Virginia, he dutifully supported Grover Cleveland for president in 1884 and 1888, although many Democrats objected to Cleveland's views on the tariff.

Opposition to Camden mounted within his own party, and he failed to win reelection in 1887. Farmers berated him for his monopolistic leanings, and twelve Agrarian state senators from eastern counties refused to participate in a nominating caucus or be bound by its decision. On May 7, 1887, the legislature elected Charles J. Faulkner, Jr., of Berkeley County as a compromise candidate.

Although he devoted increasing attention to his burgeoning industrial empire, Camden remained a loyal party man. Aided by the unpopular McKinley

Tariff of 1890, he contributed significantly to Cleveland's victory in West Virginia in 1892 and to Democratic control of both houses of the legislature. Since the location of the state capital was then settled and it was politic to select both United States senators from north of the Kanawha River, the legislature rewarded Camden by electing him to the short term at the same time that it chose Faulkner, the incumbent, for the long term.

Sharing power with Camden in the party organization was Davis, who ultimately emerged as the most powerful man in the party. Beginning as a brakeman on the Baltimore and Ohio Railroad and as station agent at Piedmont, West Virginia, Davis moved into the mercantile business and obtained lucrative United States Government contracts during the Civil War. He expanded his enterprises to include farming, banking, timbering, and coal mining and by 1871 was the leading business and political figure in the upper Potomac Valley.

Elected to the state senate in 1868, Davis, a Unionist, urged removal of restrictions against ex-Confederates and in 1871 was elected to succeed Waitman T. Willey in the United States Senate. An uninspiring speaker, he exerted more influence behind the scenes than in the Senate chamber. His estate at Deer Park, Maryland, was a mecca for the prominent and powerful. President Grover Cleveland and his bride spent part of their honeymoon there in 1886, and President Benjamin Harrison and Secretary of State James G. Blaine were frequent visitors. Davis's connections with Harrison won him an appointment to the Intercontinental Railway Commission in 1890 and the chairmanship of the Pan-American Committee.

The ascendancy of Camden and Davis in Democratic party affairs was one of the main features of West Virginia politics from 1871 to 1897. Their dominance, however, was never absolute, and factionalism continued to disrupt party harmony.

Other Party Leaders. The challengers of Camden and Davis for leadership of the Democratic party included Redeemers, Agrarians, and the Kanawha Ring. Redeemers, who represented an older political culture of West Virginia, included Samuel Price, a lieutenant governor of Confederate Virginia; Charles James Faulkner, Jr., an ex-Confederate who was elected to the United States Senate in 1887; Jonathan M. Bennett, a former auditor of Virginia; and Allen T. Caperton, "in appearance, manners, and education . . . a perfect type of old Virginia gentleman," who had been a member of the Confederate Senate.[2]

The Redeemers disdained the methods of Camden and Davis. Many regarded Davis as a mere merchant, and Charles James Faulkner, Sr., considered his rise in party councils "a subject too painful and disgusting to be dwellt [sic] upon."[3] One of Camden's opponents deplored his election to the United States Senate on the ground that the position should be filled only by "a man of

[2]Quoted in John Alexander Williams, "The New Dominion and the Old: Ante-Bellum and Statehood Politics As the Background for West Virginia's 'Bourbon Democracy,' " *West Virginia History* 33(July 1972):375.

[3]Quoted from Williams, "The New Dominion and the Old," 376.

education and political attainments" who could "shed honor on the State and the party."[4] Many Redeemers rejected the "proposition . . . that none but those who build or promise to build a railroad shall be eligible to the United States Senate from this State."[5]

Agrarian leaders, often allied to the Redeemers, generally opposed monopolies. Henry S. Walker, a Charleston newspaper editor, was first a Regular, but he differed with the industrialist element and for a time deserted the Democrats for the Greenback party, which in fusion with Republicans in 1878 and 1880 made serious inroads in Kanawha, Putnam, and Mason counties. Fusionist popularity stemmed in part from its stand on the national currency question, but it also sprang from discontent over the privileges of the railroads and monopolies in the state, always seen by the Agrarians as enemies. E. Willis Wilson, first of Berkeley and later of Kanawha County and the most successful of the Agrarians, was a perennial foe of monopolies, particularly the railroads. His position was a significant factor in his election to the speakership of the House of Delegates and in 1884 to the governorship. Daniel Bedinger Lucas, widely known as the poet of the Lost Cause, was, except for his hatred of industrial combinations and the Baltimore and Ohio Railroad, essentially a Redeemer.

The Kanawha Ring combined a concern for strong party organization with the traditional political style of the Redeemers and Agrarians. Centering in two Charleston law firms, Kenna and Watts and Chilton, MacCorkle, and Chilton, it originated in 1872 and achieved its most notable successes in the victory of John E. Kenna over Davis for the United States Senate seat in 1883 and the election of John D. Alderson to Congress and William A. MacCorkle, its youngest member, to the governorship in 1892. Following the victory of Wilson in the gubernatorial race in 1884, the Kanawha Ring made overtures to the Regulars. Out of the overtures came what seemed to be an alliance between the Camden forces and the Kanawha Ring.

The Democratic Party and State Government. Regardless of factionalism in the party, Democrats had a relatively solid basis for control of state government during the quarter of a century following their victory in 1870. The overwhelmingly rural character of the state and party devotion to Jeffersonian principles of low taxes, economy in government, and states' rights provided the mortar of unity.

During the Bourbon era state government rested lightly upon West Virginia citizens. The elective officers of the executive branch included, in addition to the governor, the auditor, treasurer, attorney general, and superintendent of free schools, whose limited duties enabled him to serve also as adjutant general and quartermaster general until 1877. The governor appointed the secretary of state, who was a mere clerk. The only ex officio administrative boards were school

[4]Quoted in Festus P. Summers, *Johnson Newlon Camden: A Study in Individualism* (New York: G.P. Putnam's Sons, 1937), 229.

[5]Quoted from *Huntington Advertiser* in *Wheeling Register,* December 28, 1882.

finance, which managed the "School Fund," and public works, comprised of all elective state officials.

Governor Henry Mason Mathews. The first of the Bourbon governors, Henry Mason Mathews (March 19, 1834–April 28, 1884), represented the Redeemers. Born at Frankford, Greenbrier County, Mathews studied at the University of Virginia and Judge John W. Brockenbrough's Law School at Lexington and practiced law at Lewisburg. Since he had served as a major in the Confederate Army, Mathews was not permitted to take a state Senate seat to which he was elected in 1865. Following removal of restrictions upon ex-Confederates, he was a prominent member of the constitutional convention of 1872 and attorney general of West Virginia.

In the election of 1876 Mathews defeated popular Nathan Goff, Jr., of Clarksburg, the Republican nominee, for the governorship, and supporters of the Lost Cause won seven of the eight elective state offices. "A patriotic, broad and liberal minded ex-Confederate who had fully accepted the results of the Civil War and was well-fitted to lead in meeting living issues,"[6] Mathews embodied the very essence of Bourbonism. He recognized the need for a more favorable industrial climate and urged legislation to encourage immigration, particularly from Germany and Switzerland, promote internal improvements, improve the Ohio River and its tributaries, and finance a geological survey of the state.

Mathews generally adhered to party positions on the troublesome Virginia debt question. The principle of assumption by West Virginia of a part of the public debt of Virginia in 1861 had been set forth in the dismemberment ordinance, the West Virginia constitution, and the act of Congress creating the new state. By the time that Mathews became governor, the question had assumed political dimensions. Republicans generally urged the state to pay its share of the debt, but Democrats, fearful of popular disapproval, procrastinated.

In 1870 Virginia had offered to submit the debt queston to arbitration, but West Virginia insisted that her share be determined by commissioners, as provided in the dismemberment ordinance. Faced with an impasse, Virginia authorities calculated that West Virginia should assume about one-third of the state debt as of January 1, 1861. They agreed to pay her bondholders about two-thirds of the total and issued certificates of indebtedness against West Virginia for the remainder. Mindful of a decision of an authorized commission that West Virginia owed only $953,360.32 and of a calculation by Jonathan M. Bennett that Virginia actually owed West Virginia $525,000 on the basis of benefits received, Mathews pursued a policy, followed by his successors, that kept the entire matter open.

Early in his administration Mathews was confronted with a railroad strike at Martinsburg, which touched off the great national railroad strike in July 1877.

---

[6]James Morton Callahan, *History of West Virginia, Old and New,* 3 vols. (Chicago: American Historical Society, Inc., 1923), vol. 1, 554.

Supporters of the strikers included a rowdy element, and in short order they disrupted train service and inflicted considerable property damage. When state forces proved unable to control the situation, Mathews appealed to President Rutherford B. Hayes for federal troops, which quickly restored order. His action suggested to industrialists that the Bourbons were committed to a favorable climate for business activity.

Governor Jacob Beeson Jackson. A native of Parkersburg, Jacob Beeson Jackson (April 6, 1829–December 11, 1893) was the son of John J. Jackson, Sr., a distinguished jurist, and the grandson of John G. Jackson, a prominent congressman and federal judge. Jackson, a lawyer, served as prosecuting attorney of Wood County, member of the House of Delegates, and mayor of Parkersburg. In the gubernatorial race of 1880 Jackson, a Copperhead during the Civil War, defeated Republican George C. Sturgiss of Monongalia County, who had steadfastly opposed reenfranchisement of ex-Confederates. His margin of victory, 60,074 votes to 44,838 for Sturgiss, might have been greater had not Napoleon B. French, the Greenback–Labor party candidate, won 13,027 votes, chiefly from Democratic voters in the Kanawha Valley.

Jackson considered advances in education, recodification of West Virginia laws, and tax reforms important accomplishments of his administration. On January 14, 1885, a few weeks before the end of his term, he declared, with more enthusiasm than accuracy, that the state then had "an efficient [school] system, comfortable school houses in each neighborhood, with an adequate supply of teachers and home talent educated in our normal schools."[7]

Tax reforms were also modest, although Jackson urged the legislature to undertake a comprehensive study of tax problems. Between 1870 and 1880 the state had experienced remarkable growth, with an influx of capital, construction of railroads, opening of mineral resources, expansion of agriculture, rise of the timber industry, and a forty percent increase in population. The net gain in real and personal property, however, rose only five percent. Moreover, thousands of acres of land were offered for sale in eastern cities at ten cents an acre, with deeds, plats, and abstracts made in New York City. Jackson urged the enactment of laws to prevent county clerks from certifying titles to forfeited and delinquent lands and to clarify titles to tracts held under grant from Virginia, but the legislature, bound by old patterns, failed to respond.

Other problems arose from tax exemptions. As a means of ameliorating the effects of the Panic of 1873, the legislature excluded certain farm properties from taxation. When prosperity returned, the beneficiaries objected to reimposition of the taxes. Perhaps more serious were exemptions granted to railroads. The Baltimore and Ohio long claimed exemption under its Maryland charter, but in 1869 Henry Gassaway Davis and other lobbyists arrived at a compromise

---

[7]Quoted in John G. Morgan, *West Virginia Governors, 1863-1980,* 2d ed. (Charleston: Charleston Newspapers, 1980), 40.

with the state. The Chesapeake and Ohio Railroad claimed similar advantages under West Virginia laws of 1866 and 1867. The constitution of 1872 provided for taxation of railroad property, and Grangers pressed for rate regulations, but the legislature failed to give real effectiveness to constitutional provisions. In 1882 the supreme court of appeals, in the case of *Miller* v. *Chesapeake and Ohio Railroad,* ruled that all property not specifically excluded by the constitution must be assessed for tax purposes. Despite an assessment order from Jackson, assessors continued to drag their feet. Through airing the tax problems, however, the governor drew attention to the need for reforms and accelerated demands for greater regulation of monopolies.

Governor Emanuel Willis Wilson. The most noted foe of corporate privilege during the Bourbon era was Emanuel Willis Wilson (August 11, 1844–May 28, 1905). Born at Harpers Ferry, Wilson practiced law in Jefferson County, represented the county in the House of Delegates for a single term, and in 1872 was elected to the state Senate. In a filibuster against a bill, reportedly backed by Camden and Davis, to transfer control of public improvements in the Kanawha River to a private corporation, he earned his nicknames "Windy" and "East Wind." In 1874 Wilson moved to Kanawha County, from which he was elected to the House of Delegates two years later. In 1880 he became speaker of the House.

Wilson's denunciation of monopolies was primarily responsible for his nomination for governor in 1884. He defeated his Republican opponent, Edwin Maxwell of Harrison County, by a vote of 71,438 to 66,149, even though large numbers of immigrants from neighboring northern states and Negroes from the South, who found employment in mining, lumbering, and manufacturing industries, had begun to swell Republican ranks.

The concerns and tone of the Wilson administration were entirely predictable. Wilson continued to agitate for revision of the tax laws to reduce burdensome inequities, an end to oppressive trusts and business combinations, and bans upon the distribution of railway passes to state officials and delegates to political conventions. He intensified his battle against trunk line railroads, which through discriminatory passenger and freight rates nullified West Virginia's favorable geographical position with respect to eastern markets and stifled her economic progress. Wilson urged the 1889 legislature to enact a more effective act to prevent corruption during elections, provide for the Australian ballot, regulate the adoption and sale of school textbooks, which had become the source of numerous abuses, and take steps to prevent the pollution of West Virginia streams. His farsighted proposals, however, were premature, and another generation or more passed before most of them were enacted into law.

Wilson's Agrarian ideals and crusading spirit undoubtedly heightened factionalism in the Democratic party and state government. In 1887 twelve members of the legislature refused to vote for the return of Camden to the United States Senate on the ground that he had used improper and corrupt political methods to obtain his position. The legislature ended its session without selecting a senator or passing a general appropriations bill. Wilson appointed Daniel Bedinger Lucas to the vacant Senate seat and called the legislature into special session to deal with fiscal problems. A recalcitrant legislature, however, took up the question of the Senate seat and, after seven ballots awarded it to Charles J. Faulkner, Jr.

Governor Aretus Brooks Fleming. By 1888 power in the Democratic party began to swing away from Populistic elements represented by Wilson and back toward the Regulars. The Democratic nominee for governor, Aretus Brooks Fleming (October 15, 1839–October 1, 1923), a Fairmont native, was the associate and legal adviser of Camden, who had extensive mining and timber operations in the Monongahela Valley. Camden became Fleming's political mentor and urged his nomination for governor.

Without doubt, the gubernatorial election of 1888 was the most exciting in West Virginia history. Official returns gave Nathan Goff, Jr., the Republican candidate, 78,904 votes and Fleming 78,798. Fleming challenged Goff's election on the ground that many of his votes had been obtained by fraud. He charged that several hundred Negroes, who had recently arrived or been brought to mining towns in Mercer and McDowell counties, had voted without the required period of residence and that many of them were, in fact, migratory or transitory workers with no fixed places of abode. Fleming asked the legislature to examine the returns of the two counties and determine their validity.

Inauguration day arrived without a legislative decision, and both Goff and Fleming took the oath of office. Robert S. Carr, the Greenback-Labor president of the Senate, claimed the governorship under a constitutional provision that the Senate president should fill the office in case of a vacancy. Governor Wilson refused to relinquish the office until the results of the election were determined. Carr and Goff instituted mandamus proceedings against Wilson in the supreme court, but the court upheld Wilson. On January 15, 1890, more than a year after the election, the legislature, in special session, voted along strict party lines, forty-three to forty, that Fleming was the victor.

The bitterness engendered by the contested election persisted through Fleming's abbreviated term. One of the few constructive acts during his administration was the adoption of the Australian ballot, repeatedly urged by his predecessor. A voters' registration amendment recommended by Fleming, however, had to await a constitutional alteration in 1902. Much of Fleming's energy was devoted to advertising the advantages of West Virginia resources for industry.

Governor William Alexander MacCorkle. The last of West Virginia's Bourbon governors, William Alexander MacCorkle (May 7, 1857–September 24, 1930), was born near Lexington, Virginia, and graduated from Washington and Lee University. He was elected prosecuting attorney of Kanawha County and in 1892 defeated Thomas E. Davis of Ritchie County for the governorship by a vote of 84,585 to 80,663.

MacCorkle's election marked the pinnacle of success of the Kanawha Ring, but it also proved a transition to rule by Republicans, who in 1894 gained control of the legislature. MacCorkle worked with Republicans to raise standards of state institutions and to reduce baneful political influences upon them. Throughout his term he engaged in vigorous advertising of the resources of West Virginia and efforts to correct misrepresentations regarding the state.

MacCorkle was well aware of the dangers of unbridled industrial exploitation of West Virginia. In his inaugural address he declared, "The state is rapidly passing under the control of large foreign and non-resident land owners" interested only in "the usufruct" of its land. He expressed fear that "In a few years, at the present rate of progress, we will occupy the same position of vassalage to the North and East that Ireland does to England."[8]

Bourbon Ideals and Realities. Whatever their background, Bourbon governors usually retained the political forms and traditions of the past while compromising with new political, social, and economic forces. They were natural concomitants of a transitional era. By the time they came to power wartime and Reconstruction politics had fallen into disarray. When they left office, industry had already begun to take precedence over agriculture. Sensing the importance of industry to their future, West Virginians were ready by 1896 to entrust the future of the state to the Republicans, whose principles and policies were already identified with the industrial and business growth of the nation.

[8]William A. MacCorkle, *Public Papers of Governor Wm. A. MacCorkle, of West Virginia* (Charleston: Moses W. Donnally, 1897), 9.

Agriculture and Rural Life

Agriculture in the New State. West Virginia entered the Union as a rural state, with about eighty percent of her people engaged in general agriculture, which included both horticulture and animal husbandry. Corn was by far the most important crop, but wheat, oats, hay, particularly timothy and bluegrass, and potatoes were also produced in abundance. Small acreages were put to rye, and buckwheat flourished in higher elevations in Greenbrier and Preston counties. Tobacco, which had thrived in southwestern sections before the war, had begun to decline because of labor shortages and soil depletion. Sorghum, or Chinese sugar cane, first introduced into the state in 1857, was grown in most sections and converted into molasses, which was consumed at home. Maple sugar and maple syrup continued as important farm-related products.

Wheat and livestock dominated the marketable farm products of West Virginia. Wheat production gave rise to numerous flour mills along the upper Ohio River and the South Branch of the Potomac. Those on the Ohio shipped flour to Pittsburgh, Cincinnati, Louisville, New Orleans, and other inland cities, and those in the Potomac section supplied Washington, Alexandria, and other eastern centers. Baltimore, Richmond, Pittsburgh, and Cincinnati provided important markets for West Virginia livestock. The western market for West Virginia whiskey declined as the temperance movement gained momentum in the country.

Insufficient attention to scientific practices hampered the development of commercial agriculture. In 1851 W.S. Miller of Garrardstown introduced a business aspect into fruit growing and eventually had thousands of apple and peach trees, as well as large numbers of cherry, pear, and plum trees, in the vicinity of Apple Pie Ridge. The Shenandoah Valley achieved a reputation for its apples before the Civil War, and the Northern Panhandle also produced fruit of good quality. Improved strains of livestock had been brought into the state early in the nineteenth century, and by the mid-1850s the Ludington, Renick, and Rogers families had introduced Shorthorn cattle into the Greenbrier region. Cattlemen along the South Branch of the Potomac had also gained a significant place in the improvement of livestock and often had close connections with breeders in Kentucky and southern Ohio.[1]

[1] Otis K. Rice, "Importations of Cattle into Kentucky, 1790-1860," *Register of the Kentucky Historical Society* 49(January 1951):36-38.

Late Nineteenth Century Growth. After devastating setbacks during the Civil War, West Virginia agriculture revived rapidly with the return of peace. Between 1869 and 1879 the number of farms increased from 40,000 to 63,000, and the number of acres of improved land rose by more than one million. Average farm size, however, decreased from 214 to 173 acres, indicating a trend toward more intensive forms of agriculture. With the lifting of the depression in the 1870s, the increased use of commercial fertilizers in the 1880s, the introduction of improved farm machinery, and greater attention to improvement of seed and breeds of livestock, agriculture began to surge forward.

One evidence of the new interest in agriculture lay in the cultivation of fruits. Berkeley, Hampshire, Jefferson, and Morgan counties took the lead in apples, while Hampshire, Mineral, and Berkeley led in peach crops. Older commercial orchards featured York, Imperial, Ben Davis, Grimes Golden, and Yellow Transparent apples. Newer ones leaned toward Stark's Delicious, Golden Delicious, and Stayman Winesap. The Grimes Golden was developed on the farm of Thomas Grimes in Brooke County, and the Golden Delicious apple originated on the farm of A.H. Mullins on Porters Creek in Clay County.

In 1869 Joseph H. Diss Debar, the state commissioner of immigration and author of a valuable handbook on West Virginia, described stock farming as "the pulsating artery of agricultural prosperity in West Virginia."[2] Each year thousands of cattle were driven from the South Branch, Greenbrier, and upper Monongahela valleys into the glades of the Alleghenies, where they grazed during spring and summer months. In the autumn they were sent on the hoof to eastern markets or returned by the graziers to their owners for wintering and further conditioning.

West Virginia cattlemen gave increased attention to improvement of breeds. During the 1870s Hereford cattle were introduced into Summers County and breeding stock was sold throughout the state. Shorthorns, imported into Jefferson, Mason, Greenbrier, and other counties, gained rapidly in popularity. The Aberdeen Angus, probably first bred in Mineral and Randolph counties, was accepted somewhat more slowly. By World War I Herefords accounted for nearly one-third of the blooded cattle in the state, Shorthorns for about one-sixth, and Aberdeen Angus for about one-tenth.

The beef and dairy industries were never sharply differentiated in West Virginia. The dairy business centered in the Northern Panhandle, in Jefferson and Berkeley counties, and around the larger cities. Jersey and Holstein were favored dairy cattle, but Guernsey, Brown Swiss, Devon, Red Polled, and Ayrshire were also popular.

Mechanization of farm work increased agricultural productivity in West Virginia, but rugged terrain and the smallness of mountain farms prevented the use of machinery on a scale comparable with that of midwestern states. Axes, hoes, rakes, pitchforks, plows, harrows, horse mills, and tub mills common in

[2]J[oseph] H. Diss Debar, *The West Virginia Hand Book and Immigrant's Guide* (Parkersburg: Gibbens Brothers, 1870), 79.

pre–Civil War times remained on many farms. After the war the ingenious "bull tongue plow," capable of throwing soil into rows where corn had been dropped by hand, enabled one man and a horse to do the work of three men covering the corn with hoes. The grain cradle generally replaced the sickle and about 1880 the steam thresher and horse-powered reaper became common.

Some of the most significant changes in West Virginia agriculture after the Civil War centered in efforts to retain or restore soil fertility. Very little commercial fertilizer was used before 1880, but its application increased by about three hundred percent by 1909 and by nine hundred percent by 1919.

The Quality of Rural Life. Farm life in the nineteenth century was marked by endless toil and times of intense loneliness. Machinery relieved families of some of the drudgery, but many worked from sunrise to sunset. Large families were the rule, and each member had responsibilities. The frontier habit of community cooperation in some arduous work still prevailed and relieved the monotony of the daily routine.

For all its hardships, farm life had its compensations. Close bonds of affection and concern united families. Isolation and loneliness fostered hospitality and friendliness. Church meetings and social gatherings brought neighbors together in wholesome activities and gave the people a sense of community. Concerns for land, crops, and livestock fostered an appreciation for environmental matters. Moreover, closeness to land and family inspired a sense of durability and continuity often lacking among those dependent upon industry and business.

Because of their long reliance upon agriculture, values regarded as essentially rural became deeply ingrained in the character of the people of West Virginia. They sprang in part from the emphasis of country churches upon righteous living, the role of the common school in undergirding morality and character, and the necessity of maintaining standing with lifelong neighbors by conforming to prevailing customs and mores.

Industrial expansion in the late nineteenth and early twentieth centuries gradually undermined many agrarian values and ways of life. Yet in small industrial communities the old ways often persisted for several generations and blended with those spawned by the new society. Even yet, despite strong urban and technological influences, they remain in subtle forms in many parts of the state.

The Grange. West Virginia farmers eagerly embraced the Patrons of Husbandry, or Grange, and its principles. The organization was founded by Oliver Hudson Kelley, a Minnesota farmer and Indian trader who worked as a clerk in the Post Office Department in Washington, D.C. Kelley hoped to relieve the tedium of farm life and to promote education and self-improvement of rural Americans, but the Grange met more urgent needs, particularly those arising from lingering effects of the Panic of 1873, soaring tariffs, and monopolistic practices by American railroads and other businesses. The first lodge in West Virginia was formed in 1872 at Summit Point, Jefferson County, and by 1876 the number had grown to 378, with 10,752 members, or about eleven percent of the voting population of the state. The Grange was strongest in northcentral counties, particularly Harrison, Lewis, Barbour, Doddridge, Marion, and Upshur, and weakest in the rugged, undeveloped region south of the Kanawha River.

Among the goals of the West Virginia Grange were the establishment of a state board of agriculture and the creation of a college of agriculture under provisions of the Morrill Act of 1862. Dissatisfied with courses in agriculture at West Virginia University, the Grange lent its support to the Jefferson County Agricultural College, which the legislature incorporated in 1875, with an office at Leetown. In 1877 Daniel Bedinger Lucas, one of its staunchest advocates, dealt the proposed college a severe blow when he became a member of the Board of Regents of West Virginia University and his brother-in-law, St. George Tucker Brooke, was named to a new chair of law and equity at the university.

As in the western states, the West Virginia Grange battled for legislative reforms of benefit to farmers. It secured laws forcing the Baltimore and Ohio Railroad to abandon some of its rate discriminations and requiring that railroad and the Chesapeake and Ohio to pay taxes on their West Virginia properties.

The West Virginia Grange achieved some of its most notable successes under the leadership of Thomas Clark Atkeson, the owner of a prosperous farm near Buffalo, in the lower Kanawha Valley. Atkeson served as master of the West Virginia Grange from 1897 to 1920, dean of the College of Agriculture at West Virginia University from 1897 to 1910, and member of the State Board of Agriculture. By endorsing candidates for political office sympathetic to its objectives and effective lobbying in the legislature, the Grange, under Atkeson, aided in the establishment of the Public Service Commission and a more equitable distribution of taxes in the state. It also advanced the institution of rural free delivery service by the United States Post Office Department.

The West Virginia Farmers' Alliance. From the early 1880s until about 1897, when it was revitalized by Atkeson, the West Virginia Grange was in decline. The causes lay in falling farm prices, exploitation of the state's resources by monopolies, continued discrimination against short hauls by the railroads, scarcity of money, an increase in farm tenancy, and other concerns that undermined faith in the organization. Many farmers turned to the Farmers' Alliance, which had already made headway in western and southern states. At its height, from 1889 to 1892, the Alliance had organizations in forty-one West Virginia counties and a membership of at least ten thousand in the state.

Many of the goals of the West Virginia Alliance were attainable only through federal action and hinged upon the success of the Northern and Southern alliances. Some of these goals were identical to those of the Grange, but the Alliance also had other objectives, including a subtreasury plan by which farmers could deposit nonperishable crops in government warehouses and borrow money against them and expansion of the money supply through the free and unlimited coinage of silver.

Like the Grange, the West Virginia Alliance turned to political action. It worked primarily through the Democratic party, which had a strong agrarian element. Some members favored the Populist party, which never won key elections in the state but sometimes held a balance of power between the major parties. The Alliance had its greatest opportunity in 1896, when the Democrats adopted most of the Populist platform and Populists supported William Jennings Bryan, the Democratic nominee, for president of the United States. Agrarian and industrial workers, however, were divided on many issues, and Republican William McKinley carried West Virginia. Both the Alliance and the Populist party soon disintegrated in the state.

An Era of Transition. The year 1896 marked something of a turning point in West Virginia agriculture. The raising of crops and livestock on family-owned farms, once the backbone of the West Virginia economy, fast gave way in the 1880s and 1890s to extractive industries and manufacturing. Ralroads opened new coal fields, oil and gas industries expanded, and timber production moved toward its peak years. Capitalists, urban workers, and labor unions gained dominance in political and economic affairs, and farmers, already becoming a minority, in 1896 lost their last major opportunity to wield genuine control over the destiny of the state and the nation.

In spite of the changes, agriculture in West Virginia appeared healthy as late as 1900, with 151,000 of the 326,000 gainfully employed persons in the state. There yet remained 93,000 farms, seventy-eight percent of them owned by their operators. The value of industrial products, however, excceeded by $30 million that of farm products, a clear indication of future trends. As William D. Barns has observed, "West Virginia gradually experienced a drastic status revolution, in which the agriculturist became subordinated to the capitalist and . . . rural ethics were modified by urban influences."[3]

One of the most striking changes lay in the increasing loss of self-sufficiency of West Virginia farmers. More and more farmers and their hired hands turned to the mines and factories for the major part of their income and kept their farms as residences and as sources of supplemental earnings. As the coal, oil, and gas industries penetrated rural areas, many farmers leased or sold part of their lands or mineral rights and resorted to more intensive and scientific agriculture on their dwindling acreages. In doing so they contributed to destruction of the land, pollution of streams, and other environmental problems that would plague the state by the mid-twentieth century.

Despite the declining importance of agriculture, West Virginia farmers, like those nationally, generally remained prosperous from 1897 to 1914. Farm income compared so favorably with that of industrial workers between 1909 and 1914 that the federal government later used the period as a base for parity prices for several important agricultural commodities.

Twentieth Century Developments. Shortly before World War I, West Virginia farmers began to take a new interest in agricultural organizations. The

[3]William D. Barns, *The West Virginia State Grange: The First Century, 1873-1973* (Morgantown: Morgantown Printing and Binding Company, 1973), 17.

West Virginia Farm Bureau, founded in 1918, quickly replaced the Grange as the leading agricultural body in the state. Among its accomplishments were sponsorship of the Tax Limitation Amendment of 1932, which halted an appalling loss of property by farmers delinquent in taxes as a result of the Great Depression. In 1907 the 4-H Club movement began in Monroe County, and in later years its stress upon farm-related projects and summer camping made it one of the most popular youth organizations in the state. By the 1950s thousands of youths were enrolled in the Future Farmers of America, Future Homemakers of America, and corresponding Negro youth organizations.

A major achievement of farm organizations was the creation in 1891 of a bipartisan State Board of Agriculture. The new board pursued policies in harmony with those of the Grange and cooperated with the West Virginia Agricultural Experiment Station and the West Virginia University College of Agriculture in conducting farmers' institutes. It also published numerous farm bulletins. In 1911, upon recommendation of Atkeson, the Grange, and other organizations, the legislature replaced the board with a commissioner of agriculture elected by the people.

Later developments included the growth of the West Virginia University College of Agriculture, with a wide range of programs in agricultural economics, animal husbandry, plant industry, and teacher training programs in vocational agriculture and home economics. Federal assistance through the Smith-Lever Act and other legislation of later years vastly extended the functions and services offered by the college and the Agricultural Extension Service.

Agriculture steadily declined in relative importance in the economy of West Virginia after the Great Depression. Under revised definitions of farms in 1978, the acreage of the state classified as farmland dropped from 4.6 to 4.2 million. During the 1970s West Virginia generally ranked low among the states in the value of her grain crops, but she held relatively high positions in apples, peaches, and tobacco. Livestock maintained its preeminent place in her agriculture, with cattle and calves valued at about three times that of hogs and pigs. Chickens (particularly commercial broilers) and turkeys made up about thirty percent of its total value. In addition, milk and milk products and eggs ranked high among farm products of the state.

The Mountaineer. Very different from the fruit grower of the Shenandoah Valley, the cattleman of the South Branch Valley or the Greenbrier plateau, or the diversified farmer of the river valleys was the mountaineer, who combined farming with timbering, hunting, and other forest-related occupations. Local color writers drew attention to his unique qualities as early as the 1870s and 1880s in leading magazines of the country. Moreover, West Virginia writers such as Margaret Prescott Montague penetrated the mind of the mountaineer, as did John Fox, Jr., and James Lane Allen, whose accounts of the Kentucky mountain folk were equally valid for parts of West Virginia.

In the mid-1880s northern Protestant churches also found the Appalachian region a fertile field for activity. Originally interested in Negro freedmen after the Civil War, they could not ignore the Appalachian whites, in whose lives they saw little except poverty, illiteracy, and degradation. Their endeavors and the writings of local colorists conveyed the impression to many Americans that the mountain region was, in the words of Will Wallace Harney, "a strange land" with "a peculiar people" in need of attention.[4]

Except for John C. Campbell, author of *The Southern Highlander and His Homeland,* who recognized its diversity, most writers after 1900 viewed Appalachia as a coherent region with a homogeneous people, who, through isolation from the mainstream of American development, had degenerated from the hardy, independent pioneer stock. William Goodell Frost, president of Berea College, contended that the region had its own peculiar population, often referred to as "our contemporary ancestors." Ellen Churchill Semple, in anthropogeographic studies, stressed the adaptiveness of mountain culture and social structure and their interaction with environmental forces.

Regardless of their perceptions of Appalachia, observers were struck by the persistence of traits and characteristics from earlier times. Speech patterns from sixteenth and seventeenth century England and folk music, which preserved ballads and tunes hundreds of years old, attracted wide interest. Sir Cecil Sharp, the noted British authority, established the folk character of Appalachian culture in *English Folk Songs from the Southern Appalachians,* published in 1917.

The poverty and unemployment that attended mechanization of coal mines and ghost towns left in the wake of widespread emigration from mining towns in the 1950s accentuated the special problems of Appalachia. John F. Kennedy made the most of them in the West Virginia primary election of 1960, and the federal government infused vast amounts of money into the region during the following decades. Sociologists, folklorists, self-styled folk singers, and other individuals and organizations discovered the region anew, and many sought and received federal funds for projects and studies relating to it. Unfortunately many of the grantees proved more adept at obtaining federal money than in ameliorating the problems of Appalachia.

The Hatfield-McCoy Feud. A rash of family and political feuds in southern Appalachia in the late nineteenth century produced a wave of national revulsion, even in an era marked by unusual violence. The most famous of the vendettas was between the Hatfields and the McCoys. Both families were pioneers in the isolated Tug Fork, and each clan had numerous members living on both sides of the river in West Virginia and Kentucky. Prolific and intermarried with most other families of the area as well as with each other, the Hatfields and McCoys belonged to the yeoman class, owning their own lands and living by farming, hunting, rafting timber to downriver markets, and sometimes making moonshine whiskey.

[4]A detailed account of the "discoveries" of Appalachia by outsiders is Henry D. Shapiro, *Appalachia on Our Mind: The Southern Mountains and Mountaineers in the American Consciousness, 1870-1920* (Chapel Hill: University of North Carolina Press, 1978), particularly 1-84, 113-43.

As in some other parts of the Appalachian Highlands, social institutions such as schools and churches were weak and law enforcement was often capricious in the Tug Valley. Close-knit and clannish families such as the Hatfields and McCoys were sensitive to affronts and quick to seek revenge. They had little patience with societal restraints or the slow processes of legal redress. This imbalance of social influences produced a climate conducive to conflict, but it cannot be said to have caused the feud.

The event that touched off the feud, which disrupted the peace of the Tug Valley for two decades, cannot be identified precisely. Some writers have attributed it to the alleged theft by Floyd Hatfield of a razorback hog belonging to Randolph McCoy. Others have stressed the romance between Rose Anna McCoy, the daughter of Randolph, and Johnson, or Johnse, Hatfield, the son of Anderson Hatfield, better known as "Devil Anse." Pike County court records, however, suggest that a residue of hard feelings had existed since the Civil War, when members of both clans engaged in guerrilla and home guard activities. Assertions that the Hatfields and McCoys fought on opposite sides in the war have no foundation, since both were originally Confederate in sympathy.[5]

Smoldering hostilities, whatever their source, might have burned themselves out had not events in the Kentucky elections of 1882 caused them to take new fire. Elections were social as well as political occasions, and West Virginia Hatfields regularly attended those held on Blackberry Creek in Pike County, Kentucky. In 1882 three sons of Randolph McCoy killed Ellison Hatfield, a brother of Devil Anse, after an argument, and the Hatfields gained their revenge by killing the three McCoys. Pike County authorities issued warrants for the arrest of twenty persons indicted for the murders. The Hatfields continued to visit Pikeville, but always in large bands with guns visible, and the authorities made no arrests.

In 1888, after six years marked by intermittent violence, Perry Cline, a Pikeville lawyer with McCoy connections, enlisted the aid of Governor Simon Bolivar Buckner of Kentucky, whom he had supported in the preceding election. Buckner sought to extradite the twenty persons indicted for the McCoy murders, but West Virginia Governor E. Willis Wilson, convinced that Cline was engaged in duplicity and that the Hatfields would not receive an impartial trial, refused Buckner's request. When Pike County authorities, under Frank Phillips, made illegal forays into West Virginia and seized several of the men charged, Wilson instituted habeas corpus proceedings in the federal courts. Ultimately the Supreme Court held that there was no positive federal law regarding actions by the Pike County officials and no way in which West Virginians taken by them could be returned.

Fearing the outcome of the impending trials in Pike County, several Hatfield partisans, led by Jim Vance, an uncle of Devil Anse, attempted to

---

[5]For a detailed examination of the origins of the feud, see Otis K. Rice, *The Hatfields and the McCoys* (Lexington: University Press of Kentucky, 1978), 1-29.

remove witnesses who might testify against them. On New Year's night of 1888 they burned the house of Randolph McCoy on Blackberry Creek, killed his daughter Alifair and son Calvin, and left his wife Sarah in what appeared to be a dying condition. The trials proceeded, however, with new charges against many Hatfields. One defendant, Ellison Mounts, was sentenced to death by hanging, and several others received prison sentences.

The Pike County trial climaxed the long and bloody vendetta. By then most Hatfields and McCoys were weary of fighting and ready to respond to new opportunities arising from the entry of railroads and industry into the Tug Valley. Even Devil Anse, who appears to have been more humane than many writers have pictured him, confessed that the war spirit in him had abated. He moved from the Tug Valley to Island Creek near Logan, where in 1911 he became a member of the Baptist Church. By the time of his death in 1921 and that of his old adversary, Randolph McCoy, seven years earlier, the feud had become for most Hatfields and McCoys but a memory of an unhappy and best forgotten era. Allegations that as many as a hundred or more persons were killed were highly exaggerated. In fact, no more than a dozen deaths can be positively associated with the vendetta.

The end of the Hatfield-McCoy feud coincided with the waning of rural life in West Virginia. It was a way of life that encompassed great diversity, ranging from the peaceful, almost idyllic modes of the state's eastern agricultural areas to the turbulence that sometimes marked relationships in interior and southern sections of the state. It provided many of the images that still, in the minds of many outsiders, characterize much of West Virginia.

The Industrial Age

Post–Civil War Economic Life. West Virginia entered the Union with some ninety percent of its people engaged in agriculture and an economy yet in the domestic stage. Most industrial and commercial establishments, including gristmills, sawmills, carding factories, woolen mills, tanneries, blacksmith shops, and even general stores were farm related. This agrarian economy prevailed in many parts of the state well into the twentieth century. West Virginians, however, had for decades pressed for solutions to problems of capital, labor, and transportation that would unlock their vast mineral and timber resources.

River Transportation. Critical to the growth of industry in West Virginia were adequate transportation facilities, including river improvements. Of major importance were federal inland navigation projects on the Ohio, Monongahela, Kanawha, Little Kanawha, and Big Sandy rivers in the late nineteenth and early twentieth centuries. Engineering difficulties and opposition from coal shippers and large coal-tow operators delayed improvements on the Ohio, in which the only lock and dam in 1900 was at Davis Island, five miles below Pittsburgh. In contrast, the Monongahela had fifteen locks and dams that gave it a navigable depth of nine feet from Pittsburgh to Morgantown and of seven feet from Morgantown to Fairmont. The Kanawha by 1898 had ten locks and dams, built under the direction of Addison M. Scott, that provided a six-foot depth to Deepwater, above Montgomery and some ninety miles from its mouth.

Improvements in the Big Sandy and Little Kanawha were less satisfactory. Those on the Big Sandy, begun in 1883, envisioned three locks and dams on the main stream and one each on its Levisa and Tug forks to maintain six feet of water. Because of competition from railroads, including the Norfolk and Western and the Chesapeake and Ohio, the original plans were abandoned, and in 1914 work on the river ceased. The Little Kanawha, primarily a carrier of petroleum and forest products, had four locks and dams built by the Kanawha Navigation Company by 1874 and a fifth erected by the federal government in 1891. The structures afforded four feet of water from Parkersburg to Creston, forty-eight miles upstream.

Even with improvements, the rivers could not handle the mounting volume of coal traffic in West Virginia. As early as 1901 coal tows on the Kanawha were "double-locked," or broken in two for passage through lock chambers, and by 1926 "triple-locking" was common. By 1912 railroads had captured most of the industrial transport business. Only 688,939 tons of coal moved down the Kanawha, and none was shipped from West Virginia mines via the Monongahela. When railroads proved inadequate to the nation's needs in World War I, rivers again assumed importance. Every available boat and barge was pressed into service, and such firms as the Charles Ward Engineering Company of Charleston and the Marietta Manufacturing Company of Point Pleasant were kept busy producing needed rivercraft.

Wartime experiences revived interest in a network of deep waterways from the Gulf of Mexico to the Great Lakes. The completion in 1929 of a new series of locks and dams in the Ohio, twenty-eight of them within the borders of West Virginia, gave the Ohio a nine-foot slackwater navigation for its entire 981 miles. These improvements stimulated activities on West Virginia rivers. Beginning in the mid-1920s the Monongahela carried the largest volume of freight of any river in the United States and was second only to the Rhine among rivers of the world. Its traffic, mostly in coal, exceeded that of the Panama Canal.

Until 1926 coal exports down the Kanawha were hampered by unsatisfactory facilities on the Ohio, but after that time barges from the Kanawha could not take full advantage of the nine-foot depth of the Ohio. With the completion in 1939 of new dams, each with two locks, at Winfield, Marmet, and London, the Kanawha had a nine-foot navigation to Deepwater. The new structures encouraged other industries, including chemical manufacturing, and started an upward spiral of traffic that made the Gallipolis locks and dams, the largest in the world when they were completed in 1938, obsolete within two decades.

With the inland river system strained by carrying three to four times the tonnage for which it had been designed and diesel-powered boats of all-steel construction replacing stern wheelers of the passenger-packet type, the United States Army Corps of Engineers began about 1950 to plan a new series of fifteen high-lift dams in the Ohio. The new structures increased the lift from 9.5 to 23 feet and extended lock chambers from 600 to 1,200 feet in length. Largely complete by 1979, they included locks and dams at New Cumberland, Pike Island, Hannibal, Willow Island, Belleville, and Racine and improvement of the Gallipolis locks and dam, all on the West Virginia segment of the Ohio River.[1]

Railroad Transportation. Railroads had an even greater impact than river improvements upon the economic development of West Virginia. Their importance had been demonstrated before the Civil War by the Baltimore and Ohio, which promoted the growth of such towns as Pruntytown, Grafton, Fairmont, Mannington, Cameron, and Wheeling, and by the Northwestern Virginia, which connected Grafton and Parkersburg.

[1]By far the best account of West Virginia river improvements is Leland R. Johnson, *Men, Mountains, and Rivers: An Illustrated History of the Huntington District, U.S. Army Corps of Engineers, 1754-1974* (Washington, D.C.: U.S. Government Printing Office, 1977), particularly 81-96, 102-19.

The Chesapeake and Ohio was the first great railroad in southern West Virginia. Designed to link the Atlantic with the Midwest farmland via the New, Kanawha, and Teays valleys, it grew out of two older lines, the Virginia Central, complete from Chesapeake Bay to Covington in 1867, and the languishing Covington and Ohio. In November 1869 Collis P. Huntington, a western railroad magnate, revitalized the proposed line, and on January 2, 1873, its first train sped west via Charleston to Huntington. The railroad led to mine openings on the New River at Quinnimont, Stone Cliff, Fire Creek, Sewell, Nuttallburg, and Hawks Nest. In 1879 New River and upper Kanawha mines shipped 365,523 tons of coal and 19,748 tons of coke eastward by rail.

After the Panic of 1873 other railroad entrepreneurs turned to West Virginia coalfields and timberlands. In 1881 Frederick J. Kimball of Germantown, Pennsylvania, a businessman of unusual versatility and judgment of character, joined with Philadelphia capitalists to purchase the Atlantic, Mississippi and Ohio Railroad, a floundering combination of three old Virginia lines. Kimball developed his holdings into the Norfolk and Western railway to open the Pocahontas coalfield and to serve as the nucleus of a great coal-carrying transportation system. He opened the New River branch of the railroad in 1881–1882, and the first Pocahontas coal reached Norfolk in March 1883. Extensions were completed to Flat Top Mountain in 1886, to Kenova in 1892, and later to Columbus and Cincinnati.

The Norfolk and Western transformed much of southern West Virginia into wealthy and populous centers. Bluefield, the "gateway to the Pocahontas coal field," was only a flag station on the farm of John B. Higginbotham in 1888. In December 1889 it was incorporated as a town with a population of 600, which increased to 4,644 by 1900 and to 11,188 by 1910. Equally meteoric was the rise of Welch. Laid out on "wild lands" purchased for forty dollars in 1885, it was voted the seat of McDowell County in 1891. Williamson, the site of a cornfield in 1891, became an incorporated town the next year and a few years later one of the largest coal shipping centers in the state. Similar growth occurred at Bramwell, Matoaka, Maybeury, Keystone, Gary, Iaeger, and Matewan.

Two railroads that tapped West Virginia coal and timber, the Western Maryland and the Coal and Coke, sprang from the dreams of Henry Gassaway Davis. When he conceived the idea of the Western Maryland, Davis was working as a station agent for the Baltimore and Ohio at Piedmont, West Virginia, and living in a boxcar. Begun as the West Virginia Central and Pittsburgh Railway, the line was completed to Gormania in 1883, to Elkins in 1888, and later to Beverly and Belington. In 1905, as part of the Western Maryland system, it was extended to Durbin to join the Chesapeake and Ohio and to Webster Springs. Other coal and lumber towns on its route included Bayard, Thomas, Davis, and Parsons.

With the Charleston, Clendenin, and Sutton Railway as its nucleus, the Coal and Coke Railroad was completed by Davis and Stephen B. Elkins in 1906. It provided a much-needed north–south route through the heart of the state and connected with the Western Maryland at Elkins and with the Kanawha and Michigan at Charleston. The 175-mile line, later part of the Baltimore and Ohio system, assured central West Virginia coal an outlet on the Great Lakes and an alternate route to Atlantic ports.

Unique among West Virginia railroads was the Virginian, completed in 1909 by Henry H. Rogers, who with a Standard Oil fortune built the $40 million line on his own resources. Instead of following the meanderings of mountain valleys, the Virginian made maximum use of gravity and the downward slope of the terrain from the coalfields to the Atlantic coast by bridging rivers and tunneling through mountains. As a coal carrier from the upper Guyandotte area to Norfolk via Roanoke, it became a formidable competitor of both the Chesapeake and Ohio and the Norfolk and Western. The Virginian also extended its lines to Deepwater, where they connected with the Kanawha and Michigan, and reached the New River and Winding Gulf coalfields. It contributed to the growth of Mullens and Princeton and other towns such as Pax, Glen Jean, and Page. Later, with electrification of the line between Mullens and Roanoke, Virginian tracks carried some of the largest locomotives and heaviest freight trains in the world.

Other rail lines stimulated the economic growth of West Virginia. In 1893 the Kanawha and Michigan connected Corning, Ohio, and the Great Lakes with Gauley Bridge via Point Pleasant and Charleston. It gave new impetus to mining on the north side of the Kanawha. Later, as the New York Central, it was built to Nallen and Enon. The West Virginia and Pittsburgh Railroad, organized in 1890 by Johnson N. Camden, tied the Baltimore and Ohio, which leased it for ninety-nine years, to the Chesapeake and Ohio by way of Weston, Clarksburg, Buckhannon, Sutton, and Richwood. The Baltimore and Ohio also acquired another Camden line, the Monongahela Railroad, built in 1889–1890 between Clarksburg and Morgantown to develop intervening coalfields.

The Coal Industry. Minable seams of bituminous coal lie beneath seventeen thousand square miles, or more than two-thirds, of West Virginia. Major coalfields include the Kanawha, New River, Winding Gulf, Flat Top–Pocahontas, Logan, Williamson, Fairmont, Elkins, Northern Panhandle, and Greenbrier. Most of those worked in southern West Virginia are in the Pottsville and Allegheny-Kanawha series, while those of the central and northern sections lie in the Allegheny-Kanawha, Monongahela, and Conemaugh series. Recoverable coal reserves were estimated at 55,124,762,308 tons in 1990.

At the end of the Civil War West Virginia mining was in its infancy. In 1870 there were only eighty-five small operations, some described as "quarrying, oil-boring, and peat-cutting."[2] Of their 1,527 laborers, 646, including 69 boys, worked underground. With a capital investment of some $2.5 million, they

---

[2]U.S. Department of Commerce and Labor, *Mines and Quarries* (Washington, D.C.: Government Printing Office, 1902), 338.

produced about 608,000 tons of coal valued at about $1 million. In 1880 production had reached only 1,568,000 tons, valued at approximately $2 million.

Transportation improvements in the 1880s had a dramatic impact in the New and Kanawha valleys, where the Chesapeake and Ohio Railroad and the newly locked and dammed Kanawha River opened vast coal resources. With the railroad and its rich Fire Creek and Sewell seams in the heart of the New River field, Fayette in 1888 became the first West Virginia county to mine more than one million tons of coal annually. It led all counties until 1902 and held second place until World War I. In 1903 fifty-six mines operated along the railroad west of Prince, and Fayette and Kanawha counties produced about thirty percent of the coal mined in the state. The Kanawha and Michigan line further encouraged mining in the Kanawha field. In 1888 Kanawha County, with a production of 982,310 tons, was second only to Fayette. In 1890 it, too, passed the million-ton mark. From 1904 to 1912 Kanawha generally ranked third among the counties in coal mined.

Even more dramatic growth occured in the Flat Top–Pocahontas coalfield. Jed Hotchkiss, publisher of the influential trade journal *The Virginias,* and some other mining engineers and geologists considered it one of the finest coalfields in the world. Following its penetration by the Norfolk and Western Railway, capital, chiefly from Pennsylvania, began to pour in. From three mines with an output of 32,341 tons in April 1885, coal production soared to 1,210,723 tons from thirty-three mines in Mercer and McDowell counties in 1891. In 1903 McDowell, with 5,249,913 tons, became the leading coal-mining county in West Virginia. In 1912 tonnage from its 103 mines reached 13,768,977.

Development of the Fairmont field, one of the oldest mining areas of the state, was slow until the arrival of railroads in the 1890s. Capital then began to flow in from New York, Philadelphia, Baltimore, Cleveland, and other centers. Between 1890 and 1900 coal production in Marion County, the leader in the field, rose from 406,960 to 2,925,907 tons and that in Harrison County from 128,964 to 1,088,175 tons. The two counties, in which the famed Pittsburgh seam predominated, usually held fourth and fifth places, respectively, in the state until World War I.

Other coalfields, particularly the Winding Gulf, Logan, and Williamson fields, also expanded rapidly, and by 1914 coal output in the state reached 65,783,088 tons. McDowell, Fayette, Marion, Logan, Kanawha, Harrison, and Raleigh, in that order, each produced more than five million tons, and Mercer, Mingo, Preston, Tucker, Barbour, and Taylor each mined more than one million tons.

About ten to fifteen percent of the coal mined in West Virginia was converted into coke at thousands of beehive ovens. Coke production increased from 190,899 tons in 1883 to 4,217,831 tons in 1910. Pocahontas, or Smokeless, and New River coals had excellent coking qualities, but, except for some

Preston County coals, those of the Fairmont field found little favor. McDowell County usually accounted for about one-half of the coke made in the state. By about 1910 many companies began to abandon wasteful beehive ovens and to ship coal eastward to by-product ovens, where it was mixed with coal of higher volatility to produce fuel gases, coal tar, ammonia, and other products.

With the exception of a brief decline during the economic readjustments following World War I, coal production in West Virginia mounted steadily until the Great Depression, rising from 69,783,088 tons in 1914 to 139,297,146 tons in 1929. Output in the 1930s remained substantially below that of the 1920s. World War II stimulated a strong resurgence, but the peak year was 1947, when 173,653,816 tons was mined. Thereafter, tonnage fluctuated widely, but McDowell County remained the leader, with Monongalia, Boone, Wyoming, Kanawha, and Logan following.

Mining and the Socioeconomic Structure. Mining profoundly changed the social and economic structure of most coal areas of West Virginia. It superimposed upon a rural, agrarian society industrial establishments with thousands of landless wage earners, a managerial class, and a new elite of wealthy and politically influential coal barons. The new mining towns introduced a paternalism that had no counterpart in the yeoman farmer spirit that had prevailed in the state. Although company towns have been described as drab and enervating places "imposed on helpless miners by rapacious operators,"[3] most mine owners built them because workers had to live near minable seams of coal, which were often found in isolated areas. Many, to be sure, consisted of dwellings without variety of design except for those of managerial personnel, doctors, and a few other officials.

The company store, often the only retail outlet within reach of mining families, stocked food, clothing, household furnishings, mine supplies, and most other necessities. Companies usually made use of scrip, a form of currency negotiable only at their stores. Many exerted pressure upon employees to trade at their stores, frequently charging excessive prices, but some endeavored to promote trade by providing good merchandise at more competitive prices.

Life in many mining towns bore a resemblance to that in notorious gold and silver towns of the West, where law enforcement was weak and saloons were plentiful. Centers such as Thurmond and Keystone gained unenviable reputations as veritable dens of iniquity. Some operators built saloons and cared little about the behavior of their employees as long as it did not affect coal production. Justus Collins, a pioneer in the New River and Winding Gulf fields, disclaimed any intention of "running a Christian Endeavor Camp Meeting or a Sunday School."[4]

[3]W.P. Tams, Jr., *The Smokeless Coal Fields of West Virginia: A Brief History* (Morgantown: West Virginia University Library, 1963), 51.

[4]Quoted in John Alexander Williams, *West Virginia: A Bicentennial History* (New York and Nashville: W.W. Norton & Company, Inc., and American Association for State and Local History, 1976), 140.

Enlightened operators sought to provide an environment conducive to the sobriety and the well-being of miners and their families. Motivated more by a belief that such policies were good business than by elaborate social theories, they contributed to schools and churches, built theaters, often called "opera houses," clubhouses, and YMCAs, and subsidized athletic teams and community bands. Several of the larger companies, particularly between 1910 and the Great Depression, established model towns in which they and their employees took great pride. Conspicuous among them were Holden, Gary, and Tams.

West Virginia coal mines attracted a variety of races and nationalities. Of 69,611 persons employed in the mines in 1912, only 31,696 were native white Americans. Native miners also included 13,403 Negroes, mostly migrants from the South after the Civil War. In 1912 McDowell County mines employed 5,394, or over 40 percent, of the black miners of the state, and Fayette and Mercer 3,091 and 1,214, or 23 and 9 percent, respectively.

Slightly over 35 percent of West Virginia miners in 1912 were foreign born. They were part of the New Immigration to the United States that began in the 1880s and drew millions of distressed people from southern and eastern Europe in the ensuing decades. Immigrant miners in the state in 1912 included 9,701 Italians, 4,492 Hungarians, 2,293 Poles, 2,120 Slavs, 1,091 Austrians, 863 Russians, and 3,502 laborers representing at least twenty other nationalities. A few counties had disproportionate numbers of certain nationalities. McDowell, for instance, had 1,886 Italians, Fayette 1,390, Harrison 1,244, and Marion 1,136. The four counties accounted for over 58 percent of all Italian miners in the state. Similarly, over 43 percent of the Austrians were in Marion and Harrison counties, and nearly 47 percent of the Hungarians were in McDowell, with another 24 percent in Logan, Fayette, Marion, and Harrison counties.

Some coal companies actively recruited foreign laborers. In 1907 the legislature created a new immigration bureau to replace an earlier one, under Joseph H. Diss Debar, which had become defunct. John H. Nugent, the commissioner, was in reality little more than an agent of the coal companies. From 1907 to 1913 the New River Company and the Consolidation Coal Company paid his salary and expenses. His connection with the coal companies does much to explain why 475 of 1,390 Italian miners in Fayette County in 1912 were employed by the Boomer Coal and Coke Company and 825 of 1,126 Italians in Marion County and 411 of 1,244 in Harrison County worked at operations of the Consolidation Coal Company.

Foreign-born miners, like Negroes, often lived in restricted sections of mining communities, usually those with the least desirable housing. Not uncommonly, an immigrant miner and his family devoted one room of a four-room house to kitchen purposes, another to a family bedroom, and the other two to recently arrived workers from their native land, for whom they provided board and lodging. In time the newcomers brought their own families or married and began homes of their own. The process of Americanization and assimilation normally took about three generations. During that time immigrant families abandoned much of their Old World culture, including their language, but most retained their religious ties, usually with the Catholic Church.

The Era of Corporate Consolidation. Until about the beginning of the twentieth century relatively little capital was needed to open a coal mine. Following the penetration of the coal regions by railroads, scores of small companies began operation, often with no more than twenty or thirty thousand dollars, subscribed by a few men and borrowed from local banks with company stock as collateral. Many of these entrepreneurs were natives of Wales, England, and Scotland who had gained experience in Pennsylvania mines.

Typical of the operators who began business "on a shoestring" was Joseph L. Beury, the pioneer in the New River field. Of Welsh background, Beury left a position as mine superintendent in Pennsylvania during the Molly Maguire disturbances. With little more than a mule and a borrowed harness, he opened the Fire Creek seam at Quinnimont in 1873, when he shipped the first New River coal eastward by way of the Chesapeake and Ohio Railroad. With Jenkin Jones and others he developed the Fire Creek mines and in 1884 was among the organizers of the first coal company in the Flat Top field.

Local investors also found opportunities in the coalfields alluring. Successful pioneers in northern West Virginia included Henry Gassaway Davis, Stephen B. Elkins, Johnson N. Camden, and James O. Watson, whose empires included coal mines, railroads, and other enterprises. Davis and Elkins, his son-in-law, had extensive businesses in Randolph, Mineral, and Tucker counties. Watson, the leading entrepreneur in the Fairmont field, with his son Clarence W. and his son-in-law A. Brooks Fleming, built a rail line from Fairmont to Morgantown in 1886 and organized the Montana Coal and Coke Company, which constructed the first beehive coke ovens in West Virginia. The success of the Watsons attracted the attention of Camden, who, having disposed of his oil properties, began in 1888 to buy coal lands along the West Fork River and build a railroad from Fairmont to Clarksburg.

The twentieth century ushered in an era of consolidation in West Virginia coalfields. In 1901 Watson and his partners formed the Fairmont Coal Company, which acquired Camden's coal interests, including his mine at Monongah. By 1903 they owned thirty-seven "well located and fully equipped mines, with 1,060 coke ovens and the necessary stores, tenements," and other appurtenances.[5] With the Hanna Coal Company of Cleveland and the Pittsburgh Coal Company, a Mellon organization, the Fairmont Coal Company acquired control of the North Western Fuel Company, the largest coal distributing firm in the upper Midwest, with docking facilities at Duluth and Superior, Minnesota, and Milwaukee, Wisconsin. In 1903 the company merged with the Consolidation Coal Company, controlled by a syndicate of Baltimore and Ohio and Pennsyl-

[5]Charles E. Beachley, comp., *History of the Consolidation Coal Company, 1864-1934* (New York: [Consolidation Coal Company], 1934), 140.

vania Railroad executives. From then until 1928 Watson or his son served as president or chairman of the board of the Consolidation Coal Company, which became one of the largest producers in West Virginia.

The pattern of combination, formation of well-organized sales companies, and identification with powerful railroads also prevailed in other fields. In the New River area Thomas G. McKell, originally of Chillicothe, Ohio, acquired twenty-five thousand acres of land underlaid by the Fire Creek and Sewell seams. In 1893 the Chesapeake and Ohio Railroad built a branch line to his properties. For the next seven years McKell leased tracts to various operators, but after 1900 he himself engaged in mining, with headquarters at Glen Jean. His most famous development was the town of Thurmond, one of the major shipping points on the Chesapeake and Ohio line and the site of the Dunglen Hotel, a popular hostelry with attractions that gave it a dubious reputation as the Monte Carlo of the East.

More closely connected with consolidation in the New River field was Samuel Dixon, a native of Yorkshire, England, who arrived in America in 1876. After ten years as a bookkeeper near Montgomery, Dixon moved to the New River area. He and others formed the MacDonald Colliery Company and in 1893 opened mines on land leased from McKell. Dixon purchased other tracts, including lands of Justus Collins and John A. McGuffin. In 1899 he built the White Oak Railroad from Glen Jean to Carlisle and opened additional mines. With a later rail extension, his operations acquired outlets by way of both the Chesapeake and Ohio and the Virginian railroads.

The formation of the New River Fuel Company, with capital supplied by Dixon and by capitalists of Boston and Scranton, Pennsylvania, marked a significant enlargement of Dixon's coal empire. Known as the New River Company after 1906, it brought twenty-two mines into a single organization. It marketed its coal through a subsidiary sales company, the White Oak Coal Company, of which Dixon was president, and through C.H. Sprague and Son of Boston, which handled coastal and foreign sales. When Dixon resigned as president in 1912, the New River Company controlled over seventy thousand acres of coal land in Fayette and Raleigh counties, a figure increased to ninety thousand in 1940 with the acquisition of the McKell estate.

Aside from personalities, a veritable web of relationships often tied together coal companies, railroads, and other industries in West Virginia. For instance, a syndicate composed of Elbert H. Gary and William Edenborn, both connected with the United States Steel Corporation, and Isaac T. Mann, a Greenbrier native then serving as president of the Bank of Bramwell, purchased properties of the Flat Top Coal Land Association in 1911. It ultimately owned over three hundred thousand acres, or eighty-two percent, of the Pocahontas coal lands. The syndicate sold its holdings to the Norfolk and Western Railway, which discouraged competing lines and exerted, through leases and other methods, decisive influence over coal production in the Pocahontas field. Among its lessees was the United States Steel Corporation, which through its subsidiary, the United States Coal and Coke Company, obtained sufficient land to meet its coking needs for thirty years.

Coal magnates exerted enormous influence upon political affairs of the state. Davis, Elkins, Camden, and Goff were themselves dominant political figures, and numerous members of the legislature owed their seats to powerful corporations, whose interests they served. Coal company executives often controlled county politics. Samuel Dixon was long regarded as the kingpin in Fayette County affairs. Don Chafin kept a tight rein on Logan County matters and, as sheriff, reportedly had five hundred men deputized for service in mining areas.

Powerful coal operators outside the state also took a hand in West Virginia politics. John C.C. Mayo of Kentucky was as much at home in Charleston as in Frankfort and attended most sessions of the state legislature. In 1911 he and his associates lobbied successfully for the election of Clarence W. Watson, then president of the Consolidation Coal Company, to the United States Senate. Their success drew from one outraged state resident the remark that "It beats hell that a coal miner from Kentucky can come over here in West Virginia and elect a Maryland citizen as senator from West Virginia."[6]

Surface Mining. Long practiced in its simplest forms, surface mining increased rapidly in West Virginia after World War II. In 1950 only 12,821,160 tons, or 8.8 percent of the total output, were mined by strip and auger methods. By 1980 surface mining accounted for 25,174,782 tons, or 20.7 percent, of the total. The upsurge was due partly to the development of heavy equipment and new technologies that made surface mining more economical than conventional mining. Opponents objected to scarred hillsides and ugly highwalls; the almost irreparable damage to wildlife, soils, and water; and increased danger from flooding along streams, such as occurred in the Buffalo Creek disaster in 1972.

In 1939 the legislature enacted a regulatory measure requiring strip mining operators to obtain permits from the Department of Mines and to post bonds of fifty dollars per acre toward reclamation of disturbed lands. Inspection was inadequate, and many companies forfeited the bond rather than undertake costly programs of restoration. A new law in 1959 raised the cost of mining permits, created a special surface mining reclamation fund from forfeited bonds, and increased the number of inspectors. In order to reclaim thirty thousand acres already stripped, the legislature in 1963 authorized a special fund, obtained from a tax of thirty dollars per acre upon surface mines. The new law required operators to file plans for reclamation before they disturbed the land, refrain from depositing soil on steep slopes, where it might be washed away or be unrecoverable, and begin restoration within sixty days after stripping or thirty days after auger-mining.

[6]Quoted in Carol Crowe-Carraco, *The Big Sandy* (Lexington: University Press of Kentucky, 1979), 88.

Surface mining and the mechanization of underground mines drastically reduced the labor force in the West Virginia coal industry. From 125,699 in 1948, the number of miners dropped to 41,941 in 1969. Thousands of older miners took advantage of a United Mine Workers of America pension plan embodied in their 1946 contract and financed through a ten-cent levy on each ton of coal mined. Younger members of mining families left the coal regions in an unprecedented exodus to industrial centers such as Cleveland, Akron, Dayton, Detroit, and Chicago, where they joined other Appalachian expatriates. Scores of mining communities became ghost towns. With their crumbling houses, stores, and coal tipples, unsightly slate piles, and rusting railroad tracks, they added their own dimension to national perceptions of Appalachia.

The Oil Industry. Long before the arrival of white men, Indians in West Virginia had obtained oil for medicinal purposes form seepages along the Hughes River. Upon learning of the success of the Drake well at Titusville, Pennsylvania, Charles H. Stattuck, a coal-oil producer at Tarentum, leased land on the Hughes River, about twelve miles from Parkersburg, and drilled for oil in 1859. His well came in only fifty-nine days after the Drake well, but it did not yield enough oil to continue pumping.[7]

More important was a well drilled by Samuel D. Karnes of Pittsburgh on land leased from John Valleau Rathbone near the mouth of Burning Springs Run in Wirt County. Karnes cleaned out an abandoned salt well known as the "old greasy waterhole," pumped out the brine, and about a week later began to produce seven barrels of oil a day, which he sold for twenty dollars a barrel. His success inspired the Rathbone family, then engaged in mercantile, lumber, and milling businesses, to sink a well. Their well came in with about one hundred barrels a day in July 1859 and laid the basis for the Burning Springs oil field.

Although the only proven oil deposits were on the Hughes River and in the Burning Springs area, an epidemic of "oil fever" swept over much of northern West Virginia. The population of Burning Springs skyrocketed from some twenty families in the spring of 1860 to about six thousand people by August of that year. Hundreds of families lived in jerry-built huts that gave but minimum protection from the cold and storms of winter. Prospectors swarmed over the area and into the Northern Panhandle above Wheeling.

By the spring of 1863 about 225 wells had reached paying sands and were pumping an average of 116 barrels of oil per day. At Burning Springs, Confederate raiders under General William E. Jones on May 9 destroyed an estimated 150,000 barrels of oil awaiting a rise in the Little Kanawha for shipment to Parkersburg. Thereafter the oil industry languished. Numerous landowners sold their properties, but a few oil men, including the Rathbones

[7]For the oil and gas industries of West Virginia, the most satisfactory account is Eugene D. Thoenen, *History of the Oil and Gas Industry in West Virginia* (Charleston: Education Foundation, Inc., 1964). Much of the material in this chapter is drawn from this source.

and Johnson N. Camden, retained and even expanded their holdings, confident of a bright future ahead.

Interest in oil revived after the Civil War. Production in West Virginia began to shift northwesterly from Burning Springs and the Little Kanawha–Eureka anticlinal, or "oil break," through Wirt, Wood, and Pleasants counties. Centers of activity were Burning Springs, Oil Rock, California House, Volcano, Sand Hill, and White Oak. The most promising well, at Horseneck, Pleasants County, for a time yielded one thousand barrels of oil a day. In 1870 Ritchie became the premier oil-producing county, followed by Wirt, Wood, and Pleasants.

The speculation and excitement of the oil industry bore little relationship to actual production in the 1870s. In 1879 the daily output in West Virginia was about 800 barrels, an impressive figure when compared with 212 in Ohio and 175 in Kentucky but insignificant when measured against Pennsylvania's 40,000. Only along the "oil break" on the Little Kanawha and Hughes rivers were the rocks sufficiently hard and the walls of the borings firm enough to permit drilling techniques used in Pennsylvania. Elsewhere oil-bearing strata in West Virginia were higher and softer, and drillers often suffered costly losses of tools and equipment from collapsing walls until they devised new and effective methods.

Acceptance of a theory advanced by Dr. Israel C. White, a professor of geology at West Virginia University, that large deposits of oil tended to collect under great arches of rock known as anticlines led to a dramatic upsurge in oil production. White's anticlinal theory received its first major test in the state at Mannington, where a well drilled by T. Madison Jackson in 1889 proved to be a gusher. Its success sent real estate prices soaring and led to a scramble for oil leases, largely by New York and Pennsylvania investors. When the boom peaked in 1893, over two hundred wells had been sunk in a massive oil belt extending from Mount Morris, Pennsylvania, deep into West Virginia. Oil transformed Mannington from a sleepy town of some five hundred people into a bustling shipping center with more than three thousand residents.

Meanwhile, explorations along the Ohio River pushed the older Volcano–Burning Springs oil region toward Saint Marys and led to the opening of the Belmont-Eureka field in Pleasants County in 1885. Numerous towns, including Eureka, Vaucluse, Waverly, Willow Island, Soloma, Raven Rock, and Bens Run, became distributing points for supplies and provided lodgings for workmen, but Saint Marys remained the major commercial center for the field.

The most rapid growth along the Ohio occurred in the Sistersville field. By 1893, two years after its first successful well came in, it had become the largest producing field in the world. Operating wells spread outward to join others in Wetzel, Doddridge, Harrison, and Pleasants counties, as well as to Monroe and Washington counties, Ohio. As a transportation and supply center for the entire oil region and headquarters of several companies, Sistersville had strong banks and a newspaper that was almost a trade journal for the industry.

In 1900 preeminence in oil production in the state passed from Sistersville to Lewis County, the last and one of the most flamboyant of the oil regions. In that year the Copely well, on Sand Fork, a small tributary of the Little Kanawha, erupted as a gusher. Its flow reached 7,920 barrels a day after only five days and filled the banks of Sand Fork for a distance of eight miles. The Lewis County wells reached their maximum production in 1902.

The spectacular growth of the Mannington, Sistersville, and Lewis County fields combined with increases in Ritchie, Doddridge, Wetzel, Pleasants, Harrison, and Monongalia counties to raise oil output in West Virginia from 120,000 barrels in 1888 to 16,195,675 in 1900, the peak year. Already, in 1898, West Virginia oil output had surpassed that of Pennsylvania.

The West Virginia oil industry entered an era of consolidation in the 1890s. Powerful companies absorbed scores of smaller competitors, many of them names almost lost to memory. Major corporations such as the South Penn Oil Company, the Forest Oil Company in the Northern Panhandle, and the Carter Oil Company in the Sistersville field were subsidiaries of the Standard Oil Company, which acquired independent refineries in West Virginia and southern Ohio. By 1895 the National Transit Company, another subsidiary of Standard Oil, controlled most of the oil output of the state and also pipelines from its fields.

In West Virginia, Standard Oil formed alliances with prominent local oil men, influential lawyers, and politicians. A. Brooks Fleming, a corporation lawyer, coal and oil producer, and governor of the state from 1890 to 1893, became its chief counsel. Johnson N. Camden, who shifted his oil interests from production to refining, became John D. Rockefeller's chief lieutenant in the state after his Consolidated Oil Company became a subsidiary of the Standard Oil Company in 1875. Camden orchestrated moves by which the larger company gained control of most of the oil wells and refineries in the state and established dominion over Baltimore markets.

Oil production in West Virginia steadily declined in the twentieth century. By 1990 it had dipped to 2,143,000 barrels. Discoveries in Roane, Kanawha, and Lincoln counties shifted the oil fields southwestward in the state in the early part of the century. For a time natural gas pressure was used to stimulate the flow, and in 1953 the legislature authorized the use of water pressure, but the oil business failed to recover. By then the oil centers of the country had moved to other areas, particularly the southwestern and Gulf states.

Even as the oil industry of West Virginia lost its vigor, Michael L. Benedum launched a career seldom equaled in the business. Born at Bridgeport, he made his debut in the oil fields as an agent of the South Penn Oil Company in northern West Virginia. At the height of his career his own interests extended from Pennsylvania and Ohio to Oklahoma and Texas and from Central America to eastern Europe. Generous grants from the Benedum Foundation, which he created, later benefited his hometown, the state's colleges and universities, and numerous charitable, religious, scientific, and cultural enterprises.

The Natural Gas Industry. Natural gas fields in West Virginia generally coincide with the oil regions. Anticlines often yield natural gas at their upper strata, oil at intermediate levels, and water or brine at greater depths. Prior to 1882 most natural gas was discovered accidentally by oil and salt drillers, who considered it a nuisance and made no effort to conserve it. Unwelcome gas flows sometimes discharged into the air for months, with thunderous sounds that could be heard for miles. Gas ignited by chance burned drilling equipment, scorched surrounding vegetation, and illuminated the skies for great distances. The most spectacular of these flambeaus, "Big Moses," on Indian Creek in Tyler County, erupted for more than a year after it was "drilled in" on September 6, 1894, with an initial flow estimated at more than 100 million cubic feet per day.

West Virginia was relatively slow in putting natural gas to commercial and industrial uses. In 1841 William Tompkins introduced it as a fuel at his Kanawha Valley salt furnaces, and in 1864 a carbon black industry at New Cumberland turned to gas. Later consumers included other carbon black burning sheds, iron and steel mills, and glassworks. Wheeling glass plants began to use gas in 1879, and Wellsburg operations three years later. Between 1870 and 1900 most West Virginia towns introduced gas lighting.

From 1906 to 1924 West Virginia ranked first among the states in output of natural gas. It became the keystone of the Appalachian region, embracing also New York, Pennsylvania, Ohio, and Kentucky, which for many years was the most important gas-producing region of the world and the supplier of ninety-nine percent of the nation's needs. From 1897 to 1937 the value of natural gas marketed from West Virginia was nearly one-half that of all gas produced in the United States.

Until 1914 West Virginia also led other states in the manufacture of casinghead, or "wet," gasoline from vapors that accumulated between inner and outer tubings of gas wells and in pipelines. To avoid condensation in their lines, gas companies installed outlets to drain off this "drip" gasoline. After the advent of the automobile, however, most made use of a new oil-absorption method. As late as 1916 the state had fourteen oil-absorption plants, but successful cracking processes in refining crude oil ended production of casinghead gasoline.

As in the coal and oil industries, large numbers of small natural gas operations in West Virginia gave way to a few giants that controlled production and distribution. The Pittsburgh and West Virginia Gas Company, formed in 1894, purchased the properties of the Philadelphia Company of West Virginia, a subsidiary of George Westinghouse's Philadelphia Company, and in the 1950s and 1960s became part of the Equitable Gas Company. The Hope Natural Gas Company, organized in 1898 with stock held by Standard Oil's National Transit Company subsidiary, in 1943 became a component of the Consolidated Natural Gas Company, made up of properties of Standard Oil. By 1910 the Standard Oil Company also controlled fifty-one percent of the stock of the United Fuel Gas

Company, a major firm in the southern part of the state, which later became part of the Columbia Gas System.

In recent decades depleted wells have served as underground storage facilities. Initiated in 1932 at Bridgeport by the Hope Natural Gas Company, the use of storage pools grew at a rate of about ten percent per year. Thirty years later West Virginia had thirty-five underground reservoirs with a capacity of more than 377 billion cubic feet.

Forest Industries. Historically, West Virginians, like most Americans, have equated recession of the forests with progress. Pioneers destroyed valuable trees indiscriminately in clearing land and constructing farm buildings. Early industrialists selected choice trees for American and British shipyards, made millions of barrel staves and hoop poles for Baltimore and Ohio Valley markets, and sent out vast amounts of tan bark. Their whipsaws, water-powered sash saws, and steam-driven circular sawmills, however, had limited capacities and allowed West Virginia forests a reprieve from the onslaught that occurred later.[8]

Until the twentieth century the rafting of sawlogs and crossties was an important occupation on the Little Kanawha, Elk, Guyandotte, Big Sandy, Cheat, and Tygart Valley rivers and Middle Island Creek. Raft capacities varied from about thirty-five to seventy logs, depending upon the size of the streams. In 1881, for instance, more than forty million board feet was rafted down the Guyandotte, most of it for mills at Cincinnati and other places along the Ohio. Lumber, staves, hoop poles, and tanbark were usually sent out in small barges.

Log drives were common on the Greenbrier, Cherry, and Shavers Fork of the Cheat River, as well as on other streams that did not lend themselves to rafting. During the summer, construction crews built splash dams across smaller streams; woodsmen cut and trimmed trees into logs, which filled the impounded waters; and other workmen built arks, seventy to one hundred feet long, with cabins and bunks for rivermen. The log drive began as soon as winter ice in the streams broke up and the main floes passed. Then the gates of the splash dams were opened, and the rushing waters carried the logs swiftly downstream. Rivermen kept the logs adrift until they reached great booms, where they were caught. Shantyboat residents and others living along the streams earned money by capturing stray logs for their owners. West Virginia law permitted booms in all unnavigable streams except the Cheat in Monongalia County and the Elk in Kanawha County, gave companies the right to condemn land for booms, and provided stiff penalties for theft of logs.

The assault upon the forests reached unprecedented proportions in the 1880s with the extension of railroads into the heart of the timberlands and the introduction of the band saw. Narrow-gauge logging railroads that used Heisler, Shay, and Climax engines fed into larger lines such as the Baltimore and Ohio,

[8]The lumber industry of the state during its most productive era is described and pictured in Roy B. Clarkson, *Tumult on the Mountains: Lumbering in West Virginia, 1770-1920* (Parsons, W.Va.: McClain Printing Company, 1964), a source of special value for this chapter.

Chesapeake and Ohio, and West Virginia Central and Pittsburgh. In an eleven-hour work day band saws, costing upwards of $60,000, could cut 100,000 to 140,000 board feet of lumber and consume the virgin timber from seventeen acres of forestland. The two largest operations in th state, the Meadow River Lumber Company at Rainelle and the Blackwater Boom and Lumber Company at Davis, operated triple band mills. The Meadow River Company, organized by John Raine, erected the largest hardwood lumber mill in the world at Rainelle. A double band mill of the Saint Lawrence Boom and Manufacturing Company at Roncevere consumed much of the white pine of the Greenbrier Valley.

With the coming of railroads and the band saw, lumber companies, chiefly from New York, Pennsylvania, Michigan, and Minnesota, bought most of the choice timberlands of West Virginia, usually at two to five dollars an acre. A yellow poplar tree for which they paid perhaps fifty cents might yield two thousand board feet of lumber, which sold for eighty to one hundred dollars per thousand board feet. In 1909, the peak year of the West Virginia lumber industry, eighty-three band mills were in operation, and production soared to 1,483 million board feet. Ten years later West Virginia ranked third among the states in hardwood production but seventeenth in lumber of all kinds. Oak, chestnut, hemlock, yellow poplar, maple, and spruce, in that order, were her most important varieties.

By 1920 most of the virgin timber was gone, and the lumber industry began a steady decline. Production in the 1950s dropped to about one-fourth that of the pre–World War I era. Band saw mills remained in operation only at Bluefield, Clarksburg, Charleston, Kenova, Williamson, Rainelle, Richwood, Pineville, Swandale, Camden-on-Gauley, and Riverton. Depletion of hemlock, the source of tanbark, forced the closing of most tanneries except at Frank, Marlinton, Petersburg, and Parsons. By midcentury several companies had built kilns to convert slabwoods into charcoal, in increasing demand for indoor and outdoor fireplaces. Some prosperous towns, such as Richwood and Rainelle, survived the changes, but others, including Davis and Cass, suffered the loss of their major economic base and steady decreases in population.

In 1980 some twelve million acres, or about seventy-eight percent, of West Virginia remained in forests. Three national forests lay wholly or partly within the state. The Monongahela embraced 1,673,590 acres, the George Washington 157,568 acres, and the Jefferson 29,782 acres. Nine state forests covered another 79,308 acres. State nurseries provided ever-increasing numbers of seedlings for reforestation, but fires continued to take a heavy toll of timberlands. In spite of efforts at reforestation and conservation, timbering and related industries, like coal mining and other extractive businesses, left a legacy of depleted resources, scarred terrain, and fleeting prosperity.

Manufacturing Before World War I. When West Virginia entered the Union, most indicators pointed to an increasingly important role for manufacturing in its economy. In 1870 its 2,444 small industrial establishments had a capital investment of $11 million and employed 11,600 workers. Ohio County produced nearly forty percent of its industrial goods, followed by Mason, Marshall, Jefferson, Berkeley, Kanawha, and Wood, in that order. The number of establishments declined by 1900, but capital investment increased to $49 million, wage earners to 33,000, and the value of finished products to $67 million. Yet, in its relative position in manufacturing West Virginia shifted from thirty-first among thirty-seven states to twenty-eighth among forty-four.

During the late nineteenth century Wheeling stood out as the preeminent industrial town in West Virginia. As early as 1885 nearly one-half of its thirty thousand residents depended upon industry for a livelihood. Its numerous enterprises included wood processing, bronze and brass fabricating, textile manufacturing, tobacco factories that made the famous Mail Pouch tobacco and Wheeling "Tobies," meat-packing, and pottery-making. Its nail factories were the first to turn from iron to steel. Other major industrial towns were Parkersburg, an oil-refining center; Newell and New Cumberland, with brickyards and potteries; Wellsburg, with paper, glass, and cotton and woolen mills; Benwood and its iron and nail factories; Hartford and Mason City, with salt and bromine works; and Charleston, where foundries, brickyards, mine car factories, and other industries were developing.

On the eve of World War I, West Virginia had 2,749 industrial establishments with 71,000 employees. The most important enterprises and the value of their products were iron and steel, $21 million; tinplate and terneplate, $15 million; glass, $14.5 million; and flour and grist mills, $7 million. In number of employees glass held first place with 9,000, followed by car and general repair work with 8,500; iron and steel, 5,300; and pottery, 3,300. By 1914 thousands of West Virginians had left their farms, partly for new opportunities in industry and partly to escape the austerities, boredom, and growing insecurities of agricultural life.

World War I acted as a great catalyst on West Virginia industry. The manufacture of pottery, iron and steel, and textiles had a relatively long history in the state, with glassmaking of a somewhat shorter duration. The war gave new stimulation to most of them, but it really marked the birth of others, such as the chemical and electric power industries.

Glass, Stone, and Clay Industries. Clay resources have long been a basis of West Virginia industry. From the earliest days, brickmaking occurred in every part of the state, with scores of old dwellings built of brick fired on their sites attesting its importance. By the late nineteenth century the manufacture of face brick, firebrick, paving brick, drainage tile, and furnace linings had become important. Perhaps the most widely recognized use of clay resources, however, had been in the making of pottery, with Wheeling, Mannington, Grafton, Paden City, Huntington, Parkersburg, and Ravenswood remaining important centers as late as the 1950s. The industry was at its best at Newell, which was long noted for high-quality chinaware.

The abundant sandstones and limestones gave rise to other industries. Sandstone occurs throughout the state, but especially north of the Kanawha River. The most valuable limestones lie along the length of the Allegheny Mountains, on the Cacapon and upper South Branch rivers, and in the lower Shenandoah Valley. West Virginia limestone has for many years been used in the manufacture of Portland cement, insulating materials, road ballast, and aggregates and as a source of agricultural lime, riprap, fluxing stone, and crushed stone. In 1977 the output of sandstone and limestone reached 10,499,000 tons.

Vast deposits of sand, some of it 99.89 percent pure silica, and availability of natural gas and limestone, assured West Virginia an important place in the glass industry. Wellsburg had a glass factory as early as 1815, but the industry remained limited until the introduction of natural gas as a fuel. The invention of a bottle-making machine by Michael J. Owens, a native of Mason County, significantly speeded up production, reduced costs, and revolutionized the bottle-making process. Bottle and sheet glass plants at Charleston during the World War I era were among the largest in the world and forced small hand blown glass plants out of operation. Other glass centers have included Clarksburg, Fairmont, Weston, Morgantown, Moundsville, Parkersburg, Williamstown, Grafton, Pennsboro, Paden City, Wheeling, Huntington, and Milton. Fostoria, made at Moundsville, Fenton at Williamstown, and Blenko at Milton are among well-known glass products of West Virginia.

The Chemical Industry. No industry of West Virginia has had a more rapid or continuous growth in the twentieth century than the manufacture of chemicals and their by-products. The industry rests upon extensive brines in the Kanawha Valley and great beds of rock salt, particularly in the Northern Panhandle, along the upper Ohio River, and a belt extending eastward from Ritchie to Monongalia County. Rock salt, found at depths varying from five thousand feet at Chester to more than ten thousand in Monongalia County, cannot be mined profitably, but it is obtained by pumping water into the strata and forcing to the surface brines that in many ways are better suited to industrial purposes than natural brines.

As early as 1876 John P. Hale, a Charleston saltmaker, predicted that the time would soon come when the chief use of West Virginia salt would lie in the manufacture of alkalies and other chemicals. Salt production in the Kanawha Valley had by then dropped to 967,465 bushels, barely thirty percent of that of 1846, the banner year, although 2.5 million bushels were yet made along the Ohio River. A steady decline, which in 1907 left only the Dickinson works at Malden and three plants in Mason County in operation, verified the accuracy of Hale's prediction.

Although a few small chemical plants were built prior to 1914 at Clarksburg, Huntington, and Moundsville, World War I gave the chemical industry its first great impetus. When the war cut off supplies from Germany, upon which Americans had relied heavily, the United States faced the necessity of producing its own chemicals and essential by-products. During the war the federal government itself laid the basis for the chemical industry in the Kanawha Valley by undertaking construction of a high-explosives plant at Nitro and a mustard gas plant at Belle. Other major chemical firms of the Kanawha Valley, including Union Carbide and Du Pont, had their origins in World War I or the years immediately following, making the valley a center for production of bromine, magnesium, sodium, barium, ammonia, and many intermediate compounds used in the manufacture of rubber, plastics, rayon, nylon, automotive anti-freezes, and other substances.

The chemical industry also expanded into the Ohio Valley from Huntington to the Northern Panhandle, with abundant supplies of coal and either brine or rock salt providing such basic substances as chlorine and carbon. Stimulated by World War II, chemical production in both the Kanawha and Ohio valleys grew rapidly. In 1976 it employed 25,200 persons, but by 1991 employment had dropped to 17,500. In value added by manufacturing, however, chemicals and allied industries have remained leaders in the state.

Iron, Steel, and Other Metals. Prior to the Civil War the major iron-making centers were in the Northern Panhandle at Wheeling and Weirton and on the Cheat River near Morgantown. The introduction of the open hearth and Bessemer processes after the war, however, gave rise to a steel industry that had a significant impact upon West Virginia. By the end of the century Wheeling, Charleston, Parkersburg, Huntington, Clarksburg, and a few other towns boasted foundries that turned out a variety of iron and steel products. Several foundries engaged in the manufacture of rail and mine cars and mining equipment. The Kelly Axe factory, later established at Charleston, became the largest of its kind in the world. By 1920 a few giant operations, particularly at Wheeling and Weirton, had absorbed most smaller competitors.

The two world wars further stimulated the steel industry in West Virginia, with Wheeling and Weirton remaining the major centers. In 1932 construction began on a large plant at Alloy, which produced more than fifty alloys used in making high-grade steel and ferrochrome alloy. The Kaiser Aluminum plant, built at Ravenswood after World War II, added diversity to these industries. The state's primary metals industries employed nearly 25,000 persons in the 1970s, but the number fell to about 19,500 by 1991.

The Textile Industry. Like the iron industry, textile manufacture in West Virginia dated back to pioneer times, when it was carried on by families as a domestic enterprise. In the years before World War I, Wheeling was noted for excellent calicos, Martinsurg and Berkeley Springs for hosiery, Charleston for its blankets, and Huntington for upholstery and work clothes, particularly overalls for men.

The manufacture of synthetic yarns and fibers assumed major proportions after World War I. Plants at Nitro and Parkersburg made rayon by chemically processing raw cotton and wood pulp, and the Du Pont Company at its Belle plant developed and produced nylon, a synthetic fiber derived from coal, nitrogen, and water, which because of its durability replaced silk for many purposes. The textile industry slipped in relative importance in the economy of West Virginia and by the mid-1970s it ranked thirteenth in value added by manufacturing.

Electric Power Production. Following World War I, electric power began to compete with coal, oil, and natural gas as a source of energy in West Virginia. In 1950 the state produced nearly eight billion kilowatt-hours of electricity, most of it in coal-fired plants at Beech Bottom, Graham Station, Rivesville, Cabin Creek, Albright, Willow Island, Logan, and Kenova. At Hawks Nest a private corporation diverted water from the New River through Gauley Mountain by means of a tunnel one and one-half miles long, but few other industries made use of abundant water power. After World War II, production of electricity rose rapidly to 68.4 billion kilowatt-hours in 1977, a 1,900 percent increase over that of 1940.

By the 1980s most West Virginians obtained electric power from the Appalachian Power Company and the Wheeling Electric Company, subsidiaries of the American Electric Power System; the Monongahela Power Company and the Potomac Edison Company, subsidiaries of the Allegheny Power Company; and the Virginian Electric and Power Company. Major new generating plants were the John Amos near Saint Albans, Kanawha River at Glasgow, Philip Sporn at New Haven, and Kammer-Mitchell in Marshall County, all built by the Appalachian Power Company; the Monongahela Power Company's Fort Martin operation in Monongalia County; and the Mount Storm plant of the Virginian Electric and Power Company. Like their predecessors, most of the new plants were coal-fired.

Transportation Changes. Although railroads and rivers remained critical to the expansion of industry, the arrival of the automotive age and an ever-growing motor truck business necessitated improvement of West Virginia highways. In 1917 the legislature designated 4,600 miles of roads as Class A highways and authorized distribution of state road funds to counties on the basis of their Class A, or intercounty mileage. In 1933 the state assumed responsibility for 31,166 miles of roads and vested control in a single commissioner. The Good Roads Amendment of 1942 earmarked all revenue derived from motor vehicles and motor fuels for road construction and maintenance. Periodically, voters of the state had approved constitutional amendments for funding both primary and secondary roads in the state.

Aside from United States and state routes, several massive road-building projects have upgraded West Virginia highways. In 1954 the West Virginia Turnpike, an 88-mile span connecting Charleston and Princeton, was opened. Built at a cost of $133 million and financed through the sale of bonds, the road quickly became obsolete, and part of it was later incorporated into the Interstate system. The Interstate and Appalachian Corridor systems have had dramatic impact upon the state. The Interstate highways, begun in the 1950s, include portions of Routes 64, 68, 70, 77, 79, and 81. By 1992 the system was complete, with 546.91 miles. Of the 393.4 miles proposed in the Appalachian Corridor system, 252.2 were open. Highways were not only vital to business and industry but they were also essential to the promotion of tourism, which by the 1980s had become a $1 billion business in itself.

Efforts to Attract Industry. As coal mining and other extractive industries declined in relative importance in the economy of West Virginia, manufacturing enterprises received increased attention. By the mid-1970s more than 120,000 persons were employed in manufacturing. Value added by manufacturing amounted to $3.5 billion, with the chief components being, in order, chemicals, primary metals, and stone, clay, and glass products. Major industrial areas centered in the Ohio, Kanawha, and Monongahela valleys and in the Eastern Panhandle. Large corporations, which accounted for much of the manufacturing, included Union Carbide, Wheeling-Pittsburgh Steel, E.I. Du Pont de Nemours, PPG Industries, Owen-Illinois, Mobay Chemical Company, Monsanto Company, FMC Corporation, Kaiser Aluminum and Chemical Company, International Nickel Company, and American Cyanamid Company, some of which had closed or changed hands by the 1990s.

Since World War II, West Virginia has made special effort to draw new industries. The tax structure generally relied upon a business and occupations tax, carrier income, and corporation net income taxes. By the 1980s parts of the system were considered unusually cumbersome and regressive, paticularly the business and occupations tax, and the legislature initiated steps to abolish it and replace it with other forms of taxation.

Viewed more favorably was the West Virginia Industrial Development Authority, which was authorized to make loans up to thirty percent of the costs of land, buildings, and equipment at low interest up to twenty-five years and to cooperate with banks, development corporations, and federal agencies to provide one hundred percent plant financing. The Business Development Corporation offered new and existing industries loans for working capital as well as facility financing over long terms at favorable interest rates. Local development corporations, as well as the Small Business Administration and conventional loans, provided other methods of financing industrial enterprises.

West Virginia and the National Energy Crisis. In the 1970s the United States began to experience a serious energy crisis. With only six percent of the world's population, it consumed about thirty percent of the world's energy. As an oil importing nation its difficulties were compounded when the Organization of Petroleum Exporting Countries, or OPEC, raised prices to unprecedented levels with disruptive effects on the economies of the United States, Japan, and western Europe.

Once again coal loomed large as a possible solution to the nation's energy needs. In the 1970s interest developed for erection of plants for liquefaction and gasification of coal. A promising plan by which West Germany agreed to provide twenty-five percent of the capital for a liquefaction plant near Morgantown fell through, however. At the same time, the acute need led to reassessment of surface mining in West Virginia. In the 1960s and early 1970s opponents generally were divided between those favoring outright abolition and those willing to accept its methods but only with strict regulation. By the mid-1970s many abolitionists, including John D. Rockefeller, IV, had shifted their positions and became supporters of regulated surface extraction. In 1979 clean air standards in the state, which had greatly reduced pollution, were relaxed to conform to less stringent federal standards. They permitted the use of high-sulfur West Virginia coals in industrial plants in the state with a view to reducing competition from low-sulfur western coal.

Despite increasing energy demands, the West Virginia coal industry lost ground in the 1970s. Production in 1978 was the lowest since 1922. The state, which had long held first place in the nation in bituminous coal mined, ranked third in that year. Strikes and troubled labor-management relations accounted for part of the reduced output. Moreover, a nearly fifty percent increase in the work force between 1969 and 1977 resulted in no corresponding advance in productivity. Faced with depressed conditions nationally in the 1980s and severe cutbacks in steel and other heavy industries, West Virginia mining fell upon its most difficult times since the Great Depression. Many companies closed their mines or drastically reduced operations in the state.

The Fruits of Industrialization. The growth of industry, both primary and secondary, in the late nineteenth and twentieth centuries placed West Virginia in the mainstream of American economic life to a far greater extent than is commonly acknowledged. Although it retained many of its rural qualities during the age of industrialiation and urbanization, the state experienced in its own modest way the movement from the farms to towns and cities that characterized American life at the time. Morever, during the era of the New Immigration, the mines and manufacturing establishments of the state drew large numbers of people from southern and eastern Europe and thousands of Negroes from the South, giving it a cosmopolitanism often overlooked by those preferring to nourish stereotypes regarding the Appalachian area. Industry also drew to the state thousands of professional and skilled workers, who brought with them new ideas and outlooks, and at the same time provided opportunities for native sons and daughters to advance both professionally and economically.

On the other hand, industry, particularly in its extractive aspects, has left a residue of scarred and ravaged lands and impoverished people. Many have contributed to air and water pollution and serious environmental and ecological changes, with all their baneful effects on human life. In short, in spite of positive contributions of industry to the economic, civic, and cultural life, the full potentialities of alliance between the people and industry in many parts of the state may be seen as possibilities for the future rather than solid achievements of the past.

Progressivism and Reaction

Disarray in the Republican Party. Following the Democratic victories in 1870, the Republican organization in West Virginia rapidly fell apart. The constitution of 1872 ended procedures which had enabled the Republicans to maintain control of the state during the Reconstruction era. In 1872 the party did not nominate a candidate for governor, but supported John J. Jacob, the Democratic incumbent, who ran as an Independent. Although Republicans took some comfort in the victory of President Ulysses S. Grant in West Virginia, his vote stemmed in part from the unpopularity of Horace Greeley, the Democratic candidate.

The debate on the Civil Rights bill in Congress in 1874 produced further setbacks for the Republicans. In a typical reaction to the bill, which forbade discrimination against Negroes in public places and transportation, the *Buckhannon Delta* declared on January 24, 1874, that "We consented willingly to granting political and legal rights to . . . the colored men, but we will *never* favor forcing social equality upon us."[1] Resentment against federal intervention in racial matters was so great that many Republican politicians declined to run for office in 1874. At its state convention the party endorsed independent Democrats for most legislative races. Waitman T. Willey, long a Republican wheelhorse in the state, refused to accept his party's nomination for Congress. Similar conditions prevailed in 1876.

Nathan Goff and the Republican Party. Republican leaders in the Appalachian states gradually realized that in order to return to power they must ignore the racial policies of their party in Washington and concentrate on issues of local interest. One of the first West Virginians to perceive this necessity was Nathan Goff, Jr., scion of a wealthy Clarksburg family, who served as United States District Attorney for West Virginia from 1868 to 1881. With an impressive record as a Union captain in the Civil War, a gift for oratory, and a handsome appearance, Goff unsuccessfully sought high elective office three times during the 1870s. He was defeated for Congress from the state's First District in 1870 by John J. Davis and again in 1874 by Benjamin Wilson. In 1876 he won the Republican nomination for governor and ran well ahead of his party, but he lost to Democrat Henry Mason Mathews.

[1]Quoted in Gordon B. McKinney, *Southern Mountain Republicans, 1865-1900: Politics and the Appalachian Community* (Chapel Hill: University of North Carolina Press, 1978), 43.

At the Republican state convention of 1880, Goff, who controlled federal patronage in West Virginia, established his dominance in party affairs. Later, at the national convention, West Virginia delegates bowed to his wishes and supported James G. Blaine for president and Goff for vice president, but the convention chose James A. Garfield and Chester A. Arthur. In the state election of that year a coalition of Republicans and Greenbackers, favored by Goff, reduced the Democrats to a mere fifty-one percent of the vote.

Old-line Republicans challenged Goff's leadership. In 1881 he accepted an appointment as secretary of the navy, and when James A. Garfield became president, Goff again became District Attorney for West Virginia. He antagonized many financial backers of the party by insisting that George W. Atkinson, a major coordinator of the Republican and Greenback campaigns in 1880, be named United States marshal for West Virginia. In a purge of Blaine supporters in 1882, President Chester A. Arthur removed Goff himself from his federal post.

Despite his break with the Arthur administration, Goff held his organization together and in 1882, with Greenback assistance, won election to Congress. Like other Republicans from the Appalachian area, he gained strength by concentrating upon local matters, including special claims and pension bills for his constituents, aid for flood victims along the Ohio River, and protection of jobs of local beneficiaries of federal patronage. He so successfully reinvigorated his political machine that the 1884 state convention by a vote of 229 to 190 endorsed Blaine over the administration. Although Republicans lost both national and state races in West Virginia, Goff won reelection to Congress. The party was edging closer to victory in the state, and Goff was its master.

Goff reached the pinnacle of his political career in 1888, when, on the basis of original returns and with the aid of black voters, he defeated A. Brooks Fleming, his Democratic opponent, for the governorship by the narrow margin of 110 votes. Fleming challenged Goff's election, and more than a year after inauguration day, the legislature, by a strict party vote, declared Fleming the victor by 237 votes. Goff's ambitions for a United States Senate seat then ran into conflict with those of Stephen B. Elkins, a prominent figure in national affairs of the party who was then seeking a political base in West Virginia. Neither desired a rupture in the party, and Elkins withdrew. Goff, however, lost the seat by a single vote to the incumbent, Democrat John E. Kenna of Kanawha County.

Following the disappointments of 1888, Goff's influence in the Republican party in West Virginia declined rapidly, and that of Elkins rose correspondingly. Elkins believed that he had discharged any obligations to Goff as party leader by supporting him for governor and yielding to him in the senatorial contest. Moves by Goff supporters to block a cabinet appointment for Elkins in the Benjamin Harrison administration and clashes over patronage widened the rift between the two men. Goff's strong support of the Republican ticket in 1890 proved unwise, since the Republicans, particularly Elkins partisans, were committed to the unpopular Lodge Bill, which increased federal authority over elections. Keenly aware of his waning influence, Goff found a graceful way of relinquishing party leadership, when in 1892 he became judge of the Fourth United States Circuit Court, which included South Carolina, North Carolina, Virginia, Maryland, and West Virginia. Elkins by then had emerged as the recognized leader of West Virginia Republicans.

Goff was typical of many new political leaders of the state in the late nineteenth century. He added to his wealth through coal mines, oil and gas properties, electric power operations, and other ventures. He nevertheless built a broad political base by blending the interests of the new industrial age with old political patterns. In rejecting unpopular national issues, especially federal intervention in racial matters, he enabled the Republican party to overcome identification with the black population and hated Reconstruction policies and to gain adherents among mountain whites. When he stepped aside as its leader, the party constituted a genuine threat to Democratic supremacy in West Virginia.

Stephen Benton Elkins and the Republican Party. The emergence of Stephen B. Elkins as the leader of the Republican party in West Virginia marked a major triumph for its business and industrial elements. Born in Ohio, where his Virginia grandparents had moved in order to liberate their slaves, Elkins grew up in Missouri. There he taught school and was admitted to the bar. He defied his parents and joined the Union army. After the war he went to the New Mexico Territory, where he entered Republican politics and was elected the territorial representative to Congress. In Washington he met and married Hallie Davis, the daughter of West Virginia Senator Henry Gassaway Davis.

Elkins, already on the way to wealth, prospered enormously as the business partner of his Democratic father-in-law in railroad and coal interests. His growing wealth enabled him to indulge his political ambitions, and he quickly became influential in the national councils of the Republican party. He served as an adviser to James G. Blaine and in 1880 had an important part in Blaine's nomination for the presidency. In 1888 he visited West Virginia in search of a political base from which to advance his own career. He took part in a West Virginia Boom Convention at Wheeling and delivered a scholarly address at West Virginia University. He further strengthened his position by purchasing a large share of stock in the *Wheeling Intelligencer,* the leading Republican newspaper in the state.

In establishing his political base in West Virginia, Elkins moved with consummate political skill. He acted with restraint in his victory over Goff for party control in 1890 and avoided antagonizing Goff's supporters. Unable to win a United States Senate seat as long as Democrats controlled the West Virginia legislature, he accepted in 1891 the post of secretary of war in the cabinet of President Benjamin Harrison, whom he had supported in the previous election.

Taking advantage of the depression of 1893 and hoping to harmonize divergent interests within the party, Elkins in 1894 made the protective tariff the central goal of the Republicans. He supported Philippi lawyer Alston G. Dayton, who ran against Democrat William L. Wilson, a cosponsor of the Wilson-Gorman Tariff of that year, even though George Sturgiss, one of his own men, endeavored to stop Dayton. Republicans not only won all four West Virginia congressional seats, but they also gained sufficient strength in the state legislature to assure the election of a Republican as United States senator, a position that naturally went to Elkins.

Invigorated by its leader's flexibility and his refusal to insist upon rigid party discipline, the Elkins machine later won even greater triumphs. In 1896 it concentrated upon educating voters on the professed evils of free silver and the need for a protective tariff. Elkins assured party unity by supporting a Goff partisan, George W. Atkinson, for governor. Republicans captured not only the governorship but also the state's electoral vote, their first great victory since Reconstruction. Elkins, now the undisputed leader of the party, retained the United States Senate seat that he won in 1896 until his death in 1911. His close ally, Wheeling industrialist and banker Nathan Bay Scott, held the state's other Senate seat from 1899 to 1911. Because of his support, George W. Atkinson, Albert B. White, William M.O. Dawson, and William E. Glasscock, who served between 1897 and 1913, have often been called the "Elkins governors."

Essentially a business-minded conservative, Elkins was not an implacable enemy of all reform. As chairman of the Senate Committee on Interstate Commerce, he sponsored the Elkins Act of 1903, which set penalties for railroad rebates, and the Mann-Elkins Act of 1910, which extended the jurisdiction and increased the power of the Interstate Commerce Commission. Moreover, he exerted influence to promote tax and administrative reforms during the administrations of the governors associated with the era of his dominance in party affairs.

Governor George Wesley Atkinson. Already well known in the state when Elkins achieved supremacy in the Republican party was George W. Atkinson (June 29, 1845–April 4, 1925) of Kanawha County. He had served as postmaster at Charleston, United States Internal Revenue agent, and United States marshal. After opening a law office at Wheeling, he was elected congressman from the First District. Moreover, he was a writer of considerable note and a prominent leader in the Methodist Episcopal Church.

Atkinson was not comfortable when the mantle of power passed from Goff to Elkins, but his desire for high public office and his inability to match the vast sums that Elkins and Scott poured into party coffers stifled any thoughts of leading dissident elements. Elkins, however, recognized Atkinson's popularity and, never desiring open breaks in the party, accepted his nomination for governor in 1896. Atkinson defeated his Democratic opponent, Cornelius C. Watts of Kanawha County, by 12,070 votes.

As governor, Atkinson made no sharp departures from the policies of the Bourbon Democrats with respect to business and industry. In his inaugural address he declared that "It is a mistake to create prejudice against men who organize for legitimate purposes and pursuits" and that he would "take no stock . . . in the nonsensical cry of 'Down with the rich men and corporations.' "[2] Although seeking to promote a favorable climate for industry, Atkinson recognized the problems of labor. Concerned over the "total absence of industrial legislation for the welfare and preservation of life and health of the wage earners,"[3] of the state, he later called upon the legislature to provide an eight-hour workday, prohibit the employment of children under fourteen years old, require proper working conditions for women, and mandate additional safety regulations, especially in coal mining. Although the legislature failed to enact most of his recommendations, Atkinson continued to press for changes, including coal mine safety laws and even abolition of company stores.

Throughout his administration, Atkinson set a tone of moderate progressivism that generally characterized the Elkins governors. At the outset, he renounced some of the worst features of the spoils system. He announced that he would appoint representatives of the minority party to state boards even though the law did not require him to do so and promised that he would not tolerate politics in the public schools. He urged legislation to curb "corruption at the ballot box, the very fountainhead of all free institutions," and warned lawmakers against the influence, "born of selfishness or greed," of professional lobbyists.[4] At a time when racism had begun to engulf some neighboring states, Atkinson spoke out against Jim Crowism, declaring with more fervor than accuracy that "West Virginia has never adopted a law which abridged the rights and privileges of any of its citizens, and I hope it never will."[5]

One of the most serious problems confronted by Atkinson was a financial crisis that gripped the state government. Many years in the making, it stemmed from an expansion of government services, policies of past governors and the Board of Public Works that kept property valuations low in order to attract new industry, a general property tax system that had become an inadequate patchwork, and efforts of many counties to pay the smallest possible share of the state levy. To deal with the problems, Atkinson advocated abolition of the fee system, whereby certain state and county officials received shares of the revenue they collected; a rise in corporate taxes, which were based on grossly undervalued real estate and some personalty; and an increase in the license tax on all corporations, with a graduated scale based on capitalization and landholdings.

Stephen B. Elkins and Henry Gassaway Davis, then seeking an increase in

[2]John G. Morgan, *West Virginia Governors, 1863-1980*, 2d ed. (Charleston: Charleston Newspapers, 1980), 61.

[3]Quoted in *Wheeling Intelligencer*, January 12, 1899.

[4]Quoted in Morgan, *West Virginia Governors*, 62.

[5]Ibid.

capitalization of their West Virginia Central Railroad and repeal of a ten thousand–acre limit on corporate landholdings, opposed Atkinson's proposals. Elkins agreed to a plan drawn up by Secretary of State William M.O. Dawson, one of his lieutenants, to increase the corporation tax, but only if the limit on landholding were removed and there were no graduated tax scale on capital stock.

In February 1901 Elkins himself conferred with legislators and lobbyists in Charleston and worked out informal agreements that separated the need for immediate revenue from the broader question of tax reform. Bowing to his wishes, the lawmakers killed proposals for a severance tax on natural gas and oil and restrictions on specific corporations. They also accepted his suggestion that they create a special commission to study tax reform and report to the legislature in 1903. Elkins's visit divided the reformers, undermined the assault upon corporate privilege, and assured his organization a powerful voice in future tax reform movements in the state.

Governor Albert Blakeslee White. Hopes for constitutional and tax reform at the turn of the century rested with a new governor, Albert B. White (September 22, 1856–July 3, 1941). A native of Cleveland, Ohio, White began his career as a newspaper editor in Lafayette, Indiana, where his father was president of Purdue University. In 1883 he purchased the Parkersburg *State Journal,* which he edited until 1899, in later years as the leading spokesman for the Elkins machine. In 1894 White managed the successful campaign of Elkins for the United States Senate. After serving as governor, he returned to public life as state tax commissioner and state senator.

In the gubernatorial contest of 1900, in which he defeated Democrat J. Homer Holt of Cabell County by 19,516 votes, White made it clear that tax reform would be the major concern of his administration. He reiterated his resolve in his inaugural address, in which he declared the tax laws of the state "so crude and defective" that there had been very little increase in income during the previous ten years despite a twenty-five percent growth in population and a doubling of actual wealth. White expressed a desire to "treat the developing corporations, such as railroads and mining and manufacturing enterprises, employing labor and building up the state, with the utmost liberality," but also to "relieve, if possible, the burdens on modest home owners and small farmers."[6]

Soon after his inauguration White appointed members of the Tax Commission, authorized the previous year. He offered the chairmanship to Elkins, who declined, and then to Henry Gassaway Davis, who accepted. Made up of conservatives, including an industrialist, a banker, and a corporation lawyer, the commission in November 1902 made a surprisingly moderate report that embodied proposals in line with plans in effect in other states, including Indiana,

[6]Quoted in *Parkersburg Daily Sentinel,* March 5, 1901; *Wheeling Register,* March 5, 1901.

Pennsylvania, and Massachusetts. It recommended separation of state and local revenue, with property taxes reserved to local governments and annual assessments under the supervision of a state tax commissioner; retention of the licensing tax on corporations; and imposition of a small severance tax on coal, oil, and natural gas, with assurances in a constitutional amendment that it would not become burdensome upon those industries. White himself added a proposal for a railroad commissioner to expedite collection of taxes from rail carriers.

Although a Davis-Elkins attorney drafted the report of the Tax Commission and the bills to put its provisions into effect, their presentation to the legislature by Governor White on January 15, 1903, was greeted by a storm of opposition from corporations charging betrayal by both Davis and White. Senator E.C. Colcord, a member of the Kanawha Republican ring known as the "Hog Combine," introduced a resolution calling for their rejection, even if they were constitutional, on the ground that they threatened the continued prosperity of the state. The Senate Finance Committee promptly scheduled hearings at which corporation lawyers and lobbyists challenged the views of White and Secretary of State Dawson, his chief tax expert. The Senate adopted the Colcord Resolution and ended all chance of adoption of the integrated tax proposals advocated by the governor and the Tax Commission.

During the spring and summer of 1903 White and William P. Hubbard, the new chairman of the Tax Commission, took their case to the people. Former Governor A. Brooks Fleming, who had alerted the Rockefeller interests, assembled representatives of Standard Oil, the Fairmont and Pocahontas coal corporations, and the Western Maryland, Pennsylvania, Norfolk and Western, Baltimore and Ohio, and Chesapeake and Ohio railroads in Washington. Members of the conference agreed to raise funds to fight the proposed changes and issued an "Anti-Tax Manifesto," signed by twenty-eight prominent West Virginians and published in all major newspapers of the state on August 19, 1903. The following year anti-tax Republicans, encouraged and financed by Democrat Fleming, united behind Charles F. Teter in a move to deprive Dawson, the leading contender, of the Republican nomination for governor.

On January 18, 1904, Elkins summoned the two factions to Washington, where they worked out a compromise version of the tax bills. Hoping that they might be enacted into law, White called the legislature into special session in July. In an eighteen-day session, the legislature created the office of state tax commissioner, with authority to compel all county assessors to rate all property at its true and actual value. The legislature also set maximum rates per one hundred dollars assessed valuation for school purposes, increased the tax on corporation charters and on inheritances and transfers, directed the Board of Public Works to assess public utilities, and forbade state institutions, county courts, and boards of education to contract debts in excess of available funds.

Although tax reform claimed much of his attention, White pressed for other reforms clearly in the Progressive tradition. He urged a pure food and drug act, and election reforms, including the short ballot, compulsory publication of campaign expenses, and stricter laws to reduce corruption. He favored an antilobby law modeled on one in Massachusetts. White, like Governor Wilson nearly twenty years previously, deplored the pollution of West Virginia streams. He drew attention to the Kanawha and New rivers, once "beautiful, pellucid, and sparkling streams," already so contaminated that fish could not live in them, and asked the legislature to provide money to gather evidence in case suits were needed to stop the "great defilement and pollution of the most important river lying wholly within our State."[7] One of White's recurring themes was the need for railroad regulation, which he regarded as scarcely less important than his tax program.

Governor William Mercer Owens Dawson. White's successor as governor, quite appropriately, was William M.O. Dawson (May 21, 1853–March 12, 1916), the chief architect of the tax proposals of 1902. Without a college education, Dawson entered the newspaper business as a young man and in 1873 became owner and editor of the Kingwood *Preston County Journal*. Prior to his inauguration in 1905, he had served as state senator, chairman of the Republican state executive committee, clerk of the House of Delegates, and secretary of state.

Dawson was an early supporter of Elkins, whom he welcomed to the state in 1889. As chairman of the Republican state executive committee by the choice of Elkins, Dawson proved a superb organizer, perhaps superior to Elkins himself. He gave the Republicans a modern organization, with lines of authority extending to every county of the state. By 1904 he had emerged as a skilled political leader in his own right, but he retained close ties with the Elkins machine.

Refusing to withdraw from the Republican gubernatorial race in 1904, even though Elkins suggested that he do so, Dawson not only captured the nomination but defeated Democrat John J. Cornwell by a vote of 121,540 to 112,457. The Republican candidate for president, popular Theodore Roosevelt, carried West Virginia by almost 32,000 votes, although Henry Gassaway Davis was the running mate of the Democratic candidate, Alton B. Parker. For the eighty-one-year-old Davis, who had incurred condemnation from both advocates and opponents of tax reform, the humiliating loss ended a long and influential career in West Virginia politics.

Tax reform, which Dawson had made the central issue in the campaign of 1904, became a primary concern of his administration. He called upon the legislature for taxes on alcoholic beverages, increased valuations of banks, a progressive inheritance tax, an excise tax on gross earnings of public service corporations, and a tax on coal, oil, and natural gas production. The legislature enacted only a small part of his recommendations, but it expanded the powers and duties of the state tax commissioner and gave the governor authority to

[7]Albert Blakeslee White, *Public Addresses . . . during His Term of Office, Including Proclamations and Other Official Papers* (Charleston: Tribune Printing Company, 1905), 198-99.

remove assessors who refused to comply with the law. It retained corporate protection from excessive burdens by setting maximum rates on assessed valuations for specific purposes.

Anticipating Theodore Roosevelt's New Nationalism by several years, Dawson maintained that the state government must be powerful enough to deal effectively with large corporations, including railroads. Under his direction, assessments of railroads rose from $36 million to $177 million, but the major carriers successfully appealed the higher valuations.

Although the legislature took positive steps in enacting a corrupt practices act in 1908 and a year later in authorizing the governor to appoint a bipartisan Board of Control with supervision over the financial affairs of all state educational, charitable, penal, and correctional institutions, it generally lagged far behind the progressive governor. It rejected Dawson's requests for laws for conservation of natural resources, a pure food and drug act, the employment of experts to draft legislation, workmen's compensation, and a public service commission "to regulate rates of express companies, sleeping-car companies, telegraph and telephone companies, and other like common carrier and public service corporations."[8] Deeply disappointed in the legislative record, Dawson endeavored to place West Virginia firmly in the progressive tradition by incorporating many of the rejected proposals in the Republican platform of 1908, of which he was the principal author.

Governor William Ellsworth Glasscock. The last of the Elkins governors was William E. Glasscock (December 13, 1862–April 12, 1925). After serving as superintendent of Monongalia County schools, clerk of the circuit court, and collector of internal revenue, Glasscock was selected as chairman of the state Republican committee. In 1903 he was admitted to the bar and became attorney for Stephen B. Elkins in Monongalia County.

Glasscock's nomination for governor in 1908 resulted from a bitter contest between Secretary of State Charles W. Swisher and Attorney General Arnold C. Scherr. In order to avert an almost certain victory for Democrat Louis Bennett, Elkins persuaded both Swisher and Scherr to withdraw. With the election only six weeks away, the Republicans accepted Glasscock as a compromise candidate. Glasscock waged a campaign based on defense of Republican policies of the previous twelve years, reaffirmation of the progressive reforms advocated by his predecessors, and condemnation of Democrats who urged disfranchisement of Negroes and institution of Jim Crow laws. He defeated Bennett by a vote of 130,807 to 118,674.

Glasscock's first biennial message to the legislature contained a familiar recital of needed reforms. Glasscock urged a tax on natural gas; greater aid to education, including free textbooks; mine safety laws; a public service commis-

[8]Nicholas C. Burckel, "Progressive Governors in the Border States: Reform Governors in Missouri, Kentucky, West Virginia, and Maryland, 1900-1918" (Ph.D. diss., University of Wisconsin, 1971), 317.

sion; an antilobby law; an antitrust law; and legislation to reduce pollution and preserve wildlife. The legislature, particularly the Senate, showed little enthusiasm for his recommendations, but it assented to improvements in education, including longer school terms, and agreed to submit a prohibition amendment to the voters in 1912. With his term approaching its end, Glasscock convened the 1913 legislature a week early to consider nine essential reforms, including two new ones, woman suffrage and an end to capital punishment. Once again he was disappointed, but, with the support of Governor-elect Henry D. Hatfield, the legislature at last created a public service commission and enacted a workmen's compensation law, both along lines proposed by Glasscock.

The most dramatic events of Glasscock's administration revolved around the organization of the Senate in 1911 and the selection of two United States senators by the legislature. With the connivance of Glasscock, Republicans attempted to prevent the Democrats, who had a majority of the total membership of the legislature, from choosing successors to Senators Nathan B. Scott, whose term expired in that year, and Elkins, who died three days after the legislature convened. To prevent the Democrats from organizing the Senate, which had fifteen members of each party, the Republican senators were hidden in Glasscock's office. After the Democratic nominee for sergeant-at-arms attempted to force his way into the office and compel at least one Republican to attend the sessions which the Democrats were holding daily, Glasscock approved a plan by which the fifteen Republican senators went to Cincinnati for two weeks.

The two parties at last agreed to a compromise by which Republicans organized the state Senate and Democrats chose both United States senators. The Republicans promptly elected Henry D. Hatfield president of the state Senate. Passing over aged but still active Henry Gassaway Davis, the Democrats chose Clarence W. Watson of Fairmont, the president of the Consolidation Coal Company, for the unexpired term of Elkins, and William E. Chilton of Charleston for the seat formerly held by Scott. The ties between Watson and the Kanawha Ring led to charges of bribery, which persisted throughout the two years that Watson remained in the Senate. John J. Cornwell, a spokesman for Bryanite and working-class Democrats, predicted that Watson's out-of-state connections would lead to new attacks upon corporate interests, but Chilton branded foes of "Watsonism" as enemies of West Virginia prosperity.

As his term progressed, Glasscock became increasingly disenchanted with President William Howard Taft. Early in 1912 he and six other governors appealed to Theodore Roosevelt to seek the Republican nomination. Once Roosevelt agreed, his supporters formally organized at Parkersburg on February 28 under the leadership of former Governor Dawson. Dawson worked with Glasscock and Hatfield to achieve a solid Roosevelt victory at the state convention in Huntington and served as chairman of the West Virginia delegation to the Republican national convention. Despite urging by some state delegates, he declined to seek the vice presidency on a ticket with Roosevelt.

Capitol at Wheeling, 1876-1885

Arthur Ingram Boreman, first governor of West Virginia. Both engravings on this page from *West Virginia Archives and History Report, 1908*

Dickinson locks and dam, completed in 1880, was one of a series that stimulated coal and other industries in the Kanawha valley. *The Virginias* (1884), p. 104

Logging arks and crews on Greenbrier River at Cass

Above, Capitol at Charleston, 1885-1921, until its destruction by fire

Left, Henry Gassaway Davis, industrialist and Democratic nominee for vice president of the United States in 1904

Below, steamboat Chesapeake, which participated in the removal of the state capital from Charleston to Wheeling in 1875 and back to Charleston in 1885

Above, Booker T. Washington home at Malden, where Washington spent part of his youth.

Left, birthplace of novelist Pearl Buck, the home of her grandparents, Hillsboro

Below, "Old White," famous nineteenth-century spa and predecessor of the equally famous Greenbrier resort

Left, "Mother" Mary Jones, labor activist who supported the cause of West Virginia coal miners

Below, National Guard encampment at Pratt during Paint Creek coal strike, 1912-1913

Bottom, mine explosion at Monongah, 1907

Union Carbide Corporation plant at South Charleston. Courtesy Charleston Newspapers

Modern coal preparation plant and the mining town of Gary

West Virginia state capitol, designed by Cass Gilbert and completed in 1932. The sculpture in the foreground is "Abraham Lincoln Walks by Midnight" by Fred M. Torrey. Photograph by Stephen W. Brown

National Radio Astronomy Observatory, with its Reber Radio Telescope, Greenbank (collapsed November 16, 1988)

New River Gorge Bridge, the longest steel arch bridge in the world and, 876 feet above the river, the highest span east of the Mississippi River. West Virginia Travel Development Division

Although deeply disappointed when Taft was renominated, Glasscock did not join those who bolted the party. He and Hatfield met with Dawson, the founder of the West Virginia Bull Moose Party, and the two Republican factions agreed to run the same ticket for state offices. Glasscock campaigned actively for Hatfield, the Republican nominee, and other Republican candidates, but he voted for Roosevelt. His course reflected the feeling of the majority of West Virginia Republicans. Roosevelt won 94,360 of the state's popular votes and Taft only 56,754. The rift enabled Woodrow Wilson, the Democratic candidate, to carry the state with 113,097.

The demands of the gubernatorial office, heightened by a prolonged and bloody coal strike on Paint and Cabin creeks in 1912–1913, contributed to deterioration of the already precarious health of Glasscock. When he left office, he gave up his active role in Republican politics.

Governor Henry Drury Hatfield. The last of the Republican governors in the Progressive Era was Henry D. Hatfield (September 15, 1875–October 23, 1962) a nephew of "Devil Anse," the leader of the Hatfield clan in its bloody feud with the McCoy family of Kentucky. Hatfield, a medical doctor, practiced extensively in railroad and mining towns and in 1899 led a move in which the state established a miners hospital at Welch under his direction. His record as a member and president of the McDowell County court, where he insisted upon clean and efficient administration, control of notorious saloons, more humane treatment of criminals, and improved sanitation at the county jail, led to his election to the state Senate, of which he became president in 1911. In 1912 he defeated William R. Thompson of Cabell County for governor by some fifteen thousand votes.

Committed by campaign promises to continuation of progressive reforms, Hatfield met with the Republican legislative caucus in January 1913, before his inauguration, and urged immediate action to provide a public service commission, a primary election law, an employers' liability law, abolition of the mine guard system, and a tax on coal, oil, and natural gas, most of which his predecessors had sought. He threatened to call a special session of the legislature as soon as he was inaugurated if the lawmakers did not act in the meantime.

Under the whip that Hatfield cracked, the legislature began to stir. One of its first acts was the Slemaker Blue Sky Law, which empowered the auditor to investigate and prosecute companies selling fraudulent securities in the state. In February 1913 the legislature at last agreed to a public service commission with authority to determine reasonable rates for public utilities, set standards of service, suspend announced rate increases, and appraise property of utility companies covered by the law, with the right of appeal from commission decisions directly to the state supreme court. The same legislature also passed an employers' liability law, ratified the income tax amendment to the federal Constitution, and endorsed the principle of popular election of United States senators, but it went on record as opposing woman suffrage.

With many of the reforms he advocated enacted into law before he assumed office, Hatfield confidently declared in his inaugural address that "the great tendency of the American people today is toward more constructive socialism than ever before."[9] Under his prodding, the legislature enacted a primary election law designed to eliminate the "imperious and corrupt influence of bosses" who had dominated the nominating conventions of the major parties;[10] a corrupt practices act; a liberalized workmen's compensation law; and a more comprehensive child labor law that forbade employment of boys under fourteen years old in the coal mines and of those between fourteen and sixteen in communities in which a free school was in session.

Especially close to the heart of the governor was the establishment of a state department of health, with authority to enforce public health laws; examine foods, drugs, and drinks available to the public; and to make rules and regulations covering more than a score of matters affecting the health of citizens of the state. To offset the loss of revenue with the advent of prohibition, the legislature authorized increases in tax rates on real and personal property, broadened the inheritance tax, raised the tax on corporations, and levied an excise tax on the net incomes of businesses operating in West Virginia. In 1913 the legislature created the state road bureau, with general supervision over road-building programs in the state. It refused to authorize the short ballot or judicial reforms advocated by Hatfield, but it did agree to submit the woman suffrage amendment to the voters. When Hatfield left office, "West Virginia had as much progressive legislation on her books as most of her northern and western sister states."[11]

Governor John J. Cornwell. Ironically, the success of the Hatfield admin-istration in progressive legislation contributed to the defeat of the Republicans in the gubernatorial election of 1916. The Hatfield wing of the party nominated state supreme court Judge Ira E. Robinson for governor, but conservative industrial interests, especially the coal operators, who opposed many of the reforms, united behind former state Attorney General Abraham A. Lilly. The rift in the party was too deep and was repaired too late to prevent the election of Democrat John J. Cornwell (July 11, 1867–September 8, 1954), although Charles Evans Hughes carried the state over Wilson in the presidential race.

Like White and Dawson, Cornwell moved into politics by way of the field of journalism. After teaching school for seven years, he and his brother pur-chased the Romney *Hampshire Review,* in which Cornwell retained an interest for the remainder of his life. In 1895 he was admitted to the bar and soon began to participate actively in Democratic politics. After two terms in the Senate, he won the nomination for governor in 1904, but he was defeated by Dawson.

[9]Quoted in Burckel, "Progressive Governors in the Border States," 387.

[10]Quoted in Charles H. Ambler and Festus P. Summers, *West Virginia, the Mountain State*, 2d ed. (Englewood Cliffs, N.J.: Prentice-Hall, Inc., 1958), 385.

[11]Burckel, "Progressive Governors in the Border States," 406.

In his inaugural address, delivered only a month before the United States declared war on Germany, Cornwell called upon West Virginians to lay aside partisanship and unite behind the president and the needs of the nation. He himself set an example. Cornwell was forced to work with Republicans, who controlled both houses of the legislature and handicapped his efforts by "ripper" legislation, which prevented him from removing large numbers of Hatfield appointees and was not repealed until 1921, when another Republican became governor. He nevertheless established amicable relations with the legislature.

Even in wartime Cornwell continued the progressive tradition. During his administration the legislature strengthened the mining code; prohibited employment of children under fourteen years old in any gainful occupation except agriculture and domestic service and those under sixteen in hazardous or night work; created the State Board of Education, with control over the entire public educational system; and established a Department of Public Safety with a force of two hundred men under a superintendent appointed by the governor. The state police system, modeled on that of Pennsylvania, seemed essential for dealing with law enforcement problems arising from the increasing use of the automobile and crime and labor unrest in the wake of World War I. Although organized labor opposed the state police, Cornwell maintained that they would "eliminate the private guards and the company-paid deputy sheriffs and substitute real public officials in their stead" in labor-management troubles.[12]

Cornwell's administration brought other changes. The legislature established the Virginia Debt Sinking Fund and authorized the Board of Public Works to levy not more than ten cents on each one hundred dollars valuation of general property to discharge the debt. A constitutional amendment of 1918 placed the budget-making power in the Board of Public Works, although Cornwell had become convinced that "the responsibility of framing the budget belongs with the governor and should be placed squarely upon him."[13] Other amendments authorized a $50 million road bond issue to "Help Pull West Virginia Out of the Mud" and dubious "cleft" sessions of the legislature in which members met for fifteen days to introduce bills, recessed for fifteen days to study them, and returned for forty-five days to deliberate upon them.

Quite apart from wartime exigencies, the Cornwell administration had its excitements. During the last two years a violent coal strike engulfed much of Logan and Mingo counties. Some irate miners apparently even plotted to assassinate Cornwell on September 30, 1919. Later, on January 3, 1921, a spectacular fire destroyed the state capitol, forcing government agencies into temporary quarters that soon included the hastily constructed ninety-day wonder known as the "Pasteboard Capitol."

Cornwell's administration in many respects marked the end of the Progressive era in West Virginia. The Progressive governors had given the state an

[12]Quoted in Ambler and Summers, *West Virginia, the Mountain State*, 386.
[13]West Virginia Senate *Journal, 1917, 2d Extraordinary sess.*, 94.

impressive body of reforms and made government more responsive and serviceable to the people. Yet, for all the accomplishments, industrial and other special interests retained great power over the state and its affairs. Postwar readjustments and the prevailing philosophy in Washington set a different mood for the 1920s.

Governors Morgan, Gore, and Conley. West Virginia returned to the Republican fold in 1920 with the election of Ephraim F. Morgan (January 16, 1869–January 15, 1949) as governor. Morgan received a majority of 57,565 over Arthur B. Koontz, but Samuel B. Montgomery drew 81,330 votes as a Non-Partisan and M.S. Holt 2,695 as a Socialist. When Morgan assumed office, southern West Virginia was yet in the throes of a violent coal strike, roads were in need of attention, funds were required for liquidation of the Virginia Debt, and a major outlay was needed for a new capitol. To meet some of the financial needs, the legislature established a state sinking fund and retained a ten cent levy per $100 evaluation on general property for the use of the Board of Public Works. Morgan appointed a Capitol Commission, which engaged world-famous architect Cass Gilbert to design a new capitol to be located on the banks of the Kanawha River in east Charleston. The west wing of the structure was completed in 1925, along with a handsome new Governor's Mansion, into which Morgan and his family moved about one week before he left office.

Howard M. Gore (October 12, 1887–June 20, 1947) of Clarksburg left the post of secretary of agriculture under President Calvin Coolidge to become governor after defeating Democrat Jake Fisher by a vote of 304,587 to 261,846 and Socialist J.W. Bosworth, who received 7,218 votes. Sensitive to the needs of agriculture, Gore diverted more state funds to rural areas, returned portions of taxes from public utilities to counties and municipalities, and legalized agricultural credit and cooperative associations. Efforts to modernize the state's tax system, however, met with little success.

William G. Conley (January 8, 1866–October 21, 1940) succeeded Gore in 1929 by defeating the Democratic candidate, J. Alfred Taylor, by a vote of 345,909 to 296,673. During the first part of Conley's administration the legislature amended numerous laws, including the state banking code and prohibition laws, and approved a general revision of the West Virginia Code. The new capitol was completed. The last years of Conley's governorship were overshadowed by the Great Depression and measures to relieve mounting distress in the state.

In national affairs, West Virginians generally supported Republican policies. They registered their own desire for "normalcy" in 1920 by voting 282,007 for Warren G. Harding for president to 220,789 for Democrat James M. Cox and 5,618 for Socialist Norman Thomas. Four years later they gave incumbent Calvin Coolidge 288,635 votes to 257,232 for Democrat John W. Davis and 36,723 for Robert M. LaFollette, who ran as an Independent. In 1928 they endorsed the Republican administration even more strongly, with 375,551 votes for Herbert Hoover to 263,784 for Alfred E. Smith. The prosperity associated with Republican rule undoubtedly accounted for the rather dramatic increase in the Republican vote, but Smith's failure to capture a proportion of the total vote approximating that of the party in contests for state offices suggests that many West Virginians opposed his Catholicism, his stand on prohibition, or his big city background. Norman Thomas, the Socialist, received only 1,313 votes.

Ironically, West Virginians in 1924 rejected John W. Davis, the state's only native son to receive the nomination of one of the major political parties. Davis, a native of Clarksburg, served in the West Virginia House of Delegates and as a member of Congress prior to his appointment by President Woodrow Wilson as solicitor general of the United States, a position which he filled with genuine distinction. Later, Wilson named him ambassador to England, and he received serious consideration for the United States Supreme Court, but he evinced little interest in a place on the bench, and the appointment went to Louis D. Brandeis. Davis had all the qualifications for the presidency, but perhaps no Democrat could have captured the office from Coolidge, who in only two years had become associated in the public mind with prosperity and honesty in government. Davis, like Coolidge, generally held a conservative political philosophy. He opposed the nomination of Franklin D. Roosevelt in 1932, objected to much of the New Deal, helped organize the Liberty League, and argued the case against desegregation before the Supreme Court in 1954. In many respects a product of his times, Davis served both the state and the nation with dignity and responsibility.

Three other West Virginians, each of whom first achieved stature in national rather than state affairs, have served in presidential cabinets in the twentieth century. Newton D. Baker of Martinsburg served as secretary of war under Woodrow Wilson; Louis Johnson of Clarksburg became the second secretary of defense under Harry Truman; and Cyrus Vance, also of Clarksburg, was secretary of state under Jimmy Carter.

Labor Problems and Advances

Genesis of the Labor Movement. A labor consciousness began to stir in West Virginia as early as 1830, when a diversified economy had produced a distinct wage-earning class in the Wheeling area. In 1829 William Cooper Howells, father of the novelist William Dean Howells, founded at Wheeling *The Eclectic Observer, and Working People's Advocate,* which called for public education and for voting and office-holding rights for unpropertied laborers. In the same year, workers in Wheeling petitioned the Virginia legislature for mechanic's lien laws to assure payment of wages through the sale of property of employers in default. The labor movement languished after the Jacksonian era and, except for a few later unions, including those of Wheeling typographical workers and stogie makers, did not revive substantially until after the Civil War.

A more durable growth of unionism in West Virginia coincided with the rise of the Knights of Labor, a national union formed in 1869 by Uriah S. Stephens. The union received a major test in the railroad strike of 1877, the first nationwide industrial strike. On July 18, the day a ten percent wage reduction for railway workers became effective, members of the Trainmen's Union at Martinsburg took possession of the Baltimore and Ohio lines and refused to allow trains to move. The strike spread rapidly, with mounting violence in such cities as Baltimore, Pittsburgh, Buffalo, Chicago, Saint Louis, and San Francisco. When state militiamen proved unable to quell the troubles at Martinsburg, Governor Henry M. Mathews requested President Rutherford B. Hayes to send in federal troops. The federal forces dispersed the strikers, and by August 3 most of the violence was over.

Short-lived though it was, the railroad strike gave workers a new sense of solidarity. In 1877 the Knights of Labor established a district assembly at Paden City, and within the next few years Stephens himself organized sixteen more in the state. In 1891 the Knights had forty assemblies in West Virginia. Meanwhile, the American Federation of Labor (AFL), composed of craft unions, was founded at Columbus, Ohio, in 1886 by Samuel Gompers and Adolph Strasser. Affiliated craft unions in West Virginia increased from twenty-six in 1889 to fifty-four in 1899.

Many industrial workers joined with farmers in 1878 to support the new Greenback-Labor party, which advocated cheap money, bureaus of labor in each state and in the federal government, and discouragement of monopolies. The party elected no West Virginians to federal office, but it made deep inroads into both the Democratic and Republican parties in some parts of the state, particularly the Kanawha Valley. In 1878 Democrat John C. Montgomery of Coal Valley, now Montgomery, who ran as a Greenbacker, and two Republicans who had Greenback support unseated prominent Democratic legislators James H. Ferguson, William A. Quarrier, and E. Willis Wilson of Kanawha County. Republican stalwart Romeo H. Freer addressed a Greenback rally in Braxton County, and dyed-in-the-wool Democratic newspaperman Henry S. Walker introduced James B. Weaver, the Greenback presidential candidate, at a dinner in Charleston.

For several years the Greenbackers preserved their organization in the state. In 1880 their candidate for governor, Napoleon B. French, received 13,027 of the 118,873 votes cast. In 1886 the party elected six members of the state legislature and enabled Robert S. Carr, an Independent Republican from Charleston, to win the presidency of the state senate. Some Democrats, such as Montgomery, concluded that Greenbackism actually aided the Republicans, since the two parties often supported the same candidates, and returned to the Democratic fold. There was no clear line of movement from Greenbackism to Populism in West Virginia, although they shared many of the same principles. During the 1890s party alignments generally returned to their customary patterns.

Workers usually responded more favorably to concerted union activity at municipal and state levels than to political approaches. The Ohio Valley Trades and Labor Assembly, organized at Wheeling in 1885, had forty-two craft unions and over four thousand members in 1903. Other cities with central labor unions in 1904 included Fairmont, Clarksburg, Charleston, Hinton, Morgantown, and Parkersburg. Goals of central organizations included ordinances banning employment of children under fourteen years old, an eight-hour workday, arbitration of labor disputes, and establishment of reading rooms featuring labor-related materials.

A further consolidation of union efforts occurred with the founding of the West Virginia Federation of Labor in 1903. By then Gompers and other leaders of the American Federation of Labor were convinced that a state organization could do more than municipal bodies to obtain desired legislation and influence state labor policies. The new state organization represented 152 craft locals, 46 trades, and 9,535 members, with special strength among iron, steel, and tin employees; transportation, railroad, and street railroad personnel; and glass workers. Wheeling had over forty percent of the craft union members in the state, with Huntington, Hinton, Bluefield, Parkersburg, and Fairmont, in that order, trailing far behind. In 1914 West Virginia had 270 craft unions, enrolling 31,315 members.

Early Union Activities in the Coalfields. In the early 1880s the coalfields had the largest pool of nonunion labor in West Virginia. The Knights of Labor stepped into the vacuum in 1877 by creating West Virginia District No. 5 at

Raymond City, with locals there and at Coalburg, Cannelton, and Lewiston. Some locals included laborers and even farmers in addition to miners. Coal operators resisted such efforts. In the Flat Top–Pocahontas field they dismissed and blacklisted miners who promoted unionism and imported foreigners, chiefly Hungarians, to replace them. As elsewhere, they capitalized on racial and ethnic divisions to thwart the union movement.

Unionism entered a new phase in 1886, when the new National Federation of Miners and Mine Laborers attempted to organize the Kanawha–New River fields. The National Federation included black as well as white miners and attacked the widespread "free turn" system whereby mine cars were allotted or withheld as a means of keeping coal loaders in line. A typical meeting, at Coal Valley, attracted eighty-nine miners and received strong endorsement from the local black minister.

Spurred by its success in southern West Virginia, the National Federation founded a statewide organization in 1888 and the following year merged with the Knights of Labor Trade Assembly 135 of coal miners to form the National Progressive Union, or NPU. President Michael F. Moran of the West Virginia Federation organized some twenty locals with more than one thousand members in the Kanawha–New River, Wheeling, Flat Top–Pocahontas, and other fields. In emphasizing the commitment of black miners to the union cause, the NPU proved an important link in activities that led to the founding of the United Mine Workers of America.

The United Mine Workers of America to 1914. Although it was an industrial rather than a craft union, Samuel Gompers encouraged the formation of the United Mine Workers of America, or UMWA, in 1890. At a meeting in Wheeling on April 21 West Virginia became District 17 of the new union. Partly because of conditions arising from the Panic of 1893, the UMWA made little immediate headway in the state. Scarcely more than half of West Virginia miners participated in a nationwide coal strike in 1894, and then for only varying periods of time. Most of the strike activity, including violence, centered in Kanawha, Fayette, Marshall, Ohio, and Brooke counties. The union, with its small treasury, was unprepared for a prolonged work stoppage and failed to bring the operators to terms. UMWA membership in West Virginia began to decline and fell to only 206 by 1897.

The UMWA faced a crisis, with West Virginia as its focal point. Wages ranged from only forty to sixty percent of those in 1894, with rates in West Virginia the lowest in the nation except for the Pittsburgh area, where immigrant labor from southern Europe was abundant. Union president Michael D. Ratchford took a long shot and called a nationwide strike for July 4, 1897. Operators in the Central Competitive Field, made up of western Pennsylvania, Ohio, Indiana, and Illinois, were already alarmed by the increase in superior and cheaper nonunion West Virginia coal in Midwest and Great Lakes markets. They offered to unionize their mines on a standard wage basis if the UMWA

would organize West Virginia and Kentucky mines on the same basis. Their
interests coincided with those of the UMWA, which recognized that nonunion
West Virginia and Kentucky mines jeopardized organizational efforts elsewhere.

Ratchford appealed to Gompers for aid in organizing West Virginia mines,
and on July 27 Gompers, Ratchford, John R. Sovereign, president of the
Knights of Labor, "Mother" Mary Jones, and Eugene V. Debs addressed some
seventeen thousand miners at Wheeling. Yet, only 5,134 of the 15,049 miners of
the state took part in the strike. Operators divided them by raising wages and
giving bonuses to those who remained at work. The failure to unionize West
Virginia mines left wages, hours of labor, and working conditions inferior to
those in the central parts of the country.

The 1897 strike marked the beginning of antilabor injunctions by West
Virginia judges, a practice condemned at the Wheeling meeting as "unjustified,
unwarranted, and unprecedented."[1] On July 26 Judge John M. Mason of the
Marion County Circuit Court had, at the request of former Governor A. Brooks
Fleming and Johnson N. Camden, both coal operators, forbidden Debs and his
associates to interfere in any way with mining in that county. On August 15
Judge John J. Jackson of the United States District Court enjoined Ratchford,
Debs, and others from entering property of the Montana Coal and Coke
Company to induce or intimidate miners into accepting the union. Three days
later United States Circuit Judge Nathan Goff, Jr., ruled that strikers using a
public highway near a mine named in Jackson's injunction were guilty of
contempt of court and should be punished.

At about the same time, companies began to use special police, mine
guards, and detectives to thwart union organizers. These hirelings, many of
notorious reputation, sometimes made it dangerous even for neutral persons to
venture on or near company properties. In 1907 Governor William M.O.
Dawson declared to the legislature that "Many outrages have been committed
by these guards, many of whom appear to be vicious and dare-devil men who
seem to aim to add to their viciousness by bull-dozing and terrorizing people."[2]

None of the union organizers captured more attention than Mary Jones,
known to laborers everywhere as "Mother" Jones. Born in Cork, Ireland, in
1830, she possessed in more than ample measure the fiery temperament often
associated with the sons and daughters of Erin. When she was five years old her
family migrated to America. As a young woman, Mary, née Harris, taught in a
convent in Michigan and later in Memphis, Tennessee. Following the death of
her husband and four children in a yellow fever epidemic in Memphis, she began

---

[1]G. Wayne Smith, *Nathan Goff, Jr.: A Biography* (Charleston: Education Foundation, Inc.,
1959), 256.

[2]William M.O. Dawson in West Virginia, *Special Message of Governor Dawson Concerning
Cases of Peonage and Labor Conditions to the Legislature of 1907* (Charleston: Tribune Printing
Co., 1907), 34.

to attend meetings of the Knights of Labor and soon became a passionate crusader for the rights of workers. For the next fifty years she was in the thick of union battles, whether in the coal mines of West Virginia, Pennsylvania, and Colorado; the railroads of Idaho; the copper mines of Arizona; or the streetcar business in New York City.

Accounts of Mother Jones are legion. Her diminutive stature, white hair, pleasant face, and unpretentious dress bespoke a certain dignity. When she dwelt upon injustices suffered by labor or sought to spur workers to action, however, the venerable little lady tore loose in torrents of invective and profanity that both shocked and delighted her audiences. Her methods were no mere theatrics; they were the means of drawing to the surface the thoughts, feelings, and longings of laboring classes to which she was able to give eloquent expression. Her sincere concern for their hardships, deprivation, and sufferings engendered trust and in the long run contributed as much to her success as her rousing exhortations. When she died in 1930 at the age of one hundred, she was beloved by the working classes and admired by others for her candor and courage.

In 1902 the UMWA resumed its efforts in West Virginia. On June 7 it called a strike of some sixteen thousand coal miners in fifteen counties and closed 108 of the 408 mines in the state. Coal companies again turned to injunctions, blacklisting, and mine guards, and union organizers often found it impossible to obtain meeting places. At a gathering in Clarksburg federal marshals arrested Mother Jones and eleven others and sent them to the Wood County jail in Parkersburg. Mother Jones refused special accommodations at a hotel and insisted on going to jail with her "boys." Despite strenuous efforts, the UMWA made little progress except in the Kanawha Valley. There Mother Jones, with Montgomery as her base, waged a campaign that unionized seven thousand miners of the area.

Meanwhile, both operators of the Central Competitive Field and UMWA leaders became increasingly alarmed by the volume of nonunion coal rolling into Midwest and Great Lakes markets. Regarding unorganized West Virginia mines as a dagger pointed at the heart of the union and spurred by financial support from Central Field operators, UMWA leaders in 1907 undertook to unionize the entire Ohio Valley on the basis of a uniform wage scale and a union dues checkoff system. John Mitchell, the UMWA president, took personal command of activities in West Virginia. Operators in the state again made effective use of their proven weapons, and after three years of intensive effort the UMWA had only three thousand members in District 17. In 1912 about ninety percent of the 70 million tons of coal mined in West Virginia still was sold in competition with that of the Central Competitive Field.

The Paint Creek Strike of 1912–1913. Ironically, one of the most violent events in the labor history of West Virginia occurred on Paint Creek in the Kanawha coalfield, where the UMWA had been entrenched since 1902. When their contract expired on April 1, 1912, Kanawha miners demanded more favorable terms, but the operators refused to negotiate a new agreement and withdrew their recognition of the UMWA as a bargaining agent. Most operators soon came to terms with the union. Only those on Paint Creek declined to sign new contracts.

Determined to make a stand, Paint Creek operators employed scores of mine guards, many from the Baldwin-Felts Detective Agency in Bluefield and Roanoke, Virginia, and armed them with shotguns, rifles, and machine guns. They evicted strikers from their houses and forced them to leave company property. The miners erected temporary shelters and tent colonies along public highways and on private property at Holly Grove, near the mouth of Paint Creek. They armed themselves and prepared to meet force with force.

Tension mounted steadily. Striking miners fired at trains carrying company-imported strikebreakers to the mines. Mother Jones visited Cabin Creek and persuaded miners there to join those on Paint Creek. Later, on the steps of the state capitol in Charleston, she demanded abolition of the mine guard system and urged miners to buy every gun in the city. By the end of August shootings at night, assaults, and destruction of property were common. On September 1, armed miners from Hugheston, Cannelton, and Boomer, on the north side of the Kanawha River, massed some 1,500 to 2,000 strong for a move against Cabin Creek, where about 400 heavily armed guards waited behind breastworks.

On September 2 Governor William E. Glasscock declared martial law and dispatched 1,200 state militiamen to the troubled Paint Creek–Cabin Creek area. Within a few days the militia seized 1,872 rifles, 556 pistols, 6 machine guns, 225,000 rounds of ammunition, 480 blackjacks, and an assortment of daggers, bayonets, and brass knuckles from the opposing sides. When the militia left on October 15, violence flared anew. A month later Glasscock reimposed martial law, which remained in effect until January 10, 1913.

Under martial law scores of persons were arrested and charged with offenses ranging from violations of travel restrictions in the strikebound area to inciting unrest. Many were confined to makeshift jails such as the "bull pen" at Hansford. Although civil courts were open, they were tried by military tribunals. Civil liberties, including the rights of the accused to counsel, to refuse to give evidence against themselves, and to separate trials, were ignored. Sentences were often severe, with prison terms for mere misdemeanors.

A ray of hope for the miners appeared in November 1912 in the report of an investigative commission appointed by Glasscock. The commission called for abolition of the "vicious, strife-producing and un-American" mine guard system, as well as the practices of blacklisting miners who joined unions and docking workers who loaded unclean coal. It endorsed the right of labor to organize for its own benefit and protection, by then the central issue in the strike.[3]

Both miners and operators stiffened their positions following the lifting of martial law. Miners concealed on the hillsides fired upon trains carrying

[3]West Virginia *Report of West Virginia Mining Investigation Commission, Appointed by Governor Glasscock on the 28th Day of August, 1912* (Charleston: Tribune Printing Co., [1912], 2.

strikebreakers with such frequency that they had to cease running. On the night of February 7, 1913, a train, the "Bull Moose Special," with an armored car carrying mine guards and at least one company official, steamed through Holly Grove, where the guards fired upon the dwellings of sleeping miners and their families and killed one miner. A few days later a clash at much-troubled Mucklow, now Gallagher, resulted in the death of twelve miners and four guards. On February 12 Glasscock reimposed martial law, which remained in effect until the end of the strike.

Mother Jones, who had denounced the governor, reaffirmed her "doctrine of divine discontent," and condemned the use of military courts and violations of civil rights in the Paint Creek area, returned to Charleston. Upon her arrival she was arrested and taken to Pratt, where she was confined on charges of incitement to murder, stealing a machine gun, and attempting to blow up a train with dynamite. Her arrest and the questionable charges against her drew widespread attention in the national press, which had by no means ignored events on Paint Creek. The eighty-two-year-old Mother Jones refused to enter a plea as long as civil courts were open. With a fire and venom that the years had not dulled, she declared her willingness to die for a cause to which she had given most of her life.

Soon after he took office on March 4, Governor Henry D. Hatfield, a physician, made a personal visit to the strife-torn area. Ignoring warnings that he might be assassinated, he arrived at Pratt armed only with a doctor's satchel. There he found Mother Jones ill with rapid respiration, a cough, and a high temperature. He had her sent to Charleston for treatment, but she was later returned to Pratt, where, still under arrest, she lived comfortably with a local family.

Redeeming a campaign pledge to end the violence, Hatfield created a board of arbitration and instructed it to reach an agreement no later than May 1. His pressure resulted in the "Hatfield Contract," which included a nine-hour workday, the right of miners to organize and to trade at noncompany stores, semimonthly paydays, and checkweighmen at coal tipples. Hatfield reaffirmed the right to civil trial by jury and invalidated pending sentences imposed by the military tribunals, including a twenty-year term meted out to Mother Jones.

Prior to the settlement John W. Kern of Indiana introduced a resolution in the United States Senate for an investigation to determine whether peonage existed, postal and immigration laws had been violated, and strikers had been prosecuted contrary to federal law in the Paint Creek troubles. Mother Jones urged him to make the inquiry "for the honor of the nation."[4] West Virginia Senator Nathan Goff, Jr., who as a federal judge had upheld a contempt case against her in 1902, tried to block the resolution. Hatfield himself vehemently

[4][Mary Harris Jones], *Autobiography of Mother Jones* (Chicago, 1925; New York: Arno & The New York Times, 1969), 164-65.

declared that he would not allow Mother Jones or any other person to enter the state to make inflammatory speeches likely to produce riots and bloodshed.

On May 27, after modifications and routing through the Committee on Education and Labor, the Kern Resolution passed the Senate. A subcommittee chaired by Claude A. Swanson of Virginia visited the Kanawha Valley and took testimony from scores of persons, including Glasscock, coal operator Quin Morton, union leaders, and strikers and their families. It found extensive lawlessness in the strike area, but it uncovered no peonage or evidence of interference with the mails or violation of immigration laws. Senator William E. Borah, however, held that there had been abuses in the use of martial law.

Labor and World War I. Both craft and trade unions made progress in West Virginia during World War I. In 1916 the West Virginia Federation of Labor and the Ohio Valley Trades and Labor Assembly established *The Majority*, a significant labor journal, at Wheeling. Already, in 1906, the *Labor Argus* had been founded at Charleston. By 1918 the American Federation of Labor had 548 affiliates in the state, and in 1920 the West Virginia Federation of Labor, after a period of near collapse, had 438 affiliates with 45,000 members.

Labor gained in other ways. In 1913, on the eve of the war, the legislature passed a workmen's compensation law, which shifted responsibility for accidents to employers. In that year, too, United States Senator Clarence W. Watson, a powerful coal operator, failed to win reelection, and young Matthew M. Neely, a staunch friend of labor, made his debut as congressman from the First District. Responding to labor influence, the legislature refused its assent to an antistrike law, urged by Governor John J. Cornwell, who claimed that Bolsheviks had infiltrated labor organizations in the larger cities.

Perhaps the most serious wartime setback for labor was the decision involving the Hitchman Coal and Coke Company, which had mines near Benwood, and the UMWA. On October 24, 1907, the company asked United States District Judge Alston G. Dayton for an order to restrain union organizers from interfering with its operations. It held that under the Sherman Anti-Trust Act the UMWA was an illegal organization, that it had conspired with operators in the Central Competitive Field, and that experience had shown that they could not deal with it on a peaceful, fair, and profitable basis. The case was appealed, and on December 10, 1917, the Supreme Court ruled that the company had a right to operate its mines under any rules and regulations that it chose and without union interference.

The wartime need for maximum industrial production and the creation of the War Labor Policy Board, with authority to enforce an industrial code, delayed immediate execution of the Hitchman decision. Moreover, coal operators made unprecedented profits and did not seek to claim the benefits deriving from the case. Most mines in the state, except those in the Smokeless coalfields and Clay County, were unionized, with UMWA membership increasing from about seven thousand in 1913 to about fifty thousand by the end of the war.

The First March on Logan. In spite of unprecedented growth of union membership in West Virginia and attainment of such goals as the eight-hour day by some ninety percent of organized workers by the end of 1920, wartime gains of labor proved fragile, particularly in the coal industry. Markets declined, stockpiles of coal-consuming industries grew, benevolent government policies toward labor subsided, and veterans competed for ever fewer jobs. Operators abandoned their forced tolerance of the UMWA and turned to the Hitchman decision. Faced with an era of dangerous competition, union leaders readied their forces for action, lest they "lose in peace what they had won in war."[5]

Adding to the vulnerability of the UMWA in West Virginia was a work force in which 37,000 of 91,000 miners were not unionized. Moreover, from 1912 to 1922 the nonunion fields of West Virginia produced between seven and ten percent of all of the coal mined in the United States. The UMWA centered its attention on Logan and Mingo counties, which included about one-third of the nonunion miners in the state and, with neighboring McDowell and Mercer counties, accounted for 32.21 percent of the coal mined in the state.

Determined to maintain their competitive status, Logan and Mingo operators again resorted to yellow dog contracts, court jurisdictions, and mine guards. They paid hundreds of thousands of dollars to county sheriffs, who employed antiunion deputies. Don Chafin, the sheriff of Logan County, had as many as forty-six active deputies, who drew salaries from both the county and coal companies, and as many as five hundred on inactive duty but armed with full legal authority.

In 1919 UMWA leaders laid plans for a national strike to begin November 1 and prepared a special assault upon nonunion fields. Logan and Mingo operators took measures to prevent organizers from entering their territory, giving rise to sometimes unfounded rumors of atrocities, including the beating and killing of miners, their wives, and children. Enraged by the reports, some five thousand miners from the Kanawha Valley and other unionized areas of central West Virginia gathered on September 4 at Marmet, with the intention of marching via Lens Creek to Logan "to get Don Chafin" and operator-paid deputies and mine guards.

Faced with an explosive situation and convinced that the miners had been stirred by Bolshevist propaganda, Governor Cornwell hurriedly enlisted the aid of Frank Keeney, president of District 17 of the UMWA. Keeney could not persuade the miners to disperse or to give up their plans. Apparently at his suggestion, Cornwell himself drove to Marmet. He addressed the miners by torchlight from the back of a truck on the night of September 5. He promised a full investigation of conditions in Logan County and appealed to the miners to abandon their march. Most of them accepted his offer, but about 1,500 refused and the next day moved on to Danville.

[5]Quoted in Charles H. Ambler and Festus P. Summers, *West Virginia, the Mountain State*, 2d ed. (Englewood Cliffs, N.J.: Prentice-Hall, Inc., 1958), 453.

Cornwell acted swiftly. He provided credentials for three investigators, whom Keeney, now acting as his agent, rushed to the Logan area, and called for federal forces, including airplanes equipped with machine guns. Deterred by the possibility of facing federal troops and charges of treason and assured by Keeney that union organizers in Logan County had found reports of brutality by deputy sheriffs exaggerated, the miners agreed to return home by special trains.

The Union Advance into Mingo County. In the spring of 1920 the focus of labor discontent shifted to Mingo County, where miners received a wage cut at a time when the United States Coal Commission awarded generous increases to those in unionized areas. After an unsuccessful strike, they appealed to Frank Keeney. On May 6 Keeney, William Blizzard, and Fred Mooney, who had served on the uniform rate commission of the Bituminous Coal Commission in 1919, addressed about three thousand miners. Before the end of the month UMWA organizers established twenty-two local unions.

A few operators of small mines signed contracts with the union, but large companies refused to deal with it. On May 19 twelve Baldwin-Felts agents, whom they employed, arrived at Matewan and evicted striking miners from their houses in nearby Stone Mountain. Afterward, while they waited at the Matewan station for the train for Bluefield, Albert and Lee Felts, their leaders, got into an argument with Mayor Cabell Testerman and his chief of police, Albert Sidney Hatfield, a tough and wiry little man who had long since earned the nickname "Two-Gun Sid." With tempers flaring, one of the Felts brothers drew his gun and killed Testerman in a shot probably aimed at Hatfield. Bullets then rang from all directions. In a few seconds, seven detectives (including both Felts brothers), Testerman, two miners, and a bystander were dead.

Sid Hatfield, who had a gun blown from his hand and his hat shot off, became the instant hero of the "Matewan Massacre." With no pretense to modesty, he claimed responsibility for the death of all seven detectives and declared that he had done "no more than any other red bloodied [*sic*] American would have done in my place."[6] Later, when murder indictments were returned against him and nineteen others, he maintained that he had not shot any of the detectives.

By the time that Hatfield and his codefendants were brought to trial, civil law had broken down, and Mingo County was policed by 450 federal troops, requested by Governor Ephraim Morgan. Military police had to disarm spectators, witnesses, and officials before Judge R.D. Bailey's court could conduct business safely. Evidence against Hatfield and the other defendants was not beyond all doubt, and all were acquitted. The following year, in an unrelated incident, Hatfield was "assassinated" on the steps of the McDowell County

[6]Quoted from *Washington Times*, January 29, 1921, in Daniel P. Jordan, "The Mingo War: Labor Violence in the Southern West Virginia Coal Fields, 1919-1922," in *Essays in Southern Labor History: Selected Papers, Southern Labor History Conference, 1976*, ed. Gary M. Fink and Merl E. Reed (Westport, Conn.: Greenwood Press, 1977), 108.

courthouse at Welch, when he appeared for trial on charges of "shooting up" the town of Mohawk.

Following the Matewan killings the UMWA grew rapidly in Mingo County, with about six thousand members by July 1. At a mass meeting in Williamson in late June union leaders called for the pay scale and benefits received by union miners in the northern part of the state. Operators refused to talk with the union and with Negro and foreign-born strikebreakers restored production to normal levels before the end of 1920, which had ominous implications for the union cause.

During the twenty-eight months of the strike-lockout some three thousand evicted miners and their families lived in tent villages along public highways and on private property, the largest of which was at Lick Creek near Williamson. The union provided much of their food and other needs. Police restricted movements of the miners and forbade all assemblies except church gatherings and authorized demonstrations and parades.

Disorders were frequent and violent. A three-hour battle on August 21 left six men dead and more than a score wounded. On January 31, 1921, strikers rained "a veritable hail of bullets" on Williamson.[7] They also fired into the towns of Merrimac, Rawl, Sprigg, and Matewan and neighboring McCarr, Kentucky. By July 1921 Frank Keeney placed the death toll at more than one hundred, and in later testimony before a United States Senate investigating committee, a spokesman for the operators asserted that between July 1920 and July 1921 there were at least 125 "disturbances, assaults, killings, explosions, burnings, and so forth."[8] Leading newspapers across the country treated their readers to details of events in what had by then become known as "Bloody Mingo."

Three times during the strike governors of the state called for federal troops. The first contingent, numbering 450, served from August 29 to November 3, 1920. Union leaders contended that their presence aided the operators, and Keeney threatened a statewide strike unless they were removed. Governor Cornwell yielded on the condition that the Mingo County sheriff appoint enough deputies to maintain order. Once the troops departed, violence broke out anew. Cornwell then proclaimed "a state of insurrection" in the county, and at his request, five hundred federal troops were sent in and remained there from November 28, 1920, until January 16, 1921. When troubles erupted again in May 1921, Governor Morgan asked President Harding for federal forces. Harding refused, asserting that West Virginia had not exhausted its own resources and that the United States Army was not a police force. Left to his own devices, Morgan reimposed martial law, which was to be enforced by state police and a "vigilance committee" of over five hundred citizens, nearly all antiunionists.

[7]Quoted in Ambler and Summers, *West Virginia, the Mountain State*, 455.
[8]Jordan, "The Mingo War," 109.

The Second March on Logan. Prospects for the miners deteriorated in July and August 1921. Governor Morgan rejected a petition by several hundred miners urging him to end the strike on favorable terms. The state Supreme Court upheld martial law and the imprisonment of miners and union officials in Williamson.

Armed miners from the Kanawha Valley, chiefly Paint and Cabin creeks, again gathered, five thousand strong, at Marmet on August 20 for a supportive march on Logan. Many were veterans of World War I and wore either their military uniforms or blue denim overalls and red bandannas. They were well organized, with sentries, patrols, passwords, and marching songs, and were accompanied by loaded commissary wagons, nurses, and chaplains. Most traveled on foot, but some went by automobile or horseback. A few commandeered freight trains and gave them such names as "Blue Steel Special" and "Smith and Wesson Special."

The following day Don Chafin warned that he would not allow any "invasion" of Logan County by an "armed mob." On August 23 Mother Jones, then ninety-one years old, arrived at Marmet and urged the miners to disperse. She waved a paper, purportedly a telegram from President Harding promising a full investigation of conditions in the troubled area. It quickly became known that Harding had sent no telegram, and a discredited Mother Jones lost control of the determined miners. The motive for her deception has remained a mystery.

Alarmed by the turn of events, Governor Morgan alerted state police and the militia and appealed to President Harding for assistance. Harding dispatched General Henry Bandholtz, who arrived in Charleston at 3:05 in the morning of August 25 and called at once upon the waiting governor. Bandholtz then conferred with Keeney and Mooney and warned that he would hold them responsible for any illegal acts by the marchers. Keeney and Mooney left at 5:30 by taxi and persuaded the miners, whom they overtook at Madison, to disperse. Bandholtz met with them the next day and informed Harding that troops would not be necessary.

On the night of August 28, while miners at Madison awaited transportation home, about 130 state police from Logan, in an ill-timed move, tried to arrest forty-two miners accused of interfering with their work sixteen days earlier. The resulting "Sharples Massacre," which left two miners dead and three wounded, enraged those at Madison. Ignoring pleas from Harding and union leaders to disperse, more than five thousand again took up the march. On August 31 some twelve to thirteen hundred state police, deputy sheriffs, armed guards, and "volunteers" intercepted them at Blair Mountain, near the Boone-Logan county line. For four days the "battle of Blair Mountain" raged over a twenty- to thirty-mile front, with reporters, some of them World War I correspondents, providing full coverage.

Federal intervention ended the battle. On September 1, the secretary of war dispatched the Eighty-eighth Light Bombing Squadron under General Billy

Mitchell from Langley Field, Virginia, and 2,100 troops, including a chemical warfare unit and eight trench mortars, from Fort Thomas, Kentucky. Confronted by the possible use of such force, the miners surrendered and returned home. Losses among the Logan forces were light, with three men killed and about forty wounded. Those of the miners were never ascertained.

Aftermath of the Mingo Troubles. Once the miners were defeated, the operators turned to the courts. A Logan County grand jury indicted 543 persons on charges ranging from "pistol toting" and murder to treason against the state. A Boone County grand jury also indicted 302 persons. The most serious cases were tried, through a change of venue, by the Jefferson County Circuit Court at Charles Town in the courthouse where John Brown had been found guilty of treason.

The trials excited great interest. The operators, aided by a friendly press, emphasized charges that the UMWA had made war against the state and that its leaders had engaged in treason. Union leaders contended that they opposed not the state but an industrial autocracy that had usurped both civil and military power for its own purposes. Union lawyers made the most of an admission that some attorneys for the prosecution were paid by coal operators.

From April 24, 1922, until well into 1924 the trials commanded public attention. Attorneys for the operators leveled some of their heaviest legal artillery at William Blizzard, the alleged leader of the march on Logan, who was charged with treason. When Blizzard was acquitted, the American Legion in the town held a celebration and carried the union leader through the streets. The murder trials of Blizzard and Keeney were moved first to Berkeley Springs and then to Lewisburg, where Blizzard was saved by a deadlocked jury. Keeney's case was then moved to strongly prolabor Fayette County, and the charge against him was dropped from the docket. Prison terms for most others convicted of serious charges were later reduced, or the defendants were pardoned.

On June 21, 1921, the United States Senate authorized its Committee on Education and Labor to investigate labor conditions in southern West Virginia. A subcommittee chaired by William S. Kenyon of Iowa reported that coal operators constituted an industrial autocracy and condemned their domination over county and municipal governments and their use of mine guards. It singled out the payment of deputy sheriffs by operators as "a vicious and un-American policy and a practice that should cease." The subcommittee termed as "absolutely indefensible" lawlessness of the miners, including murders, destruction of property, commandeering of railroad trains and crews, and armed marches.[9] It recommended, however, that if miners had the right to bargain collectively under the code of the National War Labor Board, they should be protected in that right.

The right of coal miners to belong to a union, the central issue in the

[9]U.S. Congress, Senate "Personal Views of Senator William S. Kenyon," *Report No. 457*, 67th Cong., 2d sess., 4-6.

troubles, remain unresolved despite the gubernatorial investigation and the senatorial inquiry. Miners held that such a right was beyond question in the twentieth century. Coal operators, however, never conceded their rights to use mine guards and paid deputy sheriffs, to obtain court injunctions, and to suppress union activity by indictment. Labor battles in the mining areas were far from won.

An Era of Labor Losses. As an aftermath of the defeat of the miners in Logan and Mingo counties, UMWA membership in District 17 dropped sharply from 42,000 in 1921 to about 21,000 in 1924. Officers of the bankrupt district asked that they be removed from their positions and the district revert to a provisional status in the national organization. In 1929 the secretary-treasurer of the State Federation of Labor declared that "within the last three or four years, the coal companies have been successful in wiping out the last vestige of collective bargaining in the coal mines of West Virginia."[10]

The Great Depression further undermined union strength in West Virginia. In 1932 craft unions had less than three thousand dues-paying members, and those affiliated with the State Federation of Labor seemed near extinction. Of 23,000 miners, organized into 220 locals, less than one thousand were paying dues. More than one-third of the miners of the state were jobless, thousands of others worked only part-time, and scores of operators had declared bankruptcy.

Believing the UMWA incapable of solving the problems of state miners while it was under the leadership of John L. Lewis, Frank Keeney organized the rival West Virginia Mine Workers Union, which soon enrolled some twenty thousand miners. The new organization staged hunger marches on the state government, forced operators to place checkweighmen on coal tipples, and obtained wage scales above those paid in northern West Virginia. In the summer of 1931, however, miners refused to support a general strike to force acceptance of collective bargaining. After passage of the National Industrial Recovery Act in 1933, he urged members to return to the UMWA, but he himself never did so. Other unions, including the stogie makers, also faced the threat of dualism, which the State Federation of Labor consistently opposed.

Labor and the New Deal. Departing from practice, the State Federation of Labor in 1932, at the urging of Van A. Bittner, a leader of UMWA District 31, called upon member unions to support Thomas C. Townsend as a nonpartisan prolabor candidate for governor. Townsend, who had defended Blizzard and Keeney in their treason trials, also received the nomination of the Republican party and the endorsement of AFL President William L. Green, John L. Lewis, and leaders of most other labor organizations. As usual, workers followed their own political preferences. They supported the Democratic party, adding to the margins of victory of Franklin D. Roosevelt and Herman Guy Kump, its gubernatorial nominee.

[10]Quoted in Ambler and Summers, *West Virginia, the Mountain State*, 460-61.

The National Industrial Recovery Act of 1933 (NIRA), designed to stabilize industry during the nation's worst depression, provided for an eight-hour work-day and minimum wage scales, both of which enabled industry to absorb large numbers of unemployed persons. More far-reaching was a section, hailed as the "magna carta of labor," which guaranteed employees the right to bargain collectively and outlawed yellow-dog contracts, stimulating a resurgence of unionism in West Virginia. The State Federation of Labor added 641 new affiliates with 106,175 new members in its 1933–1934 fiscal year. UMWA membership rose from 16,000 in May 1933 to 107,000 in July 1935. Even Logan County miners organized under the aegis of the act.

The state legislature also showed a new responsiveness to labor needs. In 1935 it abolished the mine guard system, approved a prevailing wage rate, improved workmen's compensation, and provided for victims of silicosis. In later years it regularly refined and liberalized workmen's compensation and a comprehensive unemployment compensation act passed in 1936.

The new federal legislation, particularly the NIRA, enabled John L. Lewis to gain new stature among coal miners of the state. In 1933 he negotiated the first of a series of industrywide contracts known as the Appalachian Agreements, which narrowed and eventually eliminated unfavorable wage differentials for West Virginia miners. Coal operators objected to the contracts, but the Wagner Labor Relations Act of 1935 and the Guffey Coal acts of 1935 and 1936 reinforced the gains of the miners. Two years later the UMWA organized captive mines belonging to steel companies, with Governor Matthew M. Neely disciplining state police rather than pickets when violence flared at United States Steel mines at Gary.

In 1935 Lewis himself introduced the disruptive force of dualism into the union movement. Claiming that craft unions were incompatible with labor goals under conditions of mass production, he founded the Committee on Industrial Organization, later the Congress of Industrial Organizations, or CIO. The AFL repudiated the CIO, and President Green revoked the charter of the State Federation of Labor, which refused to dissociate affiliates of the CIO. The State Federation applied for membership in the CIO and in 1937 became the West Virginia Trades Council, of which the UMWA was the chief component. In 1938 opposing unions revived the West Virginia Federation of Labor with an AFL affiliation. Within five months it had 152 locals.

For all his accomplishments, the brusque and imperious Lewis owed much of his success to Roosevelt, whose New Deal made possible many of his gains for labor. In 1940 Lewis opposed Roosevelt's bid for a third term, but most miners remained loyal to the president. Lewis soon resigned as head of the CIO and led the UMWA out of the organization and in 1946 back into the AFL, only to withdraw again in 1947.

The Hawks Nest Tragedy. One of the most unfortunate experiences of labor during the depression era involved construction of the Hawks Nest tunnel through Gauley Mountain. Built to divert part of the waters of the New River to a hydroelectric generating station of the Union Carbide Corporation about three miles downstream, it was begun in 1930 and completed in 1935.

Hundreds of men desperate for jobs, many of them Negroes from southern states, made their way to Gauley Bridge, the headquarters of the construction company. Unfortunately, the rock through which the tunnel was cut ranged up to ninety-nine percent pure silica. Few precautions, including relatively simple wet-drilling techniques, were taken. Workers inhaled tiny dust particles, which were trapped in their lungs, causing breathing impairment and even death. Local doctors, later accused of lack of medical knowledge and even of intent to conceal its nature, failed to diagnose the condition as silicosis. Investigations by a United States Senate subcommittee revealed that scores of workers died during construction and that many of the bodies were taken to Summersville for burial by a local undertaker, who had an agreement with the contractors. The widely hailed engineering achievement was accomplished at a frightful human cost.

The Hawks Nest tragedy had equally inglorious sequels. Governor Homer A. Holt, who was shown the manuscript of *West Virginia: A Guide to the Mountain State*, prepared by the Federal Writers' Project, branded the account of silicosis at Hawks Nest "distinctly discreditable to the State and its people."[11] His refusal to permit use of the state seal or other marks suggesting official approval forced alterations before the book went to press. Later, Hubert Skidmore, a state author, made the tragedy the theme of a novel, *Hawks Nest*, but criticisms and threats of lawsuits caused the publisher to withdraw all available copies.

Mine Disasters and Safety Legislation. The Hawks Nest problem created temporary excitement, but the hazards of coal mining left a long and bloody stain upon the labor history of West Virginia. The mines claimed 4,309 lives between 1883 and 1919. Of that number 2,181 were victims of coal, slate, and roof falls; 1,175 of gas or dust explosions; 529 of mine car accidents; and 424 of other causes. Prior to World War I, the fatality rate in West Virginia mines exceeded that of competing states. In 1911 it stood at 5.17 per one thousand workers compared with 4.09 in the anthracite mines and 3.23 in the bituminous mines of Pennsylvania, 2.14 in Illinois, and 2.35 in Ohio.

Major disasters did more to draw attention to dangers in mining than did the appalling number of both fatal and nonfatal accidents with relatively few casualties. The first great tragedy in the state occurred at Newburg, Preston County, in 1886, when an explosion killed thirty-nine men. Twenty-one major disasters darkened the pages of coal-mining history by 1917 and another twenty-one occurred from 1917 to 1968.

The greatest single loss of life in the mines occurred at Monongah on

[11]Quoted in John Alexander Williams, *West Virginia: A Bicentennial History* (New York and Nashville: W.W. Norton & Company, Inc., and American Association for State and Local History, 1976), 163.

December 6, 1907, when 361 men were killed in a blast, the cause of which was hotly disputed by miners and officials of the Fairmont Coal Company. Other explosions that resulted in great losses occurred at mines at Switchback, where 50 men died on December 29, 1908, and another 67 were killed two weeks later; Eccles, in 1914, with 183 deaths; Layland, in 1915, with 112 deaths; Benwood, in 1924, where 119 men died; Everettville, in 1927, with 97 deaths; and more recently, Farmington, where 78 men died in 1968. Some of the explosions were of such magnitude that they blew mine cars and other equipment out of the mines. The spectacle of tearful families waiting at mine entrances for news was a common sight. In earlier years survivors faced the gloomy prospect of cessation of family income and dependence upon charity and the goodwill of coal companies, friendly relatives and neighbors, and any relief funds that might have been established.

With its politically powerful operators and weak miners' unions, West Virginia for decades had only rudimentary mine safety laws. Reflecting a prevailing laissez-faire attitude toward industry, Governor Atkinson, by no means an unfeeling man, declared that "it is but the natural course of mining events that men should be injured and killed in accidents."[12] Even in the wake of an explosion at Red Ash that took forty-six lives, the legislature in 1900 killed bills that would have made mine bosses legal agents of the operators, provided examinations for key management persons, subjected operators convicted of willful neglect to large fines, and required a license tax on the mining of coal, with proceeds set aside for inspection services and miners' hospitals.

Following a series of relatively small mine accidents and an explosion of a mine at Courrières, France, in 1906 that killed 1,230 men, sentiment for safety legislation grew rapidly in West Virginia. In 1907 the legislature passed laws defining the responsibilities of mine foremen for safety conditions, requiring the use of locked safety lamps in mines with dangerous levels of explosive gases, increasing ventilation standards, and giving district mine inspectors authority over solid-shooting of coal. After explosions at Stuart and Thomas, the lawmakers created a committee to investigate safety problems in state mines. The committee, however, declared that excessive solid-shooting and ignition of coal dust by blown-out shots, two major causes of explosions, could not be corrected by law. Under pressure from operators who feared competition from other states, the legislature rejected every reform proposed in 1908 and enacted no major mine laws for the next seven years.

The legislature at last, in 1915, approved several mine safety measures, including regulation of shooting of coal in gaseous mines, but it refused to place curbs upon dangerous solid-shooting. John Laing, the state mine inspector, responded by issuing administrative regulations that required the use of compe-

[12]Quoted in William Graebner, *Coal-Mining Safety in the Progressive Period: The Political Economy of Reform* (Lexington: University Press of Kentucky, 1976), 73.

tent shot-firers, permitted only approved explosives in unwatered dusty mines, and mandated examinations for mine foremen and fire bosses. Hoping to forestall further state action that might place them at a disadvantage vis-à-vis other states, many West Virginia operators began to press for federal mine safety laws. They included A. Brooks Fleming, a major owner of the Fairmont and Consolidation coal companies, Walter N. Page, and George H. Caperton. The creation of the United States Department of Mines in 1910 was in part a result of their efforts.

Mine safety improved, but slowly. From the beginning of the twentieth century to the end of 1980, there were 19,826 fatal accidents in West Virginia mines. Of that number 11,457 occurred before the end of 1930, another 5,721 before the end of 1950, and the remaining 2,548 after 1950.

The mines have taken a heavy toll in human health and life in other ways. In 1946 John L. Lewis negotiated a contract with operators that included a Welfare and Retirement clause by which the federal government agreed to pay into such a fund five cents for each ton of coal mined. Through the fund, augmented by subsequent increases, miners' hospitals were built throughout the coalfields. The identification in Great Britian in 1942 of pneumoconiosis as a distinct type of dust disease led to another significant achievement in miner welfare. In 1970 West Virginia enacted "black lung" legislation, but the previous year, federal action had already recognized pneumoconiosis as an occupational disease, provided funds for benefits to its victims, and set ceilings on acceptable dust levels in coal mines.

Labor After World War II. Organized labor reached one of its plateaus of success in 1940. Coal miners, with such leaders as Bittner and Blizzard, made important contributions to the election of Matthew M. Neely as a prolabor governor. Yet even Neely began to rely less on the labor vote after his defeat for the United States Senate two years later. Moreover, the moves of Lewis and the UMWA in and out of the AFL and a series of defiant wartime strikes lost the union much public support, with other politicians, including United States Senator Harley M. Kilgore, loosening their ties to Lewis.

Antiunion sentiment engendered by strikes that caused inconvenience and hardship to millions of Americans produced a backlash in the passage of the Taft-Hartley Act by a Republican-dominated Congress in 1947. Labor leaders criticized provisions that outlawed the closed shop, gave state right-to-work laws precedence over union shops if approved by a majority of the workers, restored the power of "discretionary injunctions" to the courts, and allowed unions to be sued as entities. The West Virginia Federation of Labor applauded President Harry Truman's veto of the act, praised John L. Lewis for opposing a requirement that union officials sign an affidavit that their organizations were free of Communists in order to share legal benefits, and called upon affiliates to work for repeal of the act.

The powerful unions suffered some reverses in West Virginia in the 1950s.

After victories in the "Big Steel" and "Little Steel" settlements, the CIO in 1950 lost a battle to organize employees of the Weirton Steel Company at Weirton and Steubenville, Ohio, to the Employees Security League. In 1952 the UMWA agreed to assist the Employees League of Widen Miners, after failing to supplant it as the bargaining agent with the Elk River Coal and Lumber Company at Widen. The Widen strike dragged on for months, with destruction of property, at least one death, and much criticism of company owner Joseph G. Bradley. By December 1953 the strikers abandoned their fight, and the UMWA ceased to aid them.

Both federal and state action enabled labor to make steady gains in the 1960s and 1970s. The Federal Coal Mine Health and Safety Act of 1969 was a substantial victory for coal miners. In 1973 the West Virginia legislature, under Title IV of the act, established a pneumoconiosis, or "black lung," fund for miners from premiums paid by employers. Comprehensive revisions in 1974 brought further gains for labor.

In spite of advances, West Virginia suffered from a reputation as a strike-prone state. In 1971 the legislature created a bipartisan Labor-Management Relations Board of three members with authority to hear, investigate, and prosecute unfair labor practices in private industry. In 1977 it established the West Virginia Labor-Management Advisory Council, representing labor, management, and government and charged with improving the labor climate and attracting new industry.

The 1980s brought new troubles for labor in West Virginia. The decline in oil prices of OPEC countries and production of low-sulfur western coal undermined potential markets for West Virginia coal, pushing the state below even Wyoming in coal mined and reducing available jobs. Moreover, several coal companies, led by the Consolidation Coal Company, one of the nation's largest producers, rejected the Bituminous Coal Operators Association as the corporate bargaining agent with the UMWA and threatened the continuance of favorable contracts of the past. Employees in smokestack industries, particularly those in primary metals, also fared poorly. One of the potentially promising developments was the sale of the Weirton Steel plant to its employees, making it the largest employee-owned business of its kind in the country.

The recession of the 1980s further weakened the economy of West Virginia and undermined the well-being of its workers. The state by 1984 had the highest rate of unemployment in the nation. Worse still, economic indicators pointed to continuing difficulties, with recovery trailing far behind that of other states. In this gloomy context, labor and management both seemed to have arrived at a time when new outlooks and a new spirit of cooperation would be needed to restore the state to the more favorable conditions it had known in the preceding decades.

The Transformation of Education

The Free School Idea in the First Constitution. Free public education made little progress in West Virginia before the Civil War. Only Kanawha, Ohio, and Jefferson counties provided free schools for all children, although a few others were contemplating adoption of the plan when the war came. Many West Virginians, nevertheless, shared a common American belief that a close link existed between education and material progress, and they did not want to be left farther behind than they were.

When the question of public schools came before the Committee on Education of the West Virginia Constitutional Convention of 1863, Gordon Battelle, chairman of the committee, turned for advice to the Reverend Alexander Martin, a professor at Allegheny College in Meadville, Pennsylvania. Within two weeks Martin presented "An Outline of a System of General Education for the New State," based upon the premise that "the education of the people . . . is the only exhaustless mine which the people possesses" and should be "as free as the air . . . and the light of Heaven."[1] His plan called for a system financed through state appropriations, income from a permanent school fund, and local taxes and administered by a state board of education, a state superintendent, county superintendents, and local officials.

The convention adopted the Martin outline, but it declined to accept proposals for funding recommended by the Education Committee. It limited sources of school revenue to net proceeds from the sale of delinquent or forfeited lands; the new state's share in the Literary Fund and in moneys, stocks, and properties owned by Virginia for educational purposes; the proceeds of estates escheating to the state; possible grants and bequests for educational purposes; and such sums as the legislature might appropriate. Fearing that "the bottom had dropped out of the whole scheme," Battelle offered a resolution that the legislature should "as soon as practicable" provide for "a thorough and efficient system of free schools."[2]

[1]Charles H. Ambler and Festus P. Summers, *West Virginia, the Mountain State*, 2d ed. (Englewood Cliffs, N.J.: Prentice-Hall, Inc., 1958), 299.
[2]Charles H. Ambler, Frances Haney Atwood, and William B. Mathews, eds., *Debates and Proceedings of the First Constitutional Convention of West Virginia, (1861-1863)*, 3 vols. (Huntington: Gentry Brothers, 1942), vol. 1, 388-89.

Legislative Provisions for Free Schools. On December 10, 1863, the legislature adopted a more detailed plan presented by Andrew F. Ross, principal of West Liberty Academy. The statute authorized a six-month school term for all youth of the state, provided for division of counties into townships and the latter into subdistricts in which school matters could be decided in mass meetings, and specified procedures for election of county superintendents and district commissioners. The election of a state superintendent was set for February 16, 1864, when William Ryland White, a Methodist minister and principal of Fairmont Male and Female Academy, was chosen for the term ending March 3, 1865. To finance the new system, the legislature authorized a general property tax, with the rate not to exceed ten cents on each one hundred dollars of assessed valuation. It required townships with more than thirty eligible Negro children to provide for their education, but not in the schools attended by white children.

In some respects the new system proved disappointing. Meetings of citizens in sparsely populated mountain townships were often not feasible, and in 1867 the legislature vested responsibility for organizing and maintaining schools in township boards and supervision of each school in local trustees. Local tax revenues were inadequate, and in 1867 the minimum school term was reduced to four months.

Despite severe handicaps, the schools made progress during the first years of statehood. The average term increased from 2.7 months in 1865–1866 to 4.1 in 1869–1870. In 1870 the 2,257 schools were staffed by 2,405 teachers, of whom 641 were women. Of the 2,113 schoolhouses, 1,104 were frame structures. A few towns, including Clarksburg and Parkersburg, established public schools for Negroes, and others founded with aid from the Freedmen's Bureau later became public institutions. Except in a few towns, such as Wheeling, salaries of teachers were low, the average being only slightly more than thirty dollars per month.

An Era of Change. Rapid advances in education occurred during the years between adoption of a new constitution in 1872 and World War I. The constitution placed control of the school fund in a board composed of the governor, superintendent of free schools, auditor, and treasurer; required county sheriffs to collect all school levies and make annual settlements with county courts; and continued the requirement of separate schools for white and black pupils. The term of the state superintendent was extended to four years, but the office became political, leading to a request by the State Teachers Association that it be permitted to designate "some able, efficient and practical educator" for the position.[3]

The legislature made few changes as a result of the new constitution. It retained the minimum four-month term, but inequalities in taxable wealth caused great variations among the counties. In the interest of economy, the lawmakers assigned the state superintendent the responsibilites of the adjutant

[3]Quoted in Charles H. Ambler, *A History of Education in West Virginia from Early Colonial Times to 1949* (Huntington: Standard Printing and Publishing Company, 1951), 149.

general. County superintendents became little more than low-paid clerks, who could supplement their salaries by teaching without certification and by conducting sessions that those seeking certification were expected to attend. In an effort to eliminate abuses in the adoption of textbooks by counties, selection was entrusted to a bipartisan state commission of nine members that included the state superintendent of schools.

An important innovation of the late nineteenth century was a graduating plan for rural schools devised by Alexander L. Wade, a superintendent of Monongalia County. Drawing upon experiences of graded schools then being established throughout the nation, Wade's plan included grades, promotions, and graduation and provided new incentives for countless pupils. His ideas won applause from the National Education Association and educational leaders and in 1881 appeared in print as *A Graduating System for Country Schools*. In 1891 a modified form of the plan was made compulsory throughout the state.

At about the same time, teachers' institutes gained importance in the professionalization of teaching. Usually held for a week or so in late summer, they provided thousands of instructors, most of them in one-teacher schools, with professional fellowship and knowledge of advances in their fields. Following a grant of five hundred dollars by the legislature in 1879, Barnas Sears, the agent of the Peabody Fund, provided three thousand dollars for the purpose of assuring an institute in each county. In 1903 the legislature enacted a law requiring uniform teachers' examinations, which ended much of the corruption that had attended the granting of certificates by county superintendents.

The state assumed a major role in the preparation of teachers with the establishment of normal schools. In response to a declaration by Governor Boreman in 1866 that the scarcity of trained teachers was one of the "greatest difficulties in the way of putting into successful operation our free school system," State Superintendent White made teacher training the focus of secondary education.[4] In 1868 Marshall College reopened as the State Normal School. In 1869 the Fairmont State Regency Normal became the Fairmont Branch Normal, and the following year West Liberty Academy opened as West Liberty State Normal. Two years later branch normals were established at Athens, Glenville, and Shepherdstown.

With little popular support for professional preparation of teachers and depressed economic conditions of the early 1870s depriving them of necessary operating funds, the normal schools at first had a precarious existence. A movement in the 1880s to establish a unified state educational system reduced them to little more than preparatory schools for West Virginia University. In 1885 the normal school regents concluded that it was impracticable to develop the institutions into teachers colleges and accepted a uniform course of study based on that of the preparatory department of the university.

[4]West Virginia Senate, *Journal, 1866*, 15.

The elevation of the normal schools to genuine teacher training institutions evolved in the ensuing decades. An increasing number of teachers educated at George Peabody College and at Columbia University, with support from leaders in other walks of life, induced the Board of Regents to create a teacher training department at Marshall College in 1901 and soon afterward one at Fairmont. Two preparatory schools for West Virginia University, established at Montgomery in 1895 and at Keyser in 1901, also provided courses for teachers. Contributing to the staffing of Negro schools were Storer College, founded at Harpers Ferry in 1867 by the Freedmen's Bureau, with support from John Storer, a Maine philanthropist; the West Virginia Colored Institute, established at Institute in 1892; and Bluefield Colored Institute, founded in 1895.

At the urging of State Superintendent of Schools Virgil A. Lewis and the State Education Association, the legislature in 1901 required county superintendents to have skill and experience in teaching and forbade them to teach in a public or private school while holding office. It also mandated that the superintendent visit the schools annually and report to the state superintendent.

Amidst these modest achievements, one glaring defect remained. In 1910 the state had only fifty "so-called high schools." Part of the problem lay in a constitutional provision requiring approval of three-fifths of the voters in a school district for the establishment of a high school and setting a ceiling of thirty cents on each one hundred dollars assessed valuation of general property for their support. Curricula varied widely, as did the quality of instruction.

Financing the Public Schools. Inadequate financing greatly impeded the progress of public education in the late nineteenth century. The state levy for teachers remained constant at ten cents on each hundred-dollar valuation until 1904. Three years later the state property levy was eliminated, and minimum district levy rates were reduced from fifty to forty cents for teachers and from twenty-five to fifteen cents per hundred dollars valuation for maintenance. The law of 1907, however, stressed local effort by allowing voters in a school district to increase the teacher levy sufficiently to ensure a six-month term and the new building levy to twenty-five cents per hundred dollars valuation.

In 1882 West Virginia adopted the "first minimum salary law for teachers ever placed on the statute books of an American commonwealth."[5] The scale was set at $25, $22, and $18 per month for first-, second-, and third-grade certificates and remained unchanged until 1901, when the pay for first-grade certificates was raised to $30 and that for second-grade certificates to $25 per month.

The traditional aversion of farmers to taxes and devices used by large landowners and corporations to avoid payment of school taxes did much to retard education. A.S. Dandridge, a Shepherdstown dealer in farm implements, believed that he could weaken the candidacy of ex-Governor E. Willis Wilson

[5]Quoted in Ambler, *History of Education in West Virginia,* 235.

for the Senate in 1894 by "quietly using the fact among our farmers that he has always been a warm advocate for the increase of the state school tax, which is particularly obnoxious to our people."[6]

The legislature itself, through the creation of independent school districts, which numbered forty-seven in 1900, fostered serious inequities in length of school terms and teacher salaries even within counties. In 1890, for instance, Wyoming County had 55 days of school; Boone and Raleigh, 70 days; Ohio and Brooke, 155 days; and Jefferson, 180 days. The effect was "to give one half of the people 'thorough and efficient schools' and require the other half to provide just such schools as they may."[7] In 1904–1905 the average school term in West Virginia was 125 days, the average monthly salary of teachers $36.70, and the per capita expenditure for education $3.23. Corresponding national figures were 150.3 days, $47.08 monthly salary, and $3.49 per capita expenditure.

Higher Education to World War I. Unfortunately for higher education in the new state, West Virginians had traditionally favored the use of tax money for common schools rather than colleges, which many regarded as elitist. Problems for higher education were compounded by a lingering rural conservatism that provided no more support than outside industrial interests concerned chiefly with profits. Moreover, the absence of even one first-class high school as late as 1897 afforded no real basis on which to build sound collegiate education and left newly established colleges and the six normal schools little more than high schools. Marshall College, under the leadership of Lawrence J. Corbly, remained the leader in teacher education, but it was not authorized to grant baccalaureate degrees until 1920. About that time other normal schools discontinued high school work.

The conditions that fostered the growth of the normal schools also gave encouragement to private and denominational institutions. Bethany College survived the Civil War but had a precarious existence for the next three decades. More than once it was on the verge of bankruptcy. Beginning in 1901 under President Thomas E. Cramblet and his successors, Cloyd Goodnight and Wilbur H. Cramblet, it entered an era of stability, with an increasing endowment, a competent faculty, and a reputation for strong liberal arts programs.

Because of the influence they wielded at West Virginia University, the Methodists were somewhat slow to found their own college. When Alexander Martin, a Methodist minister, was dismissed as president of the university, however, they took steps to establish the West Virginia Conference Seminary at Buckhannon in 1890. In 1906 the institution became West Virginia Wesleyan College. Guided by several able presidents and emphasizing liberal arts and teacher education in the context of Christian ideals, West Virginia Wesleyan assumed an important place in higher education in the state.

[6]Quoted in ibid., 236.
[7]Quoted in ibid.

Morris Harvey College, established in 1888 as Barboursville Seminary and known from 1890 until 1901 as Barboursville College, was affiliated with the Southern Methodists for over half a century. In 1901 it changed its name to Morris Harvey College in honor of a Fayetteville industrialist who provided an endowment that for a time had an invigorating effect. From 1910 to 1919, in the face of new difficulties, it lapsed to the status of a junior college.

Salem College, founded in 1890 by Seventh-Day Baptists, grew out of an academy. During its early years it maintained both normal and academic departments. Under Presidents Charles E. Clark and S. Orestes Bond, it expanded its curricula to include preprofessional courses and expanded its facilities.

Davis and Elkins College grew out of missionary efforts of the Lexington, Virginia, Presbytery to provide educational opportunities for mountainous areas of West Virginia after the Civil War. Success was limited until 1901, when Henry Gassaway Davis and Stephen B. Elkins donated land at Elkins and thirty thousand dollars for the founding of a college for resident West Virginia Presbyterians. Davis and Elkins began operation in 1904 as a small liberal arts college and experienced slow but steady growth during the following decade.

Less durable institutions claiming college status included West Virginia College, maintained by Free Will Baptists at Flemington from 1865 until about 1885; Shelton College at Saint Albans, an outgrowth of the Baptist Coalsmouth High School, which flourished from 1877 until the Baptists withdrew their support and then limped along until 1911; Carbondale College at Big Chimney, Kanawha County, which existed from 1884 to 1887; Wheeling Female College, an antebellum institution that remained active until 1889; and a few other pre–Civil War academies reopened later as collegiate institutes.

West Virginia University to World War I. On February 7, 1867, less than four years after West Virginia became a state, the legislature accepted an offer of the trustees of Monongalia Academy at Morgantown to donate its property and that of nearby Woodburn Female Seminary to the state, provided it located a proposed agricultural college at Morgantown. In June the Board of Visitors of the institution complied with provisions of the Morrill Act, under which it became a land-grant college, with an award of 150,000 acres of land, mostly in Minnesota and Iowa. The following year its name was changed to West Virginia University.

West Virginia University opened its doors on September 2, 1868, under the presidency of Alexander Martin. Only six of its 184 students at the end of its first year were in the college proper, the remainder being in the preparatory and primary departments. Prospects, nevertheless, were encouraging. Martin Hall, with accommodations for instruction and student residences, was completed in 1870. By 1872 the faculty had grown in number and quality, and instruction was offered in ancient and modern languages, English literature, mathematics, military tactics, natural science, physics, chemistry, agriculture, natural history, belles lettres, elocution, history, political science, and civil and constitutional law. Peabody funds supported a "Teacher's Course."

Unfortunately, the university was wracked by internal dissension, rooted in part in deep political animosities, Republican influence in its affairs, and efforts of Methodists to control it. Serious conflict also arose over whether the university should follow Northern or Southern models in its organization and policies. Northerners generally favored coeducation, rigid discipline, prescribed curricula, and retention of the preparatory department; Southerners preferred separate campuses for men and women, a more relaxed discipline, greater use of the elective system, and abandonment of the preparatory department. Declining enrollments, financial exigencies accentuated by the Panic of 1873, an increase in "Virginia," or Southern, influence among faculty and students, and a stern and tactless puritanism on the part of President Martin forced the conflict to a head and resulted in Martin's dismissal.

After Waitman T. Willey declined the presidency, the regents employed John R. Thompson, the twenty-four-year-old pastor of the Morgantown Methodist Church and a man of character and commanding personality. Thompson thwarted a move by Agrarians, particularly Grangers, led by Daniel Bedinger Lucas, to divert Morrill funds to the Jefferson County Agricultural College, incorporated by the legislature in 1875. Lucas was named to the university Board of Regents and his brother-in-law, St. George Tucker Brooke, to the chair of law at the university.

Faculty insubordination and intrigue seriously disrupted the university in the 1880s and 1890s. They undermined the effectiveness of Presidents William Lyne Wilson, who served briefly before entering Congress; Robert C. Berkeley, who was designated simply as chairman of the faculty; E. Marsh Turner, who, along with defiant faculty against whom he preferred charges, was fired by the regents through letters delivered by an insolent janitor; and James L. Goodnight, whose position was declared vacant after he refused to resign in the face of faculty pressures. Jerome Hall Raymond, a twenty-eight-year-old import from the new University of Chicago, fared no better. After two years of attempted reform, in which he incurred opposition from faculty, students, and townspeople, the legislature refused to make any part of the university appropriation available until the regents required Raymond's resignation.

A conservative era followed Raymond's departure. Daniel B. Purinton, his successor, attempted to instill "harmony, unity, and economy"[8] into university affairs, but appropriations, salaries, and faculty-student ratios compared unfavorably with those of other universities. Moreover, Purinton had the outlook of a nineteenth century educator and was unable to deal effectively with the rising power of New School educators. In 1911 he resigned.

Tumultuous though they were, the first four decades of West Virginia

---

[8]Quoted in ibid., 340.

University were not without accomplishment. Presidents such as Wilson and Goodnight made important organizational changes. In 1889 the university admitted women to its collegiate department, and in 1897 it opened all other departments to them. In 1895 the alumni association, with Waitman T. Barbe as field agent, became an active force in university affairs. The State Geological and Economic Survey, created in 1897, became closely identified with the university. Leaders of the university, nevertheless, generally had narrow views concerning its functions, and its service to the state remained limited.

Transitions in the Public Schools. By World War I education in West Virginia had become involved in a titanic struggle between Old School educators, who stressed the values of discipline, character, and scholarship, and Progressive educators, who placed their faith in methodology and professional training for teachers. The latter drew inspiration from the philosophy of John Dewey, Edward L. Thorndike, William H. Kilpatrick, and others, who called for development of inquiring and critical minds, shared experiences in a democratic classroom atmosphere, and learning through problem situations.

The leader of the Progressive forces in West Virginia was Jasper N. Deahl of West Virginia University. For years Deahl had yielded to no one in his zeal for discipline and mastery of subject matter. Once he gained his doctorate, at the age of forty-seven, from Teachers College, Columbia University, one of the centers of Progressive ideas, he "threw former practices to the winds in pursuit of the new light."[9] Assertive and convincing in his arguments, he won a devoted following, particularly among younger educators.

Deahl and his allies, like Progressive educators elsewhere, endeavored to gain control of administrative bodies at the state level. When in 1909, in the interest of economy, a single five-member Board of Regents was created for the state's institutions of higher learning, Deahl's friends Morris P. Shawkey and Joseph Marsh, Sr., served as president and secretary, respectively. Once they captured control, the Progressive educators introduced far-reaching changes. Completion of prescribed courses in professional education became the basis for teacher certification. Between 1915 and 1921 legislation that they supported authorized school districts, cities, and towns to establish and maintain public libraries, expanded vocational education, gave new authority to county superintendents, and provided for employment of district supervisors of schools.

High schools experienced unprecedented growth in the early twentieth century. In 1910 State Superintendent Shawkey created a division of high schools in the Department of Education. Despite wartime interruptions, the number of high schools increased from twelve in 1910 to 233 and an enrollment of 32,075 in 1925. Junior high schools, encouraged by the Smith-Hughes Act, grew from four in 1917 to eighty-eight and an enrollment of 12,565 in 1928.

Serious impediments yet stood in the way of educational progress in West

[9]Ibid., p. 393.

Virginia. A comprehensive study made in 1929 by Charles H. Judd of the University of Chicago and L.V. Cavins of the State Department of Education included recommendations for an appointed state board of education with financial as well as professional control over education; appointment of the state superintendent by the state board of education; creation of county boards with authority to name superintendents; higher qualifications for county superintendents and their assistants; and the county unit for purposes of taxation and administration.

Contributing to professionalization of teaching was the State Education Association, which in 1931 included 13,341 of the 15,556 white teachers of the state, and the West Virginia Teachers Association, its Negro counterpart. In 1923 the State Education Association acquired the *West Virginia School Journal,* which was first a privately owned journal and later a semiofficial organ of the State Department of Education. Its employment of a full-time executive secretary, the emergence of a delegate assembly as its policy-making body, and after 1904 its election of an outstanding educator as president enabled the organization to take a more vigorous approach to educational issues and problems.

An Era of Reforms in Public Education. The Great Depression, which descended upon the country in 1929, produced a crisis in public education in West Virginia. Large amounts of taxable real estate, the principal source of school revenue, were forfeited to the state for nonpayment of taxes. Scores of schools were closed, terms were shortened, and many systems failed to pay teachers. In 1932 voters approved a constitutional amendment limiting tax rates on real property, which seriously reduced school revenues.

The crisis hastened adoption of the county unit plan, which the legislature approved on May 22, 1933, partly as an economy measure. The plan replaced 398 school districts, 54 of which were independent, with 55 county systems, each administered by a single five-member board. It was hailed throughout the country as a promising departure in administration and financing of public education.

The tax limitation amendment and the county unit plan drastically altered school financing in West Virginia. The old magisterial and independent districts had provided about ninety-five percent of the total expenditures for schools. The limits on county taxing power now necessitated a strong infusion of state aid, which in 1933–1934 amounted to nearly one-half of the $22 million needed to ensure nine-month terms in all counties. The new sharing of responsibility led to formulation of a "foundation program" in which the state contributed forty-five percent of the educational costs of a county. The county raised as much of the remainder as possible and the state made up any deficiency. In 1947 the legislature made the share of each county contingent upon its ability to raise funds, based upon a variety of economic indices.

Reforms continued throughout the 1940s and 1950s. They included a state

retirement plan for teachers in 1939, continuing contracts in 1940, free textbooks for all elementary grades in 1941, election of school boards on a nonpartisan basis, and nomination of all teachers, principals, and assistant superintendents by county superintendents rather than by board of education members.
In 1947 the legislature created a nine-member nonpartisan state board of
education, with the state superintendent serving as a nonvoting member, and
vested it with control over all free public schools and state colleges, with the
exception of West Virginia University and its branch, the Potomac State School,
which had their own board of governors. In 1958, by constitutional amendment,
the state superintendent of schools was made appointive by the State Board of
Education, but he remained a member of the Board of Public Works, the budget-
making body of the state.

One of the most critical decisions affecting education in West Virginia was
that of the United States Supreme Court on May 17, 1954, in the case of *Brown* v.
Board of Education of Topeka, Kansas. The court ruled that segregated schools
were "inherently unequal" and unconstitutional. Although there was minor
sporadic resistance to integration, West Virginians generally accepted the
decision as the law of the land. Twelve counties integrated their schools in the
ensuing year, and most others took preparatory steps in that direction.

Maturing Years in Higher Education. The rapid growth of high schools
between 1910 and 1925 profoundly affected higher education in West Virginia.
Both state-supported and private institutions discontinued their preparatory
departments as rising high school enrollments provided a reservoir of students
for college-level courses. The number of high school graduates who attended
college rose steadily, reaching 2,426 out of 5,963, or nearly forty-one percent, in
1928.

The normal schools and colored institutes emerged into colleges in the
1920s, with legislative authorization to grant baccalaureate degrees. Their
continued emphasis upon teacher education, however, was reflected in name
changes in which Concord, Fairmont, Glenville, Shepherd, and West Liberty
normal schools and Bluefield Colored Institute became state teachers colleges.
About the same time West Virginia Colored Institute became West Virginia
State College, and Montgomery Preparatory School, after a brief and precarious
existence as the West Virginia Trades School, became the New River State
School, with junior college status. In 1931 it was renamed New River State
College to reflect its new baccalaureate status. President Morris P. Shawkey and
his supporters aspired to make Marshall College into the state university for
southern West Virginia on a coordinate basis with West Virginia University but
were unsuccessful.

Although the state colleges continued to stress teacher education, they
added programs in liberal arts, physical education, home economics, journalism, commercial fields, and preprofessional areas. In 1943 the legislature
dropped the word "Teachers" from the names of Bluefield, Concord, Glenville,

Shepherd, and West Liberty. Two years earlier it had changed the name of New River State College to West Virginia Institute of Technology in response to a new emphasis, begun under President Edward S. Maclin, upon technological programs to serve the needs of the Kanawha Valley and other industrial areas of the state.

State-supported colleges underwent rapid change following World War II. An unprecendented influx of students, many of them taking advantage of the "G.I. Bill," necessitated further expansion of programs and facilities. The Supreme Court ruling striking down segregation laws further altered the clientele of most colleges. Previously all-white colleges accepted black students virtually without incident. The impact of desegregation was greatest on West Virginia State College, where the number of white students, drawn from the industrialized Kanawha Valley, soon exceeded that of blacks. Even before mandatory desegregation, West Virginia University had opened its graduate programs, which had no parallel at Negro institutions, to black students.

Faced with competition from the state colleges for faculty and facilities and with the ambitions of President Shawkey for Marshall University, friends of West Virginia University succeeded in 1927 in having its governance transferred from the state Board of Education to a bipartisan Board of Governors. Already, under President Frank B. Trotter, the university had entered an era of stability, marked by increasing enrollment, greater faculty participation in policy decisions, and a successful athletic program. John R. Turner, who followed Trotter, hoped to establish a graduate school, but the legislature, faced with the Depression, diverted funds that might have been used for that purpose to the public schools.

Under President Chauncey S. Boucher, West Virginia University experimented with the "Chicago College Plan," established the College of Pharmacy and the School of Physical Education and Athletics, and vested policy decisions in a university senate composed of certain administrators, department heads, and full professors. Boucher's successor, Charles E. Lawall, devoted much attention to expansion of the physical plant, but he allowed the administrative machinery established by Boucher to fall into disrepair. Responding to claims by some faculty and students that the university had not advanced under his leadership, Governor Matthew M. Neely attempted to remove Lawall from office by obtaining a subservient Board of Governors. Lawall sucessfully defended his legal right to office, but many believed that his resignation a few months later was in the best interests of the university.

Private and Denominational Colleges. In most respects development of the private colleges from the 1920s to midcentury paralleled that of state institutions. Most of them stressed liberal arts, but some, such as Morris Harvey, West Virginia Wesleyan, and Salem, were important teacher training colleges. Private as well as public colleges suffered declines in enrollments and revenues during the Great Depression. Beset also by problems arising from an ambitious building program in the 1920s, Morris Harvey moved from Barboursville to Charleston in 1935. The leadership of President Leonard Riggleman and support of the Charleston community enabled it to survive, and in 1951 it occupied an imposing new campus on the south side of the Kanawha River opposite the state capitol.

In 1931 the West Virginia Baptist Convention merged two struggling institutions, Alderson Junior College at Alderson and Broaddus College at Philippi, into Alderson-Broaddus College at Philippi. Alderson-Broaddus stressed liberal arts and pioneered in nurses' training in the state.

Other private colleges include Beckley, Wheeling, and Ohio Valley. Beckley, a junior college, was founded in 1933 to make low-cost education available to area youth with a view to increasing their skills. Ohio Valley, a junior college emphasizing liberal arts curricula, was established at Parkersburg in 1960. Wheeling College was founded in 1954 by Archbishop John J. Swint of Wheeling and operated by the Jesuit Fathers of the Maryland Province as a four-year liberal arts institution.

Several institutions offering collegiate work closed their doors in the later twentieth century. Greenbrier College, a junior college for women that traced its origins to Greenbrier Academy, and Greenbrier Military School ceased to operate in 1972. Kanawha College at Charleston merged with Morris Harvey in 1939, and Mason College of Music and Fine Arts, also in Charleston, ended its existence in 1956. Storer College at Harpers Ferry, under the direction of Henry T. McDonald from 1899 to 1944, became a degree-granting institution in 1938, but declining enrollment and withdrawal of a state subsidy in 1955, in the wake of the *Brown* v. *Board of Education* decision, hastened its demise.

Later Developments in Public Education. Major changes in public education began in the 1950s. A decrease in population in the state from 2,005,552 in 1950 to 1,744,237 in 1970 resulted in a twenty-two percent decline in elementary school enrollment, which dropped from 298,148 in 1954–1955 to 231,886 in 1977–1978. Public kindergartens, required by the legislature beginning in 1973, enrolled 17,846 pupils and partially offset the loss. Partly because of greater retention of students, secondary school enrollments during the same period actually increased from 159,600 to 161,425.

Consolidation of schools, both elementary and secondary, has been a significant trend in education since the 1930s. One of its casualties was the one-teacher, or one-room, school. In 1930–1931 West Virginia had 4,551 one-room schools. In 1978–1979 only one, at Auburn in Ritchie County, remained. One-room schools provided instruction for 76,904 pupils in September 1938. By contrast, the Auburn School enrolled only twenty-two forty years later.

Numerous innovations in philosophy and procedures in education appeared in the 1960s and 1970s, many associated with federal programs. Head Start provided preschool children from low-income families educational experiences that presumably enabled them to compete more favorably with others when they entered school. Upward Bound allowed economically disadvantaged high school students to spend several weeks during the summer on selected college campuses, with the presumption that those of sufficient ability would be stimulated to enter college. Teacher aides relieved elementary school instructors of many routine tasks and enabled them to concentrate on teaching.

Other new departures, some of them experimental, included the ungraded system in primary grades, the open classroom plan in elementary schools, and a flexible organization for high schools that emphasized student freedom and responsibility. In certification of teachers, the State Department of Education turned from emphasis on college credits in teaching fields to attainment of certain competencies as determined by educationists and subject matter specialists.

Public response to educational changes ranged from enthusiastic approval to downright hostility. In 1974 a controversy with nationwide implications arose in Kanawha County over adoption of language arts textbooks, which Alice Moore, a member of the Board of Education, and others considered destructive of American moral, religious, and patriotic values. Opponents charged Mrs. Moore and her supporters with efforts at censorship and insensitivity to the views and cultures of minorities. Critics of the books, however, succeeded in having them withdrawn at least temporarily from use, but not before incidents of violence erupted.

The Kanawha County controversy provided a focus for a rising disenchantment with the public schools and contributed to the growth of private schools, most of them founded by Protestant denominations, which five years later enrolled 7,632 elementary and 11,097 secondary students. By the 1970s many parents and educators were urging a "back to the basics" approach to education. In 1979 State Superintendent Roy W. Truby proposed an increase in credits required for high school graduation, with special attention to English and other substantive courses. There seemed little likelihood, however, that the new developments would reverse the course set by Progressive educators half a century earlier.

By 1980 teachers appeared to be on the threshold of new political power. The West Virginia Education Association had become much more militant, with collective bargaining a major objective. Disappointed in legislative action on salaries and other benefits, it was largely responsible for the defeat of Senate President William T. Brotherton, Jr., of Kanawha County and John Pat Fanning of McDowell County, who had opposed its program. Two years later the teacher vote combined with the labor vote to defeat other veteran legislators, including Senators Lafe P. Ward of Williamson and Alan Susman of Beckley.

In 1982 Judge Arthur Recht of the Ohio County Circuit Court handed down a landmark decision in education in a case involving Lincoln County, which had taxed itself to legal limits but still could not provide adequate education for its youth. Recht detailed gross inequalities in educational provisions by the counties and held that they stemmed from failure of the state to comply with a constitutional mandate to provide "a thorough and efficient system of free schools." His decision, which in essence extended to the state the principles used to justify the county unit plan half a century earlier, implied heavy expenditures, estimated as high as $1.5 billion, over the next decade and substantial tax increases. Inevitably, it produced strong reactions. Teacher organizations generally hailed it as a critical victory, but opponents and skeptics regarded many of its features as impractical, unwarranted, or too expensive. Governor Rockefeller withheld immediate judgment, but by 1984 he, Superintendent Truby, and legislative leaders had accepted its principles as guides for the future.

Later Developments in Higher Education. One of the most significant changes in higher education in the state was the creation of the West Virginia Board of Regents in 1969. The legislature vested the board with authority over all public colleges and universities and charged it with welding them into a comprehensive state system of higher education.

In an attempt to place a college within reach of every West Virginian and to expand curricula well beyond traditional offerings of four-year institutions, the Board of Regents, acting upon a recommendation of Chancellor Prince Woodard, established a system of community colleges. Parkersburg Community College grew out of a branch of West Virginia University; West Virginia Northern Community College from centers operated by West Liberty State College at Wheeling and Weirton; and Southern West Virginia Community College from branches of Marshall University at Logan and Williamson. The Board also set up community college components on the campuses of West Virginia Institute of Technology, Marshall University, Fairmont State College, and West Virginia State College and established the Greenbrier Center of Bluefield State College at Lewisburg.

Other innovations of the Board of Regents included an external baccalaureate degree program and the West Virginia College of Graduate Studies at Institute. The Board of Regents degree allowed students to receive credit for relevant work experience and to graduate without a formal major from participating colleges. The College of Graduate Studies at first had no campus or buildings of its own but used facilities at West Virginia State College and Morris Harvey College. With only a small instructional staff, it relied heavily upon adjunct faculty drawn from nearby colleges and universities and from industry and business. Its programs in teacher education, business, sciences and liberal arts filled needs in the Kanawha Valley and southern West Virginia that extension offerings from West Virginia and Marshall universities had not met. The awarding of 1,963 Board of Regents baccalaureate degrees and 1,825 graduate degrees by the College of Graduate Studies by June 1980 attested to the popularity of the two actions.

Many actions of the Board of Regents engendered heated controversy. In

1972 its "Plan for Progress," which envisioned reallocation of functions of institutions under its jurisdiction, drew fire from both advocates of greater institutional autonomy and proponents of ruthless elimination of duplication and overlapping programs. The merger of Concord and Bluefield colleges in 1973, purportedly in the interest of economy, produced such bitterness that they were restored to their previous status in 1975. Although many parts of West Virginia had an acute shortage of physicians, strong opposition arose to establishment of a medical school at Marshall University in 1974 on the ground that the state could not afford two medical schools. Criticism of the board became even more intense in 1975 when it accepted, under gubernatorial pressure, jurisdiction over the West Virginia School of Osteopathic Medicine at Lewisburg.

Attacks upon the Board of Regents, which had developed into a powerful governing body, mounted in the late 1970s. They stemmed in part from the rapid changes and uncertainties that characterized academic life in the nation, often leaving the board caught between public demands for economy and accountability and institutional concerns for professional quality and program security. Part of the problem, however, arose from a growing bureaucracy insufficiently sensitive to public, academic, and other constituencies and to ill-conceived pressures for consolidation of institutions and application of rigid cost-effective business practices. The legislature, however, ignored a recommendation in an independent study, which it commissioned, to reduce the board to a coordinating body.

The private and denominational colleges also felt the economic and social strains of the 1970s. Some emulated larger institutions elsewhere by drawing into their administrations men with experience outside academe. In 1972 Bethany College named as its president Cecil H. Underwood, who had held administrative posts at Salem and Marietta colleges and high positions in industry and had served as governor of the state. The following year John D. Rockefeller IV, a member of one of the nation's wealthiest families, became president of West Virginia Wesleyan College after being defeated for governor a few months earlier. At Morris Harvey College financial exigency gave rise to a proposal to convey the college and its resources to the state to be administered by the Board of Regents. Fierce opposition arose from those who desired the college to remain independent, and the state ultimately refused the offer. Later President Thomas G. Voss introduced sweeping changes, including renaming the institution the University of Charleston and drastically altering its mission and purpose.

Although some faced severe retrenchment and reorientation, West Virginia colleges weathered the troubles of the 1970s and in many cases expanded their offerings. Joining West Virginia University, Marshall University, and the College of Graduate Studies in providing graduate study was West Virginia Institute of Technology, with programs in engineering. West Virginia Wesleyan College and the University of Charleston also initiated graduate studies on a limited scale. As a result of a merger in 1996, the Montgomery college was renamed West Virginia University Institute of Technology.

Education in West Virginia faced troubled times in the 1980s. With an economy that was especially vulnerable to the deep national recession that engulfed the nation and the highest rate of unemployment in the country, state revenues were inadequate to the demands upon them. Salaries of public school teachers and college and university professors were at or near the lowest levels in the nation. Yet the Recht decision regarding public education and a growing belief that higher education must be accessible to a greater proportion of the people, who already ranked among the lowest of the states in percentage of population attending college, offered some hope that education might ultimately receive a higher priority than in past years. If the faith that Americans professed in education had validity, it seemed possible that the progress of the preceding twenty-five years, tempered by reflective judgement and evaluation, might yet prove to be one of the most significant influences in the last years of the twentieth century.

Literary Endeavors

The Civil War Era. The birth of West Virginia during the tragedy of civil war provided a setting for a great literature, but the conflict left little time for literary pursuits. The most important West Virginia novel set in a wartime context was *David Gaunt* (1862) by Rebecca Harding Davis (1831–1910). In it Mrs. Davis, the mother of the noted writer Richard Harding Davis, portrayed the attitudes of Wheeling area farmers toward the war. She found nothing romantic in war, "for the shadow of death has fallen on us; it chills the very heaven." She added, "Men had forgotten to hope, forgotten to pray; only in the bitterness of endurance they say in the morning, 'Would God it were evening!' and in the evening "Would God it were morning!'"[1]

Mrs. Davis was also attracted to the effects of industrialism on Wheeling and its vicinity. "Life in the Iron Mills," published in the *Atlantic Monthly* in 1861 is said to have been the first work in American fiction to deal with the problems of labor. *Margaret Howth* (1865) contrasted the wretchedness of life in the mills with the beauties of the countryside. Although "crude and amateurish in workmanship," the novels of Mrs. Davis have been seen as "Russian-like in their grim and sordid realism" in an era given to excessive sentimentality and as a "distinct landmark in the evolution of American fiction."[2]

The Civil War also gave rise to valuable personal narratives. They included *Nine Months in the Quartermaster's Department* (1862) by Charles Lieb; *Four Years A Soldier* (1867) by David E. Johnston, a sergeant major in the Confederate Army; and *The Flying Gray-Haired Yank* (1868) by Michael Egan, a Union soldier from Parkersburg who was confined to a Confederate prison.

Poetry, much of it of no enduring value, was the most popular literary form during the Civil War. The best poetry of the era came from the pen of Daniel Bedinger Lucas (1836–1909) of Charles Town, a member of the staff of General Henry A. Wise and later of the West Virginia Supreme Court of Appeals. The title poem of *The Land Where We Were Dreaming* (1865) perhaps caught better

---

[1]Quoted in Mary Meek Atkeson, "West Virginia Literature and Literary Writers," in James Morton Callahan, *A History of West Virginia, Old and New,* 3 vols. (Chicago: American Historical Society, 1923), vol. 1, 684.

[2]Fred Lewis Pattee, "Rebecca Blaine Harding Davis," in *Dictionary of American Biography,* ed. Allan Johnson, Dumas Malone, and others, 26 vols. (New York: Charles Scribner's Sons, 1928-1980), vol. 5, 143.

than any other the spirit of the Lost Cause, which provided themes for other works of Lucas, including *The Wreath of Eglantine* (1869). The romantic poetry of Beuhring H. Jones (1823–1872), a native of Pratt and longtime resident of Lewisburg, was written in a "quiet pensive vein, recalling loved ones at home, and pathetic scenes in battle and camp" while Jones was in a federal prison at Johnson's Island. His best work was published as *The Sunny Land; or Prison Prose and Poetry* (1868).

Late Nineteenth Century Prose and Poetry. No great literary flowering accompanied the achievement of statehood in West Virginia, the triumph of western political and economic ideas, or the arrival of the new industrial age. The literary climate of the state in the late nineteenth century, however, was by no means arid. William Leighton (1833–1911), a resident of Wheeling, combined literary pursuits with a manufacturing business. *The Sons of Godwin* (1877) and *At the Court of King Edwin* (1878) were written in expressive and beautiful English in Shakespearian form, and three other works, *A Sketch of Shakespeare, Shakespeare's Poems,* and *The Subjection of Hamlet,* published between 1879 and 1882, established Leighton as a leading Shakespearian scholar. His most ambitious work, *Change: The Whisper of the Sphinx* (1879), was a poem of great power in which he saw "The works of man sink crumbling back to dust, From which, with painful toil, his hand hath raised them."[3]

Frank R. Stockton (1834–1902) lived at "Claymont," Jefferson county, the last three years of his life. His most important literary works, including *Rudder Grange* (1879), *The Casting Away of Mrs. Lecks and Mrs. Aleshire* (1876), and his most famous story, *The Lady or the Tiger* (1882), were behind him. In the last, he left readers arguing whether a barbaric princess sacrificed her lover to a lady bound to marry him or to a tiger certain to devour him, an accomplishment Stockton could "never live down" or again equal. His West Virginia writings included "Tales Out of School."

William Hope, commonly known as "Coin," Harvey (1851–1936), a native of Buffalo, Putnam County, had a varied career. After practicing law in Barboursville, Huntington, and Gallipolis, he turned in the 1880s to silver mining in Colorado, where he became painfully aware of falling silver prices. In 1893 he moved to Chicago and founded the Coin Publishing Company. There he made a "sudden leap onto the stage of history" with *Coin's Financial School* (1894), a simplistic but compelling defense of the free silver movement then sweeping the country. The book became the bible of its advocates, chief of whom was William Jennings Bryan.[4]

Major West Virginia poets included Danske Dandridge (1854–1914), Waitman T. Barbe (1864–1925), and Thomas Dunn English (1819–1902). The works of Mrs. Dandridge, a resident of Shepherdstown, included *Joy and Other Poems*

[3]See, for instance, Warren Wood, *Representative West Virginia Authors* (Ravenswood, W.Va.: Worth-While Book Co., 1926), 125.

[4]Introduction to William H. Harvey, *Coin's Financial School,* ed. Richard Hofstadter (Cambridge: Harvard University Press, 1963), 12.

(1888) and *Rose Brake* (1890). Written with uncommon literary grace, they reflected a strain of mysticism and a deep love of nature. Barbe, a professor of English at West Virginia University, first gained attention with "The Song of the Centuries" (1888), but *Ashes and Incense* (1892) established his literary reputation. In later years he turned increasingly to literary analysis and wrote three important works, *The Study of Poetry* (1905), *Famous Poems Explained* (1909), and *Great Poems Interpreted* (1913). English, a mayor of Logan, wrote numerous poems of the Guyandotte and Gauley rivers. "Ben Bolt," his best known poem, was one of the most popular love songs of its era.

Early Twentieth Century Novelists. About the beginning of the twentieth century, Romantic approaches to literature faded and a new era of Realism arrived. Foremost among the new novelists was Melville Davisson Post (1869–1930), a native of Romine's Mills. Post received a law degree from West Virginia University and practiced criminal law in Wheeling for about eight years. In 1901 he turned to corporate law and formed a partnership with John T. McGraw, a powerful leader in the Democratic party. By then Post had given up his own fleeting political ambitions and embarked upon literary pursuits.

Post achieved success with *The Strange Schemes of Randolph Mason* (1896) and its successor, *The Man of Last Resort* (1897). Inverting the usual plots of detective story writers such as Edgar Allan Poe and A. Conan Doyle, he created in Randolph Mason a clever and unprincipled lawyer who used extraordinary intelligence and legal skill to find imperfections in laws to protect wrongdoers. Critics applauded Post's literary skill, but some feared that his exposure of legal flaws would encourage villains to seek them out as ways of escaping justice. Post contended that the stories emphasized the need for greater care in framing laws, but in *The Corrector of Destinies* (1908) a reformed Randolph Mason turned his great talents to legal methods of correcting injustices.

Twenty-two short stories, collected as *Uncle Abner, Master of Mysteries* (1918), enhanced Post's literary reputation. Uncle Abner was a shrewd and unpretentious hill country detective, whose devotion to justice led him to draw a sharp distinction between statute law and God's law. On the basis of his Randolph Mason and Uncle Abner stories, many critics consider Post second only to Poe among American writers of detective fiction.

Although Post enjoyed cosmopolitan Eastern and European society, he found inspiration for many of his works in the hills of West Virginia. *Dwellers in the Hills* (1901) was reputedly based on actual experiences in the Harrison County cattle country. Its strength lay in the authenticity of its characters and their society and in its well-constructed plot. A minor classic in American literature, it never achieved widespread popularity in the United States, but it won Post an appreciative audience in Great Britain.

Perhaps influenced by the untimely death of his wife, Post turned to a religious theme in *The Mountain School-Teacher* (1922). He based the story on the life of Jesus, but with reverence and skill he gave it a modern setting, with

Jesus assuming the form of a mountain schoolteacher. Often described as an allegory, the work gave Post new stature as a novelist and won him a nomination for the Nobel Prize for literature. Deeply distressed by the materialistic and immoral society of the 1920s, Post is said to have been considering at the time of his death another allegorical novel with Satan as the central figure.

Like Post, Margaret Prescott Montague (1878–1955) of White Sulphur Springs possessed unusual literary versatility, particularly in use of the short story and local color. Her first success, *The Poet, Miss Kate and I* (1905) was an idyllic but almost plotless story set in the West Virginia hills. *The Sowing of Alderson Cree* (1907), a convincing character study, revolved around the murder of Alderson Cree and its effects upon his twelve-year-old son, whom he swore to avenge his killing. *Closed Doors* (1915) and *Home to Him's Muvver* (1916) dealt sympathetically and artistically with the lives of deaf and blind children. Two works, *Up Eel River* (1923) and *To-Day Tomorrow* (1923), were fanciful tales of Tony Beaver, a mythical lumberjack. Following World War I, Miss Montague won the O. Henry Memorial Prize for *England to America* (1920), an eloquent plea for closer cooperation between England and the United States, and a commendation from President Woodrow Wilson for *Uncle Sam of Freedom Ridge* (1920), which urged preservation of the fruits of the Allied victory through support of the League of Nations.

Other well-known novelists who made extensive use of West Virginia themes and settings included Granville Davisson Hall (1837–1934), Albert B. Cunningham (1888–1962), and Mary Meek Atkeson (1884–1971). Hall's *Daughter of the Elm* (1899) made a venerable elm tree in Shinnston the focus of a love story and of the activities of a band of horse thieves and robbers who operated with impunity in the area. Cunningham provided authentic and probably autobiographical accounts of life along the Elk River, where he grew up, in *The Manse at Barren Rocks*(1918) and its sequel, *Singing Mountain (1919)*. He wrote more than twenty light mystery novels and other works, some under the pseudonyms of Garth Hale and Estil Dale. Miss Atkeson, a native of Buffalo, left vivid pictures of life in rural West Virginia, particularly the lower Kanawha Valley, in *The Cross Roads Meetin' House* (1919), *The Good Old Days* (1922), and *The Woman on the Farm* (1924).

Henry Sydnor Harrison (1880–1930), formerly headmaster of a school in New York and a journalist in Richmond, spent his most productive literary years in Charleston. In *Queed* (1911), the best-selling novel of the year, he told the story of an introverted and bookish young man who left New York for a sleepy Southern town to write a definitive work on evolutionary psychology, the conflict between his ideas and the practicalities of life, and the romance and mystery surrounding him. *V.V.'s Eyes* (1913) examined the differing values of self-effacing and humanistic Dr. V. Vivian and Carlisle Heth, a young woman of great wealth, who through Vivian gained a sense of social responsibility and a new appreciation of the meaning of life. In addition to these distinctly didactic novels, Harrison's works included *Angela's Business* (1913), *When I Come Back* (1918), *Saint Teresa* (1922), and *The Good Hope* (1931).

Herbert Quick (1861–1925), a longtime resident of Morgan County, had a greater interest in the problem novel than most contemporary West Virginia writers. *The Broken Lance* (1907) dealt with a Midwest schoolteacher-minister and disciple of Henry George, who, with disastrous consequences for his personal life, made opposition to "private earth-holding" a religion instead of an economic philosophy. *The Good Ship Earth* (1913) examined resources and economic institutions in their social implications by depicting the earth as a vessel on which all men were embarked. *Vandemark's Folly* (1922), generally regarded as Quick's best work, and its sequels, *The Hawkeye* (1923) and *The Invisible Woman* (1924), constituted a saga of American life as reflected in the dreams and achievements of pioneers from the Erie Canal to the farmlands of Iowa.

Prose and Poetry Since 1930. The foremost West Virginia novelist of the twentieth century was Pearl Sydenstricker Buck (1892–1973). A native of Hillsboro whose connections with the state were minimal throughout her life, she was taken to China by her missionary parents when she was about two years old. She returned to the United States for her college education, but soon afterward went back to China. There she married Dr. John Lossing Buck, a missionary who also taught agriculture. While she and her husband were teaching at the University of Nanking, Mrs. Buck wrote her first novel, *East Wind, West Wind* (1929).

Mrs. Buck's greatest work, *The Good Earth* (1931), won her a Pulitzer Prize and international acclaim as a literary interpreter of Chinese civilization to the Western world. Her greatest recognition came in 1938 when she became the first American woman to receive the Nobel Prize for literature. In the meantime she completed *The Exile* (1936) and *Fighting Angel* (1936), biographies of her mother and father, which critics have ranked among her best works.

A prolific writer, Mrs. Buck was the author of at least thirty-four novels and scores of other literary pieces. Her earlier fiction was marked by probing character studies and objectivity, but after 1939 she embraced numerous causes, and some critics charged that she became more a crusader than a novelist. Her interests, however, were essentially humanitarian, and her novels remained more than mere best-sellers.

One of the most promising West Virginia writers was Hubert Skidmore (1911–1946), whose career was cut short by a tragic accident at his mountain cabin. Skidmore drew upon his own background for *I Will Lift Up Mine Eyes* (1936), *River Rising* (1939), *Hill Doctor* (1940), and *Hill Lawyer* (1942). His *Hawk's Nest* (1941) dealt with the silicosis scourge among workers who built a tunnel to divert waters of the New River through Gauley Mountain. The book was a searing indictment of either negligence or apathy of the construction company and public officials, whose protests caused the publisher to withdraw the book from sale. Hobart Sidmore (1909–1969), an elder brother of Hubert, also wrote novels descriptive of life in the West Virginia hills or of World War II in the South Pacific.

During the 1930s other West Virginia novelists gained national attention. John Peale Bishop (1892–1944) wrote about his native Charles Town and the Shenandoah Valley in *Many Thousands Gone* (1931) and *Act of Darkness* (1935), but he was better known for his poetry, published over more than a quarter of a century. Eleanor Carroll Chilton (1898– 1949) of Charleston was the author of *Shadows Waiting* (1927), *Follow the Furies* (1935), and *The Burning Fountain* (1939), and Stella Morgan (b. 1889) of Fairmont attained her greatest success with *Again the River* (1939).

Among post–World War II novelists, Mary Lee Settle (b. 1918) a native of Charleston, thinly disguised as Canona in some of her books, has received special recognition. Her *Beulah* quintet (1954–1982) traces the fortunes and changing values of a West Virginia family over three centuries. *Blood Tie* (1977), which dealt with expatriate Americans and Europeans in a Turkish coastal town, was given the National Book Award in 1978.

Other postwar novelists include Alberta Pierson Hannum (b. 1905), Davis Grubb (1919–1980), and Warren E. Blackhurst (1904–1970). Mrs. Hannum, of Moundsville, used Appalachian themes in most of her writings, including *Thursday April* (1931) and *The Hills Step Lightly* (1934), her earliest works. *Spin a Silver Dollar* (1945), *Roseanna McCoy* (1947), and *Look Back With Love* (1970) are among her later novels. Grubb, also of Moundsville, won attention with *The Night of the Hunter* (1954) and later with *The Watchman* (1961), *Voice of Glory* (1962), and *Fool's Parade* (1969). Less adept in the literary arts, Blackhurst, of Cass, caught the spirit of life in the timber and lumber industries of bygone days in *Riders of the Flood* (1954), *Sawdust in Your Eyes* (1963), *Of Men and a Mighty Mountain* (1965), and *Mixed Harvest* (1970).

Louise McNeill Pease (b. 1911), who was born near Marlinton, has held first place among West Virginia poets for forty years and in 1978 was appointed poet laureate of the state. In 1938 she won an Atlantic Monthly prize for her "Mountain Corn Song." She gained further acclaim with *Gauley Mountain* (1939), which dealt with the pioneer era of the Kanawha Valley perceptively and appreciatively. In *Paradox Hill* (1972) Mrs. Pease returned to "Gauley" and its people, who as Americans had traveled since she first wrote of them, "from the cornfield to the Hiroshima cloud; from the blackberry patch to the lunar shore."[5] In *Elderberry Flood* (1979) she essayed a portrait of West Virginia through a series of poetic sketches of persons and events.

West Virginia's most noted author of books for children and juveniles is Jean Lee Latham (b. 1902) a native of Buckhannon. After 1952 most of her books dealt with historical figures. They included *Carry on, Mr. Bowditch*

[5]Foreword to *Paradox Hill from Appalachia to Lunar Shore* (Morgantown: West Virginia University Press, 1972), vii.

(1955), which won the Newberry Award; The *Story of Eli Whitney* (1953); *Medals for Morse* (1954); *This Dear-Bought Land* (1957); and *Trail Blazer of the Seas* (1956), a biography of oceanographer Matthew Fontaine Maury.

Nineteenth Century Historical Writing. In spite of the scientific approaches advanced by the German historian Leopold von Ranke and his disciples, historical writing in the United States at the end of the nineteenth century was still considered a branch of literature and left to poorly prepared amateurs. Most state and county histories were accumulations of unassimilated materials, lacking in proportion or careful organization and stressing settlements; Indian wars; military events, particularly those relating to the Revolutionary and Civil wars; pioneer life; and prominent families. Yet many of these antiquarians, faced with scattered sources and difficult and expensive travel, produced works that have remained useful to the present day.

One of the greatest services to historians of the pioneer era of West Virginia and many of its neighboring states was rendered by Lyman C. Draper (1815–1891). Inspired by *Chronicles of Border Warfare* by Alexander Scott Withers, Draper spent a lifetime visiting towns, obscure farms, and isolated hollows to ferret out and save from oblivion or destruction hundreds of thousands of manuscripts that have illuminated or made possible the reconstruction of pioneer history. The Draper Collection, at the state Historical Society of Wisconsin, is a major repository of sources for West Virginia and Appalachian history.

Of the numerous writers of county and regional histories, two Charleston historians produced works of more than ordinary merit. John P. Hale (1824–1902) was the author of *Trans-Allegheny Pioneers* (1886) and *History of the Great Kanawha Valley* (1891). Prior to becoming governor of the state, George W. Atkinson (1845–1925) published *The History of Kanawha County* (1876) and *Life Among the Moonshiners* (1881), the latter providing insights into the lives and thinking of mountaineers obtained through his work as a revenue agent. His *Prominent Men of West Virginia* (1891), done in collaboration with Alvaro F. Gibbens, and *Bench and Bar of West Virginia* (1919) remain valuable reference works.

Early Twentieth Century Historical Writing. Although antiquarian techniques long remained in vogue with many county and local historians, the semi-centennial of statehood drew attention to broader aspects of West Virginia history, particularly to the formative years. In 1902 Granville Davisson Hall (1837–1934), who had kept stenographic notes of the First Constitutional Convention, stimulated interest with *The Rending of Virginia: A History.* Virgil A. Lewis (1848–1912), who was the first historian and archivist of the state, published *How West Virginia Was Made* (1909) and other works, including *A History of West Virginia* (1889) and *A History of the Battle of Point Pleasant* (1909). Among later works were *The Disruption of Virginia* (1922) by James C McGregor and *The Borderland in the Civil War* (1927) by Edward C. Smith.

Meanwhile, the history faculty at West Virginia University advanced research into state history. James Morton Callahan (1864–1956) followed *Semi-Centennial History of West Virginia* (1913) with the more comprehensive *History of West Virginia, Old and New* (1923). Charles H. Ambler published numerous works on the statehood movement and its background, including *Sectionalism in Virginia from 1776 to 1861* (1910), *Francis H. Pierpont: Union War Governor of West Virginia and Father of West Virginia* (1937), and *Waitman Thomas Willey: Orator, Churchman, Humanitarian* (1954). Among other writings of the prolific and versatile Ambler were *A History of Transportation in the Ohio Valley* (1932), *A History of West Virginia* (1933), later revised with Festus P. Summers, *George Washington and the West* (1936), and *A History of Education in West Virginia* (1954).

Festus P. Summers (1895–1971), who succeeded Ambler as chairman of the history department at West Virginia University, made important contributions in *The Baltimore and Ohio in the Civil War* (1939) and *Johnson Newlon Camden: A Study in Individualism* (1937), a biography of a leading industrialist and politician. His *William L. Wilson and Tariff Reform* (1953) illuminated the tariff question in the nation and the state in the late nineteenth century.

Prominent among writers outside the academic world was a Charleston triumvirate. Roy Bird Cook (1886–1961), a pharmacist, was a recognized authority on Stonewall Jackson and the author of *The Family and Early Life of Stonewall Jackson* (1924), *Washington's Western Lands* (1930), and *The Annals of Fort Lee* (1935). Boyd B. Stutler (1889–1970) amassed a valuable collection of John Brown manuscripts and memorabilia and wrote extensively on Brown and the Civil War in West Virginia. Phil Conley (1887–1979) compiled *The West Virginia Encyclopedia* (1929), a useful reference work.

West Virginia scholars tilled fields other than state history. Callahan, a pioneer in American diplomatic history, received acclaim for such works as *American Foreign Policy in Mexican Relations* (1932) and *American Foreign Policy in Canadian Relations* (1937). Oliver P. Chitwood (1874–1971) of West Virginia University was the author of *A History of Colonial America* (1931), an admirable survey and widely used college text, and *John Tyler, Champion of the Old South* (1939) and coauthor of *The American People: A History* (1945), a popular textbook. Cornelius C. Regier (b. 1884) published *The Era of the Muckrakers* (1932), a standard work on the Progressive period, while he was at New River State College. *French Policy and Development in Indo-China* (1936) and *Eastern Asia* (1946) established Thomas E. Ennis of West Virginia University as an authority on the Far East.

Among black historians, Booker T. Washington (1856–1915) and Carter G. Woodson (1875–1950) were outstanding. Washington, the influential leader and educator, wrote of his youth in the Kanawha Valley in *Up From Slavery* (1901). Woodson, one of the significant black historians of the twentieth century, was for a time dean of West Virginia Collegiate Institute. He wrote numerous books on black history, completing *The Negro in Our History* (1922) while in West Virginia, and founded the *Journal of Negro History*.

Contemporary Historical Writing. Interest in state history has remained strong since World War II. In *A Banner in the Hills: West Virginia's Statehood* (1963), the centennial commemorative work, George E. Moore of Fairmont State College provided an updated and balanced account of the Civil War in West Virginia and the attainment of statehood. Richard O. Curry, a native of Greenbrier County and professor at the University of Connecticut, advanced fruitful new interpretations in *A House Divided: A Study of Statehood Politics and the Copperhead Movement in West Virginia* (1964) and in an edited work, *Radicalism, Racism, and Party Realignment: The Border States During Reconstruction* (1969).

Earlier periods of history received attention in *The Allegheny Frontier: West Virginia Beginnings, 1730-1830* (1970) and *Frontier Kentucky* (1975), both by Otis K. Rice. Rice also provided a broad historical context for a famous Appalachian vendetta in *The Hatfields and the McCoys* (1978). Stephen W. Brown retrieved from obscurity an important West Virginian in *Voice of the New West: John G. Jackson, His Life and Times* (1985).

Most of the scholarly work on the later history of the state is of recent vintage. William D. Barns of West Virginia University distilled extensive research in agricultural and economic history in *The West Virginia State Grange: The First Century, 1873-1973* (1973). His colleague, John Alexander Williams, documented the close relationship between major industrial leaders and politics in *West Virginia and the Captains of Industry* (1976) and provided an interpretive study in *West Virginia: A Bicentennial History* (1976). G. Wayne Smith of Fairmont State College dealt with a significant political figure in *Nathan Goff, Jr.: A Biography* (1959), as did Robert Maddox of Marshall University in *The Senatorial Career of Harley Martin Kilgore* (1981). Labor history, an area of increasing interest, has attracted such scholars as Edward M. Steel, Jerry Thomas, Fred Barkey, Kenneth Bailey, and David T. Javersak.

Professional historians of West Virginia have added substantially to other areas of history. At West Virginia University, Wesley M. Bagby provided a perceptive account of the election of 1920 in *The Road to Normalcy* (1968); John A. Caruso undertook a multivolume synthesis of American frontier history, beginning with *The Appalachian Frontier: America's First Surge Westward* (1959); and Mortimer Levine established himself as an authority on Tudor England with such works as *The Early Elizabethan Succession Question* (1966) and *Tudor Dynastic Problems* (1973). James David Barber, a native of Charleston and a Duke University political scientist, received favorable attention with *The Presidential Character* (1972), and Paul D. Casdorph of West Virginia State College produced careful studies in *Republicans, Negroes, and Progressives in the South, 1912-1916* (1981), *Let the Good Times Roll: Life at Home in America during World War II* (1989), and *Lee and Jackson: Confederate Chieftains* (1992). Roy W. Curry of West Virginia Wesleyan College added to diplomatic historiography with *Woodrow Wilson and Far Eastern Policy, 1913-1921* (1957).

Periodical publications also did much to stimulate interest in state history.

West Virginia History: A Quarterly, established in 1939 with support from the West Virginia Department of Archives and History and the West Virginia Historical Society, has remained the major scholarly journal devoted to state history. For nearly forty years Cecile R. Goodall served as its editor. The *West Virginia Archeologist,* founded largely through the efforts of Delf Norona and the West Virginia Archeological Society, its sponsor, enhanced interest in the remote past.

Folklore and Music. West Virginia has shared a growing interest in folklore in recent decades. Patrick W. Gainer of West Virginia University devoted a lifetime to folklore and folk music of the region. His publications included *Witches, Ghosts, and Signs: Folklore of the Southern Appalachians* (1975). Ruth Ann Musick of Fairmont State College gathered state materials in *Folk Songs and Folk Tales of West Virginia* (1960), *The Tell-Tale Lilac Bush* (1965), and *Green Hills of Magic* (1970).

Folk music also gained in popularity. Sir Cecil Sharp, the British authority, did much to inspire collection and preservation of Appalachian folk music. John Harrington Cox of West Virginia University collected folk songs of European and early American origins in *Folk Songs of the South* (1925) and added others in *Folk-Songs Mainly from West Virginia* (1939). Louis W. Chappell, of the same institution, stressed newer folk songs in *John Henry: A Folk-Lore Study* (1933). In 1950 Patrick W. Gainer organized the West Virginia Folk Festival at Glenville State College. Gainer drew a sharp distinction between authentic folk music and hillbilly music and rejected the pseudo-folk music that swept the country in the 1960s and 1970s.

The Newspaper Press. During the first half-century of statehood, the number of newspapers grew rapidly in West Virginia. In 1860 there were forty-three newspapers in nineteen counties, only three of which were daily journals. With introduction of new machinery, including the linotype, in the 1880s, printing costs declined, and by 1912 the state had 223 newspapers with at least one in each county. In 1980 there were twenty- five daily publications in twenty cities and towns and seventy-six weekly papers in forty-eight counties. Six cities had more than one daily newspaper, but in five of them competing papers were owned by the same company. The Ogden Newspapers owned six of the daily papers in the state.

West Virginia produced no towering giants during the nation's era of personal journalism. Albert B. White of the Parkersburg *State Sentinel,* William M.O. Dawson of the Kingwood *Preston County Journal,* and John J. Cornwell of the Romney *Hampshire Review,* however, moved to the governor's mansion by way of the editor's chair. Few editors have enjoyed more personal popularity than Calvin Price of the Marlinton *Pocahontas Times* and Jim Comstock of the Richwood *West Virginia Hillbilly,* whose wit and folksy observations struck responsive chords.

Several West Virginia journalists have won national recognition. Holmes Alexander, who grew up in Clarksburg, was a senior editor of the *Kiplinger*

Magazine, later *Changing Times,* and a syndicated columnist for some 140 daily newspapers. John Daniell "Jack" Maurice of the *Charleston Daily Mail* won a Pulitzer Prize for editorial writing in 1976 with a series of temperate editorials concerning the Kanawha County school textbook controversy, which had drawn nationwide attention.

As the century advanced, the newspaper press encountered increasing competition from radio and television. In 1980 West Virginia had fifty-five AM radio stations and forty-two FM stations. They and its ten television stations, including educational stations at Beckley, Huntington, and Morgantown, did much to change patterns of life surviving from bygone times and to draw West Virginians into the mainstream of American life.

Scientific Writings. The natural environment of West Virginia stimulated interest in its flora and fauna. William H. Edwards of Coalburg, Kanawha County, produced a pioneer work in *The Butterflies of North America* (1879–1897). Scholarly studies of the twentieth century included *West Virginia Trees* (1920) by A.B. Brooks; *Common Forest Trees of West Virginia* (1959), *Outlines of the Flora of West Virginia* (1954), and *Spring Wild Flowers* (1958), all by Earl L. Core; *Common Seed Plants of the Mid-Appalachian Region* (1931) by Perry D. Strasbaugh, Earl L. Core, and Nelle Ammons; and *Flora of West Virginia* (1952–1953) by Strasbaugh and Core.

Writings on the state's mineral resources have been voluminous. Israel C. White (1848–1927), whose anticlinal theory relating to oil and gas deposits was regarded as "epochal," spurred the creation of the West Virginia Geological Survey with his "Notes on the Geology of West Virginia." Eminent among later professionals in the field was Paul H. Price (1898–1980), state geologist and director of the West Virginia Geological and Economic Survey for some thirty-five years. Price was the author of *Geology and Natural Resources of West Virginia* (1938) and, with others, of *Salt Brines of West Virginia* (1937). Raymond E. Janssen of Marshall University made a valuable contribution to literature of the field with *Earth Science: A Handbook on the Geology of West Virginia* (1973).

Twentieth Century Politics: Kump to Marland

Depression Politics. Prolonged economic depressions have always been deadly enemies of elected governments, and it was inevitable that the economic collapse of 1929, unprecedented in scale or duration, would seriously affect the political situation in both the nation and the states. Moreover, the euphoria of the late 1920s and a naive belief that want and privation would be banished from the land left most Americans unprepared pyschologically or materially for the worst crisis the nation had faced since the Civil War.

The depression fell upon West Virginia with unusual severity. Employment in coal mining dropped from 119,937 in 1926 to 86,378 in 1932, with an approximate forty percent decline in production. Thousands of mining families, caught in towns where mines ceased to operate or worked only one or two days a week, depending upon erratic orders for coal, fled to places where work was reportedly available, even to such deadly opportunities as Hawks Nest tunnel construction. Others lived precariously, with emergency aid from the Red Cross or volunteer or religious organizations. Similar conditions existed in industrial towns. Wages in all industries plummeted precipitously. Farmers fared little better. They seldom faced the destitution of industrial workers, but their cash income dwindled, and many faced the loss of their farms for nonpayment of taxes.

Neither the federal nor the state government provided effective responses to the depression. Both were attuned to the corporate values and laissez-faire doctrines of the 1920s. The Reconstruction Finance Corporation, for instance, was predicated on the "percolator theory" and offered no immediate relief to millions of distressed Americans. In West Virginia the state government suffered from an antiquated system of financing that left its treasury with a $4 million deficit and its credit impaired. County governments and boards of education were on the verge of bankruptcy. Suffering a near-paralysis, state and local governments also failed to devise effective strategies for the emergency.

In spite of the crisis, the election of 1932 offered reassurances that the people retained faith in the political system. West Virginians followed national patterns in turning Republicans out of office and replacing them with Democrats. The election ended a thirty-six-year Republican reign in the state and ushered in a predominantly Democratic era that continued for the next half-century. West Virginians, who had voted 375,551 for Herbert Hoover to 263,784 for Alfred E. Smith for president in 1928, cast 405,128 votes for Franklin D. Roosevelt to 330,731 for Hoover in 1932. They gave only 5,133 votes to Norman Thomas, the Socialist candidate, and 442 to William Z. Foster, the Communist.

Governor Herman Guy Kump. Voting in the gubernatorial race in 1932 followed closely that of the presidential contest. Democrat H. Guy Kump (October 31, 1877–February 14, 1962) defeated Thomas C. Townsend, a Republican with strong labor support by a vote of, 402,325 to 342,660. J.N. Snider, the Socialist candidate, received only 2,788 votes, and Mike Stone, the Communist, a mere 452. Kump, a successful lawyer, farmer, and banker in Randolph County, had served as county prosecutor and mayor of Elkins. He resigned the judgeship of the Twentieth Judicial Circuit, which included Randolph and Upshur counties, to seek the governorship.

On March 24, 1933, Kump, a man of quiet strength and efficiency, called a special session of the legislature, which convened on April 10 and continued in session for 240 days, making it the longest in state history. Its thorniest problem, the need for revenues to cover the treasury deficit, meet interest and sinking fund requirements, and maintain essential public services, was complicated by a tax-limitation amendment, approved the preceding November by a vote of 335,482 to 43,931. A response to an appalling loss of farms and homes for nonpayment of taxes during the depression years, the amendment limited tax rates for each class of real property and reduced local revenues to such levels that the state had to provide supplemental aid for schools, relief of the destitute, and highways.

In grappling with the financial crisis, the legislature was forced to tap new sources of revenue. It provided some additional income from increase in gross sales and capitation taxes, but it moved in a new direction with a consumers sales tax of two percent on retail sales, earmarked for public schools, and a personal income tax, initially set at one percent on gross income. New taxes were also imposed on chain stores; manufacturers, distributors, and retailers of beer, wine, and liquor; and horse racing. The new taxes permitted general property tax reductions in keeping with the tax limitation amendment.

The constitutional requirement of a balanced budget, as well as his campaign promises, forced Kump to reduce the costs of the state government. The measures he instituted included cutbacks in the number of state employees, reduction of salaries, institution of a central mailing system at the capitol, and creation of a central Department of Purchases for state agencies and institutions. Economy, as well as efforts to assure more equitable educational opportunities for all children, lay behind legislation that made the county the unit of school administration in the state.

The restructuring of the tax system and economies in government had gratifying results. In 1937 when Kump left office, West Virginia finances appeared as sound as those of any state in the Union. Although the net income of state and local governments in 1936 was about $10 million less than it was in 1929, stringent financial measures had provided the state with a small surplus in spite of expenditures of more than $13 million in state aid to public schools, $5.5 million for public welfare, and $4 million, in addition to fixed charges, for primary and secondary roads.

In 1934 voters approved amendments to the West Virginia constitution that brought it in line with changes at the federal level. One repealed the prohibition amendment adopted by West Virginia in 1912 and coincided with the Twenty-first Amendment to the federal Constitution, which again permitted the manufacture, transportation, and sale of intoxicating beverages. The other amendment, patterned after the federal Lame Duck Amendment, changed the date on which the governor and other elected state officials assumed office from March 4 to the first Monday after the second Wednesday of January following their election.

The impressive reforms of the Kump administration by no means matched the dramatic changes in Washington, where Roosevelt's New Deal led to sweeping departures from the past with respect to the role of government in economic affairs. In fact, the federal programs had an impact upon the state that sometimes obscured the more traditional actions in Charleston. The Federal Emergency Relief Administration, or FERA, provided jobs for at least sixty thousand unemployed West Virginians and spent $51 million in the state between 1933 and 1936. The Civil Works Administration, or CWA, and the Public Works Administration, or PWA, spent additional millions on major projects, such as Kanawha Boulevard in Charleston. The Works Progress Administration, or WPA, had more than four thousand small projects and in 1936 employed thirty-six thousand persons. The Civilian Conservation Corps, or CCC, emphasized conservation of forests and other natural resources at camps in the state, and the Farm Security Administration, or FSA, established homestead projects at Arthurdale, Eleanor, and Tygart Valley, where displaced workers might purchase homes and combine limited farming with part-time work in handicrafts and local industries.

For all its benefits, West Virginia did not participate fully in federal relief and recovery programs. State revenues did not permit matching all available federal money, particularly PWA funds. Differences between federal and state officials over administration of WPA funds prevented the state from obtaining its proportionate share of federal relief. Conservative influences remained strong among state leaders, many of whom looked with extreme misgiving upon the paternalistic policies of the federal government. Nevertheless, West Virginia shared fully in the benefits of the Social Security Act of 1935, and in 1936, the legislature passed a Public Welfare Law that authorized maximum participation in federal programs. In 1936, too, it passed an unemployment compensation act, which Kump called "the greatest movement in our history to protect those who toil from the hazards and the punishments of the economic cycle."[1]

---

[1]Quoted in Charles H. Ambler and Festus P. Summers, *West Virginia, the Mountain State*, 2d ed. (Englewood Cliffs, N.J.: Prentice-Hall, Inc., 1958), 482.

Undoubtedly more inspired by the bold and decisive action of President Roosevelt than by the restrained approaches of Governor Kump, West Virginians gave the Democrats a ringing endorsement in the election of 1936. Roosevelt received 502,582 votes, or nearly 100,000 more than in 1932, even though the 325,388 cast for his Republican opponent, Governor Alfred M. Landon of Kansas, fell only about 5,000 short of the number given Hoover four years earlier. The popularity of Roosevelt remained intact in West Virginia. In 1940 he defeated Wendell L. Willkie by a vote of 496,530 to 373,238, and four years later, in the midst of war, he won by a vote of 392,777 to 322,819 against New York Governor Thomas E. Dewey.

The Democrats and Congress. Democratic ascendancy in West Virginia was also reflected in its congressional delegations. From 1933 to 1982 only two Republicans, Henry D. Hatfield and Chapman W. Revercomb, elected in 1928 and 1942, respectively, served complete terms in the United States Senate. The deaths of three Democratic incumbents, however, gave three other Republicans opportunities to serve partial terms. Hugh Ike Shott, Sr., was elected to replace Joseph Rosier in 1942; Jack D. Hoblitzell was appointed in 1958 by Governor Cecil Underwood to complete the term of Matthew M. Neely; and Revercomb was elected in 1956 to succeed Harley M. Kilgore. In contrast, Democrats usually enjoyed long tenure. Neely served from 1923 to 1929; from 1931 to 1941, when he resigned to become governor; and from 1949 until his death. Kilgore served from 1941 until his death. Jennings Randolph and Robert C. Byrd, an incumbent, began their senatorial duties in 1959. Randolph retired in 1985 and was succeeded by John D. Rockefeller IV.

Since 1933, Democrats have usually held the state's seats in the House of Representatives. Except for one Republican in the Seventy-sixth Congress, state delegations were solidly Democratic from 1933 until 1945. From then until 1948 Republicans held three or four of the six seats allotted to the state. Since 1949, however, only four Republicans have represented the state in the House. Dr. Will E. Neal served two consecutive terms; Arch A. Moore, Jr., a skilled and popular figure, served from 1947 to 1969, when he became governor; and Cleveland K. Benedict and David Michael "Mick" Staton were both elected in 1980. In 1982, however, the congressional delegation once again became solidly Democratic.

The Kee family of Bluefield held the Fifth District seat for forty years, a record in state politics. John Kee won election in the Democratic landslide in 1932 and held the seat until his death in 1951. His widow, Elizabeth, was appointed to succeed him. When she relinquished the position in 1965, their son James was elected and continued in office until 1973. In that year the state lost one congressional seat, and in the redistricting Kee faced Congressman Ken Hechler, who defeated him. Other congressmen with long tenures included Jennings Randolph, Joe L. Smith, Cleveland M. Bailey, Robert Mollohan, Harley Staggers, Sr., John Slack, and Ken Hechler, whose service ranged from Smith's twelve years to Staggers's thirty-two years, the record for any West Virginia congressman.

Governor Homer Adams Holt. In the Democratic landslide of 1936, Homer A. Holt (March 1, 1898–January 16, 1976), the attorney general of the state, defeated Judge Summers H. Sharp of Pocahontas County for governor by a vote of 492,333 to 383,503. A native of Lewisburg, Holt had taught at the Washington and Lee University Law School, his alma mater, and practiced law at Fayetteville.

In his inaugural address Holt declared an intention to concentrate on finance and administration and improvement of services already established. He advocated that the consumers sales tax, a temporary measure, become permanent. Fortunately, an expanding economy enabled his administration to meet most demands for additional funds for schools and roads without new taxes.

At the outset of his administration Holt, a man of tenacious convictions, aroused the displeasure of the school lobby, which Kump had as early as 1933 excoriated as "the most disappointing, the most unyielding, the most unrelenting" of all pressure groups and "as selfishly intent upon maintaining its advantages as any utility in maintaining its rate."[2] Holt in 1937 bluntly rejected demands from educators and the press for a special session of the legislature to raise additional revenue for schools and advised those in education to work with funds available "to promote happiness and contentment in the system."[3] During his administration, however, the legislature revised the state school aid formula and took steps toward supplying free textbooks for elementary schools, and in October 1938 Holt told the State Education Association that he considered himself "now among friends."[4]

Holt had more serious differences with organized labor, particularly the United Mine Workers. When some 2,500 miners in Fayette, Raleigh, Mercer, and McDowell counties remained idle after settlement of a strike in the spring of 1939, over a closed shop issue, Holt, believing that most of them disagreed with the position of their leaders, promised them the support of his office if they returned to work. In a Labor Day address at Wheeling, he charged that un-American influences and totalitarian methods had crept into the labor movement. He elaborated on his ideas in a written message to miners the following day. His assertions drew angry responses from Van A. Bittner, leader of District 17 of the UMWA, and John B. Easton, president of the West Virginia CIO. Holt emphatically disclaimed any intention of obstructing the labor movement, but union leaders were convinced that the next governor must be a trusted friend of labor.

Strife Among the Democrats. As Holt's term drew to an end, serious factionalism disrupted the Democratic party. The rift had its origins in the Kump

---

[2]H.G. Kump, *State Papers and Public Addresses,* comp. and annotated James W. Harris, Jr. (Charleston: Jarrett Printing Company, [1937]), 164.

[3]Homer Adams Holt, *State Papers and Public Addresses,* comp. and annotated Willliam E. Hughes (Charleston: Jarrett Printing Company, [1942]), 153.

[4]Ibid., 319.

administration. A liberal element led by Senator Neely and supported strongly by labor spokesmen, especially Bittner and William M. Blizzard of the UMWA, endeavored to gain control of federal programs in the state. Opposing it was a "statehouse" faction headed by Kump, Holt, and Robert G. Kelly, the Democratic state chairman. Philosophically, the statehouse wing objected to leftward tendencies of the New Deal, which Kelly blamed on "a small group of labor leaders and social workers."[5]

Kump, who praised President Roosevelt on August 1, 1933, as the "greatest blessing" that could have come to the oppressed of the nation and the world, in his last biennial message to the legislature admonished, "We must raise our guard against placing a penalty upon industry or a premium upon indolence. We must cut off special privilege and governmental concession, but we must neither shackle individual initiative, not stifle honest enterprise. We must not permit our people to believe that the government will do for men what they should do for themselves and thus foster a race of weaklings where strong men should stand."[6]

In spite of the general popularity of New Deal programs and the infusion of federal money into West Virginia, the statehouse faction had major resources in the struggle for control of the Democratic party. The power of the patronage had vastly increased with state assumption of responsibility for roads, the introduction of the county unit system and increased reliance upon state funds for education, and the creation of a state liquor monopoly. Moreover, federal programs, including welfare and conservation, were administered through the state. Out of this burgeoning power was born the "statehouse machine."

The struggle in the Democratic party reached a head in the election of 1940. In precampaign sparring, Neely called upon the party to nominate a liberal for governor and suggested about thirty acceptable persons. The conservative faction, now headed by Holt, supported R. Carl Andrews, the Democratic state chairman. Then, on the last day for filing in the primary election, Byron B. Randolph of Clarksburg, president of the state Senate, appeared at the office of the secretary of state to file a certificate of candidacy, apparently with the blessings of Neely. Before he did so, however, he was intercepted, and Neely announced to reporters that he himself would enter the gubernatorial race.

In becoming a candidate, Neely made "the greatest political sacrifice of his life," giving up a secure United States Senate seat and significant seniority in that body.[7] Rumors persisted that UMWA leaders pressed Neely into the race, but Neely gave as his major reason his belief that "the Democratic Party of West

[5]Quoted in John Alexander Williams, *West Virginia: A Bicentennial History* (New York and Nashville: W.W. Norton & Company, Inc., and American Association for State and Local History, 1976), 166.

[6]Kump, *State Papers and Public Addresses*, 153.

[7]Quoted in John G. Morgan, *West Virginia Governors, 1863-1980*, 2d ed. (Charleston: Charleston Newspapers, 1980), 166.

Virginia is worth rescuing from a handful of ambitious, selfish, willful dictators who now have a stranglehold upon it and are apparently determined to rule it or ruin it during the next four years."[8]

Neely waged a colorful campaign with, as one admirer stated, "a Bible in one hand and Mother in the other."[9] With rousing oratory and labor support, he won the primary, defeating Andrews, his nearest competitor, by a plurality of more than 48,000 votes. Liberals won another victory when Harley M. Kilgore, a relatively unknown Beckley judge, defeated Kump for nomination for United States senator. In the general election Neely won over Republican D. Boone Dawson, the mayor of Charleston, by a vote of 496,028 to 383,608.

Governor Matthew Mansfield Neely. When Neely (November 9, 1875–January 18, 1958), assumed his duties as governor on a cold January 13, 1941, he had already attained a pinnacle of political success unknown to any of his predecessors at the time of their inaugurations. Born in a log cabin in Doddridge County, he had served as mayor of Fairmont, clerk of the House of Delegates, congressman, and United States senator. After losing his congressional seat in the Harding landslide of 1920, Neely won election to the Senate in 1922. Defeated by Republican Henry D. Hatfield in 1928, he returned to the Senate in 1930 with a 133,000-vote majority over his opponent and the largest vote ever cast to that time for any candidate on any ticket in West Virginia. He was an easy victor in subsequent elections and remained in the Senate until January 12, 1941, when he became governor.

One of Neely's first official acts as governor exacerbated the gaping party wounds. Both he and retiring Governor Holt endeavored to fill the Senate seat that Neely was vacating. A genuine difference of opinion existed as to which of them had authority to make the appointment, and both sought to cover all contingencies. Holt appointed Clarence E. Martin, Sr., of Martinsburg, a former president of the American Bar Association, and gave him three commissions— one to take effect upon Neely's "ceasing to have the office," one when a vacancy occurred, and another at the "first moment after midnight Jan. 13, upon Neely having resigned."[10] In order to protect his own appointee, Dr. Joseph Rosier, president of Fairmont State College, Neely took four oaths of office. One was at 11:35 on the night of January 12, one about ten minutes later, one "instantly after midnight," and the fourth at noon, January 31, at the formal inauguration ceremonies.[11] Martin and Rosier went to Washington to claim the Senate seat. After deliberation, the Senate Elections Committee by a vote of eight to seven recognized Neely's right to make the appointment and recommend seating Rosier.

The first legislature of the Neely administration passed several important

[8]Quoted in ibid.
[9]Quoted in ibid.
[10]Ibid., 167.
[11]Ibid.

acts that provided a court of claims, permanent registration of voters, nonpartisan county boards of education, a teachers retirement fund, and certificates of competence for coal miners. Nevertheless, Neely claimed too much when he told a convention of Young Democrats that the factional strife that "bedeviled our party as boils bedeviled Job, has at last been buried in a grave so dark and deep and wide that . . . Gabriel and his trumpet will never resurrect its wicked spirit no matter how loud and long he may blow."[12]

Midway in his governorship, in 1942, Neely clearly made a serious political miscalculation in seeking to return to the United States Senate. He defeated former Governor Kump by more than seventy thousand votes in the primary. Public disapproval of his willingness to desert a duty to serve out his gubernatorial term and a drift toward the Republican party in the state cost Neely heavily, and he suffered the greatest humiliation of his career by losing the general election to Chapman Revercomb by more than fifty thousand votes.

Although the last two years of Neely's administration brought achievements such as establishment of the Andrew Summers Rowan Home for the Aged, better facilities for the care of tuberculosis victims, and an Inter-Racial Commission, differences in philosophy and politics led to deterioration in relations between the governor and the legislature. Neely vetoed fourteen acts of the 1943 legislature, which passed several over his veto. In refusing assent to repeal of the income tax, Neely declared, in a populistic vein, that "plutocracy, blind, heartless and needless, with its army of paid agents, swarming lobbyists and subsidized instrumentalities" had for months marched over the state and flooded it with propaganda in order to avoid bearing a fair share of government expense. He vetoed the act, he said, "with the fervor with which I would feed a starving Lazarus at a merciless rich man's gate."[13]

One of Neely's most controversial actions as governor was an attempt to remove Charles E. Lawall from the presidency of West Virginia University on the ground that the university had not made progress comparable with that of other state universities and that a change of administration was essential. The Board of Governors of the university on June 9, 1944, bowed to gubernatorial pressure and voted four to three to remove Lawall. Neely quickly found that the interested public might be more tolerant of stagnant university administration than of political interference in its affairs. Lawall brought suit in the Kanawha County Circuit Court and won a temporary injunction preventing his dismissal. The Supreme Court refused to hear an appeal by the Board of Governors, and Lawall retained his office. In August 1945, seven months after Neely's term expired, Lawall resigned. Both sides claimed victory, Lawall in maintaining academic integrity and Neely in stirring the university to a new sense of responsibility.

[12]Matthew Mansfield Neely, *State Papers and Public Addresses* (Charleston: Mathews Printing and Lithographing Co., n.d.), 185.
[13]Ibid., 86.

Neely's political career extended beyond his governorship. When he was seventy years old he returned to the House of Representatives, but by only a 250-vote majority. He lost the seat two years later. The old warrior, however, could not be counted out. In 1948 he was elected to the United States Senate, after defeating incumbent Rush D. Holt, his former protégé, for the nomination and crushing his old rival, Revercomb, by a 106,000 majority in the general election. Neely was reelected in 1954.

In late 1956 rumors that Neely was seriously ill began to circulate. Actually, he had terminal cancer. He arrived at the opening session of Congress on January 8, 1958, in an ambulance and remained there in a wheelchair for about forty-five minutes before returning to the hospital, where he died ten days later. His passing marked the end of one of the most colorful careers in West Virginia politics.

Governors Meadows, Patteson, and Marland. Chastened by self-inflicted wounds and Republican victories, the Democrats recognized the need for unity. Neely began to restructure and revitalize the statehouse machine along lines less conservative but short of the desires of liberal Democrats. Responsibility for drawing the warring factions together fell to Homer W. Hanna, who through the intercession of Neely had been active in party councils since the early days of the New Deal. Affable, efficient, and working from relatively obscure positions that gave little clue to his real power, Hanna perfected an organization that remained a major force in state politics for more than two decades.

With new harmony, the Democratic party united behind Clarence W. Meadows for governor in 1944. Meadows easily crushed the hopes of Rush D. Holt for the nomination and defeated the Republican nominee, Charleston mayor D. Boone Dawson, by a vote of 395,122 to 330,649. The political pendulum, which had swung leftward in 1940, moved closer to center with Meadows (February 11, 1904–September 12, 1961), who had served as prosecuting attorney of Raleigh County, attorney general, and judge of the Tenth Judicial Circuit.

The administration of Meadows was generally tranquil. Meadows made effective use of radio in reaching the people, demonstrated skills as a mediator in industrial disputes, and chose as his executive assistant Okey L. Patteson, a popular and astute politician. The legislature created the office of state insurance commissioner, abolished the practice of allowing county sheriffs to feed prisoners at profits to themselves, and authorized cities and municipalities to levy gross sales taxes. It extended retirement benefits for school personnel, revised the state school aid formula, and raised teachers' salaries, but not without intense lobbying by the State Education Association. Seeking long-range solutions to educational problems, the lawmakers created an interim committee, which engaged Dr. George D. Strayer of Columbia University and a team of experts to make a detailed study. Then, as so frequently happened, the lawmakers disregarded most of the recommendations in the Strayer report.

Unlike his immediate predecessors, Okey L. Patteson (September 14, 1898–July 3, 1989) entered politics by way of the business world rather than the legal profession. He had served on the Fayette County court and as sheriff of the county before becoming executive assistant to Meadows. With statehouse support, Patteson, who had been widely regarded as the "crown prince" of the Meadows administration, defeated James K. Thomas, a former attorney general, for the nomination and Republican Herbert S. Boreman, a grandnephew of the first governor of the state, by a vote of 438,752 to 329,309 in the general election. Patteson carried to the governorship tact and affability that produced a smooth administration and harmony between his office and the legislature. He also commanded admiration for personal courage and determination despite the loss of both legs below the knees in a hunting accident in 1932.

Generally optimistic about the state, Patteson, like many of his predecessors, emphasized highway improvements and education. The voters ratified a $50 million farm-to-market roads amendment in 1948, the year of his election, and under legislation of 1947, Patteson set up the West Virginia Turnpike Commission for construction and operation of an 88-mile toll road between Charleston and Princeton. Educational legislation included continuing contracts for schoolteachers and establishment of the West Virginia University Medical and Dental School. Patteson, to whom the legislature gave responsibility for selecting the site for the medical school, chose Morgantown, although many experts urged its location in one of the larger cities such as Charleston or Huntington. Among other achievements were a constitutional amendment for a bonus for World War II veterans and provisions for inclusion of employees of the state and its subdivisions in the federal social security system.

Early in 1952 Patteson announced that he would support William Casey Marland (March 26, 1918–November 26, 1965), the attorney general, for governor in the coming elections. A native of Illinois who grew up in Wyoming County, Marland had worked in the coal mines and received his law degree from West Virginia only five years previously. Many older Democrats resented Patteson's support for the relatively inexperienced Marland, but the young attorney general won the primary with some thirty-nine thousand more votes than Congressman E.H. Hedrick, his closest opponent. Democratic strength in the state, as in the nation, had begun to erode, and Marland's victory over Republican Rush D. Holt, a former Democrat, was by a vote of only 454,898 to 427,629, the smallest margin for any Democratic governor since the Great Depression. Nevertheless, it compared favorably with that of the 453,578 to 419,970 victory of Adlai Stevenson over Dwight D. Eisenhower in West Virginia and attested to the strength of the statehouse organization.

Marland's political future seemed bright and assured, but three days after his inauguration he stunned older and more cautious politicians when he called upon the legislature to enact a severance tax upon the extractive industries of the state. The proposed tax would have fallen most heavily upon the coal industry.

Marland's proposal had the support of labor, including the UMWA and John L. Lewis, the West Virginia Education Association, and all but one member of the West Virginia congressional delegation. The coal industry and the West Virginia Chamber of Commerce rose in an almost solid phalanx against the tax. They had strong support from the press, including the *Charleston Gazette,* the leading Democratic newspaper of the state, whose editor charged that John L. Lewis was "the real mastermind" behind the tax and would use it to control the coal industry and ultimately state government. Most Republican and a substantial number of Democratic legislators, many under intense pressure from the West Virginia Coal Operators Association, lined up against the proposal.

With the severance tax in imminent danger of defeat, Senator Neely hurried to Charleston to appeal for its passage. He declared that the battle was "largely between absentee captains of industry on the one hand and the men, women, and children of West Virginia on the other."[14] On February 22 Marland, in another impassioned plea to the legislature, argued that the state should derive some permanent benefits from industry in the form of improved schools and roads to offset perennially burning slate piles and polluted streams. Five days later the governor caucused with Senate Democrats, but his last-ditch effort proved in vain. In early March the House of Delegates dealt the tax a death blow by voting fifty-six to forty-one to postpone consideration indefinitely.

The severance tax battle produced an enduring rift between Marland and the legislature. The Board of Public Works, charged with constitutional responsibilities in budget preparation, presented a document for the 1953–1955 biennium in which expenditures exceeded estimated revenues. In spite of a constitutional requirement of a balanced budget, the legislature rejected Marland's proposal for a state personal income tax, earmarked for schools, and refused to assent to additional taxes on automobiles and gasoline for roads until a reorganization plan for the State Road Commission had been adopted. When the Supreme Court declared the budget unconstitutional, Marland called a special session of the legislature, which adopted a budget along the lines he suggested. The legislature and Marland approved a measure to place constitutional amendments on the ballot in 1956 that provided a bonus for Korean war veterans, enabled women to serve on juries, and allowed counties to double the direct property tax for schools for five-year periods with the approval of sixty percent of the voters participating in an election. The voters ratified only the first two amendments.

Marland left the governorship with many of his goals unattained. He might have done more to turn politics in the liberal direction he desired had he been willing to compromise on some major issues. Perhaps, as one observer stated, he was "plucked too green."[15] Had his experience and political seasoning been

[14]Quoted in Neal R. Peirce, *The Border South States: People, Politics, and Power in the Five States of the Border South* (New York: W.W. Norton & Company, Inc., 1975), 192-93.

[15]Quoted in Morgan, *West Virginia Governors,* 224.

commensurate with the intrinsic worth of some of his proposals and his own sincerity, he might have achieved greater success. Also at the root of some of his difficulties was the "weak governor" concept in the constitution, which produced many of the periodic struggles between the executive and legislative branches of government, particularly in the realms of budget-making, appointments, general administration, and responsibility of state officials.

Politically, Marland never recovered from his gubernatorial experiences. In 1956 he sought the United States Senate seat left vacant by the death of Harley M. Kilgore, but he lost the election to Revercomb. Two years later, when Senator Neely died, Marland entered the race for the short Senate term, which carried more seniority than the long term, but Jennings Randolph won the seat. Marland took a position with a coal company in Chicago and later faded into obscurity. He was found driving a taxi in Chicago, after overcoming a problem with alcohol, but a few months afterward died of cancer. His valiant battles against personal adversity and illness earned him a respect and sympathy that eluded him as governor.

Marland's governorship ended twenty-four years of unbroken Democratic control in West Virginia. The liberal trends of those years in both the state and the nation inevitably produced strains within the party, which retained strong conservative elements. The controversies of the Marland administration temporarily loosened some of the bonds that held together the statehouse machine, which had partially reconciled the opposing factions, and paved the way for a Republican gubernatorial victory in 1956, the first in a quarter of a century.

Twentieth Century Politics: Underwood to Rockefeller

Midcentury Political Changes. Historically, the American people have wearied of sustained departures from traditional modes of life, including the demands of liberal idealism, the exertions and regimentation of war, and the responsibilities and frustrations of world leadership. At the beginning of the second half of the twentieth century, they had experienced twenty years of New Deal and Fair Deal policies, with their advanced social and economic programs; the most destructive war in history; and, following that war, the prospect of indefinite commitments abroad. A desire for what Warren G. Harding called "normalcy" and dissatisfactions with the Truman administration enabled Dwight D. Eisenhower, the Republican candidate, to defeat the Democratic presidential aspirant, Adlai Stevenson, in 1952 by a popular vote of 33,936,234 to 27,314,987 and an electoral vote of 442 to 81 and, like Herbert Hoover in 1928, to break into the "solid South."

Although national trends were apparent in West Virginia, the state generally remained Democratic. Stevenson and Marland, the Democratic candidate for governor, carried the state, but by the smallest margins since 1932. Except for one congressional seat, the Democrats retained all federal and statewide offices that they held and kept firm control of both houses of the legislature.

The election of 1956 in West Virginia was a different story. The Democrats, split once again and many of them deeply disappointed in the actions of Governor Marland, faced an uphill battle. On March 30, a few weeks before the primary, Okey L. Patteson, who had pressed Marland upon a reluctant party as its gubernatorial nominee in 1952, publicly declared that he had made "a tragic mistake." He stated that his associations with Marland had led him to believe that his choice for the nominee was "honest, trustworthy, highly efficient and strictly sober," but he realized that his "faith was misplaced."[1]

The Republicans made the most of their opportunity. For the first time since 1928 a Republican candidate for president carried West Virginia. Eisenhower,

---

[1]Quoted in John G. Morgan, *West Virginia Governors, 1863-1980*, 2d ed. (Charleston: Charleston Newspapers, 1980), 201.

who seemed to many Americans to embody the old-fashioned virtues of the country, was easily reelected. In West Virginia, where he had lost to Stevenson four years earlier, he won 449,297 popular votes to 381,534 for Stevenson. In state congressional races, Revercomb defeated Marland, and two Republicans, Will E. Neal and Arch A. Moore, Jr., dislodged Democrats.

The most dramatic Republican victory of 1956 was achieved by Cecil H. Underwood, who became the first Republican governor since 1929, defeating Democrat Robert H. Mollohan by a vote of 440,502 to 377,121. Republicans also made gains in the legislature, but without attaining majorities. Republican R. Virgil Rohrbough was elected state superintendent of free schools over W.W. Trent, who had held the position since 1933.

Governor Cecil Harland Underwood. The youngest man ever elected governor of West Virginia, Cecil H. Underwood (b. November 5, 1922) had a background in history and political science and from 1950 to 1956 served as vice president of Salem College. In 1944, when he was twenty-two years old, he was elected to the House of Delegates and represented his native Tyler County for six terms. From 1949 until he became governor he was the minority floor leader. The thirty-four-year-old Underwood was therefore not without a considerable amount of needed political seasoning.

Despite its Democratic complexion, Underwood generally worked harmoniously with the legislature in 1957. At the end of the session he could point to the creation of a Mental Health Department, establishment of the Department of Finance and Adminstration, reorganization of the State Road Commission, creation of a bipartisan commission on equalization and revaluation of property, and authorization for counties to levy a special school tax to a maximum of ten dollars per adult annually.

In the 1958 budget session of the legislature Underwood stressed schools and roads. He urged adoption of an incentive plan, proposed by Rohrbough, that limited state aid and rewarded initiative and planning at the county level. With respect to roads, he boldly called for a $500 million system of backbone highways, featuring expressways and aggregating some 970 miles, to interconnect with the interstate routes, with costs to be spread over ten years and met through increases in consumers sales, gross sales, racing, and highway user taxes. The state, however, was in a depressed condition, and the legislature, closely attuned to its implications in the approaching elections, rejected the plan. The following year the legislature gave approval for an Economic Development Agency, a State Temporary Economic Program, or STEP, and various tax increases, with $9 million earmarked for roads.

Political differences between the executive and legislative branches of government impeded action in several areas. The Senate in 1957 and 1959 either delayed or refused confirmation of Underwood's appointees to critical positions on sometimes flimsy grounds, and in 1959 the president of the Senate delivered a strong verbal attack on the governor. Underwood branded much of the opposition as political harassment and countered in kind with the criticism of alleged Democratic exactions from state employees, known as the "flower fund." When Underwood left office, there was general agreement that he had given the state dignified and responsible leadership. He was held in high esteem in Republican councils in both the state and the nation, and his political future seemed bright.

Politics and the Midcentury Economic Crisis. Of far greater import than political differences were the economic problems that began to press upon West Virginia and other parts of the southern Appalachian region after World War II. Forebodings of trouble appeared with migrations beginning in the 1940s from the farming sections, particularly the Little Kanawha Valley and mountain counties such as Tucker, Pendleton, and Pocahontas.

Yet more serious were changes in the coal industry. Between 1947 and 1954 production of coal in the state plunged from 173,650,000 to 113,039,000 tons, a loss of thirty-five percent. Rapid mechanization and consolidation, supported by John L. Lewis and the UMWA, increased productivity per man-day from 5.57 tons in 1945 to 10.05 in 1957. The work force, not surprisingly, fell drastically, from 117,104 in 1948 to 58,732 in 1955 and to 42,557 in 1961.

As opportunities collapsed, a migration from the coalfields began that eclipsed the movement from farming areas. Thousands of young men, who normally would have entered the mines, and experienced miners whose jobs vanished, were left without employment. Many of them left for Pittsburgh, Cleveland, Akron, Chicago, Detroit, and other cities. Between 1950 and 1960 the population of West Virginia declined from 2,005,552 to 1,860,421, a loss in excess of seven percent at a time when nearly every other state gained population. More than seventy percent of the loss occurred in the ten leading coal-mining counties, although one of them, Kanawha, had a net gain of 13,296, largely because of growth in other industries. The only other counties showing population growth commensurate with that of the nation as a whole were Berkeley and those along the Ohio River.

The economic troubles of West Virginia during the 1950s had psychological dimensions. With an unemployment rate more than double the national average, a per capita income only seventy-five percent of that of the nation, and the continuing exodus of thousands of young and ambitious citizens, West Virginia seemed to have lost step in the march of progress. The pride of West Virginians suffered in the realization that the problems were deep-rooted and in need of massive attention. An article in the *Saturday Evening Post* of February 6, 1960, entitled "The Strange Case of West Virginia," touched sensitive nerves with its contrasts of the poverty of many mining areas with the splendor of other places, notably the White Sulphur Springs resort. Public officials, particularly Governor Underwood, United States Senator Randolph, and Congressman John Slack, were deeply concerned about conditions in the state and the need for programs to alleviate them.

West Virginia and the Election of 1960. West Virginia elections usually arouse little interest outside the state, but its 1960 primary attracted attention throughout the nation as a battleground for John F. Kennedy and Hubert H. Humphrey for the Democratic nomination for president of the United States. Political analysts later agreed that Kennedy's victory in West Virginia was the turning point on his road to the White House. Arthur Edson of the Associated Press declared that "if our national disputes are ever remembered as our battlefields are now, West Virginia will become a national shrine."[2]

Kennedy needed a victory in West Virginia to demonstrate that a Catholic could win in a strongly Protestant and unionized state, especially after he encountered substantial Protestant resistance in the Wisconsin primary. Walter Lippmann predicted, "It will be a miracle if the outcome in West Virginia shows there is no religious issue which divides the people of this country."[3] Kennedy, nevertheless, was confident of victory. A Louis Harris poll conducted for him stressed the relatively small proportion of church members in the state, the tendency of many of them to separate their highly personal religion from public affairs, and their general freedom from the bigotry with which outside reporters often invested them. It also indicated that Kennedy would receive as much as seventy percent of the Democratic vote in the primary.

For strategical reasons, Kennedy and his supporters treated the religious issue as a major obstacle. Kennedy repeatedly affirmed his support for separation of church and state, knowing that the religious question was really a man of straw and that it would not be the overriding consideration for the vast majority of the voters. Time after time he pointed to the Constitutional prohibition of any religious test for public office and asked, "Is anyone going to tell me I lost this primary the day I was born?"[4] This tactic, with its implication that any vote against Kennedy stemmed from bigotry, angered supporters of Humphrey, who had long fought for equality and tolerance.

The Kennedy forces knew better than to put all their political eggs in a religious basket. Their strategists worked with West Virginia leaders to get Kennedy slated in most counties and linked him to Franklin D. Roosevelt, a revered figure in the coalfields, by having the former president's son and namesake appear at Kennedy rallies. They presented Kennedy as a man of compassion, who, though rich, took the plight of West Virginia to heart. Above all, Kennedy spent money lavishly, leading an editor of the *Charleston Gazette* to observe that he "bought a landslide, not an election."[5]

Kennedy's victory, with 60.8 percent of the vote, was a catastrophe for Humphrey, who announced his withdrawal from the presidential race on elec-

[2]Quoted in Neal R. Peirce, *The Border South States: People, Politics, and Power in the Five States of the Border South* (New York: W.W. Norton & Company, Inc., 1975), 194-95.
[3]Quoted in ibid., 195.
[4]Quoted in ibid., 196.
[5]Quoted in ibid.

tion night in West Virginia. Humphrey, who had long battled for the working classes and for civil rights, failed to win strong support from either organized labor or the black population of the state. With Humphrey eliminated from the contest and Kennedy marching on to the Democratic nomination and victory over Richard M. Nixon, there was truth in the contention that the West Virginia primary made a president.

The drama of the Democratic primary has obscured other outcomes of the 1960 elections in West Virginia. Kennedy defeated Nixon by a vote of 441,786 to 395,995, but in an uninspiring gubernatorial campaign, W.W. Barron won over Republican Harold Neely by the even greater margin of 446,755 to 380,665. By approximately the same vote, Democrats won all statewide elective offices and two seats on the supreme court. They captured twelve of the sixteen Senate seats at stake and eighty-two of the one hundred seats in the House of Delegates. Completing the sweep, Jennings Randolph defeated Cecil Underwood for the United States Senate, and Democratic incumbents retained their places in the House of Representatives.

Governor William Wallace Barron. Popularly known as "Wally," the new governor, W.W. Barron (b. December 8, 1911) had both political experience and skill. He had served as mayor of Elkins, his native town, and member of the House of Delegates. In 1956 he was elected attorney general of the state, a position that three times since 1933 Democrats had used as a springboard to the governorship.

Barron's administration began on a note of accomplishment and continued to produce solid achievements. At its regular session in 1961 the legislature established a Public Employees Retirement System, a Department of Natural Resources, and an Air Pollution Control Commission and transformed an existing agency into the Human Rights Commission. On recommendation of the governor, the legislature also created the West Virginia Industrial Development Authority and the Department of Commerce, both for the purpose of promoting and expanding industrial enterprises in the state and improving its long-range economic climate. Barron named Hulett C. Smith, his closest opponent in the 1960 primary, to head the new Commerce Department. Later legislation authorized counties and municipalities to acquire sites, buildings, and equipment for factories and processing plants and to finance the acquisitions through issuance of negotiable revenue bonds.

Unfortunately, corruption was rife in the Barron administration, and scandal eventually obscured accomplishments. Thirteen high officials who served under Barron or his successor, along with five of their friends, relatives, or business associates, were convicted of bribery, conspiracy, tax evasion, or falsification of records and sentenced to prison. They included Barron's executive assistant, the state treasurer, the attorney general, the commissioner of the Department of Finance and Administration, the liquor control commissioner, the commissioner of the Department of Motor Vehicles, the state road commissioner and his assistant, and the commissioner of the Department of Welfare. Barron himself, convicted of tampering with a jury, received a five-year prison term.

The elections of 1964, held before the scandals became known to the public, continued Democratic dominance in the state. West Virginians strongly endorsed the Kennedy-Johnson policies of the previous four years, including programs to alleviate economic problems of Appalachia, by casting 538,087 votes for Lyndon Johnson for president, more than twice the 253,953 they gave to Barry Goldwater. Robert C. Byrd received 515,015 votes to 246,072 for Republican Cooper P. Benedict in the United States senatorial race. All Democratic incumbents retained their congressional positions, as did Arch A. Moore, Jr., the lone Republican among them.

In the gubernatorial race, Hulett C. Smith defeated Cecil Underwood, still a popular political figure, but by a vote of 433,023 to 355,559, far less than the two-to-one records of most other candidates for state and federal office. Democrats won fourteen of the sixteen state Senate seats at stake and ninety-one of the one hundred places in the House of Delegates.

Governor Hulett Carlson Smith. The election of Hulett C. Smith (b. October 21, 1918) provided evidence of renewed vitality of the statehouse organization. A native and businessman of Beckley, Smith had the support of Barron, under whom he served as commerce commissioner.

Achievements of the Smith administration included abolition of the death penalty in the state, establishment of the legislative Joint Committee on Finance and Administration as a statutory body, creation of the West Virginia Antiquities Commission, and the establishment of the West Virginia Educational Broadcasting Authority. The legislature also set up the State Building Commission and authorized the sale of revenue bonds for construction of state office buildings and facilities at mental and benevolent institutions. Of utmost significance to the operation of state government was the ratification by the voters of the Modern Budget Amendment, which made the governor rather than the Board of Public Works responsible for preparation of the state budget.

West Virginians gave the Democratic leadership strong endorsement in the election of 1968. Hubert Humphrey, the Democratic nominee for president, received 374,091 votes, compared with 307,555 for Richard Nixon. George Wallace, who ran as the candidate of the American party, won 72,560 votes. Democrats won all of the state's congressional seats and positions on the Board of Public Works. They retained control of the state Senate by winning in thirteen of the eighteen races and of the House of Delegates, although by a reduced margin.

Democratic victories were clouded by loss of the governorship. Revelations of scandal in the Barron administration, the extent of which was not known at the time, handicapped the Democratic nominee, James M. Sprouse. The office went to Republican Arch A. Moore, Jr., who had a strong political base in the

northern part of the state, but he triumphed over Sprouse by only 378,315 votes
to 365,530.

Governor Arch Alfred Moore, Jr. An attorney in his native Moundsville,
Arch A. Moore (b. April 16, 1923) had demonstrated political strength by
winning six consecutive congressional terms, usually serving as the lone
Republican in the state's delegation. His election as governor was in reality a
personal rather than a party victory.

Not unexpectedly, Moore's administration was marked by frequent clashes
with the Democratic legislature, but it was not without accomplishments. Notable achievements of his first term included creation in 1969 of the West Virginia
Board of Regents, which was vested with general control over all state colleges
and universities; designation of pneumoconiosis, or "black lung," a common
disease among coal miners, as a compensable affliction under workmen's
compensation laws; creation of the Department of Highways; restructuring of
the Department of Welfare; the setting of new qualifications for the director of
the Department of Mental Health; and establishment of public kindergartens.

Several amendments to the state constitution were ratified during Moore's
first administration. The Governor's Succession Amendment of 1970 enabled
the governor for the first time since 1872 to succeed himself, but it limited him to
two successive terms. A Legislative Improvement Amendment made numerous
changes in the functioning of the legislature. It required the organization of the
two houses in odd-numbered years; specified that beginning in 1973 and each
four years thereafter the legislature should convene as usual on the second
Wednesday of January but should, after taking care of organizational matters,
adjourn until the second Wednesday of February; and set dates for submission of
the budget to the legislature by the governor.

Although voter registration for the general election of 1972 in West Virginia
favored the Democrats nearly two to one, Moore defeated his Democratic
challenger, John D. Rockefeller IV, by 423,817 to 350,462 votes. His victory
lay in part with the conservative trends that characterized the state as well as the
nation, but it also stemmed from his own political adroitness and continued
popularity. Republicans also captured the offices of secretary of state and
auditor, failed by only 2,014 votes to unseat the Democratic attorney general,
won one of the three seats at stake on the supreme court, and gained six
additional members in the House of Delegates.

Many actions of the second Moore administration were in line with
national trends. Responsibilities of a new Office of Emergency Services included those previously assigned the Department of Civil Defense Mobiliza-
tion. In addition, the state government set up programs to deal with problems
of the aging; created public service districts for water and sewage services;
passed a dam control act, a response to the disastrous Buffalo Creek flood of
1972; provided for open meetings and proceedings of government bodies; and
required disclosure of campaign contributions and expenditures by candidates
for public office.

Significant amendments to the state constitution authorized a bonus for the state's Vietnam veterans; enabled county sheriffs to succeed themselves but limited them to two terms in succession; and reorganized the judicial system. Under the judicial reorganization amendment, judges of the supreme court were designated justices, and the president became the chief justice. Of greater importance, it abolished the office of justice of the peace and created magistrate courts, with magistrates elected by the voters, for each county.

As Moore's second term drew to a close, there was speculation that he would seek another, on the ground that the constitutional limit of two con-secutive terms did not apply to his first term, during which it was adopted. The Democratic-controlled supreme court, however, ruled against Moore's inter-pretation.

The 1976 gubernatorial election pitted Democrat John D. Rockefeller IV, whom Moore had defeated four years earlier, against former Governor Cecil H. Underwood. Republicans suffered severe handicaps in voter registrations, which favored the Democrats by more than two to one; the lingering effects of the Watergate scandals; and the lack of a strong national ticket such as they had in 1972. Moreover, Underwood, who addressed issues with knowledge and candor, was handicapped by the financial resources of his opponent. Rockefeller won the governorship by a vote of 495,659 to 253,423. Democrats won all other statewide offices, including three seats on the supreme court, fifteen of eighteen Senate seats, and ninety-one of the one hundred seats in the House of Delegates.

In the national races, West Virginians gave Jimmy Carter 435,914 votes and Gerald Ford, the incumbent, 314,760 for president. Robert C. Byrd, a popular United States senator, ran unopposed and led the Democratic ticket with 566,423 votes. Democrats retained all four of the state's congressional seats, but a newcomer to state politics, Nick J. Rahall of Beckley, defeated veteran congressman Ken Hechler, who had earlier that year resigned his seat to seek the Democratic nomination for governor.

Governor John Davison Rockefeller IV. A native of New York City and a member of one of the nation's wealthiest families, John D. Rockefeller IV (b. June 18, 1937), popularly known as "Jay," served as a special assistant to Peace Corps Director Sargent Shriver, special assistant in the Bureau of Far Eastern Affairs of the Department of State, and on the President's Commission on Juvenile Delinquency and Crime, with assignment to work in West Virginia. He gained considerable public notice as a social worker at Emmons, Kanawha County. After one term in the House of Delegates, he was elected secretary of state, a position in which he campaigned for voting reforms. Following his defeat for governor in 1972, he served as president of West Virginia Wesleyan College until 1975, when he resigned once more to seek the governorship.

During his first years as governor, Rockefeller undertook administrative reorganizations designed to expedite the functioning and improve the services of state governnment. They included establishment of the Department of Cor-rections, with authority over all penal and correctional institutions; creation of the Governor's Office of Economic and Community Development, which replaced the Department of Commerce; reorganization and consolidation of health services, including mental health, under the Department of Health; and creation of the Department of Culture and History, which encompassed a wide range of historical, archival, cultural, and artistic functions.

Prior to his election as governor Rockefeller had endeared himself to environmentalists by boldly calling for abolition of strip mining. As the nation began to face acute energy shortages, however, he abandoned that position and began to advocate regulation rather than an end to that method of mining. As governor he approved adoption of federal surface control standards for strip mining in the state and limiting mining generally in the Cranberry Glades Wilderness Study Area. Rockefeller was named chairman of President Carter's commission to study the uses of coal, and in that capacity he pressed for acceleration of conversion of industrial plants to coal, not only as a solution to some of the nation's energy problems but also as a means of stimulating a West Virginia industry that had fallen upon troubled times.

In 1980 Rockefeller once again faced his old adversary, Arch A. Moore, Jr., in his bid for reelection as governor. Since both had been popular and effective governors, personalities assumed more than usual importance. Although voter registration continued to show more than twice as many Democrats as Republicans, Rockefeller waged an intensive campaign in which he spent some $11 million. He defeated Moore by a vote of 401,863 to 337,240. The Democrats won fifteen of the seventeen state Senate seats and seventy-eight seats in the House of Delegates. Victories for Republican David Michael "Mick" Staton and Cleveland K. Benedict split the state's congressional delegation evenly between the two parties, but Jimmy Carter carried the state in the presidential landslide that swept Ronald Reagan into the White House. Two years later, however, Robert "Bob" Wise and Harley Staggers, Jr., recaptured the congressional seats lost by the Democrats.

Two judicial decisions handed down during Rockefeller's second term had greater implications for the future of the state than most legislative enactments. The first, made by Judge Arthur Recht of the Ohio County Circuit Court in 1982 held that the legislature had failed to meet its constitutional obligation to provide a thorough and efficient system of free schools for all children of the state. The Recht decision originated in Lincoln County, where a limited tax base and constitutional and legal requirements made it impossible to maintain a school system of acceptable quality. Recht elaborated upon his conclusion by outlining in detail in an exhaustive document steps that must be taken to comply with the constitutional mandate. Estimates of costs of equalizing opportunities throughout the state and achieving the goals set forth ranged as high as $1.5 billion and drew from many state leaders claims that many were unnecessary and economically indefensible.

The other decision, rendered by the state supreme court a few weeks later, held that the real property assessments below the constitutional requirement of true and actual value, as represented by the selling price in 1980, must be increased to true values. Specifically, moves by various counties to raise assessments to sixty percent of actual values were rejected as unconstitutional. With hundreds of thousands of state residents suddenly confronted with the likelihood of increases of several hundredfold in their taxes, Governor Rockefeller called a special session of the legislature in July 1980 to approve placement on the ballots in the ensuing November election of amendments that placed ceilings of sixty percent on property assessments, but with authority for the legislature to increase percentages and provide exemptions of up to $200,000 for each property holder in the future if conditions warranted.

The 1984 elections found West Virginia with the worst economic conditions since the Great Depression and with the highest unemployment rate in the nation. President Ronald Reagan, however, escaped much of the blame and carried the state, which he had lost to Jimmy Carter four years earlier. Former Republican Governor Arch A. Moore, Jr., defeated Democrat Clyde See for the governorship, making him the first governor in the state's history elected to a third four-year term. Rockefeller himself won the United States Senate seat vacated by Jennings Randolph, but his margin of victory over Republican John Raese, a political newcomer, was far less than expected even though he spent an estimated $11 million of his personal fortune on his campaign.

West Virginia entered the 1980s with mixed blessings. Although many of her natural resources, including timber, oil, gas, and soils had suffered various degrees of depletion, vast reserves of coal, salt, and other natural endowments remained. Isolation, which had retarded the development of much of the state, had given way before Interstate and Corridor highways and penetrations of communications media.

Yet problems persisted. Absentee ownership of land remained conspicuous. In 1972 J. David McAteer and Jonathan A. Rowe found that twenty-five large corporations owned forty-four percent of the land in fourteen coal-mining counties, and in some counties they controlled as much as eighty-six percent. Coal, which continued to be a mainstay of the economy despite industrial diversification, failed in the 1970s to give West Virginia the leadership in energy production that many residents had anticipated. Moreover, large coal companies had become subsidiaries of giant oil corporations, with a resultant loss of the independence that they had known earlier. With reliance upon a troubled coal business and the so-called smokestack industries, West Virginia suffered acutely from the recession of the early 1980s and appeared to be one of the last states likely to experience an economic revival.

Old Problems and New Dilemmas

Continuities and Uncertainties. Most of the distinguishing characteristics of West Virginia in the 1980s and 1990s were part of trends and patterns that had been in evidence at least since the middle of the twentieth century. The population decline, which gathered momentum during the economic dislocations of the 1950s, was temporarily reversed during the 1970s but resumed in the 1980s. Between 1980 and 1990 the number of people in the state dropped from 1,949,644 to 1,793,477, a loss of eight percent, which cost the state one of its four congressional seats.

Closely related to the decrease in population was the prolonged economic malaise, which afflicted the state for more than a quarter of a century. The economic troubles, population losses, and almost inevitable financial distresses of the state and local governments gave rise to myriads of other problems that seemed to defy solution and contributed to a diminution of confidence in government and public officials.

Governor Arch Alfred Moore, Jr. When Governor Moore began his third term in January 1985, the economic conditions in West Virginia were reaching a critical state. The unemployment rate stood at fifteen percent, the highest in the nation. The coal industry, historically a mainstay of the state's economy, was sinking at an alarming rate. Moore immediately initiated a program of recovery, which centered around the revitalization of the coal industry and the attraction of new industries to the state. To improve the competitive position of West Virginia coal in national and world markets, he took steps designed to cut its production costs by two dollars on the ton. A thirty percent reduction in coal company contributions to the Workers' Compensation Fund, which took effect on July 1, 1985, resulted in savings to the industry of about $180 million during the ensuing five years. In addition, Moore and the legislature addressed the mounting criticisms of the state's Business and Occupations Tax, which, its opponents claimed, discouraged businesses and industries of all kinds from entering West Virginia and impelled many of those already in the state to leave. Effective in 1987, the tax was repealed on all businesses except utilities.

In pursuit of the goal of drawing new industries to West Virginia, Moore and the legislature made a special effort to lure a multibillion-dollar Saturn automobile plant that General Motors was planning to build. Well aware that competition for the plant, with its thousands of jobs and other economic benefits, would be extremely keen, the governor and the legislature turned to the idea of a substantial tax incentive to General Motors if the company located the plant in West Virginia. Such incentives were time-honored methods of attracting business and industry and had been used extensively by federal, state, and local governments. In 1985 the legislature passed for that specific purpose the Business Investment and Jobs Expansion Act, which Governor Moore promptly signed into law. The act, nevertheless, failed to win for West Virginia the much-desired Saturn plant.

The decision to locate the Saturn facility in Tennessee galvanized the West Virginia government into making even greater efforts to expand business investments and job opportunities in the state. In 1986 the legislature modified the 1985 law to extend super tax credits, as the tax advantage was commonly known, to businesses already in the state, provided they expanded job opportunities and modernized their facilities. By 1990 two hundred corporations, including manufacturing, retail, and service companies, were receiving super tax credits. They were awarded $6 million, or ten percent of the total credits, and created about nine thousand new jobs.

The chief beneficiaries of the super tax credits, however, proved to be coal corporations, which garnered about ninety percent of the total. Unfortunately, the credits to coal companies yielded no immediate benefits to the state. In fact, in their long-range effect, they may have actually compounded the very problems they were supposed to alleviate. A study of the super tax credits in 1990 revealed that the number of jobs in coal mining had fallen by 1,300 in spite of an increase of 13.3 percent in coal production. The adverse effects of the super tax credits on state revenues and on the general economy led in 1990 to legislation to prevent coal companies from using the super tax credits to avoid payment of severance taxes. On the other hand, coal companies that could demonstrate an investment of $10 million under the super tax credit program were allowed to apply for new credits in the future. In that same year Alan Mierke, deputy tax commissioner of the state, predicted that tax write-offs, which then amounted to $48 million annually, would increase to $70 million by the mid-1990s. More disturbing was the failure to reveal the amounts of credits received by various coal companies. The commissioner also divulged that in 1991 the coal companies had in reality reduced employment by 1,650 jobs. Moreover, tax officials estimated that about twenty percent of the coal mined in the state was produced free of any business taxes. Troubling questions regarding the efficacy of the super tax credits and even the need for them arose when it was revealed that several other important coal-producing states, including neighboring Kentucky, which had no super tax allowance, actually increased their level of coal production and retained more of their mining jobs than West Virginia, with its much-touted tax incentive.

Moore made other efforts to stimulate the coal-mining industry, which further reduced state revenues. Under new and more liberal policies regarding the Pneumoconiosis Fund, the governor returned $68.1 million to coal companies that promised to become self-insured. Furthermore, the Workers' Compensation Fund forgave debts and awarded generous refunds to companies throughout the state, and by 1992 it was underfunded by $1.2 billion. Other questionable actions included numerous secret tax settlements struck with large companies, such as CSX, which reduced their tax obligations to the state by millions of dollars.

Inevitably, losses in state revenues produced financial crises and difficulties in maintaining essential public services, including the funding of education at all levels, maintaining the teachers and public employees retirement systems in a condition of actuarial soundness, and providing necessary upkeep of the state's rapidly deteriorating infrastructure. By the end of the 1980s, West Virginia had lost about 70,000 jobs and was well over $400 million in debt. The state government had resorted to borrowing from the depleted funds of the state teachers retirement system and from other monies held as public trusts. Among the most pressing of its debts was a large backlog of medical obligations owed by the Public Employees Insurance Agency, which jeopardized medical services for thousands of state employees. The financial situation was so critical that at one point gas service to the governor's mansion was on the verge of being terminated because of overdue bills.

In one economic activity, West Virginia attained an enviable position in that her banks continued to be noted for their soundness. State law, however, mandated a unit banking system and did not permit holding companies or branch banking, which existed in most other states and were favored by most banking authorities. In 1982 the legislature permitted both holding companies and branch banking. This change resulted in an expansion in banking resources and gave West Virginia banks greater flexibility in meeting the financial needs of the businesses and industries, as well as the requirements of the citizens, of the state. By 1990 West Virginia had 69 bank holding companies and 134 subsidiaries. Her banks had assets of more than $7 billion.

An Era of Political Corruption. Super tax credits and other features of Moore's recovery program, unfortunately, were made to serve corrupt purposes. In return for tax favors, Moore and others in his administration received hundreds of thousands of dollars from unscrupulous and compliant coal operators and other businessmen for illegal "underground" political activities and for their personal profit.[1] These nefarious dealings of government officials, businessmen, their intermediaries, lobbyists, and others seeking favor con-

[1]*Charleston Gazette*, July 11, 1990.

stitute a sordid chapter in the history of West Virginia. A few examples illustrate the nature of the collusion that was rampant among Republicans and Democrats and in both the executive and legislative branches of government.

Some of the most flagrant violations of the law occurred in the governor's office. A three-year federal investigation into corruption in West Virginia politics resulted in 1990 in the conviction of former Governor Moore on charges of extortion of about $1 million from H. Paul Kizer, president of Maben Energy Corporation, who gave the governor $573,721 in return for a $2.3 million refund of black lung payments to his company. Moore also received another $150,000 in exchange for super tax credits. Documents at Moore's trial in the spring of 1990 revealed that in 1984 and 1988 he operated an "underground campaign," which raised hundreds of thousands of dollars illegally from several major coal companies and other firms. These illegal funds were used for buying votes and other questionable practices. In one highly publicized episode, Moore's 1984 campaign manager received from the governor $100,000 in cash stuffed in a ski cap.[2] For these and other offenses, the governor and several members of his administration, including his former head of Workers' Compensation and 1988 campaign manager and his chief compliance officer in the State Tax Department were convicted of various felonies. Moore was sentenced to five years ten months in prison.

The corruption on the part of the governor and other prominent officials of his administration was not generally known at the time of the election of 1988. If it had been, Moore's political career might have come to an abrupt end. His Democratic opponents, however, had troubles of their own. One of the most popular and colorful figures in the Democratic party, A. James Manchin, was presiding over the State Treasurer's Office in 1989 when the public learned of enormous losses to the state through reckless investments of monies in the Consolidated Investment Fund. Blame fell heavily upon Manchin, who was lacking in knowledge of such financial matters, but who had entrusted the investments to Arnold T. Margolin, his assistant state treasurer and a former commissioner of finance and administration under Governor Jay Rockefeller. Margolin was regarded as a financial genius, but in 1987-1988 his advice resulted in the loss of $279 million to West Virginia and placed the shaky finances of the state in an even more precarious condition. Ultimately, Margolin was sentenced in federal court to one year in prison for hiding these enormous losses. Manchin, his superior officer, was impeached by the House of Delegates, but before the Senate could act upon his case, he resigned in order to save his $2,000-a-month state pension.

While Manchin's crimes arose largely from ignorance and misplaced trust, those of several other prominent Democratic leaders were more akin to the briberies and extortions of Governor Moore. Two former state Senate presi-

[2]*Charleston Gazette,* July 3, 11, 1990.

dents were among five legislators investigated by federal prosecutors. Dan Tonkovich, who served as president of the Senate from 1984 to 1988, pleaded guilty in 1989 to extorting money from gambling interests, and, according to a statement of the prosecutor, Michael Carey, "used his office as a racketeering enterprise, doling out favors in return for money."[3] Federal judge John T. Copenhaver sentenced Tonkovich to five years in prison. Also confessing to extortion in 1989 was Larry Tucker, a nineteen-year veteran legislator and a former Senate president. Tucker was sentenced to six months in prison for accepting a bribe from racetrack officials in return for favorable votes on racing legislation. Following his prison term, Tucker admitted that he had lied to a federal grand jury and obstructed justice during his extortion trial in 1989 and received a second sentence of thirty-seven months in prison. Two other legislators, including a former Senate majority leader, were among the numerous persons in state government convicted of various crimes during the investigation by the federal government.

The corruption in state government in the 1980s had its counterparts at county and local levels. In the United States District Court for the Southern District of West Virginia alone, a three-year investigation by federal authorities led to seventy-eight convictions. They included, in addition to state officials, county and local law enforcement officers, members of county boards of education, lobbyists, magistrates, a former prosecuting attorney, a county superintendent of schools, a mayor of Charleston, and numerous others, among whom were persons associated with various federal programs. They were charged with a variety of offenses, many of them drug-related, but they also included tax evasion, civil rights violations, falsification of black lung claims, extortion, unlawful trafficking in food stamps, and mail fraud.

The Election of 1988. Since the scandals that rocked the executive and legislative branches of state government were not known to the public at the time of the 1988 elections, some of those involved still aspired to high public office, including the governorship of the state. The scandals, therefore, were not issues in either the primary or general elections. In the gubernatorial race of 1988 veteran Republican leader and incumbent Governor Arch Alfred Moore, Jr., faced forty-eight-year-old W. Gaston Caperton III, a Charleston insurance executive and a newcomer to political life. Caperton had won the Democratic nomination by defeating several seasoned politicians, including Clyde See, a former Speaker of the House of Delegates; Dan Tonkovich, who had resigned as president of the state Senate in order to pursue his gubernatorial aspirations; Gus R. Douglas, for many years the state's commissioner of agriculture; and others less well known.

In the general election, Moore sought to capitalize upon his long experience in government, including his three terms as governor, and to deprecate the qualifications of Caperton for such a high office. Caperton, on the other hand,

[3]*Charleston Daily Mail*, April 13, 1990.

emphasized Moore's past mistakes and his own freedom from alliances with other politicians. Caperton had other advantages. His youthful appearance, enthusiasm, and idealism added to his appeal. During the campaign, the wealthy Democratic nominee spent over $3 million of his own money. He justified his large personal expenditure on the basis that he could enter the governor's office free of political debts. Both candidates emphasized the need to improve education and to promote economy in government. Both declared their opposition to raising any new taxes.

Caperton inflicted upon Moore a stunning political defeat, winning the election with 382,421 votes to Moore's 267,172. Caperton carried 43 counties. Moore led in only 12, which were in the northern part of the state, his traditional political stronghold. Democrats won 80 of the 100 seats in the House of Delegates and 29 of 34 Senate seats.

In the national races of 1988, West Virginia supported Democrat Michael Dukakis for president with 341,016 votes and gave Republican George Bush 310,065. The voters returned Robert C. Byrd to his United States Senate seat with 410,983 votes to 223,564 for his Republican opponent M. Jay Wolfe. All four Democratic Congressmen—Alan B. Mollohan, Harley O. Staggers, Jr., Bob Wise, and Nick Joe Rahall II—were reelected. They retained their seats in 1990.

Governor W. Gaston Caperton III. The image of Governor W. Gaston Caperton III (b. February 21, 1940) as a young, idealistic business executive, unencumbered by political debts, who would apply fresh approaches to old problems and reverse the downward economic spirals of his predecessor began to suffer somewhat within a few months of his inauguration. The governor's divorce from his wife, Dee, soon after he took office caused widespread surprise. Dee Caperton, a former beauty queeen and member of the House of Delegates in 1987 and 1988, was a well-known legislator who gave unstinting support to her husband during his campaign for the governorship. Later, she accused Caperton and his campaign manager of defrauding her of $12 million in stock of the Caperton family insurance business. In an out-of-court settlement, Caperton agreed to pay her more than $10 million. In May 1990 the governor married Rachel Worby, the conductor of the Wheeling Symphony Orchestra.

Although the Caperton divorce, with its sometimes sensational disclosures, held the public interest, persistent problems of government continued to command attention. Overshadowing other troubles was the ever-deepening financial crisis of the state. Caperton received praise when he chose Arnold T. Margolin as his chief financial advisor and appointed a task force to study the state's financial condition. Within two months of Margolin's appointment, however, disclosures were made of the mismanagement of the state's Consolidated Investment Fund. Margolin vigorously denied the allegations, but the findings of federal investigators prompted him to resign before he assumed the duties of his office.

The governor's task force, on the other hand, probed the seriousness of the financial situation and outlined some of the major problems. The state had accumulated about $400 million in obligations that it could not pay, including $50 million in unpaid tax refunds and $200 million in commitments owed by the Public Employees Insurance Agency. Using the findings of the task force as a basis of action, Caperton called for a special session of the legislature to assemble on January 25, 1989, to deal with the state's most urgent needs. He laid before lawmakers plans that addressed the financial crisis, the reorganization of state government to centralize more power in the office of the governor, and the need for passage of a strong new ethics law.

In spite of his repeated campaign promises not to raise taxes, Caperton's plan to deal with the state's financial problems rested on a controversial $392 million tax increase. The cornerstone of the increase, the highest in the state's history, was the extension of the six percent sales tax to include food. Taxes on gasoline were increased by five cents per gallon.

At the behest of the governor, the legislature enacted an Omnibus Health Care Act. It was designed to reduce the huge backlog of state debts, especially those of the Public Employees Insurance Agency, Medicaid, and the Workers' Compensation Fund.

The governor's reorganization plan for state government grouped various state executive offices under seven newly-created cabinet-level departments, each headed by a "super secretary" with a salary of $70,000. These new departments were Administration; Commerce, Labor, and Environmental Resources; Health and Human Resources; Education and the Arts; Public Safety; Tax and Revenue; and Transportation. Caperton insisted that the new positions would streamline and enhance the functioning of the governor's office, but critics contended that they would only create an additional and expensive layer of bureaucracy.

The ethics legislation, the third major component of Caperton's plan, was enacted at the time when reports of wide-ranging federal investigations of government corruption were becoming known to the public. The new law set up a state Ethics Commission to monitor the actions of state and local officials and was praised by the governor as the strongest in the nation.

By the end of the legislative session of 1989, Caperton was under fearsome criticism for his large tax increases and for his reorganization of state government. Any illusions of unimpaired popularity were shattered in September when the electorate overwhelmingly rejected three proposed constitutional amendments that would have given the governor sweeping new powers to appoint the secretary of state, treasurer, and agricultural commissioner, all of whom were elective under the state constitution; granted the governor direct control over public education; and allowed cities and counties to choose alternate forms of government. None of these amendments received more than 20 percent approval at the polls. Also defeated was a $35 million reappraisal program for equalizing property taxes, which had been ordered by the courts.

Its failure was attributed to nearly a decade of opposition from landowners, senior citizens, and antitax groups.

Midterm elections ordinarily excite little interest, but that of 1990 generated special concerns. First of all, strong public reactions to Governor Caperton's large tax increases, which were rubber-stamped by a compliant legislature, gave the election something of the character of a referendum on the governor's program. Another matter of interest centered around the election of state treasurer made necessary by the resignation of A. James Manchin following the scandals involving the Consolidated Investment Fund. The entry of Dee Caperton, former wife of the governor, into the treasurer's race brought national coverage. Although Gaston Caperton officially remained neutral, his staff supported Larrie Bailey, the victor in the race, and opposed Dee Caperton.

Many analysts expected Democrats to do poorly at the polls. Incumbents, however, won 72 of 83 races in the primary, clearly demonstrating that voters did not hold legislators, who had overwhelmingly approved the governor's policies, responsible for the unpopular Caperton program of taxes and administrative reorganizations.

Caperton's handling of affairs concerning the Division of Energy, the environment, and related matters contributed to a further slippage of public confidence in his administration. The Division of Energy, or DOE, had been created during the administration of Governor Moore. It had an ambivalent character, with regulatory powers and responsibilities in matters concerning energy production, especially coal mining, while at the same time it was charged with the promotion of those same mining activities. Caperton's appointment of Larry George, a strong environmentalist, as commissioner of the DOE received broad approval, inasmuch as earlier commissioners had been perceived as too closely associated with the coal industry. The problems of the DOE, including a threat by the United States Office of Surface Mining to take over the state's regulatory functions, were among matters considered by the legislature in a special session which met in June 1990. At that session, the legislature altered the functions of the DOE by making it strictly a regulatory agency and transferring its responsibilities for promoting West Virginia coal to the Public Energy Authority.

The dual functions of the DOE and a struggle among various interest groups for dominance in shaping its policies lay behind a major crisis within the division in 1990 and the forced resignation of George after only a few months in office. George's second in command in the DOE was Bolts Willis, a friend of Governor Caperton and a former officer of the United Mine Workers of America, or UMWA. Suspicious that Willis might be using his position to advance the interests of the UMWA and that he might compromise the integrity of the DOE, George refused Willis's request for state funds to attend a UMWA convention in Miami, Florida. Governor Caperton, however, overruled George's decision. Some observers believed that Caperton had bowed to pressure by the union. George considered the governor's action inimical to the basic principles that should govern the DOE and publicly criticized Caperton. The governor, who was then in San Francisco en route to Japan, promptly canceled his plans explaining that he had become ill, and returned to Charleston. He immediately removed George from his position as DOE commissioner and transferred him to the Department of Natural Resources.

Among the critics of the governor's action was Gordon Caperton Morse, his cousin and press secretary. Morse defended George's contention that the DOE was a regulatory agency that should not be allowed to become politicized. The differences between Caperton and Morse resulted in a physical altercation, described as a "shoving match" and the governor's firing of Morse.[4] For the vacancy in the position of commissioner of the DOE, Caperton appointed Dr. Robert C. Gillespie, president of West Virginia Institute of Technology. Gillespie, who had no specific experience in dealing with either energy or environmental matters, resigned the position prior to taking up the duties of the office.

In spite of his rather dramatic approaches to the problems of the state, Caperton continued to face many of the same conditions that had confronted him on inauguration day. In his State of the State Address of 1990, he turned to well-tried methods of dealing with the continuing financial crisis by announcing a hiring freeze and reductions in the state payroll by 750 employees. Caperton also set forth plans to close Denmar Hospital in Hillsboro, Andrew S. Rowan Memorial Home in Sweet Springs, the Greenbrier Center for the Handicapped in Lewisburg, and Spencer State Hospital. He declared that there would be no pay raises for state workers, but he softened the blow of his announcements by promising again that taxes would not be increased. Nevertheless, the governor held forth the prospect of spending cuts in 1990 and 1991. At a special session of the legislature that the governor called for June 22, 1990, to deal with the debt-ridden Workers' Compensation Fund, the legislature also reviewed the super tax credit system but failed to take any significant steps. The legislature took little substantive action regarding the huge deficits in many departments of government.

Robert C. Byrd and Federal Projects in West Virginia. At a time when state government was struggling with severe economic problems, United States Senator Robert C. Byrd, veteran of more than thirty years experience in both the House of Representatives and the Senate, was able to bring to West Virginia a variety of federal projects that did much to infuse new vitality into the state's ailing economy. Byrd, Democratic majority leader since 1986, announced in 1988 that he intended to resign that position and become the chairman of the powerful Senate Appropriations Committee. Byrd stated that by 1995 he intended to bring to West Virginia federal projects totaling $1 billion. By 1992, however, he had already exceeded that goal. Among the new projects were a

[4]*Charleston Gazette,* November 15, 1990.

$185 million FBI fingerprint center to be transferred from Washington, D.C., to Clarksburg, bringing with it 2,500 new jobs; $197 million in federal water projects; $137 million in highway projects, which constituted 30 percent of all federal monies earmarked in 1991 for highway construction; $80 million for a new federal courthouse in Charleston; $75 million to rebuild the radio telescope at Greenbank; and $50 million for a new 750-inmate prison at Beckley.

In contrast to past criticisms for not securing enough federal aid for West Virginia, Byrd now received accolades throughout his home state. Complaints were voiced by residents of the nation's capitol, who disliked seeing facilities and jobs moving from their area to West Virginia.

Education during the Moore and Caperton Administrations. Adequate financing and maintenance of quality in public education were among the most serious problems confronting West Virginians in the last quarter of the twentieth century. After decades of insufficient revenues and budgetary austerity, compliance with the constitutional mandate for a "thorough and efficient" system of free public schools seemed about as far from realization as at any time since the Great Depression. When Arch A. Moore, Jr., was elected to this third term as governor in 1984, the average salary of public school teachers in West Virginia was $19,563, or $4,032 less than the national average of $23,595. The average per pupil expenditure for education in the state was $2,777, or $680 below the national average of $3,457.[5] By nearly every measure used to judge the quality of public schools and the adequacy of their support, West Virginia ranked low among the states.

While the state compared poorly with others, gross inequities had developed among the fifty-five county school systems, partly because highly populated industrialized counties were able to supplement their school funds through the adoption of excess levies, which many sparsely populated rural counties were unwilling to approve. Concerned that the system of excess levies contributed to an inequality of educational opportunities, Judge Jerry Cook of Lincoln County rendered an opinion in 1987 that modified portions of the Recht Decision of 1982. He ordered that voters of the state should be given an opportunity to adopt a statewide excess levy. If they failed to do so, the state must during the 1988-1989 school year seize monies derived from counties with excess levies and distribute them to all the counties of the state. In effect, the Cook decision transformed the excess levy from a county prerogative to a state prerogative. Cook's interpretation proved highly unpopular, especially in counties that had already approved excess levies. On November 23, 1988, the Supreme Court of Appeals of West Virginia overturned the Cook ruling and upheld the existing excess levy system. At the same time, it ordered the lower court to determine to what extent the property tax reappraisal program, approved by voters in 1982, might help rectify school funding problems.

[5]*Rankings of the States, 1985.* National Education Association.

Shifting the emphasis from problems and shortcomings to accomplishments and opportunities, Moore proclaimed to the legislature in January that 1987 would be the "Year of Education." He proposed significant salary increases for teachers and the establishment of "lighthouse" schools—three elementary, three secondary, and one vocational—which, he believed, would serve as models for others in the future. Moore predicted that by the year 2000 all schools in the state would operate in accordance with the patterns developed by the "lighthouse" schools. As a step toward that goal, it was anticipated that by 1990 the average achievement in basic skills should reach the sixty-fifth percentile for each grade level. The concept of "lighthouse" schools was described as "the most extensive linkage of educational research and classroom reality ever attempted in the United States."[6]

For the state's teachers, who were bitterly disappointed by the failure of the legislature in 1987 to enact Moore's proposed teacher pay raises, salary increases had the highest priority. The election of Gaston Caperton in 1988 seemed a propitious moment to press their case. They were, therefore, disappointed when he failed to recommend a teacher pay raise in his State of the State Address to the legislature in January 1989. Many teachers, including West Virginia Education Association, or WVEA, leaders, were convinced that a salary increase could no longer be deferred and that some extraordinary steps must be taken to press toward that goal. Deeply disappointed by the governor's inaction, the WVEA began to consider possible responses in case the governor and legislature did not meet their conditions at the 1990 session. State finances, however, made significant raises doubtful, and Governor Caperton recommended a five percent increase, to take effect on January 1, 1991, instead of July 1, 1990, as many educational leaders expected. This change in the effective date of the raise meant that teachers, who had not had a salary increase since 1986, would actually receive only a two and one-half percent raise in the 1990-1991 school term.

Disappointed in these actions, teacher organizations began to consider more drastic moves, including the possibility of a strike. In the hope of averting a teachers' strike, Governor Caperton met with Kayetta Meadows, president of the 16,000-member WVEA, and other educational leaders on March 5. They apparently reached an understanding in which the governor agreed to a five percent raise and no cuts in Public Employee Insurance Agency, or PEIA, benefits and the teachers would relinquish the threat of a strike. Legislative leaders, who were called into a morning caucus on March 6, still perceived the possibility of a strike and refused to support the alleged agreement. Caperton, taking the view of legislators, announced that the WVEA had reneged on its agreement and that he would not be bound by previous commitments.

The increasingly restive teachers, as represented by the WVEA and the

[6]*StatEd*, February 1987, West Virginia Education Association.

West Virginia Federation of Teachers, staged West Virginia's first statewide teachers' strike, which began on March 7 and lasted for eleven days. President of the Senate Keith Burdette and Speaker of the House of Delegates Chuck Chambers stepped into the impasse between the governor and striking teachers. They agreed to request the governor to call a special session of the legislature later that year to address the problems of education. Caperton's willingness to do so ended the strike. In the meantime, an educational summit, called by the governor, assembled on June 25, 1990. Chaired by Lewis McManus, a former Speaker of the House of Delegates, it considered issues growing out of the teachers' strike and endorsed a series of nine town meetings throughout the state, in which citizens might voice their views and feelings. Two task forces set up by the governor addressed pertinent questions, including declining school enrollments, surpluses of teachers, school consolidations, pupil-teacher ratios, exit examinations for graduation from grade, junior high, and high schools, and the need to revise property taxes, including taxes on major landowners, to obtain money for schools.

On August 22, 1990, Caperton addressed a joint session of the legislature with respect to educational matters and laid out a comprehensive program that provided teachers a $5,000 salary increase over a three-year period; established a faculty senate in each school, which would help in determining expenditures, selecting mentor teachers, and advising on administrative matters; placed computers in kindergarten and first grades throughout the state, with the anticipation that they would be added to other grades later, in order to promote the teaching of basic skills; and expanded bonding by $60 million, a portion of which might be used to facilitate school consolidation. Although there was considerable debate, the legislature overwhelmingly approved the Caperton program by a vote of 88 to 4 in the House and 31 to 0 in the Senate.

The legislature also took other steps to placate public school teachers and to address some of the concerns of other state workers. It appropriated $42 million to PEIA and established an advisory board to monitor its operations. Unable to provide money for the $3 billion unfunded liability of the Teachers Retirement System, the legislature resorted to the expedient of establishing an alternate plan for beginning teachers employed after July 1, 1991.

Although the third special session, in August 1990, concentrated most of its attention on educational matters, it also took action on other issues of major public interest. Reacting to the financial scandals that occurred under State Treasurer A. James Manchin and to the enormous losses sustained by the state through the unwise investments advocated by Arnold T. Margolin, the legislature established the State Board of Investments as a separate executive agency and removed it from the control of the treasurer's office. Increasingly aware of the inadequacies and overcrowded conditions in the state's prisons and in county and municipal jails, the legislature complied with a state Supreme Court order to rectify conditions at penal institutions. It created a State Building

Authority with power to issue $200 million in bonds for a new state penitentiary and nine regional jails. After a careful study of sites proposed for a new maximum security facility, Governor Caperton chose a location at Mount Olive near Montgomery in Fayette County.

The legislature recognized that the costs of the educational changes, modernization of the prison system, and other obligations required vast amounts of new monies. To impose heavy increases in taxes was to many lawmakers unthinkable in view of Governor Caperton's experiences and with midterm elections approaching. They, therefore, empowered the governor to borrow up to $360 million to defray the cost of the projects the special session had approved. The legislature provided some modest new business taxes, including a tax on the generation of electricity; a minimum 50-cents-per-ton tax on coal exempt from other forms of taxation; a sales tax on government construction contracts; and elimination of severance tax credits on personal and corporate income taxes. Lawmakers also enacted legislation aimed at speeding up the implementation of a statewide reappraisal of property taxes, especially on large corporate tracts of land.

Although the $5,000 salary increase temporarily pacified many teachers, Governor Caperton and the legislature still had not satisfied other public employees who had also gone without raises for several years. During the succeeding months sentiment in favor of collective bargaining and unionization of public employees gained new ground with the WVEA, labor unions, and other organizations lending support to their demands.

Higher Education. The financial exigencies that curtailed state funding for public schools had equally adverse effects upon state-supported institutions of higher learning. Concerns were voiced regarding duplication of function and programs offered by both the baccalaureate and graduate institutions. Even more criticism was directed toward the state's three medical schools, which were especially costly. In response to dwindling funds at a time of ever-increasing demands upon higher education, the Sara and Pauline Maier Foundation of Charleston, which had contributed to the improvement of higher education opportunities in West Virginia for thirty years, invited the Carnegie Foundation for the Advancement of Teaching to make an independent examination of the system in the state.

The *Carnegie Report,* issued in 1989, was supported by the executive and legislative branches of government and the Board of Regents, as well as administrators and advisory boards of most colleges and universities. The *Report* recommended that two governing boards, rather than the single Board of Regents, which then had oversight of all higher education institutions, be empowered with authority over the colleges and universities. A Board of Trustees was granted responsibility for West Virginia University; Potomac State College; West Virginia University at Parkersburg, formerly Parkersburg Community College; Marshall University; the West Virginia Graduate College, formerly the West Virginia College of Graduate Studies; and the West

Virginia School of Osteopathic Medicine. Four-year colleges, including Blue-field, Concord, Fairmont, Glenville, Shepherd, West Liberty, West Virginia Institute of Technology, and West Virginia State, along with the community colleges, were placed under a Board of Directors. Questions were raised regarding possible rivalries between the two boards, especially in competing for limited state funding; the possible creation of unnecessary and costly administrative bureaucracy; and the somewhat arbitrary placing of some in-stitutions within a particular system.

Changes also occurred in several of the state's private institutions. In 1988 Wheeling College became Wheeling Jesuit College. The following year Salem College formed a relationship with Japanese business interests. As a result of the new partnership, the institution was renamed Salem-Teikyo University. Beckley College attempted to broaden its base of support and to expand its offerings. In 1991 it changed its name to the College of West Virginia.

Environmental Issues of the 1980s and 1990s. Like many of her sister states, West Virginia in the late twentieth century faced serious environmental problems, many of which related to waste disposal, abuses by extractive industries, and air pollution. Burgeoning populations in America's highly industrialized northeastern states threatened to fill West Virginia with moun-tains of out-of-state industrial and urban wastes. Investors and trucking firms sensed a highly profitable business in hauling refuse into a state which had lax environmental standards for trash disposal and a relative abundance of sites for large inexpensive landfills. The growing volume of out-of-state refuse brought a spirited reaction from concerned residents all over West Virginia. Respond-ing to the public outcry, the legislature in 1989 limited the volume of waste that might be accepted by individual sites and set stringent new standards for protecting the environment.

Among the most controversial issues facing the state was the need to provide adequate protection to West Virginia's abundant, picturesque forests and river basins. As the century drew to an end, extractive industries, es-pecially timber and coal, attained remarkable levels of production, reminiscent of the final decades of the nineteenth century. By 1990 the United States Forest Service estimated that approximately 12 million acres of timberland, much of it highly-prized hardwoods, had reached maturity and was ready to be harvested. Environmentalists, remembering the unbridled and often irresponsible prac-tices of nineteenth-century lumber barons, made a concerted effort in the legislative session of 1990 to impose, for the first time in the state's history, strict new regulations on the timber industry. Nevertheless, the legislature failed to take any significant action, except to pass a weak law requiring companies to register and pay a small fee. Defenders of the lack of regulation of the industry pointed to the existence of a voluntary "best management pro-gram," in which about one-half of the timber firms in the state agreed to follow voluntary conservation.

At the same time that West Virginia's forests offered enormous opportunities for profit, coal output in the state reached record levels. In 1990 it rose to 171,155,053 tons, the second highest annual production in the state's history. Despite near-record tonnage, employment dropped from 55,502 in 1980 to 28,876 in 1990. The mining technologies that made possible record levels of production with fewer workers gave rise to controversies regarding mountain-top stripping, the creation of large valley fills, and the employment of longwall mining techniques.

In attempting to avoid a further weakening of a faltering economy, state government failed to take strong initiative to protect the environment. On several occasions the United States Office of Surface Mining issued stern warnings that if the state did not more adequately regulate the industry the federal government would take over responsibility for protecting the environment. As a result of this pressure, Governor Caperton in a special session of the legislature of 1991 proposed additional funding for the Department of Energy that would allow it to employ more inspectors and permit the state to retain control of mining regulation.

The most significant legislation affecting West Virginia's environment, as well as her coal mining industry, was the federal Clean Air Act, which became law on November 15, 1991. Under its provisions, aimed largely at electric power plants, sulfur emissions were to be substantially reduced over a five-year period. The law placed in doubt the future of coal production in the high-sulfur coal fields of northern West Virginia. On the other hand, the low-sulfur fields of southern counties offered new opportunities for growth and employment, and during the seceding years the region experienced a boom in the buying and selling of coal lands.

The Election of 1992. The West Virginia Democratic primary of 1992 generated nearly as much interest as the general election that followed. As was expected, Governor Caperton announced his intention to seek reelection. Caperton, however, faced strong opposition from within his own party. Charlotte Pritt, a member of the state Senate from Kanawha County, proved a formidable opponent to the governor. Upon learning of Pritt's candidacy, Mario Palumbo, the state's attorney general, who was expected to seek reelection to that position, made the surprise announcement that he too would run for the gubernatorial office. Palumbo and Pritt apparently believed that they would attract large numbers of votes from party members who were disenchanted with the leadership of Caperton. The governor raised $1.4 million, more than his Democratic opponents combined and more than six times that of Cleve Benedict, the Republican nominee. Caperton defeated his Democratic opponents, winning forty-three percent of the vote. Pritt trailed with thirty-five percent and Palumbo with twenty percent.

One result of the Democratic primary was the opening of deep divisions within the party. Satisfied with her strong showing, Pritt declined to yield to Caperton and accept the primary vote as final. In the general election she ran as a write-in candidate, hoping to draw votes from both Caperton and Benedict.

Actually, she drew from Benedict and failed to cut into Caperton's strength. As a consequence, Caperton won the governorship by a vote of 368,302 to Pritt's 48,490. Benedict, who had pledged himself to reduce the state's sales tax from six percent to three percent, abolish the super secretaries, and cut the state budget by $230 million, received 240,390 votes.

The race for attorney general proved an interesting sidelight to the election of 1992. When Palumbo announced his intention to seek the governorship, Darrell McGraw, a veteran in Democratic politics and a former member of the state Supreme Court, hurried to Charleston in a last minute move to file for attorney general. McGraw captured the nomination and went on to win the office in the general election.

In the national elections, West Virginians, in keeping with their Democratic leanings, cast 331,001 votes for Bill Clinton to 241,974 votes for the incumbent George Bush. They gave Ross Perot, the independent candidate, 108,829 votes, which was 15.9 percent of the total cast. Democratic candidates—Nick Joe Rahall II, Bob Wise, and Alan B. Mollohan—retained their seats in Congress. Harley O. Staggers, Jr., had previously lost his seat to Mollohan in the primary when their districts were combined as a result of the Congressional reapportionment mandated by the Census of 1990.

End-of-the Century Trends and Concerns. As the twentieth century drew to a close, West Virginians, like other Americans, had apprehensions regarding the future. The economic outlook was filled with uncertainties. The recuperative powers of the environment, which had been grossly abused for decades, seemed far from assured. The old confidence that each new generation would have a better life than its predecessors no longer seemed to be a tenable assumption. Journalists, cartoonists, and others continued to represent, or misrepresent, the state in ways that, like *Uncle Tom's Cabin,* were true in many of their facts but false in their impressions. Most recently, the *Washington Post* carried an article about the state perpetuating old stereotypes that contained kernels of fact but failed to probe beneath the surface or to present a balanced and convincing picture of the state.[7]

Although serious problems remained, West Virginia experienced encouraging economic developments in the mid-1990s. Coal mining remained important, and timber harvests doubled between 1987 and 1994. Several automotive parts industries, including a proposed Toyota engine plant at Buffalo, and other facilities in Jackson and Kanawha counties, pointed to greater diversification of the economy. Service industries, including finance, insurance, real estate, health care, and tourism, made up 68 percent of the gross state product. Improvements in the economy helped produce budgetary surpluses in state government in contrast to the austerity that had prevailed for many years. In the state's rich cultural heritage and scenic beauty, West Virginians discovered a treasure that had waited too long to be tapped.

[7]Peter Carlson, "The Magic and the Misery (Of West Virginia, That Is)," *Washington Post,* November 22, 1992, reprinted in *West Virginia Hillbilly,* December 10, 1992.

Selected Bibliography and Suggested Readings

Sources for the study of West Virginia history are extensive and widely scattered. Primary material for this study has been drawn from more than a score of libraries and archives. Four collections that have been indispensable are the West Virginia Division of Archives and History Library, Charleston, best for state archives and related materials; the West Virginia Collection, West Virginia University Library; the Virginia State Library; and the Draper Collection of the State Historical Society of Wisconsin. Significant amounts of West Virginia material were also gleaned from the Library of Congress, the Virginia Historical Society, the Duke University Library, the Margaret I. King Library of the University of Kentucky, and the Southern Historical Collection of the University of North Carolina.

Bibliographical tools that facilitated our research and are essential to all students of state history include Innis C. Davis, comp., *Bibliography of West Virginia* (Charleston: West Virginia Department of Archives and History, 1939); Charles Shetler, *Guide to Manuscripts and Archives in the West Virginia Collection* (Morgantown: West Virginia University Library, 1958); F. Gerald Ham, *A Guide to Manuscripts and Archives in the West Virginia Collection, No. II, 1958-1962* (Morgantown: West Virginia University Library, 1965); Earl G. Swem, "A Bibliography of Virginia, Part I," *Virginia State Library Bulletin,* vol. 8, nos. 2-4 (Richmond: Virginia State Library, 1916) and "A Bibliography of Virginia, Part II," *Virginia State Library Bulletin,* vol. 10, nos. 1-4 (Richmond: Virginia State Library, 1917); and Harold M. Forbes, *West Virginia History: A Bibliography and Guide to Research* (Morgantown: West Virginia University Press, 1981), which updates Charles M. Shetler, *Guide to the Study of West Virginia History* (Morgantown: West Virginia University Library, 1960).

The listings that follow include some of the primary sources, books, and articles especially useful in the preparation of particular chapters. Since footnotes have been confined largely to verification of quoted material, they also constitute suggested readings for further information. Full bibliographical data for published works is given only in first references to those works.

Chapter 1

Ambler, Charles H., and Festus P. Summers. *West Virginia, the Mountain State.* 2d ed. Englewood Cliffs, N.J.: Prentice-Hall, 1958.
Broyles, Bettye J. *Second Preliminary Report: The St. Albans Site, Kanawha County,*

West Virginia. Morgantown: West Virginia Geological and Economic Survey, 1971.

Janssen, Raymond E. *Earth Science: A Handbook on the Geology of West Virginia.* Clarksburg: Educational Marketers, Inc., 1973.

Inghram, Joseph W., Sigfus Olafson and Edward V. McMichael. "The Mount Carbon Stone Walls: Description and History." *West Virginia Archeologist,* no. 13 (July 1961):1-35.

Mayer-Oakes, William J. *Excavations at the Globe Hill Shell Heap.* Moundsville: West Virginia Archeological Society, 1955.

———. *The Prehistory of the Ohio Valley: An Introductory Archeological Study.* Pittsburgh: Carnegie Museum, 1955.

McMichael, Edward V. *Introduction to West Virginia Archeology.* 2d ed., rev. Morgantown: West Virginia Geological and Economic Survey, 1968.

———. "1963 Excavations at the Buffalo Site," *West Virginia Archeologist,* no. 16 (1963):12-23.

———. "Preliminary Report on the Mount Carbon Village Excavations," *West Virginia Archeologist,* no. 14 (February, 1962):36-51.

Norona, Delf. *Moundsville's Mammoth Mound.* 3d ed. rev. Moundsville: no publisher, 1962.

Olafson, Sigfus. "Petroglyphs on the Guyandot River." *West Virginia Archeologist,* no.5 (no date):1-9.

———. "Rock Carvings in Boone County." *West Virginia Archeologist,* no. 2 (March 1950):7-11.

Rice, Otis K. *The Allegheny Frontier: West Virginia Beginnings, 1730-1830.* Lexington: University Press of Kentucky, 1970.

Semple, Ellen Churchill, and Clarence Fielden Jones. *American History and Its Geographic Conditions.* rev. ed. Boston: Houghton, Mifflin and Company, 1933.

Webb, William S., and Charles E. Snow. *The Adena People.* Lexington: University of Kentucky, 1945.

Chapter 2

Abernethy, Thomas Perkins. *Three Virginia Frontiers.* University, La.: Louisiana State University Press, 1940.

Alvord, Clarence Walworth, and Lee Bidgood. *The First Explorations of the Trans-Allegheny Region by Virginians, 1650-1674.* Cleveland: Arthur H. Clark Company, 1912.

Ambler, Charles H., and Festus P. Summers. *West Virginia, the Mountain State.*

Briceland, Alan Vance. *Westward from Virginia: The Exploration of the Virginia-Carolina Frontier, 1650-1710.* Charlottesville: University Press of Virginia, 1987.

Dodson, Leonidas. *Alexander Spotswood, Governor of Virginia, 1710-1722.* Philadelphia: University of Pennsylvania Press, 1932.

Freeman, Douglas Southall. *George Washington: A Biography.* 7 vols. New York: Charles Scribner's Sons, 1948-1957.

Hart, Freeman H. *The Valley of Virginia in the American Revolution, 1763-1789.* Chapel Hill: University of North Carolina Press, 1942.

Hinke, William J., trans. and ed. "Letters Regarding the Second Journey of Michel to

America, February 14, 1703, to January 16, 1704, and His Stay in America in 1708." *Virginia Magazine of History and Biography* 24 (June 1916):289-303.

———, and Charles Kemper, eds. "Moravian Diaries of Travels through Virginia." *Virginia Magazine of History and Biography* 11 (October 1903):113-31;12 (January 1904):225-42; 12 (April 1904):370-93; 12 (July 1904):55-82; 12 (October 1904):134-53; 13 (January 1905):271-84.

Kemper, Charles E., ed. "Documents Relating to Early Projected Colonies in the Valley of Virginia, 1706-1709." *Virginia Magazine of History and Biography* 29 (January 1921):1-17; 29 (April 1921):180-81.

Lewis, Thomas. *The Fairfax Line: Thomas Lewis's Journal of 1746.* Edited by John W. Wayland. New Market, Va.: Henkel Press, 1935.

Rice, Otis K. *The Allegheny Frontier: West Virginia Beginnings, 1730-1830.*

———. *A History of Greenbrier County.* Parsons, W.Va.: McClain Printing Company, 1985.

Rights, Douglas L., and William P. Cummings. eds. *The Discoveries of John Lederer, with Unpublished Letters by and about Lederer to Governor John Winthrop, Jr.* Charlottesville: University of Virginia Press, 1958.

Tillson, Albert H., Jr. *Gentry and Common Folk: Political Culture on a Virginia Frontier, 1740-1789.* Lexington: University Press of Kentucky, 1991.

Chapter 3

Alden, John R. *Robert Dinwiddie, Servant of the Crown.* Williamsburg: Colonial Williamsburg Foundation, 1973.

Ambler, Charles H. *George Washington and the West.* Chapel Hill: University of North Carolina Press, 1936.

Bailey, Kenneth P. *Christopher Gist, Colonial Frontiersman, Explorer, and Indian Agent.* Hamden, Conn.: Archon Books, 1966.

———. *The Ohio Company of Virginia and the Westward Movement, 1748-1798.* Glendale, Calif.: Arthur H. Clark Company, 1939.

———. *Thomas Cresap, Maryland Frontiersman.* Boston: Christopher Publishing House, 1944.

Baker-Crothers, Hayes, *Virginia and the French and Indian War.* Chicago: University of Chicago Press, 1928.

Brock, R.A., ed. *The Official Records of Robert Dinwiddie, Lieutenant-Governor of Virginia, 1751-1758.* 2 vols. Richmond: Virginia Historical Society, 1881-1884.

Cometti, Elizabeth, and Festus P. Summers, eds. *The Thirty-Fifth State: A Documentary History of West Virginia.* Morgantown: West Virginia University Library, 1966.

Darlington, William M., ed. *Christopher Gist's Journals, with Historical, Geographical, and Ethnological Notes.* Pittsburgh: J.R. Weldon & Co., 1893; New York: Argonaut Press, 1966.

Eccles, W.J. *France in America.* New York: Harper and Row, 1972.

Freeman, Douglas Southall, *George Washington: A Biography.*

Henderson, Archibald. *Dr. Thomas Walker and the Loyal Company of Virginia.* Worcester, Mass.: American Antiquarian Society, 1931.

Jackson, Donald, and others, eds. *The Diaries of George Washington.* 6 vols. Charlottesville: University Press of Virginia, 1976-1980.

James, Alfred P. *The Ohio Company: Its Inner History*. Pittsburgh: University of Pittsburgh Press, 1959.

Johnson, Patricia Givens. *General Andrew Lewis of Roanoke and Greenbrier*. Blacksburg, Va.: Southern Printing Company, 1980.

Kercheval, Samuel. *A History of the Valley of Virginia*. Edited by Oren F. Morton, 4th ed. Strasburg: Shenandoah Publishing House, 1925.

Koontz, Louis K. *Robert Dinwiddie: His Career in American Colonial Government and Westward Expansion*. Glendale, Calif.: Arthur H. Clark Company, 1941.

―――. *The Virginia Frontier, 1754-1763*. Baltimore: Johns Hopkins Press, 1925.

Mulkearn, Lois, ed. *George Mercer Papers Relating to the Ohio Company of Virginia*. Pittsburgh: University of Pittsburgh Press, 1954.

Rice, Otis K. *The Allegheny Frontier: West Virginia Beginnings, 1730-1830*.

―――. "The Sandy Creek Expedition of 1756." *West Virginia History* 13 (October 1951):5-19.

Stuart, John. *Memoir of Indian Wars, and Other Occurrences*. Richmond: Virginia Historical and Philosophical Society, 1833; Parsons, W.Va.: McClain Printing Company, 1971.

Tillson, Albert H., Jr. *Gentry and Common Folk: Political Culture on a Virginia Frontier, 1740-1789*.

Walker, Thomas. *Journal of an Expedition in the Spring of the Year 1750*. Edited by William Cabell Rives. Boston: Little, Brown and Company, 1888.

Withers, Alexander Scott. *Chronicles of Border Warfare*. Edited by Reuben Gold Thwaites. Clarksburg: J. Israel, 1831; Cincinnati: Robert Clarke Company, 1903.

Chapter 4

Abernethy, Thomas Perkins. *Western Lands and the American Revolution*. New York: D. Appleton-Century Company, 1937.

Alvord, Clarence Walworth. *The Mississippi Valley in British Politics: A Study in Trade, Land Speculation, and Experiments in Imperialism Culminating in the American Revolution*. 2 vols. Cleveland: Arthur H. Clark, 1917.

Ambler, Charles H. *George Washington and the West*.

Bailey, Kenneth P. *The Ohio Company of Virginia and the Westward Movement*.

―――. *Thomas Cresap, Maryland Frontiersman*.

Callahan, James Morton. *History of the Making of Morgantown: A Type Study in Trans-Appalachian Local History*. Morgantown: Morgantown Printing & Binding Company, 1926.

Caruso, John A. *The Appalachian Frontier: America's First Surge Westward*. Indianapolis: Bobbs-Merrill Company, 1959.

Cook, Roy Bird. *Washington's Western Lands*. Strasburg: Shenandoah Publishing House, 1930.

Downes, Randolph C. *Council Fires on the Upper Ohio: A Narrative of Indian Affairs in the Upper Ohio Valley to 1795*. Pittsburgh: University of Pittsburgh Press, 1940.

―――. "Dunmore's War: An Interpretation." *Mississippi Valley Historical Review* 21 (December 1934):311-19.

Haymond, Henry. *History of Harrison County, West Virginia, From the Early Days of*

Northwestern Virginia to the Present. Morgantown: Acme Printing Company, 1920; Parsons, W.Va.: McClain Printing Company, 1973.

Jacob, John J. *A Biographical Sketch of the Life of the Late Captain Michael Cresap*. Cumberland, Md.: J.M. Buchanan, 1826; Parsons, W.Va.: McClain Printing Company, 1971.

Lewis, George E. *The Indiana Company, 1763-1798: A Study in Eighteenth Century Frontier Land Speculation and Business Venture*. Glendale, Calif.: Arthur H. Clark Company, 1941.

Maxwell, Hu. *The History of Randolph County, West Virginia, from Its Earliest Settlement to the Present*. Morgantown: Acme Publishing Co., 1898; Parsons, W.Va.: McClain Printing Company, 1961.

Palmer, W.P., and others, eds. *Calendar of Virginia State Papers and Other Manuscripts*. 11 vols. Richmond, 1872-1892; New York: Kraus Reprint Company, 1968.

Parkman, Francis. *The Conspiracy of Pontiac*. Boston: Little, Brown and Company, 1851.

Peckham, Howard. *Pontiac and the Indian Uprising*. Princeton: Princeton University Press, 1947.

Rice, Otis K. *The Allegheny Frontier: West Virginia Beginnings, 1730-1830.*.

———. *Frontier Kentucky*. Lexington: University Press of Kentucky, 1975.

Shy, John W. "Dunmore, the Upper Ohio Valley, and the American Revolution," in Thomas H. Smith, ed. *Ohio in the American Revolution*. Ohio American Bicentennial Conference Series, no. 1. Columbus, 1976.

Sosin, Jack. *The Revolutionary Frontier, 1763-1783*. New York: Holt, Rinehart and Winston, 1967.

———. *Whitehall and the Wilderness: The Middle West in British Colonial Policy, 1760-1775*. Lincoln: University of Nebraska Press, 1961.

Stuart, John, *Narrative of Indian Wars, and Other Occurrences*.

Thwaites, Reuben Gold, and Louis Phelps Kellogg, eds. *Documentary History of Dunmore's War, 1774*. Madison: Wisconsin Historical Society, 1905; Harrisonburg, Va.: C.J. Carrier, 1974.

Volwiler, Albert T. *George Croghan and the Westward Movement, 1741-1782*. Cleveland: Arthur H. Clark Company, 1926.

Wainwright, Nicholas B. *George Croghan, Wilderness Diplomat*. Chapel Hill: University of North Carolina Press, 1959.

Withers, Alexander Scott, *Chronicles of Border Warfare*.

Chapter 5

Abernethy, Thomas Perkins. *Western Lands and the American Revolution*.

Bushong, Millard Kessler. *Historic Jefferson County*. Boyce, Va.: Carr Publishing Company, 1972.

Doddridge, Joseph. *Notes, on the Settlement and Indian Wars of the Western Parts of Virginia & Pennsylvania, from the Year 1763 until the Year 1783, together with a View, of the State of Society and Manners of the First Settlers of the Western Country*. Wellsburgh, [W.]Va.: *Printed at the Office of the Gazette*, 1824; Parsons, W.Va.: McClain Printing Company, 1960.

Downes, Randolph C. *Council Fires on the Upper Ohio*.

Hart, Freeman H. *The Valley of Virginia in the American Revolution, 1763-1789.*

Higginbotham, Don. *Daniel Morgan, Revolutionary Rifleman.* Chapel Hill: University of North Carolina Press, 1961.

Kellogg, Louise Phelps, ed. *Frontier Advance on the Upper Ohio, 1778-1779.* Madison: Wisconsin Historical Society, 1916.

———. *Frontier Retreat on the Upper Ohio, 1779-1781.* Madison: Wisconsin Historical Society, 1917.

Nelson, Paul David. *General Horatio Gates: A Biography.* Baton Rouge: Louisiana State University Press, 1976.

Palmer, W.P., and others, eds. *Calendar of Virginia State Papers.*

Rice, Otis K. *The Allegheny Frontier: West Virginia Beginnings, 1730-1830.*

———. "The Ohio Valley in the American Revolution" in *The Old Northwest in the American Revolution: An Anthology.* Edited by David Curtis Skaggs. Madison: State Historical Society of Wisconsin, 1977.

Selby, John E. *The Revolution in Virginia, 1775-1783.* Williamsburg, Va.: Colonial Williamsburg Foundation, 1988.

Thwaites, Reuben Gold, and Louise Phelps Kellogg, eds. *Revolution on the Upper Ohio, 1775-1777.* Madison: Wisconsin Historical Society, 1908.

———. *Frontier Defense on the Upper Ohio, 1777-1778.* Madison: Wisconsin Historical Society, 1912.

Ward, Harry M. *Major General Adam Stephen and the Cause of American Liberty.* Charlottesville: University Press of Virginia, 1989.

Withers, Alexander Scott. *Chronicles of Border Warfare.*

Chapter 6

Abernethy, Thomas Perkins. *The Burr Conspiracy.* New York: Oxford University Press, 1954.

———. *Western Lands and the American Revolution.*

Ambler, Charles Henry. *Sectionalism in Virginia from 1776-1861.* Chicago: University of Chicago Press, 1910.

Bailey, Kenneth P. *The Ohio Company of Virginia.*

Baldwin, Leland D. *The Whiskey Rebels: The Story of a Frontier Uprising.* Pittsburgh: University of Pittsburgh Press, 1949.

Brooks, Maurice. "A Community Records Its History." *West Virginia History* 17(April 1956):252-61.

Brown, Stephen W. *Voice of the New West: John G. Jackson, His Life and Times.* Macon, Ga.: Mercer University Press, 1985.

———. "Congressman John George Jackson and Republican Nationalism." *West Virginia History* 38(January 1977):93-125.

———. "Satisfaction at Bladensburg: The Pearson-Jackson Duel of 1809." *North Carolina Historical Review* 58(January 1981):23-43.

Davis, Dorothy. *John George Jackson.* Parsons, W.Va.: McClain Printing Company, 1976.

Ford, Worthington C. "The Federal Convention in Virginia, 1787-1788." In Massachusetts Historical Society *Proceedings,* 2d series, 17(1903).

Grigsby, Hugh Blair. *The History of the Federal Convention of 1788.* 2 vols. Richmond: Virginia Historical Society, 1890; New York: Da Capo Press, 1969.
Lewis, George E. *The Indiana Company, 1763-1798.*
McDonald, Forrest. *We, the People: The Economic Origins of the Constitution.* Chicago: University of Chicago Press, 1958.
Main, Jackson Turner. "The Distribution of Property in Post-Revolutionary Virginia." *Mississippi Valley Historical Review* 41(September 1954):241-58.
Rice, Otis K. *The Allegheny Frontier: West Virginia Beginnings, 1730-1830.*
Safford, William H. *The Life of Harman Blennerhassett, Comprising An Authentic Narrative of the Burr Expedition.* Cincinnati: Moore, Anderson, Wilstach, and Keys, 1850; New York: Arno Press, 1972.
Withers, Alexander Scott, *Chronicles of Border Warfare.*

Chapter 7

Alderson, Emma Frances, ed. "The Minutes of the Greenbrier Baptist Church, 1781-1832." *West Virginia History* 7(October 1945):40-53.
Asbury, Francis. *The Journals and Letters of Francis Asbury.* Edited by Elmer T. Manning, J. Manning Potts, and Jacob S. Payton. 3 vols. Nashville: Abingdon Press, 1958.
Atkinson, George W. *History of Kanawha County, from Its Organization in 1789 until the Present Time.* Charleston: West Virginia Journal, 1876.
Barnes, I.A. *The Methodist Protestant Church in West Virginia.* Baltimore: Stockton Press, 1926.
Bates, Robert L. "Middleway: A Study in Social History." *West Virginia History* 11 (October 1949-January 1950):5-43.
Cobb, W.H. "Presbyterianism in the Tygarts Valley." *Magazine of History-Biography of the Randolph County Historical Society,* no. 2 (1925):26-36.
Cometti, Elizabeth, and Festus P. Summers, eds., *The Thirty-Fifth State.*
Cramblet, Wilbur H. *The Christian Church (Disciples of Christ) in West Virginia: A History of Its Cooperative Work:* Saint Louis, Mo.: Bethany Press, 1971.
Doddridge, Joseph. *Notes, on the Settlement and Indian Wars.*
Finley, James B. *Sketches of Western Methodism: Biographical, Historical, and Miscellaneous, Illustrative of Pioneer Life.* Edited by W.P. Strickland. Cincinnati: Methodist Book Concern, 1855.
Gewehr, Wesley M. *The Great Awakening in Virginia, 1740-1790.* Durham: Duke University Press, 1930.
Gresham, Perry E., comp. *The Sage of Bethany: A Pioneer in Broadcloth.* Saint Louis, Mo.: Bethany Press, 1960.
Guthrie, Dwight Raymond. *John Macmillan, Apostle of Presbyterianism in the West, 1752-1833.* Pittsburgh: University of Pittsburgh Press, 1952.
McAllister, Lester G., and William E. Tucker. *Journey in Faith: A History of the Christian Church.* Saint Louis, Mo.: Bethany Press, 1975.
Meade, William. *Old Churches, Ministers and Families of Virginia.* 2 vols. Philadelphia: J.B. Lippincott Company, 1857.
Michaux, F.A. *Travels to the Westward of the Allegany Mountains.* London: For J. Mawman, 1805.

Posey, Walter Brownlow. *The Baptist Church in the Lower Mississippi Valley, 1776-1845*. Lexington: University of Kentucky Press, 1957.

Rice, Otis K. *The Allegheny Frontier: West Virginia Beginnings, 1730-1830*.

Royall, Anne, *Sketches of History, Life, and Manners in the United States*. New Haven, Conn.: Printed for the Author, 1826.

Semple, Robert B. *A History of the Rise and Progress of the Baptists in Virginia*. Revised and extended by G.W. Beale. Richmond: Pitt & Dickinson, 1894.

Stevens, Abel. *History of the Methodist Episcopal Church in the United States*. 4 vols. New York: Carlton and Porter, 1864-1867.

Sweet, William Warren. *Circuit-Rider Days along the Ohio, Being the Journals of the Ohio Conference from Its Organization in 1812 to 1826*. New York: Methodist Book Concern, 1923.

————. *Religion on the American Frontier: . . . A Collection of Source Materials*. 4 vols. New York: Henry Holt and Company, 1931-1946; New York: Cooper Square Publishers, 1964.

U.S., WPA Historical Records Survey Program. *Inventory of Church Archives of West Virginia: The Presbyterian Churches*. Charleston, 1941.

————. *Inventory of the Church Archives of West Virginia: The Protestant Episcopal Church*. Wheeling: Diocese of West Virginia, 1939.

Young, Jacob. *Autobiography of a Pioneer*. Cincinnati: L. and A. Poe for the Methodist Episcopal Church, [1857?].

Chapter 8

Ambler, Charles H. *A History of Education in West Virginia from Early Colonial Times to 1949*. Huntington: Standard Printing & Publishing Co., 1951.

————. "The Clarksburg Educational Convention of September 8-9, 1841." *West Virginia History* 5(October 1943):5-54.

————. "Poor Relief (Kanawha County, Virginia, 1818-1847)." *West Virginia History* 3(July 1942):285-304.

Bond, Donovan H. "How the *Wheeling Intelligencer* Became A Republican Organ." *West Virginia History* 11(April 1950):160-84.

Brown, Stephen W. *Voice of the New West: John G. Jackson, His Life and Times*.

Dayton, Ruth Woods. *Greenbrier Pioneers and Their Homes*. Charleston: West Virginia Publishing Company, 1942; Charleston: Education Foundation, Inc., 1977.

England, J. Merton. "Some Early Historians of Western Virginia." *West Virginia History* 14(January 1953):91-107.

James, Bessie Rowland. *Anne Royall's U.S.A.* New Brunswick: Rutgers University Press, 1972.

Norona, Delf, and Charles Shetler, comps. *West Virginia Imprints, 1790-1863: A Checklist of Books, Newspapers, Periodicals, and Broadsides*. Moundsville: West Virginia Library Assocation, 1958.

Rice, Otis K. *The Allegheny Frontier: West Virginia Beginnings, 1730-1830*.

————. "West Virginia Printers and Their Work, 1790-1830."*West Virginia History* 14(July 1953):297-338.

U.S., WPA Historical Records Survey Program. *American Imprints Inventory No. 14: A*

Check List of West Virginia Imprints, 1791-1830. Chicago: The WPA Historical Records Survey Project, 1940.

Virginia. *Second Auditor's Report on the State of the Literary Fund, . . . 1837-1838.* Richmond: no publisher, no date.

Williams, Elizabeth. "Mercer Academy: A Brief History Therof, 1819-1862." *West Virginia History* 13(October 1951):41-55.

Chapter 9

Ambler, Charles H. *A History of Transportation in the Ohio Valley.* Glendale, Calif: Arthur H. Clark Company, 1932.

———, and Festus P. Summers. *West Virginia, the Mountain State.* 2d ed. Englewood Cliffs, N.J.: Prentice-Hall, Inc., 1958.

Brown, Stephen W. *Voice of the New West: John G. Jackson His Life and Times.*

Callahan, James Morton, *History of West Virginia, Old and New.* 3 vols. Chicago: American Historical Society, 1923.

———. *Semi-Centennial History of West Virginia.* [Charleston]: Semi-Centennial Commission of West Virginia, 1913.

Cometti, Elizabeth, and Festus P. Summers, eds. *The Thirty-Fifth State.*

Davis, Dorothy, *A History of Harrison County, West Virginia.* Clarksburg: American Association of University Women, 1970.

———. *John George Jackson.*

Doddridge, Joseph. *Notes, on the Settlements and Indian Wars.*

Dunaway, Wayland Fuller. *History of the James River and Kanawha Company.* New York: Columbia University, 1922.

Eavenson, Howard N. *The First Century and A Quarter of American Coal Industry.* Pittsburgh: Privately printed, 1942.

Hale, John P. *History of the Great Kanawha Valley.* 2 vols. Madison, Wis.: Brant, Fuller & Co., 1891.

Jordan, Philip D. *The National Road.* Indianapolis: Bobbs-Merrill Company, 1948.

Martin, Joseph. *A New and Comprehensive Gazetteer of Virginia, and the District of Columbia.* Charlottesville: J. Martin, 1835.

Morgan, John S. *Robert Fulton.* New York: Mason/Charter, 1977.

Newton, J.H., G.C. Nichols, and A.G. Sprankle. *History of the Panhandle, Being Historical Recollections of the Counties of Ohio, Brooke, Marshall, and Hancock, West Virginia.* Wheeling: J.A. Campbell, 1879.

Nodyne, Kenneth Robert. "A Vignette of Wheeling during the Early Republic (1783-1840)." *West Virginia History* 40 (Fall 1978):47-54.

Rice, Otis K. *The Allegheny Frontier: West Virginia Beginnings, 1730-1830.*

———."Coal Mining in the Kanawha Valley to 1861: A View of Industrialization in the Old South." *Journal of Southern History* 31(November 1965):393-416.

———, and Stephen W. Brown. *A Centennial of Strength: A History of Banking in West Virginia.* Charleston: West Virginia Bankers Association, 1991.

Sanderlin, Walter S. *The Great National Project: A History of the Chesapeake and Ohio Canal.* Baltimore: Johns Hopkins, 1946.

Stealey, John Edmund, III. *The Antebellum Kanawha Salt Business and Western Markets.* Lexington: University Press of Kentucky, 1993.

Turner, Ella May. *James Rumsey, Pioneer in Steam Navigation*. Scottsdale, Pa.: Mennonite Publishing House, 1930.

Chapter 10

Ambler, Charles Henry. *Sectionalism in Virginia from 1776 to 1861*.
Brown, Stephen W. *Voice of the New West: John G. Jackson, His Life and Times*.
Hall, Claude H. *Abel Parker Upshur, Conservative Virginian, 1790-1844*. Madison: State Historical Society of Wisconsin, 1963.
Proceedings and Debates of the Virginia State Convention of 1829-1830. 2 vols. Richmond: no publisher, 1830; New York: Da Capo Press, 1971.
Rice, Otis K. *The Allegheny Frontier: West Virginia Beginnings, 1730-1830*.
Sutton, Robert P. *Revolution to Secession: Constitution Making in the old Dominion*. Charlottesville: University Press of Virginia, 1989.

Chapter 11

Ambler, Charles Henry. *Sectionalism in Virginia from 1776 to 1861*.
Bean, William G. "The Ruffner Pamphlet of 1847: An Anti-Slavery Aspect of Virginia Sectionalism." *Virginia Magazine of History and Biography* 61 (July 1953):260-82.
Boney, F. Nash. *John Letcher of Virginia: The Story of Virginia's Civil War Governor*. Tuscaloosa: University of Alabama Press, 1967.
Brown, Stephen W. *Voice of the New West: John G. Jackson, His Life and Times*.
Dunaway, Wayland Fuller. *History of the James River and Kanawha Company*.
Mathews, Donald G. *Slavery and Methodism: A Chapter in American Morality, 1780-1845*. Princeton: Princeton University Press, 1965.
Oates, Stephen B. *To Purge This Land with Blood: A Biography of John Brown*. New York: Harper & Row, 1970.
Rice, Otis K. *The Allegheny Frontier: West Virginia Beginnings, 1730-1830*.
———. "Eli Thayer and the Friendly Invasion of Virginia." *Journal of Southern History*. 37(November 1971):575-96.
———. *Lewisburg United Methodist Church: A Bicentennial History*. Parsons, W.Va.: McClain Printing Company, 1988.
Ruffner, Henry. *Address to the People of West Virginia*. Lexington, Va.: R.C. Noel, 1847; Bridgewater, Va.: Green Bookman, 1933.
Shanks, Henry T. *The Secession Movement in Virginia, 1847-1861*. Richmond: Garrett and Massie, 1934.
Woodward, C. Vann. *The Burden of Southern History*. Baton Rouge: Louisiana State University Press, 1960.

Chapter 12

Ambler, Charles H. *Waitman Thomas Willey: Orator, Churchman, Humanitarian*. Huntington, W.Va.: Standard Printing & Publishing Co., 1954.
———, and Festus P. Summers. *West Virginia, The Mountain State*.
Boney, F. Nash. *John Letcher of Virginia*.

Callahan, James Morton, *History of West Virginia, Old and New*.

Cometti, Elezabeth, and Festus P. Summers, eds. *The Thirty-Fifth State*.

Curry, Richard Orr. *A House Divided: A Study of Statehood Politics and the Copperhead Movement in West Virginia*. Pittsburgh: University of Pittsburgh Press, 1964.

Gray, Gladys M. "The Presidential Campaign of 1860 in Virginia and Its Aftermath." Ph.D. diss. University of Kentucky, 1941.

———. "A.W. Campbell—Party Builder." *West Virginia History* 7 (April 1946):221-37.

Hall, Granville Davisson. *The Rending of Virginia: A History*. Chicago: Mayer & Miller, 1902.

Lewis, Virgil A. *How West Virginia Was Made: Preceedings of the First Convention of the People of Northwestern Virginia at Wheeling, May 13, 14, and 15, 1861, and the Journal of the Second Convention of the People of Northwestern Virginia at Wheeling*. Charleston: News-Mail Company, 1909.

McGregor, James C. *The Disruption of Virginia*. New York: The Macmillan Company, 1922.

Reese, George H., ed. *Proceedings of the Virginia State Convention of 1861, February 13-May 1*. 4 vols. Richmond: Virginia State Library, 1965.

Shanks, Henry T. *The Secession Movement in Virginia, 1847-1861*.

Sutton, Robert P. *Revolution to Secession: Constitution Making in the Old Dominion*.

Chapter 13

Ambler, Charles H., and Festus P. Summers. *West Virginia, the Mountain State*.

Casdorph, Paul D. *Lee and Jackson: Confederate Chieftains*. New York: Paragon House, 1992.

Cohen, Stan. *The Civil War in West Virginia: A Pictorial History*. Missoula, Mont.: Gateway Printing & Litho., 1976.

Cook, Roy Bird. *The Family and Early Life of Stonewall Jackson*. 5th ed. Charleston: Education Foundation, 1967.

Cox, Jacob Dolson. *Military Reminiscenses of the Civil War*. 2 vols. New York: Charles Scribner's Sons, 1888.

Freeman, Douglas S. *R.E. Lee: A Biography*. 4 vols. New York: Charles Scribner's Sons, 1934-1935.

Hayes, Rutherford B. *Diary and Letters of Rutherford B. Hayes, Nineteenth President of the United States*. Edited by Charles Richard Williams. 5 vols. Columbus: Ohio Archaeological and Historical Society, 1922-1926.

Hornbeck, Betty. *Upshur Brothers of the Blue and Gray*. Parsons, W.Va.: McClain Printing Company, 1967.

Humphreys, Milton W. *Military Operations in Fayette County, West Virginia, 1861-1862*. Fayetteville: Privately printed, 1926.

Johnson, R.U., and C.C. Buell, eds. *Battles and Leaders of the Civil War*. 4 vols. New York: The Century Company, 1884-1887.

Johnston, David E. *A History of the Middle New River Settlements and Contiguous Territory*. Huntington, W.Va.: Standard Printing & Publishing Company, 1906.

Kincaid, Mary Elizabeth. "Fayetteville, West Virginia, during the Civil War." *West Virginia History* 14(July 1953):339-64.

Klement, Frank. "General John B. Floyd and the West Virginia Campaign of 1861." *West Virginia History* 8(April 1947):319-33.

Lang, Theodore F. *Loyal West Virginia from 1861 to 1865*. Baltimore: Deutsch Publishing Company, 1895.

Lowry, Terry. *The Battle of Scary Creek: Military Operations in the Kanawha Valley, April-July 1861*. Charleston: Pictorial Histories Publishing Company, 1982.

McKinney, Tim. *The Civil War in Fayette County, West Virginia*. Charleston, W.Va.: Pictorial Histories Publishing Company, 1988.

———. *Robert E. Lee at Sewell Mountain: The West Virginia Campaign*. Charleston, W.Va.: Pictorial Histories Publishing Company, 1990.

Moore, George E. *A Banner in the Hills: West Virginia's Statehood*. New York: Appleton-Century-Crofts, 1963.

Rice, Otis K. *Charleston and the Kanawha Valley: An Illustrated History*. Woodland Hills, Calif.: Windsor Publications, 1981.

Shaffer, John W. "Loyalties in Conflict: Union and Confederate Sentiment in Barbour County." *West Virginia History* 50(1991):109-28.

Stutler, Boyd B. *West Virginia in the Civil War*. Charleston: Education Foundation, 1963.

Summers, Festus P. *The Baltimore and Ohio in the Civil War*. New York: G.P. Putnam's Sons, 1939.

———. "The Jones-Imboden Raid." *West Virginia History* 1(October 1939):15-29.

Vandiver, Frank E. *Mighty Stonewall*. New York: McGraw Hill Book Company, 1957.

War of the Rebellion: A Compilation of Official Records of the Union and Confederate Armies. 70 vols. in 128 books. Washington, D.C.: Government Printing Office, 1881-1901.

Williams, John Alexander. *West Virginia: A Bicentennial History*. New York and Nashville: W.W. Norton & Company, Inc., and American Association for State and Local History, 1976.

Williams, T. Harry. *Hayes of the Twenty-third: The Civil War Volunteer Officer*. New York: Alfred A. Knopf, 1965.

Chapter 14

Ambler, Charles H. *Francis H. Pierpont, Union War Governor of Virginia and Father of West Virginia*. Chapel Hill: University of North Carolina Press, 1937.

———, Frances Haney Atwood, and William B. Mathews, eds. *Debates and Proceedings of the First Constitutional Convention of West Virginia (1861-1863)*. 3 vols. Huntington: Gentry Brothers, 1942.

Callahan, James Morton. *History of West Virginia, Old and New*.

Cometti, Elizabeth, and Festus P. Summers, eds. *The Thirty-Fifth State*.

Curry, Richard Orr. *A House Divided*.

———. "A Reappraisal of Statehood Politics in West Virginia." *Journal of Southern History* 28(November 1962):403-21.

Hall, Granville Davisson. *The Rending of Virginia*.

Ham, F. Gerald, ed. "The Mind of A Copperhead: Letters of John J. Davis on the Secession Crisis and Statehood Politics in Western Virginia, 1860-1862." *West Virginia History* 24(January 1963):93-109.

Lewis, Virgil A. *Second Biennial Report of the Department of Archives and History of the State of West Virginia*. Charleston: no publisher, 1908.

McGregor, James C. *The Disruption of Virginia*.

Moore, George E. *A Banner in the Hills*.

Parker, Granville. *The Formation of the State of West Virginia, and Other Incidents in the Late War*. Wellsburg, W.Va.: Glass & Son, 1875.

Randall, J.G. *Constitutional Problems under Lincoln,* Rev. ed. Urbana: University of Illinois Press, 1951.

Shaffer, Dallas B. "Lincoln and the 'Vast Question' of West Virginia." *West Virginia History* 32(January 1971):86-100.

Smith, Edward Conrad. *The Borderland in the Civil War*. New York: The Macmillan Company, 1927; Freeport, N.Y.: Books for Libraries Press, 1969.

Williams, John Alexander. *West Virginia: A Bicentennial History*.

Chapter 15

Ambler, Charles H. *The Makers of West Virginia and Their Work*. Huntington: Gentry Brothers, 1942.

———, and Festus P. Summers. *West Vitginia, the Mountain State*.

Callahan, James Morton. *History of West Virginia, Old and New*.

———. *Semi-Centennial History of West Virginia*.

Cometti, Elizabeth, and Festus P. Summers, eds. *The Thirty-Fifth State*.

Curry, Richard Orr. *A House Divided*.

Curry, Richard Orr, ed. *Radicalism, Racism, and Party Realignment: The Border States During Reconstruction*.

Gerofsky, Milton, "Reconstruction in West Virginia." *West Virginia History* 6(July 1945):295-360; 7(October 1945):5-39.

Lewis, Virgil A. *Second Biennial Report of the Department of Archives and History*.

Morgan, John G. *West Virginia Governors, 1863-1980*. 2d ed. Charleston: Charleston Newspapers, 1980.

Willimas, John Alexander, *West Virginia: A Bicentennial History*.

Chapter 16

Ambler, Charles H., and Festus P. Summers. *West Virginia, the Mountain State*.

Bailey, Kenneth R. *Mountaineers Are Free*. Saint Albans, W.Va.: Harless Printing, 1978.

Barns, William D. "Status and Sectionalism in West Virginia." *West Virginia History* 34(April 1973):247-72; 34(July 1973):360-81.

Casdorph, Paul D. "The 1872 Liberal Republican Campaign in West Virginia" *West Virginia History* 29(July 1968):292-302.

———. "West Virginia and the 1880 Republican National Convention." *West Virginia History* 24(January 1963):147-55.

Cometti, Elizabeth, and Festus P. Summers, eds. *The Thirty-Fifth State*.

Goodall, Elizabeth. "The Virginia Debt Controversy and Settlement." *West Virginia History* 24(October 1962):42-74; 24(April 1963):296-308; 24(July 1963):332-51; 25(October 1963):42-68; 25(January 1964):102-29.

Jacobs, James Henry. "The West Virginia Gubernatorial Contest, 1888-1890." *West Virginia History* 7(April 1946):159-220.

Kiplinger, John Lewis. "The Press in the Making of West Virginia." *West Virginia History* 6(January 1945):127-76.

MacCorkle, William A. *The Recollections of Fifty Years of West Virginia*. New York: G.P. Putnam's Sons, 1928.

McKinney, Gordon B. *Southern Mountain Republicans, 1865-1900: Politics and the Appalachian Community*. Chapel Hill: University of North Carolina Press, 1978.

Pepper, Charles M. *The Life and Times of Henry Gassaway Davis*. New York: The Century Company, 1920.

Rice, Harvey M. *The Life of Jonathan McCauley Bennett: A Study of the Virginias in Transition*. Chapel Hill: University of North Carolina Press, 1943.

Smith, G. Wayne, *Nathan Goff, Jr.: A Biography*. Charleston: Education Foundation, Inc., 1959.

———. "Nathan Goff, Jr., and the Solid South." *West Virginia History* 16(October 1955):5-21.

Summers, Festus P. *Johnson Newlon Camden: A Study in Individualism*. New York: G.P. Putnam's Sons, 1937.

Williams, John Alexander, *West Virginia: A Bicentennial History.*.

———. "The New Dominion and the Old: Ante-Bellum and Statehood Politics As the Background of West Virginia's 'Bourbon Democracy,'" *West Virginia History* 33(July 1972):317-407.

Chapter 17

Ambler, Charles H., and Festus P. Summers. *West Virginia, the Mountain State*.

Atkinson, George W. *History of Kanawha County*.

Barns, William D. "The Granger and Populist Movements in West Virginia, 1873-1914." Ph.D. diss., West Virginia University, 1946.

———. "The Influence of the West Virginia Grange upon Public Agricultural Education of College Grade." *West Virginia History* 9(January 1948):128-55.

———. "Oliver Hudson Kelley and the Genesis of the Grange: A Reappraisal." *Agricultural History* 41(July 1967):229-42.

———. *The West Virginia State Grange: The First Century, 1873-1973*. Morgantown: Morgantown Printing and Binding Company, 1973.

Brown, William Griffee. *History of Nicholas County, West Virginia*. Richmond: The Dietz Press, 1954.

Campbell, John Charles. *The Southern Highlander and His Homeland*. New York: Russell Sage Foundation, 1929; Lexington: University Press of Kentucky, 1969.

Caudill, Harry M. *Night Comes to the Cumberlands: A Biography of A Depressed Area*. Boston: Little, Brown and Company, 1962.

Diss Debar, Joseph H. *The West Virginia Hand Book and Immigrant's Guide*. Parkersburg: Gibbens Brothers, 1870.

Frost, William G. "Our Contemporary Ancestors in the Southern Mountains." *Atlantic Monthly* 83(March 1899):311-19.

Jones, Virgil Carrington. *The Hatfields and the McCoys*. Chapel Hill: University of North Carolina Press, 1948.

Kephart, Horace. *Our Southern Highlanders*. New York: Outing Publishing Company 1913.

Rice, Otis K. *The Hatfields and the McCoys*. Lexington: University Press of Kentucky, 1978.

Shapiro, Henry D. *Appalachia on Our Mind: The Southern Mountains and Mountaineers in the American Consciousness, 1870-1920*. Chapel Hill: University of North Carolina Press, 1978.

Waller, Altina L. *Feud: Hatfields, McCoys, and Social Change in Appalachia, 1860-1900*. Chapel Hill: University of North Carolina Press, 1988.

Whisnant, David E. *Modernizing the Mountaineer: People, Power, and Planning in Appalachia*. Boone, N.C.: Applachian Consortium Press, 1980.

Chapter 18

Annual Planning Information, Program Year, 1992. Charleston: West Virginia Research League, 1991.

Beachley, Charles E., comp. *History of the Consolidation Coal Company*. New York: Consolidation Coal Company, 1934.

Bradshaw, Michael. *The Appalachian Regional Commission: Twenty-Five Years of Government Policy*. Lexington: University Press of Kentucky, 1992.

Brown, Lloyd L. "The Life of Dr. Israel Charles White." *West Virginia History* 5(October 1946):5-104.

Clarkson, Roy B. *Tumult on the Mountain: Lumbering in West Virginia, 1770-1920*. Parsons, W.Va.: McClain Printing Company, 1964.

Conley, Phil. *History of West Virginia Coal Industry*. Charleston: Education Foundation, Inc., 1960.

Craigo, Robert, ed. *The New River Company*. [Mount Hope, W.Va.?]: New River Company, 1976.

Crowe-Carraco, Carol. *The Big Sandy*. Lexington: University Press of Kentucky, 1979.

Cubby, Edwin A. "Timbering Operations in the Tug and Guyandot Valleys in the 1890's." *West Virginia History* 26(January 1965):110-20.

Dodge, Jacob R. *West Virginia: Its Farms and Forests, Mines and Oil-Wells*. Philadelphia: J.B. Lippincott, 1895.

Eavenson, Howard N. *The First Century and A Quarter of American Coal Industry*.

Hungerford, Edward. *The Story of the Baltimore and Ohio Railroad, 1827-1927*. 2 vols. New York: G.P. Putnam's Sons, 1928.

Johnson, Leland R. *Men, Mountains, and Rivers: An Illustrated History of the Huntington District, U.S. Army Corps of Engineers, 1754-1974*. Washington, D.C,: U.S. Government Printing Office, 1977.

Jones, James G. "The Early History of the Natural Gas Industry in West Virginia." *West Virginia History* 10(January 1949):79-92.

Lambert, Oscar Doane. *Stephen Benton Elkins*. Pittsburgh: University of Pittsburgh Press, 1955.

Lambie, Joseph T. *From Mine to Market: A History of Coal Transportation on the Norfolk and Western Railway*. New York: New York University Press, 1954.

Massay, Glenn F. "Coal Consolidation: Profile of the Fairmont Field of Northern West Virginia, 1852-1903." Ph.D. diss., West Virginia University, 1970.

Munn, Robert. "The Development of Model Towns in the Bituminous Coal Fields." *West Virginia History* 40(Spring 1979):243-53.

1991 Statistical Handbook. Charleston: West Virginia Research League, 1991.

Pepper, Charles M. *The Life and Times of Henry Gassaway Davis.*

Prichard, Arthur C. " 'The Jackson Mystery': Dr.I.C. White and Mannington's First Oil Well." *Goldenseal* 6(April-June 1980):47-52.

Summers, Festus P. *Johnson Newlon Camden.*

Tams, W.P., Jr. *The Smokeless Coal Fields of West Virginia: A Brief History*. Morgantown: West Virginia University Library, 1963.

Thoenen, Eugene D. *History of the Oil and Gas Industry in West Virginia*. Charleston: Education Foundation, Inc., 1964.

Thomas, Jerry B. "Coal Country: The Rise of the Southern Smokeless Coal Industry and Its Effect on Area Development, 1872-1910." Ph.D. diss., University of North Carolina, 1971.

―――. "The Growth of the Coal Industry in the Great Kanawha Basin," Master's thesis, University of North Carolina, 1967.

Thurmond, Walter P. *The Logan Coal Field of West Virginia: A Brief History*. Morgantown: West Virginia University Library, 1964.

U.S. Bureau of the Census. *1987 Census of Manufactures*. Washington, D.C.: U.S. Government Printing Office, 1991.

Williams, John Alexander. *West Virginia and the Captains of Industry*. Morgantown: West Virginia University Library, 1976.

Williamson, Harold F., and Arnold R. Daum. *The American Petroleum Industry: The Age of Illumination, 1859-1899*. Evanston: Northwestern University Press, 1959.

Chapter 19

Burckel, Nicholas C. "Progressive Governors in the Border States: Reform Governors in Missouri, Kentucky, West Virginia, and Maryland, 1900-1918." Ph.D. diss., University of Wisconsin, 1971.

―――. "Governor Albert B. White and the Beginnings of Progressive Reform." *West Virginia History* 40(Fall 1978):1-12.

Casdorph, Paul D. "Governor William E. Glasscock and Theodore Roosevelt's Bull Moose Candidacy." *West Virginia History* 28(October 1966):8-15.

Fisher, Lucy Lee. "John J. Cornwell, Governor of West Virginia, 1917-1921." *West Virginia History* 24(April 1963):258-88; 24(July 1963):370-89.

Glasscock, William E. *State Papers and Public Addresses*. Charleston: no publisher, n.d.

Harbaugh, William H. *Lawyer's Lawyer: The Life of John W. Davis*. New York: Oxford University Press, 1973.

Karr, Carolyn. "A Political Biography of Henry Hatfield." *West Virginia History* 28(October 1966):35-63; 28(January 1967):137-70.

Lambert, Oscar Doane. *Stephen Benton Elkins.*

MacCorkle, William A. *The Recollections of Fifty Years.*

Morgan, John G. *West Virginia Governors, 1863-1980.*

Penn, Neil Shaw. "Henry D. Hatfield and Reform Politics: A Study of West Virginia Politics from 1908 to 1917." Ph.D. diss., Emory University, 1977.

Tucker, Gary J. "William E. Glasscock: Thirteenth Governor of West Virginia." Ph.D. diss., West Virginia University, 1978.

————. "William E. Glasscock and the West Virginia Election of 1910." *West Virginia History* 40(Spring 1979):254-79.

Turner, William P. "John T. McGraw: A Study in Democratic Politics in the Age of Enterprise." *West Virginia History* 45(1984):1-40.

White, Albert Blakeslee. *Public Addresses . . . During His Term of Office, Including Proclamations and Other Official Papers*. Charleston: Tribune Printing Company, 1905.

Williams, John Alexander. *West Virginia and the Captains of Industry*.

————. "New York's First Senator from West Virginia: How Stephen B. Elkins Found A New Political Home." *West Virginia History* 31(January 1970):73-87.

Chapter 20.

Anson, Charles P. "A History of the Labor Movement in West Virginia." Ph.D. diss., University of North Carolina, 1940.

Bailey, Kenneth R. "A Judicious Mixture: Negroes and Immigrants in the West Virginia Mines, 1880-1917." *West Virginia History* 34(January 1973):141-61.

————. "Hawk's Nest Coal Company Strike, January, 1880." *West Virginia History* 30 (July 1969):625-34.

————. "'Tell the Boys to Fall into Line': United Mine Workers of America Strikes in West Virginia, January-June, 1894." *West Virginia History* 32(July 1971):224-37.

————. "A Temptation to Lawlessness: Peonage in West Virginia, 1903-1908." *West Virginia History* 50(1991):25-45.

Barkey, Fred. "The Socialist Party in West Virginia from 1898 to 1920." Ph.D. diss., University of Pittsburgh, 1971.

Brier, Stephen. "Interracial Organizing in the West Virginia Coal Industry: The Participation of Black Workers in the Knights of Labor and the United Mine Workers, 1880-1894." In *Essays in Southern Labor History: Selected Papers, Southern Labor History Conference, 1976*, edited by Gary M. Fink and Merl E. Reed. Westport, Conn.: Greenwood Press, 1977.

Cherniack, Martin. *The Hawk's Nest Incident: America's Worst Industrial Disaster*. New Haven: Yale University Press, 1986.

Corbin, David Alan. *Life, Work and Rebellion in the Coal Fields: Southern West Virginia Coal Mines, 1880-1922*. Urbana: University of Illinois Press, 1981.

————. "Betrayal in the West Virginia Coal Fields: Eugene V. Debs and the Socialist Party in America, 1912-1914." *Journal of American History* 64(March 1978) :987-1009.

————. "'Frank Keeney Is Our Leader, and We Shall Not Be Moved': Rank-and-file Leadership in the West Virginia Coal Fields." In *Essays in Southern Labor History: Selected Papers, Southern Labor History Conference, 1976*, ed. Gary M. Fink and Merl E. Reed (Westport, Conn.: Greenwood Press, 1977).

Dillon, Lacy A. *They Died in the Darkness*. Parsons, W.Va.: McClain Printing Company, 1976.

Fetherling, Dale. *Mother Jones, the Miners' Angel: A Portrait*. Carbondale: Southern Illinois University Press, 1974.

Graebner, William. *Coal-Mining Safety in the Progressive Period: The Political Economy of Reform*. Lexington: University Press of Kentucky, 1976.

Hadsell, Richard M., and William E. Coffey. "From Law and Order to Class Warfare: Baldwin-Felts Detectives in the Southern West Virginia Coal Fields." *West Virginia History* 40(Spring 1979):268-86.

Harris, Evelyn L.K., and Frank J. Krebs. *From Humble Beginnings: West Virginia Federation of Labor, 1903-1957*. Charleston: West Virginia Labor History Publishing Fund, 1960.

Hume, Brit. *Death and the Mines: Rebellion and Murder in the UMW*. New York: Grossman Publishers, 1971.

Javersak, David T. "The Response of the O.V.T. & L.A. to Industrialism." *Journal of the West Virginia Historical Association* 4(Spring 1980):35-45.

[Jones, Mary Harris]. *Autobiography of Mother Jones*. Chicago: Charles H. Kerr, 1925; New York: Arno Press, 1969.

Jordan, Daniel P. "The Mingo War: Labor Violence in the Southern West Virginia Coal Fields, 1919-1922." In *Essays in Southern Labor History,* ed. Gary M. Fink and Merl E. Reed. Westport, Conn.: Greenwood Press, 1977.

Lane, Winthrop C. *Civil War in West Virginia: A Story of Industrial Conflict in the Coal Mines*. New York: B.W. Huebsch, Inc. 1921: New York: Arno Press and The New York Times, 1969.

McAteer, James D. *Coal Mining Health and Safety: The Case of West Virginia*. New York: Praeger, 1973.

McCormick, Kyle. *The New-Kanawha River and the Mine War of West Virginia*. Charleston: Mathews Printing and Lithographing Company, c1959.

[Mooney, Fred.] *Struggle in the Coal Fields: The Autobiography of Fred Mooney*. Edited by J.W. Hess. Morgantown: West Virginia University Library, 1967.

Scholten, Pat Creech. "The Old Mother and Her Army: The Agitative Strategies of Mary Harris Jones." *West Virginia History* 40(Summer 1979):365-74.

Seel, Edward M. "Mother Jones in the Fairmont Field, 1902." *Journal of American History* 57(September 1970):270-305.

U.S. Congress. House. *Report No. 1381* and *Report No. 1490*. 63d Cong., 3d sess.

U.S. Congress. Senate. Committee on Education and Labor. *Conditions in the Paint Creek District, West Virginia: Hearings Before a Subcommittee on Education and Labor*. 3 vols. 63d Cong., 1st sess.

———. *Digest of Report on Investigation of the Paint Creek Coal Fields of West Virginia*. 63d Cong., 2d sess.

Welch, Jack. "Of Steel and Stock: Taking over at Weirton, One Worker's Perspective." *Goldenseal* 18(1992):39-41.

West Virginia. *Report of West Virginia Mining Investigation Commission, Appointed by Governor Glasscock on the 28th Day of August, 1912*. Charleston: Tribune Printing Company, [1912].

Chapter 21

Alexander, Ronald R. *West Virginia Tech: A History*. Charleston, W.Va.: Pictorial Histories Publishing Company, 1992.

Ambler, Charles H. *A History of Education in West Virginia.*

Bond, Sirus O. *The Light of the Hills: A History of Salem College.* Charleston: Education Foundation, 1960.

Candor, Catherine Ann. "A History of the Kanawha County Textbook Controversy, April 1974-April 1975." Ph.D. diss., Virginia Polytechnic Institute, 1976.

Doherty, William T., Jr., and Festus P. Summers. *West Virginia University: Symbol of Unity in a Sectionalized State.* Morgantown: West Virginia University Press, 1982.

Feaster, E.K., director. *A Survey of Educational Programs of the West Virginia Public Schools: A Summary of the Report.* Charleston: West Virginia Legislature, Interim Committee, 1957.

Harlan, John Clifford. *History of West Virginia State College, 1890-1965,* Dubuque, Iowa: Wm. C. Brown Book Company, 1968.

Judd, Charles H., and L.V. Cavins. *Survey of Education in West Virginia.* 4 vols. Charleston: State Board of Education, 1929.

Krebs, Frank J. *Where There Is Faith: The Morris Harvey College Story, 1888-1970.* Charleston: M.H.C. Publications, 1974.

Lord, Charles A. *Years of Decision: A History of the Organization.* Charleston: West Virginia Education Association, 1965.

Moffat, Charles Hill. *Marshall University: An Institution Comes of Age, 1837-1980.* Huntington: Marshall University Alumni Association, 1981.

Morgan, B.S., and J.F. Cork. *History of Education in West Virginia.* Charleston: Moses W. Donnally, 1893.

Plummer, Kenneth M. *A History of West Virginia Wesleyan College, 1890-1965:* [Buckhannon]: West Virginia Wesleyan Press, 1965.

Regier, C.C., ed. *West Liberty Yesterday and Today.* Wheeling: Wheeling News Lithograph Company, 1939.

Ross, Thomas Richard. *Davis and Elkins College: The Diamond Jubilee History.* Parsons, W.Va.: McClain Printing Company, c1980.

Slonaker, Arthur Gordon. *A History of Shepherd College.* Parsons, W.Va.: McClain Printing Company, 1967.

Strayer, George D., director. *A Report on A Survey of Public Education in the State of West Virginia.* Charleston: West Virginia Legislature, Interim Committee to Study Problems of Government, 1945.

Trent, W.W. *Mountaineer Education: A Story of Education in West Virginia, 1885-1957.* Charleston: Jarrett Printing Company, 1960.

West Virginia Board of Regents. *A Plan for Progress: West Virginia Higher Education in the Seventies.* Charleston: West Virginia Board of Regents, 1972.

West Virginia State Department of Education. *History of Education in West Virginia.* Rev. ed. Charleston: Tribune Printing Co., 1907.

Whitehill, A.R. *History of Education in West Virginia.* Washington, D.C.: U.S. Bureau of Education, 1902.

Woods, Roy C. "The History of the County Unit in West Virginia." *West Virginia History* 19(October 1957):49-59.

Woolery, William K. *Bethany Years: The Story of Old Bethany from Her Founding Through A Century of Trial and Triumph.* Huntington: Standard Printing & Publishing Co., 1941.

Chapter 22

Alexander, Holmes. *Pen and Politics: The Autobiography of a Working Editor.* Morgantown: West Virginia University Library, 1970.

Atkeson, Mary Meek. "West Virginia Literature and Literary Writers." In Callahan, *Semi-Centennial History of West Virginia.*

Comstock, Jim, ed. *Stories and Verse of West Virginia II.* Richwood, W.Va.: Jim Comstock, 1974.

Doyle, Paul A. *Pearl S. Buck.* New York: Twayne Publishers, Inc., 1965.

Hofstadter, Richard. Introduction to William H. Harvey. *Coin's Financial School.* Cambridge: Harvard University Press, 1963.

Hubin, Allen J. Introduction to Melville Davisson Post. *The Complete Uncle Abner.* San Diego: University Extension, University of California, 1977.

Maddox, Robert F. "Four Eminent Historians: Ambler, Callahan, Chitwood, and Summers." *West Virginia History* 27(July 1966):296-308.

Morgan, John G. "West Virginian of the Year [Mary Lee Settle]." *Charleston Gazette,* January 7, 1979.

Norton, Charles A. *Melville Davisson Post: Man of Many Mysteries.* Bowling Green, Ohio: Bowling Green State University Popular Press, 1973.

Pease, Louise McNeill. Introduction to *Paradox Hill from Appalachia to Lunar Shore.* Morgantown: West Virginia University Library, 1972.

Price, Paul H. *A Geologist at Large in Appalachia, 1923-1969.* Morgantown: Paul H. Price, 1978.

Spindler, Elizabeth Carroll. *John Peale Bishop: A Biography.* Morgantown: West Virginia University Library, 1980.

Turner, Ella May, ed. *Stories and Verse of West Virginia.* Scottdale, Pa.: Mennonite Publishing House, 1940.

Wood, Warren. *Representative Authors of West Virginia.* Ravenswood, W.Va.: Worth-While Book Co., 1926.

Chapter 23

Hardin, William H. "Elizabeth Kee: West Virginia's First Woman in Congress." *West Virginia History* 45(1984):109-23.

Holt, Homer Adams. *State Papers and Public Addresses.* Compiled and annotated by William E. Hughes. Charleston: Jarrett Printing Company, [1942].

Kump, H.G. *State Papers and Public Addresses.* Compiled and annotated by James W. Harris, Jr. Charleston: Jarrett Printing Company, [1937].

Maddox, Robert Franklin. *The Senatorial Career of Harley Martin Kilgore.* New York: Garland Publishing Company, 1981.

Marland, William C. *State Papers and Public Addresses.* Charleston: Rose City Press, n.d.

Meadows, Clarence W. *State Papers and Public Addresses.* Charleston: Jarrett Printing Company, [1950].

Morgan, John G. *West Virginia Governors, 1863-1980.*

Neely, Matthew Mansfield. *State Papers and Public Addresses.* Charleston: Mathews Printing and Lithographing Co., n.d.

Patteson, Okey L. *State Papers and Public Addresses.* Compiled and edited by Rosalind Carroll Funk. Charleston: Rose City Press, [1953].

Pierce, Neal R. *The Border South States: People, Politics, and Power in the Five Border South States.* New York: W.W. Norton & Company, Inc., 1975.

Chapter 24

Ernst, Harry W. *The Primary That Made a President: West Virginia, 1960.* New York: McGraw-Hill Book Company, 1962.

Morgan, John G. *West Virginia Governors, 1863-1980.*

[Moore, Arch A., Jr.]. *Eight Years: Official Statements and Papers: The Honorable Arch A. Moore, Jr., Governor of West Virginia, 1969-1977.* 3 vols. Edited by Carl M. Frasure and Leonard M. Davis. Beckley: B.J.W. Printers, n.d.

Pierce, Neal R. *The Border South States.*

Rockefeller, John D., IV. *The Rockefeller Years: 1977-1985: Official Papers and Policies.* 4vols. Edited by Sheri A. O'Dell. No Place: No publisher, n.d.

Smith, Hulett C. *State Papers and Public Addresses.* Edited by John A. Canfield. Beckley: Biggs, Johnston, and Withrow, 1969.

Underwood, Cecil H. *State Papers and Public Addresses.* Edited by John F. AcAllister. Beckley: Biggs, Johnston, and Withrow, n.d.

White, Theodore H. *The Making of A President, 1960.* New York: Athenaeum House, Inc., 1961.

Williams, John Alexander. *West Virginia: A Bicentennial History.*

Chapter 25

Annual Planning Information, Program Year, 1992.

Building for a New Century of Higher Education in West Virginia. Washington, D.C.: Carnegie Foundation for the Advancement of Teaching, 1989.

Carlson, Peter. "The Magic and the Misery (Of West Virginia, That Is)," *Washington Post,* November 22, 1992. Reprinted in *West Virginia Hillbilly,* December 10, 1992.

Charleston Daily Mail, 1980-1992.

Charleston Gazette, 1980-1992.

Clarksburg *Exponent,* 1980-1992.

Clarksburg *Telegram,* 1980-1992.

Huntington Herald-Dispatch, 1980-1992.

1991 Statistical Handbook.

Parkersburg *News,* 1980-1992.

Parkersburg *Sentinel,* 1980-1992.

Ranking of the States, 1985. Washington, D.C.: National Education Association, 1985.

Rice, Otis, K., and Stephen W. Brown. *A Centennial of Strength: A History of Banking in West Virginia.*

State of West Virginia, Election Returns, 1988. Charleston: Issued by Ken Hechler, Secretary of State.

State of West Virginia, Election Returns, 1989-1990. Charleston: Issued by Ken Hechler, Secretary of State.

State of West Virginia, Election Returns, 1992. Unpublished report by the Secretary of
    State.
U.S. Bureau of the Census. *1987 Census of Manufactures*.
West Virginia. *Acts of the Legislature*, 1980-1992. Charleston: State of West Virginia,
    1980-1992.
West Virginia Education Association. *StatEd*.
Wheeling Intelligencer, 1980-1992.
Wheeling News-Register, 1980-1992.

Index

Croghan, George, 28, 31-33
Crook, Gen. George, 133-34, 135, 139
Crozet, Col. Claudius, 87
Cunningham, Albert B., novelist, 258
Cunningham family, 17
Curry, Richard O., 149, 263
Curry, Roy W., historian, 263

Dandridge, A. S., 242-43
Dandridge, Danske, poet, 256-57
Darke, Capt. William, 38
Davis, Henry Gassaway, 159, 161, 165, 166,
167, 170-71, 190, 192, 210, 212, 244
Davis, John J., 113, 149, 151, 154, 155, 159, 205
Davis, John W., 218-19
Davis, Patrick, 219
Davis, Rebecca Harding, novelist, 255
Davis, Thomas E., 172
Davis, 185, 198
Davis and Elkins College, 244
Davis and McCarty, 77
Davisson, Hezekiah, 48
Davisson family, 29
Dawson, D. Boone, 272, 274
Dawson, William M.O., 208, 211, 212, 223,
264
Dayton, Alston G., 208, 227
Dayton, Spencer, 120
Deahl, Jasper N., 246
Debs, Eugene V., 223
Decker, Thomas, 21
Deepwater, 183, 184, 186
Delaware Indians, 20, 21, 34; in
Revolutionary War, 38, 40, 43, 45
Democratic Party: split in 1860, 11-12; gains
in Virginia, 102; in election of 1869, 159; in
election of 1870, 159-60; in 1871, 165; in
Bourbon era, 166-67; and West Virginia
congressional seats, 269; and the statehouse
machine, 270-71; rift in 1944, 274
Dent, Marshall M., 118
Department of Commerce, 282
Department of Highways, 284
Department of Natural Resources, 282
Department of Public Safety, 217
Dering, Henry, 145, 146
Dew, Thomas R., 103
Dewey, Thomas E., 269
Dinwiddie, Robert, 22-24
Disciples of Christ, 67
Diss Debar, Joseph H., 153, 175, 189
distilleries, 82
district free schools, 70, 71
District of West Augusta, 32, 47
Division of Energy, 295-96, 302
Dixon, John, 51
Dixon, Samuel, 191, 192

Doddridge, Joseph, 57, 60, 61, 67, 77, 78
Doddridge, Philip, 92-95
Doddridge County, 140, 177, 194
Donald, David, 110
Donnally family, 29
Dorsey, Dennis B., 121
Dorsey family, 29
Douglas, Gus, 292
Douglas, Stephen A., 112
Draper, Lyman C., 78, 261
Droop Mountain, battle of, 138
"Dublin Raid," 139
Dumont, Col, Ebenezer, 125
Dunbar, 5-6
Duncan, Edwin, 78
Dunkers, 62, 63
Dunlap, Capt. James, 24
Dunmore, Lord, 31-32, 34-35, 37, 38, 39
Du Pont, E.I. de Nemours, 203
Duquesne, Marquis, 21
Duval, Isaac, glass manufacturer, 85

Early, Jubal A., 115
Eastern Panhandle, 16, 61, 66, 72, 81, 84, 120
Easton, John B., 270
Eaton, Clement, 110
Eccles, 236
Echols, Gen. John, 104, 135, 138
Eckerlin, Gabriel, 21
Eckerlin, Israel, 21
Edenborn, William, 191
Edson, Arhur, 281
education: constitutional provisions for, 239,
240-41; professionalization of, 247-48,
under Gov. Caperton, 298-301; under Gov.
Moore, 297-98. *See also* schools
Edwards, William H., 86; 265
Egan, Michael, 225
Eisenhower, Dwight D., 278-79
Eleanor, 268
elections: (1860), 155; (1869), 159; (1870),
160; (1920), 218; (1924), 218; (1928),
218-19; (1960), 281-82; (1988), 291, 292-93;
(1990), 295; (1992), 302-3
electric power industry, 202
Elinipsico, 41
Eliza, 88
Elkins, Stephen B., 190, 192, 207, 208, 210,
214, 244
Elkins, 244
Elkins coalfield, 186
Elliott, Matthew, 35, 39
Emma Graham, 163
Employees League of Widen Miners, 238
Employees Security League, 238
English, Thomas Dunn, 73; poet, 256-57
Ennis, Thomas E., historian, 262